Critical Realist Applicati Organisation and Manag Studies

Critical realism has become increasingly important in the way organisation and management is being studied. This book argues for an alternative to the prevailing ontology and shows how positivism and its empirical realist ontology can be abandoned without having to accept strong social constructionism.

Critical Realist Applications in Organisation and Management Studies applies critical realism in four ways. First, in the removal of meta-theoretical obstacles that hinder the development of fruitful theoretical and empirical work. Second and third, as a meta-theoretical tool with which to develop appropriate methodological and theoretical frameworks which can then be used to inform appropriate empirical work. And finally, all of this is applied across a broad range of subject areas including critical management studies, accountancy, marketing, health care management, operations research, the nature of work, human resource management, labour process theory, regional analysis, and work and labour market studies.

Steve Fleetwood is a Senior Lecturer in the Department of Organisation, Work and Technology at Lancaster University Management School where he teaches Employment Relations and HRM. His publications include *Hayek's Political Economy, the Socio Economics of Order*; *Critical Realism in Economics: Development and Debate*; *Realist Perspectives on Organisation and Management* (edited with S. Ackroyd); *Critical Realism and Marxism* (edited with A. Brown and J.M. Roberts).

Stephen Ackroyd is Professor of Organisational Analysis and Head of the Department of Organisation, Work and Technology at Lancaster University Management School. He is a member of the British Academy of Management Council (BAM) and a Fellow of the Society for Advanced Management Studies (SAMS). He has published widely in the fields of organisational analysis and organisational behaviour.

Critical realism: interventions
Edited by Margaret Archer, Roy Bhaskar, Andrew Collier, Nick Hostettler, Tony Lawson and Alan Norrie

Critical realism is one of the most influential new developments in the philosophy of science and in the social sciences, providing a powerful alternative to positivism and postmodernism. This series will explore the critical realist position in philosophy and across the social sciences.

Critical Realism
Essential readings
Edited by Margaret Archer, Roy Bhaskar, Andrew Collier, Tony Lawson and Alan Norrie

The Possibility of Naturalism, 3rd edition
A philosophical critique of the contemporary human sciences
Roy Bhaskar

Being and Worth
Andrew Collier

Quantum Theory and the Flight from Realism
Philosophical responses to quantum mechanics
Christopher Norris

From East to West
Odyssey of a soul
Roy Bhaskar

Realism and Racism
Concepts of race in sociological research
Bob Carter

Rational Choice Theory
Resisting colonisation
Edited by Margaret Archer and Jonathan Q. Tritter

Explaining Society
Critical realism in the social sciences
Berth Danermark, Mats Ekström, Jan Ch. Karlsson and Liselotte Jakobsen

Critical Realism and Marxism
Edited by Andrew Brown, Steve Fleetwood and John Michael Roberts

Critical Realism in Economics
Edited by Steve Fleetwood

Realist Perspectives on Management and Organisations
Edited by Stephen Ackroyd and Steve Fleetwood

After International Relations
Critical realism and the (re)construction of world politics
Heikki Patomaki

Capitalism and Citizenship
The impossible partnership
Kathryn Dean

Philosophy of Language and the Challenge to Scientific Realism
Christopher Norris

Transcendence
Critical realism and God
Margaret S. Archer, Andrew Collier and Douglas V. Porpora

Critical Realist Applications in Organisation and Management Studies 
Edited by Steve Fleetwood and Stephen Ackroyd
Also published by Routledge

Routledge studies in critical realism

Edited by Margaret Archer, Roy Bhaskar, Andrew Collier, Nick Hostettler, Tony Lawson and Alan Norrie

1. **Marxism and Realism**
   A materialistic application of realism in the social science
   Sean Creaven

2. **Beyond Relativism**
   Raymond Boudon, cognitive rationality and critical realism
   Cynthia Lins Hamlin

3. **Education Policy and Realist Social Theory**
   Primary teachers, child-centred philosophy and the new managerialism
   Robert Wilmott

4. **Hegemony**
   A realist analysis
   Jonathan Joseph

5. **Realism and Sociology**
   Anti-foundationalism, ontology and social research
   Justin Cruickshank

6. **Critical Realism**
   The difference it makes
   Edited by Justin Cruickshank

7. **Critical Realism and Composition Theory**
   Donald Judd

8. **On Christian Belief**
   A defence of a cognitive conception of religious belief in a Christian context
   Andrew Collier

9. **In Defence of Objectivity and Other Essays**
   Andrew Collier

10. **Realism Discourse and Deconstruction**
    Edited by Jonathan Joseph and John Michael Roberts

11. **Critical Realism, Post-positivism and the Possibility of Knowledge**
    Ruth Groff

12. **Defending Objectivity**
    Essays in honour of Andrew Collier
    Edited by Margaret S. Archer and William Outhwaite

Critical Realist Applications in Organisation and Management Studies

Edited by Steve Fleetwood and Stephen Ackroyd

LONDON AND NEW YORK

First published 2004
by Routledge
11 New Fetter Lane, London EC4P 4EE

Simultaneously published in the USA and Canada
by Routledge
29 West 35th Street, New York, NY 10001

Routledge is an imprint of the Taylor & Francis Group

Typeset in Baskerville by
Taylor & Francis Books Ltd
Printed and bound in Great Britain by
TJ International Ltd, Padstow, Cornwall

British Library Cataloguing in Publication Data
A catalogue record for this book is available from the British Library

Library of Congress Cataloging in Publication Data
A catalog record for this title has been requested

ISBN 0–415–34509–X (hbk)
ISBN 0–415–34510–3 (pbk)

Contents

Illustrations

Figures

Tables

Contributors

Stephen Ackroyd is Professor of Organisational Analysis and Head of the Department of Organisation, Work and Technology at Lancaster University Management School. His current research is concerned with strategic change in large British companies, particularly those still involved in manufacturing, and the impact of the new public management on the public sector professions, particularly doctors and nurses in the NHS. His interest in the philosophy and methodology of social science is of long standing. He is author of a textbook on methodology, and editor, with Steve Fleetwood, of *Realist Perspectives on Management and Organisation*, which was published by Routledge in 2000. His other recent books include *Organisational Misbehaviour* (Sage, 1999), written with Paul Thompson, and *The Organisation of Business* (Oxford University Press, 2002).

Peter Armstrong graduated in Aeronautical Engineering in 1960. After seven years in industry, he took a Master's degree in Sociology at the University of Bath and saw active service as a sociologist in the 'Chemco' studies of the early 1970s. Subsequently his career drifted into the indirection typical of those simultaneously enthralled by sociology and repelled by what is produced in its name. Best known nowadays for his work in critical accounting, Peter found himself at one point occupying a chair in accounting at the University of Sheffield. He is now Professor of Management at Keele University, where his recent inaugural lecture was devoted to a trashing of that subject. His current research is on the interaction between heavy cycling and heavy drinking.

Peter Bain lectures in the Department of HRM at the University of Strathclyde, and worked in the engineering and car industries before entering the groves of academe. Areas in which he has researched and published include occupational health and safety, workplace technological change and contemporary developments in trade unionism. A lead applicant in a joint Scottish universities project researching work in call centres and software development, funded under the ESRC's 'Future of Work' programme, he has also studied work and employment relations in call centres in the UK, as well as in the USA, the Netherlands and India.

Phil Brown is Research Professor in the School of Social Sciences, Cardiff University. His publications include: *Schooling Ordinary Kids*, *Education, Unemployment and Labour Markets*, *Beyond Thatcherism*, *Poor Work*, *Education for Economic Survival*, *Higher Education and Corporate Realities*, *Capitalism and Social Progress* (Palgrave, 2001) and *High Skills and the Mismanagement of Talent* (Oxford University Press, 2001).

Rick Delbridge is Professor of Organisational Analysis at Cardiff Business School. His research interests include the role of shopfloor workers in contemporary manufacturing and attempts to revitalise the trade union movement. Rick is author of *Life on the Line in Contemporary Manufacturing* (Oxford University Press, 1998) and co-editor of *Manufacturing in Transition* (Routledge, 1998, with James Lowe) He is co-editor (with Ed Heery) of the Routledge series Studies in Employment Relations. Rick is a Cornishman whose hobbies of supporting Derby County and playing golf are both sources of great exasperation!

Geoff Easton is Professor of Marketing in the Management School at Lancaster University. His publications include *Managers and Competition* (Blackwell, 1993, with G. Sherman, R. Burrell and C. Rothschild), 'Marketing: a critical realist approach', published recently in the *Journal of Business Research*, and *Industrial Networks: A New View Of Reality* (Routledge, 1992), of which he was co-editor (with B. Axelsson). The title of the last of these was meant to be ironic when it was first published but it has taken on a new resonance in recent years. Geoff's research is mainly in the area of interorganisational exchange relationships and industrial networks. Currently he is focusing on issues of the everyday behaviour of marketing managers in organisational markets and the use of complexity theory simulations to model complex markets. This work involves mainly case research and his interest in critical realism stems from the way it can be used to defend this form of research from its detractors.

Alex Faria lectures in Strategic Decision and Marketing Strategy at the Brazilian School of Public and Business Administration. He is also a researcher for the National Council for Scientific Research in Brazil, and co-editor of the *Interdisciplinary Review of Marketing* (an electronic journal). His current research concentrates on marketing strategy and decision-making processes. Other research interests include strategic management and organisation studies. He enjoys playing football and his main hobby is celebrating World Cups won by the Brazilian team.

Steve Fleetwood spent many years as an amateur and professional racing cyclist before grey hair and a general lack of pace demanded a change of career. A degree in Social Studies at Liverpool Polytechnic was followed by an MPhil and PhD in the Department of Economics at Cambridge University – where he first encountered critical realism. Steve is now Senior Lecturer in the Department of Organisation, Work and Technology at Lancaster

University Management School, where he teaches Employment Relations and HRM. His publications include *Hayek's Political Economy: the Socio-economics of Order* (Routledge, 1995), *Critical Realism in Economics: Development and Debate* (Routledge, 1999), *Realist Perspectives on Organisation and Management* (Routledge, 2000, co-edited with S. Ackroyd) and *Critical Realism and Marxism* (Routledge, 2002, co-edited with A. Brown and J.M. Roberts). As well as articles on philosophy and methodology of science, he has also written on Marxist political economy and labour economics. He is currently in the process of drafting a book on the nature of labour markets.

John Hamblett is a Senior Lecturer in HRM at Leeds Business School. For three years he was an ESRC Management Teaching Fellow at that institution. The focus of his current research interests concerns the changing relationship between the organisation of work, the political organisation of the working class and the idea of education. His publications include 'The tools of freedom and the sources of indignity' (with Denise Thursfield and Rick Holden; in McGoldrick *et al.*, *Understanding Human Resource Development*, Routledge, 2002), a defence of critical realism in the research of human resource development issues, and 'Other voices' (in *Human Resource Development International*, co-authored with Denise Thursfield), which represents the preliminary findings of an ongoing research project on the Plebs League. John has just bought a new bike and is sworn to getting fit.

Debbie Harrison is an Associate Professor at the Norwegian School of Management BI, Oslo, Norway. She has published articles and chapters in books on network responses to environmental change, relationship dissolution, path dependence, case studies and critical realism. She has published in *Journal of Management Studies*, *Journal of Business Research* and *Technology Analysis and Strategic Management*. Her current research focuses upon resource interaction in business networks.

Anthony Hesketh is Lecturer in the Department of Management Learning at Lancaster University Management School. His research primarily focuses on the political economy of human resource management. Current projects include investigating the political economy of the UK north–south divide (with Bob Jessop) and a growing preoccupation with the measurement of performance inside organisations generally, and with the business process outsourcing of human resources in particular. Recent publications include *Playing to Win: Managing Employability in the Knowledge Economy* (Oxford University Press, 2004).

Jan Ch. Karlsson is Professor of Sociology in the Department of Working Life Science, Karlstad University, Sweden. His publications are concerned with the concept of work, modern work organisation, class and gender in everyday life, and critical realism and methodology in the social sciences. He is co-author of *Explaining Society: An Introduction to Critical Realism in the Social Sciences* (Routledge, 2001). Among his greatest feats he counts having caught a pike of 16 kilos, a perch of 1.7 kilos and a pikeperch of 6.4 kilos. And he thinks that anyone who has learned how to keep warm in Oslo should go to Karlstad to improve their skills.

Carole and Peter Kennedy lecture in Sociology and Social Policy in the School of Law and Social Sciences at Glasgow Caledonian University. Carole's main research interests include the sociology of health professionals and the modern history of the organisation of alternative medicine in Glasgow. Peter is currently managing editor of the journal *Critique*. He has research interests in Marxism and social change and transformation, as well as the contribution of critical theory broadly defined to an understanding of disputes inherent to the philosophy of social sciences.

Ruth Kowalczyk is a Lecturer in the Management Science Department at Lancaster University. She completed a degree in Management Science at Lancaster and has recently finished her PhD, which focused on the management of intensive care units. Her past experience as a nurse has led to her prime research interest being in health care. In this area she is particularly interested in resource management, performance management and the management of change. Other research interests include integrating hard and soft methods and realism. She enjoys good food, fell walking, sewing and reading, and now has 'a life' after completing her PhD.

Clive Lawson graduated from Cambridge University in 1983. After spending several years as a professional musician he then returned to Cambridge to pursue a PhD in industrial relations. The PhD quickly turned to methodology and philosophy of science issues when it became clear that standard economic theory was unable to deal satisfactorily with institutions and organisations. He then spent some years as a Research Fellow in the ESRC Centre for Business Research working on the clustering of high technology firms and on technology consultancies, whilst also publishing extensively on institutionalist economics and critical realism. His current research is on the philosophy of technology. He is currently banned from riding his bike for health reasons!

John Mingers is Professor of Operational Research and Systems at Warwick Business School, Warwick University. His main interests are in the philosophy of OR and Systems, and in social systems theory. His books include *Self-Producing Systems: Implications and Applications of Autopoiesis* (Plenum Press, 1995), *Multimethodology: Theory and Practice of Combining Management Science Methodologies* (Wiley, 1997, with A. Gill), *Information Systems: An Emerging Discipline?* (McGraw-Hill, 1997, with F. Stowell) and *Rational Analysis for a Problematic World Revisited* (Wiley, 2001, with J. Rosenhead). Having begun his career as a 'hard' positivistic operational researcher, and then leapt into the pit of 'soft', interpretive, systems thinking, he is grateful to critical realism as a way of reconciling the two.

Andrew Sayer is Professor of Social Theory and Political Economy and Head of the Department of Sociology at Lancaster University. His books include *Method in Social Science: A Realist Approach* (Routledge, 2nd edition 1992), *Realism and Social Science* (Sage, 2000), *Radical Political Economy: A Critique* (Blackwell, 1995), *Microcircuits of Capital* (Polity, 1988, with K. Morgan) and *The New Social Economy* (Blackwell, 1992, with R.A. Walker). The last three of these are substantive studies informed by a critical realist appproach. When the workload permits, Andrew enjoys cycling in the Lake District with Steve Fleetwood.

Phil Taylor is a Senior Lecturer in Industrial Relations in the Department of Management and Organization at the University of Stirling. Areas of recent research and publications include call centres, employment relations in microelectronics, occupational health, student part-time employment, trade unions and HRM, the white-collar labour process and prison privatisation. Current call centre research includes projects on health and safety, outsourcing to India and trade union organising. He is a lead member of an Economic and Social Research Council 'Future of Work' project based across three Scottish universities investigating the meaning of work.

Paul Thompson is Professor of Organisational Analysis at the University of Strathclyde. His recent publications include *Workplaces of the Future* (Macmillan, 1998, with Chris Warhurst), *Organizational Misbehaviour* (Sage, 1999, with Stephen Ackroyd) and *Work Organizations* (Palgrave, 3rd edition 2002, with David McHugh). Paul is co-organiser of the International Labour Process Conference and editor of *Renewal: A Journal of Labour Politics.*

Denise Thursfield is a Lecturer in Human Resource Management at Hull University Business School. Her research interests are in the area of skill and human resource development. More recently she has been conducting historical research into independent working-class education and the Plebs League. Her publications include *Post-Fordism and Skill: Theories and Perceptions* (Ashgate, 2000) and 'Mutuality, Learning and Change at Work: The Case of Employee Led Development' (2001, co-authored with John Hamblett) in *Employee Relations.* She enjoys watching Leeds United struggle to remain in the premiership!

Preface

Critical Realist Applications in Organisation and Management Studies is motivated by two beliefs: one positive and the other negative. The positive belief is that critical realism has much to offer in the analysis of Organisation and Management (O&M). Evidence for this is provided not only in the following chapters where contributors have rooted their theoretical and empirical work in critical realism to good effect, but also in the growing number of critical realist inspired articles found in the O&M studies literature. The negative belief is that a great deal of current O&M studies is committed to one of two inappropriate ontological positions. The first is the *empirical realist* ontology which privileges empirical, observable phenomena and sponsors positivist and scientistic-orientated analysis. The second is the *strongly social constructionist* ontology which privileges, often to the exclusion of all else, discursive, linguistic, or other semiotised phenomena. This ontology sponsors much postmodernist or poststructuralist orientated analysis – although not all analysis carried out under these labels is committed to this *strong* social constructionist ontology. Be that as it may, the recoil from abandoning positivism appears to have 'catapulted' many postmodernists and post-structuralists into substituting one inappropriate ontology for another and could easily take O&M studies down an alley as blind as the positivist one from which it has struggled to escape. Such a trajectory would be tragic given that critical realism can provide an ontology that allows positivism and its empirical realist ontology to be abandoned without having to accept strong social constructionism.

Apart from two chapters dedicated to ontology and methodology respectively, *Critical Realist Applications in Organisation and Management Studies* is not about critical realism *per se*. Rather it is about putting critical realism to work in four senses. First, as an underlabourer, that is in the removal of meta-theoretical obstacles that hinder the development of fruitful theoretical and empirical work. Second and third, as a meta-theoretical tool with which to develop appropriate methodological and theoretical frameworks which can then be used to inform appropriate empirical work. And finally, all of this is applied across a broad range of subjects areas including critical management studies, accountancy, marketing, health care management, operations research, the nature of work, human resource management, labour process theory, regional analysis, and work and labour market studies.

Editors' introduction

Critical realist applications in organisation and management studies

Steve Fleetwood and Stephen Ackroyd

The present work, *Critical Realist Applications in Organisation and Management Studies*, is a sequel to our earlier collection on the application of realism to this field, which was entitled *Realist Perspectives on Management and Organisations* (Ackroyd and Fleetwood, 2000). It is a measure of how far things have changed in the popularity of critical realism in the field of organisation and management studies (O&MS) recently that, in just the few years intervening since the turn of the millennium, it is now common to find researchers and writers expressing an attachment to, and respect for, critical realism. When assembling the first volume, there were a few important papers already published in the field of O&MS that were written from a critical realist point of view. But, to make up an adequate quota for a book or readings, we also had to include chapters which, though clearly realist in general approach, did not explicitly acknowledge a connection with traditional realism or its more recent, critical version. The present volume, by contrast, is a collection of academic work that is entirely new. It is work that has only recently been completed and which, almost without exception, aligns itself with a critical realist philosophical position. The wealth of material now available, written from a critical realist position, means that there were many papers for the editors to choose from to produce this volume of recent work.

There is, in fact, a significant intellectual movement now going on in the field of organisation and management studies (O&MS), in which the philosophy of critical realism is being more and more widely appreciated and put to use. This has been developing for some time, and is part of a wider intellectual movement in society and culture where similar emphases are being affirmed. These developments are, at least in part, in reaction to the radical scepticism and relativism that have been the fashion in much contemporary thinking. In some areas, of which O&MS is definitely one, this movement is concerned with reconnecting with particular traditional assumptions about this subject area and using the ideas of critical realism to deepen and extend more traditional ideas. We take the view that realism has been, for many practitioners during the last century, the orthodoxy in O&MS and related fields. Historically, studies which take an implicitly realist point of view constitute a continuous strand of research which has, only in the last two decades, tended to be devalued and sidelined by authors espousing the fashionable doctrines of post-structuralism and postmodernism – although we do recognise that it is possible to subscribe to these doctrines without simultaneously subscribing to a strong (and anti-realist) social constructionist ontology. Thus, in our view, in the field of O&MS, the movement towards critical realism connects with, adds to and reaffirms a realist emphasis that is already in existence. What is novel at the present time is that more and more writers and researchers are explicitly recognising the importance and value of the philosophy of critical realism as an alternative to both scientism and positivism and to postmodernism and post-structuralism, and using it as a reference point and source of inspiration for their work. The present collection is drawn from the best of this recent work.

Considered in some ways, the lurch into postmodern and post-structuralist O&MS, which first developed in the 1980s, was unexpected. Such movements typically emerge and develop vigorously when there is the dominance of extreme forms of scientism, reductionism and positivism. But it can hardly be said that, in Western Europe at least, scientism and positivism were dominant modes of discourse, and they had not been for some time. In the late nineteenth century belief in the efficacy of science was in the ascendant and there was a tendency to try to apply (what were assumed to be) the techniques of natural science everywhere. However, it is also true that by the first decades of the twentieth century the movement of reaction to scientism and positivism was growing strongly, and at this time we have both the development of the first effective social science disciplines and the development of a recognisable philosophical realism.

It is true that there have been strong advocates of positivism in the twentieth century, but, in the first few decades of that century, the foundations for a powerful critique and rejection of scientism were laid in the existentialist and phenomenological movements. By the last twenty-five years of the twentieth century, positivism and scientism were no longer as strong as they once had been, and had been confined to particular enclaves within particular disciplines. The field of O&MS illustrates this general point as well as any. Some pockets of research in the field of O&MS, operational research or econometrics, for example, have been totally dominated by positivism for decades without serious questioning from the inside or challenge from external critics. But the views of academics in these areas were by no means universally accepted and the critique of positivism had been strongly represented in social science in general (Giddens, 1974) and O&MS in particular (Clegg and Dunkerley, 1980) for some time. In Britain and much of continental Europe, in O&MS, positivism had been on the back foot for decades. Not content with this, there arose a widespread movement to press the critique of scientism further, to cover many branches of study, including those in which it was neither dominant nor oppressive.

However, the majority of scholars and researchers operating in O&MS have never been naively certain that social science can *easily* arrive at true accounts of the world, as positivists suggest. Nevertheless, it was widely argued by postmodernists and post-structuralists beginning in the 1980s that objectivity (see

Fleetwood in this volume) in the study of human affairs is impossible. Thus, many supposedly radical exponents of O&MS turned to relativism and down an alley as blind as the positivist one from which the subject area had, laboriously but effectively, struggled to escape in earlier decades. In the enthusiasm for radical critique, it has been forgotten by many (if they ever knew) that philosophical realism provides a viable alternative to positivism and naive realism (according to which true accounts of the world are readily available), and extreme relativism on the other (according to which the very possibility of ever arriving at a true account is denied due to the strong social constructionist ontology adopted).

Yet the work of such large groups of researchers in O&MS as those studying the labour process, or institutional writers of various kinds and the regulationists, is all informed by realism and/or their views imply realist conceptions of the subject matter. Indeed, there are contributions to this volume that show obvious continuities with the work of earlier generations of scholars. Though they are concerned with the contemporary workplace, with call centres and change in high-tech sectors of the public services for example, such studies show clear continuity with the work of earlier generations of scholars. Although it is obviously very important, providing a basis on which empirical research can be extended and develop new and exciting insights, is not the only reason for advocating critical realism in O&MS, as we will now argue.

This is not a work in which it would be appropriate to give extended coverage to the nature of critical realism itself. Nevertheless, we do include a very compact and intelligible general account of the position and its applicability to social science in the foreword by Andrew Sayer, as well as general, orientating essays at the start of the first two substantive sections of the text. As Sayer argues in his inimical way (this volume and 2000) and a number of other writers affirm (Archer *et al.*, 1998), critical realism postulates a world external to the knowing subject, but also holds that gaining even partial access to that world is not straightforward. This is so for a number of reasons, not least of which is because we cannot gain access to the world independently of the concepts we use. Nevertheless, realism not only suggests a specific point of view concerning what exists (a view on ontology) but also how to assemble knowledge of it (epistemology). As has been demonstrated before, realism allows positivism and its empirical realist ontology to be abandoned without the researcher having to accept extreme forms of relativism and its strong social constructionist ontology. In view of this, it is hardly surprising that some contemporary critical realist writing is preoccupied with the criticism of relativist writing, and its implications. Nevertheless, we have tried to avoid the sterile process of critique being met with counter-critique, in favour of showing that critical realism has direct relevance to practice in O&MS in a variety of dimensions.

In general, the value of critical realism (or any philosophy of research, for that matter) to research and knowledge creation is not direct, or, as Sayer describes it, 'loose'. We must think of critical realist philosophy as serving the researcher, much as a labourer serves a craftsman, by helping to do general preparatory work or clearing obstacles that stop work or make it more problematic than it needs to be. Thus critical realism can deal with general conceptual problems, such as how to think about subject matter, what the objectives of analysis are, what is an effective and/or an adequate explanation using such subject matter, and so on. Second, critical realism can function as a meta-theoretical tool with which to help develop appropriate theoretical frameworks and methodological procedures. Third, once it is developed, a new theory can be used, with support from critical realist ideas, to inform effective empirical work. Finally, critical realism encourages the making of connections across a broad range of subject areas, encouraging synthetic understanding as opposed to more and more specialist knowledge. Critical realism is not itself a finished doctrine that may be simply used or applied; the philosophy itself is being actively developed at the same time as the social and other science it describes and informs. Ensuring that philosophical developments in critical realism are continually, and iteratively, updated in tandem with developments in theory, methodology and empirical work guards against the possibility that we simply read off method, theory and empirical claims from a pre-ordained philosophical schema. Incidentally, the relationship between empirical knowledge and other dimensions of thought is a problem facing all thinkers and it will not be addressed by ignoring philosophical presuppositions.

Following these general guidelines, in the body of the present volume, we suggest that there are three areas in which critical realist ideas have been found to be of particular relevance to O&MS by researchers and scholars in recent years, and, after the foreword by Andrew Sayer, the book is divided into three sections along these lines:

- In the first section, we include essays which point to the relevance of critical realism in meta-theory and theory formation. Here it is shown that critical realism illuminates the ways in which researchers may fruitfully orientate themselves to the field of O&MS, and ways which are less than helpful. The relationship of critical realism as philosophy and general ideas to social scientific theory is indistinct; theory is certainly not deducible from realist doctrine. Nonetheless, realist philosophy is undoubtedly an important source of ideas feeding the creative imagination of the theorist, and indicating likely sources of bias and error. This is the only section of the book in which critique of alternative ways of thinking is given much scope.
- In the second section of the book, we give consideration to the ways in which critical realism suggests the appropriateness of changes in emphasis and practice in research methodology from what has been done in the past. Critical realism does not show a preference for either quantitative or qualitative methods, holding that neither is inherently superior. On the contrary critical realist researchers see the relevance of both kinds of data, and point to the need for the creative combination of both kinds of data in illuminating causal mechanisms. In this section it is shown that there is much more discretion in the choice of research technique and in the use of data

than scholars have so far acknowledged, and that theoretical considerations are very important in shaping both the directions of research and the specific interpretation given to research information. Here it is shown that critical realism leads to the consideration of not only new ways of thinking about research, but of new ways of utilising existing research techniques and methods. Realist-inspired research methodology combines different methods of investigation to good effect. It is suggested that critical realism allows the development of new ways of opening out wide areas of O&MS for study in ways not previously envisaged.

- In the third section of the book, we include examples of new substantive social science research written from a critical realist point of view. In some of the examples included here there are obvious continuities with kinds of organisational research that have traditionally been practised in O&MS. Other chapters are examples of applied research looking at workgroups, such as professionals and semi-professionals, and at applications such as recruitment and selection, that are very far from the traditional modes of empirical work in this field. The point is that insightful research continues to be done from a realist point of view.

References

Ackroyd, S. and Fleetwood, S. (2000) (eds) *Realist Perspectives on Management and Organisation*, London: Routledge.

Archer, M., Bhaskar, R., Collier, A., Lawson, T. and Norrie, A. (1998) *Critical Realism: Essential Readings*, London: Routledge.

Clegg, S. and Dunkerley, D. (1980) *Organisations, Class and Control*, London: Routledge and Kegan Paul.

Giddens, A. (ed.) (1974) *Positivism and Sociology*, London: Heinemann.

Sayer, A. (2000) *Realism and Social Science*, London: Sage.

Foreword

Why critical realism?

Andrew Sayer

Introduction

Critical realist philosophy offers an alternative both to the spurious scientificity of positivism and to idealist and relativist reactions to positivism.[1] In this foreword, I shall sketch key features of critical realism and suggest how they might be important for research in organisation and management studies. This is a difficult task, not only because critical realism itself needs at least a book-length introduction on its own, but also, as we shall see, because the relationship between philosophies and substantive social theories is loose rather than tight. This foreword will therefore necessarily be telegrammatic in style, cutting many corners and offering citations where further discussion can be found.

What is realism?

Contrary to what many assume, realism does not claim privileged access to the real world: it rejects such 'foundationalism'. Its most basic claim is simply that there is a world which exists largely independently of the researcher's knowledge of it. This independence implies not simple, direct access to the world but a more difficult relationship. Our knowledge of the world is always in terms of available descriptions or discourses, and we cannot step outside these to see how our knowledge claims compare to the things to which they refer. It is the experience of the fallibility of our knowledge, of mistaking things and being taken by surprise, that gives us the realist conviction that the world is not merely the product of thought, whether privately or socially 'constructed'. But it is also this experience which suggests that although it is always mediated by and conceptualised within available discourses, we can still get a kind of feedback from the world. In the realm of practice, not just anything goes: wishful thinking rarely works. At least part of the world is accessible to us, though, as we have noted, always in a mediated way.

Social constructions

Of course, the *social* world is 'socially constructed', so how can realism's basic proposition about the independence of the world hold in social science? We need first to take a critical look at what 'construction' might mean here, and to consider how it works out over time, and ask 'construction of what, by whom – actors or researchers?' There is a difference between *construal* and *construction*, or between making a mental construction *of* the world and materially constructing something. Construals or interpretations of the world can contingently inform material constructions, including practices and organisational forms. Once such social phenomena are constructed, they gain some degree of independence from their original constructors and from subsequent actors. If social scientists' knowledge is fallible, so too is lay knowledge, and hence deliberate social constructions may fail or only succeed partially. Thus, a university is a social construction based upon a set of ideas, but it is always something more than the latter, and some aspects of actual instances may be quite different from the ideas which informed them. Similarly, an employment contract is not *merely* a social construction, but an incomplete or only partly successful one, in that on its own, it cannot ensure the effects it is intended to produce, but depends on other non-contractual conditions, particularly trust and certain shared assumptions and social norms. Discourses are not mere reflections of material circumstances, but nor are material circumstances mere instantiations of discourses. Discourses are shaped through practice, in particular, through material and socio-linguistic contexts which have their own properties or tendencies, inherited from previous rounds of social construction or 'structuration'.[2]

Construal and construction may merge in acts of communication, such as conversations, but even then there is an iterative process developing over time, in which what has just been constructed (for example, a comment made within the terms of a certain managerial discourse) is re-construed by others. Just as with any other process of change, how far particular construals change that discourse is constrained and enabled by the properties and circumstances of what is being changed, which are generally not of actors' own choosing. The social phenomena that confront us today are mostly the product of activities carried out before any current observations we make, and while it is occasionally possible for researchers to influence what they study, the latter phenomena are mostly others' constructions, and not necessarily intended ones at that. Management researchers may be more likely to influence the social constructions that they study than most social scientists, but this of course presupposes that there are practices or constructions which exist independently of those which they can influence. Social constructions therefore fit with our general realist principle.

Truth

Mention of the idea of fallibility of knowledge inevitably raises the issue of truth. There is only space here to make a few brief comments: first, that the concept of truth is itself complex and is an attempt to characterise a certain kind of relationship between knowledge and its objects, though objects are generally what they are regardless of researchers' knowledge.[3] Realists don't have to assume that the truth of statements, theories or discourses is an all-or-nothing, absolute matter. The relationship has an emphatically practical character, so that we may prefer to talk of degrees of practical adequacy, and of progress in terms of 'epistemic gain' rather than establishing absolute truth about some situation once and for all, whatever that might mean (Sayer, 2000a: Chapter 2).

Often, amongst non-philosophers, merely raising the issue of truth can promote a kind of stultifying blanket scepticism about all knowledge. This is self-undermining, for to doubt anything in particular (A), we need provisionally to accept the adequacy or truth of other propositions (B) which we use as grounds for our doubts about A. And truth is not always a problem. We make judgements about the truth of propositions every time we cross the road (is there are a car coming?), and if someone gets it wrong and is run over, then that again shows that the world is not merely a product of thought. While there are some matters where it is hard to imagine ever settling on an account that is likely to escape counter-evidence and argument, there are some propositions (for example, that our blood circulates in our bodies) whose truth it is hard to imagine ever being refuted.

At any particular time, there will always be matters about which we are uncertain and where we have difficulty in choosing among alternative accounts. But we should beware of exaggerating or at least mis-characterising dissensus in social science; many such alternative accounts in social science are not straightforward, mutually exclusive rivals, but emphasise different aspects of complex, many-sided processes. I personally do not think it too much to argue that there is something to learn from each of Marx, Weber and Foucault regarding modern organisations; to be sure, such a position could lead to an eclectic combination of contradictory or incommensurable ideas, but there may be ways of avoiding such contradictions by modifying aspects of any of the contributing theories. Any totalising ambitions of such theories – and all three of the above are susceptible to such ambitions! – would need to be dropped first before such non-contradictory syntheses could be developed, but critical realism need hold no brief for imperialist approaches to theorising anyway. Personally, my hunch is that much of the dissensus in social science is attributable to theoretical imperialism and reductionism (conditions to which critics of 'grand narratives' are definitely not immune!), and a chronic tendency to underestimate the concrete or many-sided character of social phenomena.

Finally, regarding truth and dissensus, it should also be noted that where theories are in contradiction, that implies they have something in common over which they can contradict one another. The problem of incommensurability has often been exaggerated, for it is common for researchers to be able to understand apparently incommensurable theories; in any case incommensurability of discourses only matters if the rival discourses are about a common referent, otherwise their differences may be no more of a problem than the differences between tennis and football (Bhaskar, 1979).

Ontology

Almost all theorists are what might be called 'minimal realists' in that they acknowledge that the world includes things which can exist independently of any knowledge of them.[4] This inference that there is something 'other' to our knowledge is again based on the resistance which we sense from the world. However, if we think about what must be the case for this experience of resistance and for the possibility of failure of intended practices, then it can be seen that we must go beyond minimal realism. This is because for the world to make a difference, so that some attempted practices work and others do not, and hence that the world is neither merely a product of wishful thinking or 'discourse' nor universally resistant or indifferent, it must itself be differentiated. If it were undifferentiated, then it is hard to imagine how the same practices could work under some conditions and not under others, or how anything *in particular* (such as catching a cold, getting arrested or getting a pay rise) could happen to us. Particular practices *can* make a difference, and this must depend on how well they accord with the differentiated properties of the world, social and natural. This relationship is of course inherently difficult to characterise (hence the problems of both correspondence and conventionalist theories of truth), but that does not mean that there is no such relation.

Critical realists go still further and argue that the world is not only differentiated, but 'stratified'; that some kinds of objects, for example biological phenomena, are 'emergent from' their constituents (chemical and physical processes, in this case). In turn, certain interactions of biological processes may allow the development of another stratum of emergent properties which we may want to call social or cultural. In other words, from certain conjunctions or interactions of objects, new emergent properties develop which are irreducible to those of the objects on which they depend. Language, *par excellence*, illustrates this emergence, as new discourses arise through the generation of new meanings which are irreducible to those of their constituents. Faced with such emergence, we must study emergent properties 'at their own level' rather than treat them as reducible to their constituents.[5] 'Higher strata' objects may react back on lower strata objects, as when humans develop agriculture or contraception, but such interactions are always via processes at the level of the stratum being changed. Thus humans do not change ecosystems just by activating their social powers of being able to develop a discourse of agriculture, they change them by using their physical, chemical and biological powers according to their (social) ideas. Interactions such as these do not contradict the basic asymmetry which is the diagnostic characteristic of emergence: chemical processes can exist without biological processes, but not vice versa; biological processes can exist without social processes, but not vice versa.

Theorising and necessity

Theorising is often seen as beyond the scope of philosophical comment, usually on the grounds that it is an inherently ineffable activity, involving imaginative leaps which elude reconstruction. For critical realism, theorising certainly involves imagination – usually in the deployment and development of metaphors, analogies and models – and also abstraction – selecting out one-sided aspects of phenomena in order to focus upon their characteristic properties and conditions of existence (cf. Lewis, 1999; Fleetwood, 2002). While, as Max Weber suggested in his ideal type methodology, researchers select elements which are important to them in value terms, we don't select them only according to our value orientation; we also construct them according to ideas about relationships, selecting those elements which we think have to go together to produce the effects of interest, as opposed to things which merely can go together but don't have to.[6] The attempt to distinguish between 'can' and 'must', contingency and necessity, coupled with the search for better metaphors and models for representing the world, is central to theorising in social science.

This highlights a key feature of critical realism, its imputation of necessity (natural or real rather than 'logical') to objects; i.e. while there are many contingent relations in which an object X can stand, that is relationships which are neither necessary nor impossible for its existence as X, there are some which are necessary conditions of its existence as an X. Thus capitalist firms have to operate with money, employ wage-labour, accumulate capital, etc. to remain capitalist firms, but simply as capitalist firms, it is contingent whether they use this or that managerial philosophy, British or non-British, black or white, workers, and whether their business is based on call centres, hotels or steel mills. Of course, these latter relationships may make some important differences to what happens, and have their own additional necessary conditions of existence, which any concrete study of capitalism would need to analyse, but in theorising we are typically involved in making such distinctions between objects' necessary features and the various forms which they can contingently take. It should be noted here that the necessity is not merely a matter of logic or definition; for example, the ability of landlords to charge rent is not merely a product of the way the concept of landlord is defined but rather a consequence of their possession of land which others who lack land need to use. Definitions often represent these natural (here including social) necessities by setting up logical or conceptual necessities, but the latter's force derives from what they represent, not mere linguistic convention.

The confusion of this kind of necessity with logical necessity usually comes about through overlooking how and why definitional truths are constructed and why they come to have any practical adequacy in making sense of the world. We may sometimes create logical necessities in the form of definitional truths to try to represent what we believe to be natural necessities, as when we make the molecular structure of water part of its definition, though, of course, like the shape of the earth, the structure and properties of water do not depend on humans conceptualising it in any particular way (Harré and Madden, 1975: 48; Harré, 1972). Our conceptualisation – in this example drawing upon molecular theory – remains a fallible way of making sense of such things. To imagine that the world – or water, bureaucracy, patriarchy or capitalism – have whatever properties they do because of the way researchers conceptualise them is a strange intellectualist conceit.

The production of change

Necessity is also central to the critical realist approach to causation, or the explanation of what produces change. Whereas both positivists and many anti-positivists assume that causation is about regularities amongst events, to be sought out by treating social systems as closed, critical realism argues that causation is more plausibly treated as based on causal powers or liabilities (susceptibilities) possessed by objects, whose existence and exercise is not dependent on regularities among events. Thus, by virtue of their hierarchical structure, their systems of rules, and information recording and storage, bureaucracies have the power to routinise and process large volumes of standard decisions in little time. By contrast, their powers of flexibility and adaptability in dealing with diverse, novel inputs are limited by these structural characteristics. In both cases the causal powers and liabilities derive from the structure of bureaucracies, including their insertion into larger structures such as the social division of labour, and their internalisation into smaller ones, particularly the dispositions and ways of thinking of workers and clients.[7]

Causal powers are dependent on the nature of objects or structures of which they are properties. However, it is contingent whether they are exercised at any particular time or place. Thus an organisation may have the power to fire workers, but for the most part it may not need to exercise this power. When it does try to exercise it what ensues will depend on the context in which they contingently operate: whether workers are strongly organised, whether employment legislation constrains what can be done, whether unemployment is high, etc. Because of these contingencies, the effects of the activation of the causal power need not be regular. While regularities may be interesting and sometimes helpful for making observations, they are not essentially related to causation. What makes things happen has nothing to do with whether social scientists have plenty of regular instances to observe and quantify. To explain how a causal process works we are likely to need a qualitative description of the causal powers present (both the key ones of interest and those of contextual phenomena) (Sayer, 1992). The process of identifying what causal powers[8] are active in a given situation is called retroduction and, of course, there are usually several jointly responsible for particular events.

The methodological implications of this are huge, for it implies that social research should place much more emphasis on conceptualisation and description than positivism assumes, and that the search for regularities through quantitative analysis becomes relatively downgraded (though not redundant). Critical realism implies that we need to distinguish between *generalisation*, which is about finding out how extensive certain phenomena are, and may give little explanation of what produces them, and *abstraction* and *retroduction*, which are needed to explain what produces particular states and changes, but which do not necessarily indicate much about their distribution, frequency or regularity. Both are needed in social science, but their differences imply a reconsideration of many common views of the respective roles of surveys and case studies, which see the former as explanatory and the latter merely exploratory or illustrative (Sayer, 1992: Chapter 9, 2000b: 19–26).

Interpretive understanding and causation

A further distinctive feature of critical realism is that it rejects the extremes of both methodological naturalism – the view that the methods of the social sciences are or should be identical to those of natural science – and anti-naturalism – the view that they have nothing in common. This opposition has traditionally crystallised around the opposition of causal explanation and interpretive understanding or *erklaren* and *verstehen*. The former is assumed by naturalists to be universally applicable, and by anti-naturalists to be restricted to natural science. The latter – understanding – is dismissed by naturalists, but anti-naturalists view it as all that social studies require. Understanding, like reading, is not a matter of being able to identify what caused (produced) a particular text but of making sense of its meaning. It is therefore indispensable in all science since scientists or researchers have to understand one another. However, meanings do not merely externally describe social phenomena but internally influence their nature, as our discussion of social construction acknowledged. In social science, this concept-dependence[9] of social phenomena means there is therefore a 'double hermeneutic' rather than merely a single one as in natural science. While critical realism endorses this point, it rejects the inference, which anti-naturalists draw from it, that causation is irrelevant to social science. On the contrary, simply because societies involve change, and we have to account for that change, we have to attempt to identify what causes (produces) it.

This implies that it is not a matter of either causal explanation or interpretive understanding but one of using *both* in social science. However, critical realism argues that they are not merely co-present but interrelated, albeit asymmetrically. This is because communication itself produces change, at least in terms of what happens in listeners'/readers' heads, and often in prompting new kinds of thinking and action; indeed language would be redundant if it changed nothing. Particularly in the field of studies of management, where management discourse is now given such extraordinary prominence, it would be absurd to deny its causal efficacity.

Following Bhaskar (1979), critical realists argue that reasons can operate as causes, that is be responsible for producing a change. This is an unfamiliar notion in that it is a non-physical notion of causation (though there are physical changes associated with reasoning in the brain of course), but when someone tries to persuade us that we are wrong to make this argument by giving us reasons, they in turn presuppose that offering reasons can be causative. This applies, as in the physical sciences, irrespective of whether there are regularities for us to record. The causal efficacy of reasons depends on them being understood in some fashion, but not necessarily just in a single fashion. Thus, management's exhortations to workers may meet with a variety of responses. The fact that they might be construed differently by different individuals and hence do not form part of constant conjunctions or event regularities does not mean that they have no (causal) influence on behaviour (Bhaskar, 1979; Collier, 1994).

Crucial though this issue of reasons as causes has been in the philosophy of social science, it remains seriously incomplete. For it evades the question of the specific nature of 'reasons' and how they come to motivate action. In particular, it ignores the semiotic character of reasons and, in some cases, treats them as simple, singular triggers of action. Yet reasons are diffuse and hard to identify unambiguously. Indeed, it would be better to think of them as emergent elements in more extensive networks of concepts, beliefs, symbols and linguistic constructions. They presuppose languages, intentionality, particular concepts and prior understandings and interests, intertextuality, conventions of inference and evidence, and so on. In addition, if we reflect more broadly upon what kinds of discursive features and events can bring about changes in behaviour (if only at the level of how people think), we notice that it is not only reasons that change what we do. We may be influenced more by the tone (e.g. warmth, hostility) or imagery of a speech than by any reasons that may be given. We therefore need to go beyond the reasons-as-causes argument, important though it is, to examine the nature of semiosis more generally and its place within the overall logic of the social (Fairclough *et al.*, 2002). Awareness of these complexities surrounding the discursive production of effects may prompt doubts about the confidence we might put in any particular analyses, but against this we should remember we routinely overcome these problems in everyday practical communication indeed the successful reproduction of complex organisations presupposes their resolution.

Critical realism recognises that reasons and other discursive phenomena may be causally efficacious – so critical realism is compatible with a recognition of the importance of managerial and other discourses in organisations. However, in accordance with its general account of causation and causal powers, it notes that (a) it is contingent whether these causal powers are activated; and (b) and if they are, the effects depend on conditions, such as the properties of other discourses, motivations and interests. Thus, rather than use a crude, black and white distinction between the denotative and performative properties of discourses, in which they either externally describe or 'construct' phenomena, we can recognise that discourses can be performative, but don't have to be, and that intended social constructions vary in their completeness and success.

Science as a social activity

Social science is a social activity, influenced by its social relations and conditions of production, but as with any production, it is not free from constraints of practical adequacy, and it is vulnerable to empirical refutations which are not reducible to changes in fashion or power relations in the scientific community. Social science, including the sociology of science itself, could benefit from greater reflexivity about its own conditions of production, particularly, as

Bourdieu demonstrates, its scholastic relationship to its subject matter and its tendency to project this relationship onto its subject matter (Bourdieu, 2000), and critical realism would do well to explore this currently underdeveloped side of its philosophy and methodology of social science. As should be particularly clear in management research, the actors and activities under study are mainly concerned with getting things done, and not with study and academic reflection.

Why *critical* realism?

Critical realism offers a rationale for critical social science, that is one that is critical of the social practices it studies as well as of other theories. Bhaskar (1986), in particular, has argued that social science has an emancipatory potential. Social practices are informed by ideas which may or may not be true and whether they are true may have some bearing upon what happens. Thus, gender relations are generally informed and reproduced through beliefs that gender is innate rather than a product of socialisation, so that the disadvantages suffered by women are seen implicitly as natural too. Social scientists who merely reproduced this explanation uncritically in their own accounts so that they merely reported that gender was a product of biological difference would fail to understand gender. To explain such phenomena one has to acknowledge this dependence of actions on shared meanings while showing in what respects they are false, if they are. If social scientific accounts differ from those of actors then they cannot help but be critical of lay thought and action. Furthermore, as Bhaskar argues, to identify understandings in society as false, and hence actions informed by them as falsely based, is to imply that (other things being equal) those beliefs and actions, and indeed any conditions which tended to encourage them, ought to be changed.

Many terms in social science in everyday usage are simultaneously both descriptive (positive) and evaluative (normative), such as 'domination', 'subordination', 'exploitation' or 'development'. They are not merely expressions of approval or disapproval; they indicate that particular circumstances are present, and that there is something good or bad about the objects themselves in relation to human needs. There is something contradictory and frustrating about 'crypto-normative' accounts of social phenomena which use such terms without making clear *what* is wrong with or good about their objects.

Critical realism's determinedly critical stance contradicts the common taboo in contemporary social science against normative judgements. Against the view that it is a threat to objectivity, I would briefly note the following points:

1 Having and articulating normative views about social phenomena may lead one to misrepresent them but it does not *necessarily* lead to this. It is possible to accept that the world is other than what one would like it to be – indeed if it weren't, normative judgement would be redundant! It is precisely because ought does not entail is that we make such judgements. Here it is important to distinguish two different senses of 'objectivity' which are all too often

conflated, with disastrous results: objectivity in the sense of value-freedom is not necessary for objectivity in the sense of truth-seeking or telling (Sayer, 2000a: 58–62).

2 'Is' and 'ought' are not always distinct and do not always correspond to matters of fact and opinion respectively, particularly where we are concerned with needs; if a researcher claims that high levels of stress at work are bad for workers, do we merely say that that's merely the researcher's opinion or feeling which has no bearing on the facts, or do we argue about whether their claim is true or untrue?

3 Normative judgements are not reducible to subjective dispositions unrelated to the differentiations of the world. It would not make sense to say when confronted with two identical objects or practices that one was good and the other bad: it only makes sense to do so if the objects or practices are different in some respect (Norman, 1998). Valuations are about something – they are therefore not object-neutral and merely a property of subjects.

4 Normative matters are not beyond the scope of reason and antithetical to it; indeed their consideration is likely to make us reconsider – or if you prefer, deconstruct – common binaries of reason and emotion, fact and value.

It might seem that freedom and emancipation require a refusal of, or escape from, necessity or causation, and that real freedom lies in being able to redescribe ourselves and the world through new discourses. But the freedom to redescribe ourselves is worthless, unless the discourse is performative, that is causal. For changes in discourse to be causally efficacious or successfully performative, and not just accidental, we must know something about how the determinations we want to avoid work and how they can be subverted, blocked and replaced by more wanted, perhaps novel, determinations, and we must make appropriate causal interventions. Without causality any concept of responsibility, agency or freedom is meaningless, for we can only be responsible for what we can influence (Bhaskar, 1989: 163–4). 'It is not a matter of disengaging ourselves from the world so that it gets no grip on us – for by the same token, we would get no grip of it' (Collier, 1994: 192–3). Idealism or anti-realism makes discourse both inconsequential and all-powerful: inconsequential because it refuses to acknowledge that it can be causal and that its causal efficacy depends on how it relates to extra-discursive processes; all-powerful because it also makes it seem that we can re-make the world merely by redescribing it.

Critical realists are only beginning to think through the further normative implications and aspects of realist philosophy, but in the meantime, quite simply, one wonders what is the point of social science and the justification of academic labour subsidised by the general public if it is lacking in any normative implications?

Critical realism and positivism

It will be apparent that critical realism opposes relativist, idealist and strong social constructivist tendencies in social science. But on all of the matters I have discussed, critical realism also opposes positivism: its empiricist epistemology based on apparently theory-neutral observation; its confusion of matters of ontology with epistemology, as in its equating the world with what can be observed; its flat, unstratified ontology which cannot comprehend emergence; its assumption of universal closed systems and its Humean view of causation as constant conjunctions, which leads it to encourage researchers to view the search for empirical regularities as the goal of science; its contemplative, unpractical view of the relationship between knowledge and its objects; its unqualified naturalism and its incomprehension of interpretive understanding; its indifference to the nature of science as a social activity; and its subjectivist conception of values which leads it to confuse objectivity in the sense of value-neutrality with objectivity in the sense of truth-seeking.[10]

Critical realism and social theories

Critical realism is a philosophy of social science, not a social theory, like Weberianism or public choice theory. Like any philosophy, while it includes recommendations of how we should think and approach substantive subjects, it does so only in very broad terms. Some theories may be closer to critical realism in form than others, for example Marxism more than liberalism, though the latter can to some degree be construed in realist terms (Fleetwood, 1995), and it even has emancipatory potential (Nussbaum, 1999). In any case, no philosophy can guarantee the truth of substantive research done according to it. For example, critical realism's insistence on the distinction between causal powers and their exercise doesn't tell us which causal powers actually exist or what they will do when they are exercised. Social theories may therefore be consistent with critical realism, or indeed any philosophy of science, and yet turn out to be untrue – indeed they could meet the formal requirements (e.g. regarding explanatory forms) and yet be nonsense. In view of this, it is naive and unreasonable to expect critical realism, any more than any other philosophy, to provide a litmus test for distinguishing true from false or better from worse social scientific accounts. What it can do is provide guidelines for researchers grounded in ontological and epistemological arguments that avoid the pitfalls of positivism on one side and idealism and relativism on the other. There has only been space here to hint at what these involve but references have been given to literature which provides elaboration.

In conclusion I would like to comment further on the relationship between critical realism and social theories associated with post-structuralism and postmodernism.

First of all, the distinction between philosophies of social science and social theories implies that it is inadvisable to reject postmodernist and post-structuralist approaches as incompatible with critical realism, simply on the grounds that they are frequently non-realist. This is not only a matter of the virtues of encouraging criticism and openness to alternatives. It is also because theorists may or may not invoke or appeal to a particular philosophy or methodology, and even when they do it is common for them to diverge from it unknowingly in practice. Realist elements are common in a wide range of social theory, including much that is written by authors who would not count themselves as realists. Thus it is not only self-professed realists who talk of 'causal mechanisms' or who generally assume that the things they study are not dependent for their existence on how researchers conceive of them. Some post-structuralists refuse the concept of causation. However, since for realists a cause is whatever produces change, then in writing about substantive subjects such as the rise of new forms of management discourse and practice no-one can avoid referring to such matters, even though they may not recognise them as causes. In our everyday lives, we treat causal processes not simply as regularities but as the exercise of causal powers in which effects depend on contextual conditions: we don't, for example, expect the use of a new management technique in firms to have an identical impact on workers regardless of whether they are managers, secretaries, fitters or cleaners. Thus, given the heterogeneous character of social theory and the unavoidability of at least some elements of realism, it would seem unreasonable to reject approaches which are self-consciously non-realist or even anti-realist, for realist elements and assumptions are unlikely to be suppressed altogether. In this context it is interesting that Richard Marsden has provided a realist interpretation of Foucault in relation to the labour process and value (Marsden, 1999).

Instead of rejecting theoretical ideas out of hand merely because their advocates have provided non- or anti-realist ways of framing them at a meta-theoretical level, we can often recast them – albeit against the intentions of their authors – in realist form, and eliminate certain problems and contradictions that attend non-realist approaches. Thus concepts such as performativity, governmentality and capillary power, which are likely to be valuable for analysing organisations, can all be theorised in a realist way which avoids the kind of identity thinking which assumes that discourses and their effects correspond. We can accept that discourses can be performative, and note that this implies they produce change. Whilst this is a causal process, it is *not* one involving event regularities, since it can fail as well as succeed in producing the intended effects. The Foucauldian idea of power as productive rather than merely repressive fits well with the critical realist account of causal powers. The concept of governmentality and the useful metaphor of capillary power highlight forms of power which are dispersed rather than highly concentrated, and which operate partly through processes of internalisation and self-discipline by actors rather than mere external pressure. In realist terms we can acknowledge that causes can be internal as well as external, that all objects have causal powers or liabilities of some sort, and that sometimes these may not be so unequal as to produce highly concentrated sources of power (in the sense of domination or power over others) but multiple, dispersed sources. Even where, in Foucauldian style, there appear to be no particular sources of power that might be identified, it could be an emergent property of combinations of numerous elements. By such simple reconstructions we can avoid the need to invoke the peculiar (and meaningless?) notion 'that power is present in its effects'.

Similarly, Foucauldian ideas of power and resistance are again better re-interpreted within a critical realist approach. Even compliance presupposes resistance. If humans were totally plastic they could not be compliant with particular managerial or other discourses (even leaves-in-the-wind need to have certain properties, including resistances, so that they can catch the wind to be blown around): just as friction is both a condition of, and a resistance to, movement, so the acquisition/possession of certain dispositions or powers, some of which are typically extra-discursive in origin, or the product of different, earlier rounds of discursive influence, is a condition of compliance with as well as opposition to something like an audit regime. The metaphors of the 'constitution' or 'construction' of 'subjects' or bodies have rhetorical power as 'exagger-concepts', but they can easily encourage a kind of lazy thinking which assumes all-or-nothing processes of creation *ab novo*, when what is normally involved is a gradual, partial and contested process of influence, interpretation and modification of already 'constituted' objects/subjects with pre-existing causal powers. It is surely particularly important for studies of management and organisations to be able to distinguish a number of positions ranging from, at one extreme, mere parroting of elements of managerial discourses without any change in behaviour or ways of thinking, through to complete 'capture' by them at the other extreme.

Regarding Foucault's notion of 'regimes of truth', while this is self-undermining and idealist (Foucault, 1977, 1980; Sayer, 2000a: 40–9), his insights into the way discourses can influence the social world, including how actors see it, make more sense within a realist approach which recognises that the effectivity of discourses is not self-guaranteed but depends upon their having some degree of practical adequacy. This in turn depends upon their relationship to properties, some of which their objects possess independently of the discourses. Not just any objects can be shaped into self-disciplining subjects; they must be the kind of objects which can be shaped thus, for example capable of acquiring dispositions, learning and internalising norms. Success in producing such subjects depends on the relationship between the assumptions made by the discourses or putative regimes of truth and the properties (including existing self-understandings) of their objects/subjects, which will determine whether they succeed in having any effect. In these ways, one can again avoid the tendency to treat what should be empirical questions of the extent of influence of discourses into *a priori* invocations of the 'constitution of subjects'.

Finally, as regards postmodernism, this is such an indeterminate term, and one that has been applied to very diverse ways of thinking, that it would be unwise to dismiss it out of hand. Even though there are nihilist variants, there are other tendencies, which are not merely (again) capable of realist reconstruction (for example, Christopher Norris's realist reading of Derrida), but which I believe realists would do well to take more seriously, such as scepticism towards categorical ways of thinking (Norris, 1991; Sayer, 2000). In keeping with this last point, it would be singularly unhelpful for critical realists and postmodernists to assume that their positions are simple opposites with battle lines already drawn. Not least because consistent relativism and anti-realism are unsustainable, there are not only complex tangles of disagreements but of actual or potential agreements still to explore here. I hope that the contributions in this collection will serve as invitations to further debate.

Notes

1 Critical realism's primary founder is Roy Bhaskar (e.g. 1975, 1979). While his work is an extremely important contribution to philosophy, it has become more inaccessible since the 1970s. For accessible commentaries and further contributions see, for example, Archer (2000), Benton and Craib (2001), Collier (1994), Keat and Urry (1975), Sayer (1992, 2000b) and Stones (1996).

2 For realist commentaries and debates on 'structuration' or structure–agency relations, see Archer (2000), Bhaskar (1979) and Stones (2001).

3 What things are, or what is the case, or what is true of them regardless of whether we know it, is termed 'alethic truth', as distinct from the issue of whether any propositions we make about those objects are true.

4 For example, Laclau and Mouffe (1985) acknowledge this, but then, peculiarly, proceed to argue that particular objects are 'discursively constituted', as if things like water, rocks, schools and states would themselves change simply if we chose to discursively constitute them differently, in other words purely as a product of wishful thinking.

5 Linguistic capacities are emergent properties of certain complex biological organisms. Note how this stratified ontology contrasts with the flat ontologies of behaviourism and actor network theory. The latter's treatment of non-human, non-social processes as equivalent to social processes flattens the difference between them (see Benton and Craib, 2001: 69–73). It is also important to avoid reducing humans to their social characteristics, or to imagine that sociality is restricted to humans (Benton, 2001).

6 See Sayer (2000b) for a discussion of this process of theorising in relation to bureaucratic organisations and gender.

7 As Stones (2001) argues, we should not assume that structures are always large and external to actors, but recognise that some structures reach within 'agents as knowledgeability or memory traces' or, as I would add, as dispositions of the habitus related to the differentiations of actors' habitats (position within social fields), as theorised by Bourdieu (1998).

8 Critical realist terminology is a bit imprecise, and it is also common to talk of 'causal mechanisms' here instead of causal powers. The meanings are very close but causal or generative mechanism are perhaps more suggestive of *the way of working* of these capacities or powers.

9 To acknowledge that most social phenomena are concept-dependent is not to imply, in idealist fashion, that they are dependent on concepts alone, for it takes more than thinking to produce social institutions and practices.

10 There are other contrasts with positivism too; for example, critical realism opposes positivism's 'logicism' – its treatment of logical relations (which concern relationships between *statements*) as crucial for the explanation of causal relations (which involve the relationships between *things*), and hence its failure to note that causal explanations have to identify causal powers or mechanisms. Related to this, positivism denies natural necessity, mistaking the contingency of the relationship between statements and the world for contingency among objects and processes in the world itself (Bhaskar, 1975; Harré and Madden, 1975).

References

Archer, M. (2000) *Being Human*, Cambridge: Cambridge University Press.

Benton, T. (2001) 'Naturalism versus humanism in green ethics', *Journal of Critical Realism*, 4 (2): 2–9.

Benton, T. and Craib, I. (2001) *Philosophy of Social Science*, Basingstoke: Palgrave.

Bhaskar, R. (1975, 1997) *A Realist Theory of Science*, London: Verso.

—— (1979) *The Possibility of Naturalism*, Hassocks: Harvester.

—— (1986) *Scientific Realism and Human Emancipation*, London: Verso.

—— (1989) *Reclaiming Reality*, London: Verso.

Bourdieu, P. (1998) *Practical Reason*, Cambridge: Polity.

—— (2000) *Pascalian Meditations*, Cambridge: Polity.

Collier, A. (1994) *Critical Realism*, London: Verso.

Fairclough, N., Jessop, B. and Sayer, A. (2002) 'Critical realism and semiosis', *Journal of Critical Reason*, 5 (1): 2–10.

Fleetwood, S. (1995) *Hayek's Political Economy*, London: Routledge.

—— (2002) 'An evaluation of causal holism', *Cambridge Journal of Economics*, 26 (1): 27–45.

Foucault, M. (1977) *Discipline and Punish*, trans. A. Sheridan, London: Penguin.

—— (1980) *Power/Knowledge*, New York: Pantheon.

Harré, R. (1972) *Philosophies of Science*, Oxford: Oxford University Press.

Harré, R. and Madden, E.M. (1975) *Causal Powers*, Oxford: Blackwell.

Keat, R. and Urry, J. (1975, 1982) *Social Theory as Science*, London: Routledge.

Laclau, E. and Mouffe, C. (1985) *Hegemony and Socialist Strategy*, London: Verso.

Lewis, P. (1999) 'Critical realism and metaphor', in S. Fleetwood (ed.), *Critical Realism in Economics: Development and Debate*, Routledge: London.

Marsden, R. (1999) *The Nature of Capital: Marx after Foucault*, London: Routledge.

Norman, R. (1998) *The Moral Philosophers*, 2nd edn, Oxford: Oxford University Press.

Norris, C. (1991) *Deconstruction: Theory and Practice*, London: Routledge.

Nussbaum, M.C. (1999) *Sex and Social Justice*, Oxford: Oxford University Press.

Sayer, A. (1992) *Method in Social Science*, London: Routledge.

—— (2000a) *Realism and Social Science*, London: Sage.

—— (2000b) 'System, lifeworld and gender: associational versus counterfactual thinking', *Sociology*, 34 (4): 707–25.

Stones, R. (1996) *Sociological Reasoning*, London: Macmillan.

—— (2001) 'Refusing the realism–structuration divide', *European Journal of Social Theory*, 4 (2): 177–97.

Part I

Meta-theory

Critique and development

Of the three areas of into which we have classified recent contributions by critical realists in this volume, this one, which is concerned with meta-theory, could pose problems for some readers. It is widely understood that realists place special emphasis on the importance of developing theory, and suggest that much depends on developing adequate concepts and building theories. The generative mechanisms that are so important to the critical realist view of effective explanation are primarily grasped by formulating theoretical accounts of these mechanisms. Hence, there is a special approach to theory proposed by realists and, because of this, extended discussion of the nature of theory and how it should be used is only to be expected in a book of this kind. Consistent with this, concern for theory and the importance of its role is a recurrent theme in this book. As has been suggested in the Foreword to this volume by Andrew Sayer, for example, critical realist philosophy provides guidelines about the necessary form of theory. But, in this section, a more general concern than with theory is indicated: here is a suggestion that critical realists are concerned about something called meta-theory. But what is meta-theory and why should it be regarded as important?

In a nutshell, meta-theory designates any ideas or areas of general thought or argument that are beyond or outside of theory. Unfortunately, there is not an agreed terminology with which to discuss such matters, and this is a potential source of problems. Different disciplines tend to approach this area with their own special categories and assumptions. Philosophers use the category metaphysics and propose specialised subject areas within this: among these the more important are ontology, epistemology and ethics. By contrast, political scientists tend to conceptualise what lies outside of theory as ideology or different kinds of political ideas, while anthropologists propose and use the notion of culture. In general then, the idea of meta-theory is handy as a non-disciplinary category that refers to everything in the realm of thought outside theory and empirical work. Nevertheless, in general terms, meta-theory is important because realists tend to think their way through whatever is outside theory in particular ways, and tend to disagree acutely and systematically with other writers on O&MS (particularly those postmodernists and post-structuralists who presuppose a strong social constructionist ontology) on the way to understand the relationship of theory to other elements of thinking.

One of the issues that divides other thinkers from realists is the kind of assumptions they bring to the conception of the relationship between theory and other kinds of concepts. For many non-realists, the embedding of theoretical ideas in a broader matrix of culture and politics is a basic problem. It is usually true that a notion that becomes an element of theory was once part of common understanding before it was taken up, reformulated and used in conjunction with other ideas; that is, before it was made into theory. Certainly, a theory does not pop up, fully formed, out of nowhere, and theory is likely to be have been shaped by the context in which it was formed. The embedded quality of ideas in cultures and ideologies is clearly important and requires careful consideration. Realists respond by differentiating ideas, distinguishing the qualities of theories from other general ideas. For realists the embeddedness of ideas merely gives rise to what are sometimes called 'demarcation problems', in which there is difficulty in designating the extent of theoretical ideas. But, for the realist, these demarcation problems are not insoluble and must be dealt with if our ability to understand and explain is to be improved. To be able to differentiate the boundaries of theoretical ideas is clearly important, especially if there is some commitment to testing (which for realists involves far more than simply empirically testing hypotheses) theories for their adequacy. If it is not clear where the theory begins or ends, testing it is relatively more difficult.

Thus realists do not succumb to the relativism which afflicts many postmodernists and post-structuralists, which involves some basic differences in the implications of the embedding of ideas in meta-theory. For the latter the connections and linkages between general ideas in culture and ideology and more specific theoretical ideas will be impossible to disentangle; and this is one reason why, for them, objective knowledge is impossible in principle. For realists, however, the philosophy of realism is important in helping to separate theory from other things. Realism helps to reveal the reasons why theory works (when it does) and how it can be used to produce sound explanations. The main point here is that realist inspired theory is effective because it is formulated in terms of propositions concerning the way the world actually is, rather than solely in terms of the way it may be understood or interpreted. In the language of philosophy, realism is effective because it gives priority to questions of ontology rather than questions of epistemology. Many postmodernists and post-structuralists reverse this order of priority and end up reducing (ontological) questions about what exists to (epistemological) questions about how we might obtain knowledge of what exists – a move encouraged by the belief that what exists is constructed by the very processes involved with knowing. Whilst epistemological questions are, of course, perfectly legitimate, they are not the same as ontological questions and cannot be reduced to them. The upshot of reducing ontology into epistemology (termed by critical realists the epistemic fallacy) is that there can be no objective understanding and little point in trying to create such a thing.

In his contribution to this section, Steve Fleetwood argues for priority to be given to ontology. He introduces some analytical distinctions between kinds of concepts aimed at illuminating how it is possible to explain things independently of the beliefs or values of people. The chapter pays specific attention to what critical realists mean by the terms 'real' and 'reality'. The author distinguishes between what he calls different 'modes of reality'. Drawing a series of distinctions between what he calls the ideally real, the materially real, the artefactually real and the socially real, Fleetwood argues that it is important to recognise that although socially real phenomena are, in some senses, socially constructed (what else could the social world be?) in the first place, socially real phenomena exist independently of their knowledge or their identification by people and constrain and enable their behaviour. The main focus of the analysis is placed on what are termed 'socially real entities' such as class and gender relations which only exist in virtue of human activity. The key thing is to understand not only that socially real entities are activity-dependent but to clarify just which humans are and are not involved; which human activities are and are not involved; and when (i.e. the temporal location) these activities occur. From here the chapter shifts from social theory to slightly more concrete matters by considering a range of socially real entities (i.e. social structures, positioned practices, powers, mechanisms, configurations and tendencies) in the more familiar context of labour process theory. The aim of this chapter is primarily one of clarification, distinguishing what is being claimed by critical realists when they suggest accounts of the world are possible.

In the next chapter, not only does Paul Thompson resist the temptation to slip into the social constructionist ontology so fashionable within post-structuralism and postmodern circles, his chapter is devoted to highlighting the conceptual and practical confusion these perspectives have generated within the fashionable movement known as critical management studies (CMS). Thompson's starting point lies in the commitment to a social world that can exist independently of our perceptions and investigations and, in virtue of this, he is also committed to an epistemology that retains the possibility of uncovering truth, or at least of making 'reality claims'. The difficulties of establishing absolute certainty should not, he argues, be used to assert that we can make no reality claims. He then proceeds to demonstrate some of the problems facing the post-structuralist accounts of CMS such as the 'bad practice' often undertaken when faced with these problems, and the use of various 'escape hatches' that merely transpose the problem into another form. Although not the only tactic, he makes great use of showing how post-structuralists continually run into theory–practice inconsistencies; that is, they write theoretical cheques they cannot honour in practice.

Post-structuralism is also the subject of Peter Armstrong's chapter. Whilst recognition of the role of language (and/or discourse and/or semiotics) in social life is a useful antidote to vulgar materialism perhaps, it licenses a degree of linguistic freedom that can easily be misused. The problem comes when a (correct) concern for language is coupled with an (incorrect) ontology constituted, and exhausted, by phenomena such as language, discourse, semiotics, concepts, ideas, beliefs, and so on. This combination leads to a variety of anti-realist ideas and ways of conducting social science. If the very idea of an extra-linguistic realm is rejected, neglected, or deemed irrelevant, then the pushes and pulls of phenomena operating in this realm cease to be of interest. There is, therefore, no sense whatsoever in considering an appeal to an extra-linguistic realm as a datum against which to compare theoretical statements in order to evaluate them. We can compare one theoretical statement to another theoretical statement; or we can take one theoretical statement and deconstruct it. Language has broken free of its extra-linguistic moorings. Now, one of the delights of imaginative writing is the freedom it allows for a parallel world to be created according to the wishes and purposes of the writer. Whilst this is appropriate for poets and writers of fiction, it is inappropriate for social scientists. In consequence it allows considerable freedom to manipulate the meanings which it draws from the ordinary language use of these terms. It is thus a medium well suited to the writing of ideology. An event of this kind happened a few years ago in the literature of critical accounting. Armstrong suggests that contemporary social scientists, especially those seduced by post-structuralism, would do well to pay attention to this event because it demonstrates what can happen when a (correct) concern for language is coupled with an (incorrect) ontology. He shows that the rhetorical devices used in this particular specimen of idealist writing represent not social science, but a work of imaginative fiction.

Jan Karlsson's chapter has a different emphasis, in that he uses meta-theory as a source for stimulating the development of theoretical ideas. Karlsson uses ideas drawn from the meta-theory of critical realist philosophy to illuminate and develop understanding of particular issues relating to the organisation of work. He uses two insights from the ontology developed within critical realism: that social phenomena are relational; and the necessity of avoiding the social constructivist notion that activities and relations are merely discourse. He then uses these ontological insights to resolve two sets of contradiction within the way work has been conceptualised. The first contradiction is between those definitions of work that emphasise the properties of actions and those that emphasise the properties of social relations. The second contradiction is between those definitions where work is treated as an empirical category (i.e. work is what can be observed) and those where it is treated as a 'deep' category (i.e. work is what we do in the sphere of necessity). He then attempts to transcend these contradictions in two steps. A fruitful definition of work, he argues, must start in ontology, specifically with what people have to do in order to gain their livelihood. But this is not enough. In a second step, he defines the internal social relations that structure the sphere of necessity in a specific society – what he calls work forms. When an activity is performed within a work form it is work; when the same activity is performed outside a work form, that is outside the sphere of necessity, it is non-work.

The final chapter in this section, by Denise Thursfield and John Hamblett, takes a similar line in using ideas drawn from the philosophy of realism to stimulate insights into the contemporary world of work. They employ a conceptual device that is prominent in the critical realist toolbox, the morphogenetic approach proposed by Margaret Archer. They use it as a basis for reconceptualising and gaining insight into the working of human resource management (HRM) in general, and the interest of HR managers in developing functional flexibility. They make use of the basic, but powerful, critical realist idea that the social world is stratified and transformational. The orthodox, normative, developmental approach, they argue, is guilty of conflating complex elements of HRM into a flat, undifferentiated (empirical realist) ontology. It fails, therefore, to explain the disparate and multi-layered nature of what occurs in the workplace. A stratified realist ontology, by contrast, encourages a more lucid understanding of the way in which the emergent properties of structure, culture and agency generate the diverse practices and ideas immanent in HRM. They employ Archer's morphogenetic approach to demonstrate how structural, cultural and agential emergent properties interject to generate a specific form of functional flexibility in a particular organisational context. Not only do they bring ontological sophistication to what is, all too often, a rather unsophisticated, positivist-orientated subject, they also provide a way of analysing HRM that avoids the temptation to slip into the social constructionist ontology so fashionable within post-structuralism and postmodern circles.

These chapters, then, demonstrate that critical realism generates a number of debates about contemporary scholarship. The particular importance attributed to theory and the understanding of its role in particular has allowed realists to re-engage with other intellectuals operating in O&MS and to take issue with their ideas in fundamental ways. There is clearly further to go: the strong social constructionist ontology presupposed by many postmodernists and post-structuralists has had such a corrosive effect on beliefs and practices in O&MS scholarship and research in the few years it has been influential. As the work of Thompson and Armstrong suggests, there is a great deal of ground to recoup. In addition, as the chapters by Karlsson and Thursfield and Hamblett suggest, the relevance of critical realist philosophy to conceptualisation and theory construction can be surprisingly direct and deep, suggesting that the future for specifically realist O&MS is unexpectedly wide. These essays also demonstrate the extent of controversy that has been provoked by the collision between critical realism and currently fashionable ideas in O&MS, and indicate how effective critical realist ideas are as a viable alternative to much postmodernism and post-structuralism in this field.

1 An ontology for organisation and management studies

Steve Fleetwood

This collection is motivated by two beliefs: one positive and the other negative. The positive belief is that critical realism, and especially its ontology, has much to offer in the analysis of organisation and management. Evidence for this is provided not only in the following chapters where contributors have rooted their theoretical and empirical work in critical realism to good effect, but also in the growing number of critical realist-inspired articles found in the organisation and management studies literature.[1] The negative belief is that much current organisation and management study is *committed to one of two mistaken ontological positions*: the *empirical realist* ontology in which positivist-orientated analysis is rooted; and the *social constructionist* ontology in which postmodernist or post-structuralist-orientated analysis is rooted. Despite contributions that postmodernism and post-structuralism have to offer, the recoil from (correctly) abandoning positivism appears to have 'catapulted' postmodernists and post-structuralists into substituting one mistaken ontology for another. If unchecked, this could easily take organisation and management studies down an alley as blind as the positivist one from which it has struggled to escape. This would be tragic given that critical realism can provide a viable ontology of organisations and management, allowing positivism and its empirical realist ontology to be abandoned without having to accept a social constructionist ontology.[2]

This chapter opens with an attempt to clarify some of the ontological ideas, terms and concepts central to critical realism, whilst making it clear that critical realism is not positivism by another name. The second part of the chapter concretises the discussion a little by discussing social structures, positioned practices, powers, mechanisms, configurations and tendencies by exemplifying them via a brief discussion of labour process theory.

Clarification of terms and concepts

Over the past few years, when introducing critical realism to various audiences, similar comments and objections *vis-à-vis* ontology come up time after time. Many (although not all) of these comments and objections are based upon a misunderstanding of the ideas critical realists actually hold. The following section, therefore, engages with some of the more common comments and objections in an attempt to clarify them and remove as much misunderstanding as possible.

Ontology

The term ontology refers to the *study* or *theory* of being, not to being itself. To have an ontology is to have a *theory* of what exists. It is thus misleading to write things like: 'entities that really exist are ontological, or have ontological status', or some such. This is a subtle, but important point, so let us pursue it a little. Chia and King criticise the 'refusal, amongst organizational theorists to acknowledge the necessarily *ontological character of language*' (2001: 312, emphasis added). The term 'ontological' is used here to mean something akin to 'real' or 'existing'. It would be more precise to write about those who 'refuse to acknowledge the causally efficacious role of language'. Potter's (1998: 38) claim that the term 'ontological discourse' is an oxymoron is intelligible only if the term ontology is used to mean something that is real and non-discursive. If, however, we take discourse to be real (I will argue below that discourse is *ideally* real), then to have a discourse appertaining to ontology, such as a theoretical statement about what exists, is perfectly acceptable.[3]

Note finally that the moment we make a claim referring to being, to something that exists (such as a word, a text, an organisation, patriarchal relations, a computer, the planet Venus, or whatever), we have presupposed an ontology – even if it is implicit or completely unrecognised. Ontology is, therefore, non-optional.

Real and reality

Whilst the terms 'real' and 'reality' are crucial if a discussion of the ontology of O&M studies is to make any headway, these terms are almost always used in a manner that invites confusion and ambiguity. Consider a couple of examples.

> The mainstream approach to organization theory was premised, however, not simply upon a positivist epistemology, but also upon a realist ontology, according to which organizations are conceived of as objective entities akin to natural phenomena … as existing 'out there' in the real world.
>
> (Hancock and Tyler, 2001: 65)

> Mainstream organization theory assumes and takes for granted the existence of organizations as material entities 'out there' in the world … Cooper, Degot and others challenge the entitative, ontological status of organizations.
>
> (Linstead, 2001: 4)

Leaving aside the ambiguous reference to 'mainstream' approaches and theories, these comments illustrate that (an unqualified) realism is often associated with an ontology wherein organisations, structures, and so on, are conceived of as entities akin to natural phenomena or as having 'entitative, ontological status'. This is misleading. *Critical* realists do not reserve the term 'real' for things that are material, physical or 'entitative'. They do *not*, for example, think that mountains, buildings, computers and kidneys are real, but ideas, beliefs, concepts, language and discourse are non-real. So what do critical realists mean by the term 'real'? *Something is real if it has an effect or makes a difference.* Since entities such as mountains and discourses clearly make a difference, in the sense that they cause human beings to act in ways they would not in the absence of these entities, then mountains and discourses are real. Entities such as fairies are not real, although entities such as the *discourse* of fairies are real: if people think fairies are real, they may undertake actions such as trying to photograph them.[4]

Entities and their identification

Critical realists often make claims to the effect that an entity can exist independently of our *knowledge* of it. I prefer the term 'identification' to 'knowledge' because the former encompasses the latter and allows us to avoid ambiguities surrounding the activities of *knowing, observing* and *socially constructing.*

Ambiguity can arise from the claim that an entity can exist independently of our *knowledge* of it because empiricists, claiming all knowledge is derived from observation, argue the following: any entity that cannot be observed cannot be known about, and we have, therefore, no warrant to claim that it, or certain of its characteristics, exists (cf. Fleetwood, 2002). Arguments like this, however, commit the 'epistemic fallacy'; that is, they collapse ontological concerns into epistemological concerns whilst not noticing that something has gone awry in the process. What exists disappears from the analytical field as it is collapsed into knowledge of what exists.

Ambiguity can also rise from the claim that an entity can exist independently of our *knowledge* of it because postmodernists and post-structuralist often deny that entities are *independent.* For them, entities are socially constructed and hence *dependent* on us in the sense that they are dependent upon our discourse, language or whatever. But notice that some odd things begin to happen. If a person or community socially constructs an entity, then in a curious way that person or community must also observe it, and have knowledge of it and its characteristics – if not, any discussion about it would be impossible. The entity constructed and observed by that person or community is 'their' entity, an identity 'for them'. Moreover, from postmodern and post-structuralist perspectives, since no-one outside that person or community can deny the existence of 'their' socially constructed/observed entity, or any of its characteristics, then any knowledge the person or community has must be privileged. Ironically, perhaps, postmodernists and post-structuralists end up on similar terrain to empiricists, implying that observation (albeit *not* of an independent entity) gives privileged access to knowledge. In this case, the 'epistemic fallacy' has a twist to it. Ontological concerns are still collapsed into epistemological concerns; what exists is still collapsed into our knowledge of what exists; but now our knowledge of what exists is collapsed into whatever we socially construct/observe.

In many cases people are knowledgeable in the sense that they know *tacitly*. They may know *how* to perform a particular work task but they cannot explain how they do it. They know 'how' but they don't know 'that' as Ryle put it (cf. Fleetwood, 1995: Chapter 7). When, for example, rules of the workplace (such as knowing the appropriate pace of work to adopt in various circumstances) are known *tacitly*, it is misleading to say they 'exist independently of our knowledge of them'. They exist independently of *articulable* knowledge, but not of *tacit* knowledge.

In short, then, claiming that an entity can exist independently of its *identification* allows us to sidestep some of the ambiguities surrounding *knowing*, *observing* and *socially constructing*.

Concept mediation

There is no theory-neutral observation, description, interpretation, theorisation, explanation, or whatever. There is, in other words, *no unmediated* access to the world: access is always *mediated*. Whenever we reflect upon an entity, our sense data is always mediated by a pre-existing stock of conceptual resources, which we use to interpret, make sense of and understand what it is, and take appropriate action. This stock may be individual (e.g. a subjective belief or opinion) and/or social (e.g. an accepted theory, perspective or social norm) and/or rooted in practice (i.e. the result of previous encounters with entities other than ourselves). When, and if, entities do become the focus of human beings' reflection, then we may say they are *conceptually mediated*.

What critical realism is not

One stumbling block facing those attempting to introduce critical realism to organisation and management studies is the widespread belief that whatever realism is, it is associated with positivism – or related discourses such as empiricism, scientism, science, scientific objectivity, structuralism, structural functionalism, foundationalism, modernism, Enlightenment thinking, 'traditional' and 'mainstream' approaches to organisation and management studies, and so on.[5] The next section demonstrates that this belief exists and why it is mistaken.[6]

Organisation and management literature is plagued by the association of a typically *unqualified* realism (i.e. not *critical* realism, *naive* realism, *empirical* realism or *scientific* realism) with positivism. Jackson and Carter (2000: 49) associate an unqualified realism with (positivist-orientated) practices such as the measurement of social phenomena like 'motivation to work, leadership, commitment, satisfaction, efficiency, potential, psychological types, and so on'.[7] *Critical* realism is, of course, hostile to many such measurement practices. Linstead (2001: 227) identifies the 'realist approach ... orientated towards "objective" organizational, commercial and economic interests, whether bowing to the laws of physics or the logic of the market'. This associates realism with natural science and the search for laws. *Critical* realism, of course, explicitly denies that such laws exist in the social world. Boje *et al.* (2001: 138–147) associate realist narratology with 'experimental manipulation' and 'narratives as measures; narratives with rating scales'. *Critical* realism, of course, denies the validity of experimental manipulation in the social sciences and criticises measures and scales of this kind.

Often, a body of theory is first associated with positivism or modernism (or whatever) and second associated with realism. If the reader subsequently associates this body of theory with *critical* realism the latter becomes associated with positivism or modernism. In the following comments, modernism and positivism are associated with Marxism and labour process theory. All that is necessary is for the reader to associate Marxism and labour process theory with *critical* realism for the latter to be tarred with the brush of positivism and modernism:[8]

> given the modernist assumptions embedded in organizations and the rather dogmatic and exclusionary character of dominant research traditions of either a positivist or a Marxist bent.
>
> (Alvesson and Deetz, 1999: 185)

> Labour Process theory did not reject science *per se*, but grounded itself within a Marxist notion of science as a potentially liberating force. … A Marxist inspired approach to organization theory represented … only a partial break from … positivist epistemological assumptions and a realist ontology.
>
> (Hancock and Tyler, 2001: 69)

Now some commentators are aware that realism comes in more than one form. Gergen (1998: 147), for example, opens a recent essay with the words: 'In important respects, the drama of social constructionism was born of its opposition to a form of realism embodied in the dominant order of positivist/empiricist science.' Unfortunately, however, not only does the rest of the essay fail to distinguish between *forms of realism*,[9] but the usual conflation of realism and positivism or empiricism is evident. In one place he writes of the 'experimental manipulation … warranted by realist discourse' (1998: 154). Whilst he usually dichotomises (unqualified) realism and constructionism, in another place he makes a slip and writes of the warfare that characterises 'empiricists and constructionists', missing realism or conflating it with empiricism by default. He then adds a list of those who are 'set against empiricism – discourse analysts, feminist theorists and culture critics among them' (1998: 149). Not only are critical realists not included in this list, surely Gergen cannot be unaware that there are critical realist discourse analysts, realist feminist theorists and culture critics.

Let me state the following for the record: *critical realism is not synonymous with discourses such as naive realism, empirical realism, positivism, scientism or other associated empiricist paraphernalia: in fact, it is antithetical to these discourses.* Those who continue to make them synonymous, at least without offering an argument, have failed to understand *critical* realism.

Modes of reality

I avoid use of the unqualified term 'real' where necessary, and qualify it by taking into account its *mode of reality*. Whilst many things are real, they are real in different ways or *modes*. Confusion often arises from not recognising, or not specifying, the different modes of reality. It is possible to identify (at least) four modes of reality, or four different ways in which real entities may be differentiated, albeit with some overlap: *material*, *ideal*, *artefactual* and *social*. I will elaborate upon these in turn in a moment, after considering a couple of examples where confusion reigns.[10]

Comments such as: 'social problems have their feet planted firmly in the *material world of social structure*' (Burr, 1998: 24, emphasis added) elide the distinction between material and social phenomena. Writing about 'the relationships between discourse and "reality"' (Keenoy, 1997: 835) misses the point that discourse is (ideally) real. Shenhav and Weitz (2000: 377) give us the confusing phrase: '*people's objective reality is unreal*' (emphasis added). According to Chia:

> Social objects and phenomena such as 'the organization', 'the economy', 'the market' or even 'stakeholders' or 'the weather', do not have a straightforward and unproblematic existence independent of our discursively-shaped understandings.
>
> (Chia, 2000: 513)

This is confusing because whilst an organisation is a social object, the same cannot be said for the weather. Moreover, the weather itself is *not* dependent on our discursively shaped understandings – although it may be dependent on our *actions* such as the inappropriate burning of hydrocarbons. Our *understanding* of the weather, by contrast, is a social object and is, by definition, discourse dependent. Let us explore the four possible modes of reality and see how a more nuanced ontology might alleviate some confusion.

Materially real

The term 'materially real' refers to material entities like oceans, the weather, the moon and mountains that can, and often do, exist independently of what individuals or communities do, say, or think. Clearly, in some cases materially real entities are affected by our actions, hence my use of the term 'overlap' mentioned above (cf. Schmidt, 2001). Weather systems may be affected by our inappropriate burning of hydrocarbons and the surface of the moon was affected by our landing upon it, but these acts are contingent: materially real entities would continue to exist even if humans disappeared. In some cases, it might be more appropriate to classify what seem, at first blush, to be materially real entities as artefacts – e.g. a quarry. Whilst much will depend upon the context, the category 'materially real' allows us to handle those entities that do exist independently of what we do, say, or think.

Whilst materially real entities *can* exist independently of our identification of them, often we *do* identify them, whereupon we may refer to them as *conceptually mediated*. Note, however, that the act of mediation does not alter their material status: their materiality is augmented by a conceptual, perhaps a discursive, dimension.

Ideally real

The term 'ideally real' refers to conceptual entities such as discourse, language, genres, tropes, styles, signs, symbols and semiotised entities, ideas, beliefs, meanings, understandings, explanations, opinions, concepts, representations, models, theories, and so on. For brevity I refer to entities like these as *discourse* or *discursive entities*. Discourse or discursive entities *are real* because they have effects; they make a difference.[11]

Ideally real entities may or may not have a referent and the referent may be ideally or *non*-ideally real. Discourses about the management of knowledge have, as their referents, ideal entities such as knowledge and non-ideal entities such as people. Discourses about women being less intelligent than men have no referent at all. It is worth emphasising here that having no referent does not mean discourses have no cause.

Whilst critical realists claim there is more to the world than discourse, this should not be taken to suggest that they think discourse is irrelevant: far from it. Reed (2000: 529), for example, notes that discourses such as financial audit, quality control and risk management are 'generative mechanisms' with 'performative potential'. Consider the example of skill and gender. In some cases, female workers possess skills similar to those possessed by (comparable) male workers. Sexist discourse not only draws our attention to women's skills, it draws our attention to them in ways that present them as being of a lower skill level. And, of course, once these skills are discursively downgraded, discrimination in the labour market and the workplace often follows. Postmodernists and post-structuralists would say that these downgraded skills are *socially constructed*, and the point is well taken. I refrain from using the term 'socially constructed' only because it carries too much unwanted baggage. Working alongside this discourse, however, are extra-discursive factors that also cause discrimination. Many female workers simply do not possess skills similar to (comparable) male workers. There are various reasons for this such as women's restricted access to jobs where skill attainment is possible. This is often caused by intermittent labour market activity which is, in turn, caused by the requirements of child and/or dependent care. In this case, the lower skill level is not caused by sexist discourse, but by extra-discursive, socially real factors.

In the Foreword, Sayer makes an important distinction which parallels what I am getting at here, namely a distinction between *construal* and *construction*. To construe is to interpret some (non-ideal)[12] phenomenon and make a mental image *of* that phenomenon – in my terminology this is referred to as a discourse. This is a different activity than making or constructing that phenomenon itself – although the two may be necessary for practical action. Clearly, once discourses, or construals, exist, they can contingently make a difference to the world outside our imagination; they can contingently effect materially, artefactually and socially real entities, including practices and organisational forms. Hence construals, or discourses in general, are real – see Thursfield and Hamblett's use of Archer's notion of cultural emergent properties (CEPs) in Chapter 5 of this collection. I will return to this notion below.

Whilst discourse makes a difference, *not all* discourse makes a difference, and we often need to consider whose discourse counts? When the Governor of the Bank of England alters his language then a significant part of the extra-discursive world alters – e.g. the price of sterling may rise and some UK firms may cease trading. But when an obscure academic like Steve Fleetwood alters his language, it alters very little.

The following comment from Fairclough *et al.* (2002; pp. 3–4) not only gives a flavour of contemporary critical realist thought on ideally real entities (in this case semiotised entities), but also demonstrates that critical realists are not naive 'table thumpers' and can deal with non-material entities – without, it must be said, collapsing the materially, artefactually and socially real into the ideally real, as social constructionists tend to do:

> Semiosis (the making of meaning) is a crucial part of social life but it does not exhaust the latter. Thus, since texts are both socially structuring and socially structured, we must examine not only how texts generate meaning and thereby help to generate social structure but also how the production of meaning is itself constrained by emergent, non-semiotic features of social structure. For example, an interview is a particular form of communication (a 'genre' …) which both creates a particular kind of social encounter and is itself socially structured, for example, by conventions of propriety, privacy and disclosure, by particular distributions of resources, material and cognitive. In short, although semiosis is an aspect of any social practice … no social practice … is reducible to semiosis alone. This means that semiosis cannot be reduced to the play of differences amongst networks of signs (as if semiosis were always purely an intra-semiotic matter with no external reference) and that it cannot be understood without identifying and exploring the extra-semiotic conditions that make semiosis possible and ensure its effectivity. We therefore reject the Foucauldian-inspired conflation of discourses and material practices.

Artefactually real

The term 'artefactually real' refers to entities such as cosmetics, computers or the hole in the ozone layer. In an interesting paper, Reckwitz (2002: 207) refers to entities like these as 'quasi-objects'. Computers are a synthesis of the physically, ideally and socially real. Because entities are *conceptually mediated* we interpret them in various, and often diverse, ways. Violins may be interpreted as musical instruments or as table-tennis bats. But unless we are prepared to accept that any interpretation (and, therefore, subsequent action) is as good as another, that interpreting a violin as a table-tennis bat is as good as interpreting it is a musical instrument, then we have to accept that there are limits to interpretation. And these limits are often established by the materiality of the entity itself. Whilst critical realism is, in this and similar contexts, materialist, the recognition that material entities are *conceptually mediated* guards against any vulgar materialism.

Socially real

The term 'socially real' refers to practices, states of affairs or entities such as caring for children, becoming unemployed, the market mechanism, social structures and organisations. Socially real entities are *social* in two senses. First, like ideally real entities, they contain not one iota of materiality: we cannot touch, smell or hold a social entity. Second, and more importantly, they are social because they are dependent on (some) activity for their *existence*, that is for their reproduction and transformation: they are *(human) activity-dependent.* Whilst this will be elaborated upon later in the chapter, it is worth emphasising here that socially real entities such as social structures should not be conflated with conceptually real entities such as theories or explanations *of* social structures. Socially real entities may be the subject of discourse, but they have an extra-discursive dimension and so are irreducible to discourse.

I will come back to this point in a moment. But before I do, it is crucial to grasp one fundamental point here. *Socially real entities such as social structures are not reducible to discourse* (or other ideally real phenomena) and this sets the critical realist ontology apart from social constructionist ontology.

Recognising a distinction between socially (and materially and artefactually) and ideally real domains allows critical realists to recognise the complex way in which discourse is related to extra-discursive phenomena, without collapsing the latter into the former, or confusing them in various ways. Not recognising this distinction, social constructionists like Linstead (2001: 5) have little choice but to reduce the socially real to the ideally real, or in this case, structure to discourse, writing: '[o]rganization is a structure, but only when structure is recognized to be an effect of language.' Others make even stronger claims:

> For poststructuralists, it is the explanation itself that creates order, gives structure to experience. *Structure is the meaning given to experience.* Structure is immanent in the subject not in the object, in the observer not the observed. … Poststructuralists conclude that there are no real structures that give order to human affairs, but that the construction of order – of sense making – by people is what gives rise to structure. *Structure is the explanation itself*, that which *makes* sense, not that which *gives* sense. It follows from this that structure

> cannot be seen as determining action because it is not real and transcendent, but a product of the human mind.
>
> (Carter and Jackson, 2000: 41 and 43, emphasis in original)

A thoroughgoing exposition of why social constructionists are mistaken in collapsing extra-discursive entities like social structures into discursive ones cannot be undertaken here (cf. Fleetwood, 2002). Instead, what I offer is a clarification of what exactly critical realists think about socially real entities in the hope that it clarifies matters.

If socially real entities such as structures and organisations really were epiphenomena of discourse, then we could change them by changing the discourse: we could talk[13] ourselves into a completely different set of social structures. There would be no need, for example, for women to be segregated horizontally in the labour market; to be segregated vertically in the firm; or to suffer any form of employment-related discrimination – if only we refrained from engaging in those discursive practices that produce and reproduce discriminatory employment patterns. This 'solution' is, of course, unlikely to work because extra-discursive practices (such as the requirements of child and dependent care) are also in operation alongside discursive practices, and the former can only be changed by practical activity – which does not mean changed discourse plays no role.

Confusion often arises when the relation between socially and ideally real entities is broached – even if this terminology is not used. Take, as an example, a theory. In one context a theory can be an expression *about* a socially, artefactually or materially real entity (i.e. ideally real entity) whilst in another context it can be a social entity *sui generis* (i.e. a socially real entity) as well. Suppose, in the first context, we have a theory about patriarchal structures. The theory and the patriarchal structures are different things. The theory is *about* the structures; the theory expresses, reflects, or captures, *in thought*, some of the characteristics of the patriarchal structures. The theory, the ideal entity, is *epistemic*: it constitutes knowledge. The patriarchal structures are *ontic*: they exist independently of this knowledge. Critical realists refer to ideal entities such as theories as *transitive* entities or as existing in the transitive domain. Thus we can account for changing (transitive) knowledge about a *relatively* unchanging (intransitive) phenomenon – the term 'relatively' is a device for preventing the (mis)interpretation that intransitive entities are necessarily unchanging or fixed. In a second context, however, the *theory* of the patriarchal structures can itself become an entity to be analysed – i.e. used to generate knowledge. The theory, whilst still being *about* patriarchy, is now *also* an entity in its own right. In this context, the theory is ontic: it exists independently of any subsequent knowledge the analysis generates. In this context, the theory has become an intransitive entity, existing in the intransitive domain. We now have a theory (or theories) about a theory.

Thursfield and Hamblett (Chapter 5 in this collection) are alert to the role ideally real entities can play and expand on this using Archer's notion of cultural emergent properties (CEPs), which they explain as follows:

> CEPs belong to the strata of ideas, theories and beliefs, and are independent of cultural agents (people). Relations between cultural agents are causal and may be contingent. So, for example, X may or may not persuade Y of the truth of X's beliefs, or X may or may not succeed in manipulating Y. ... CEPs are objective and are the product of previous generations of thinkers and the causal relations pertaining to those thinkers. Following their emergence, CEPs have a life of their own in that they exist regardless of whether current agents comprehend them or not.

Having the ontological sophistication to recognise that an ideally real entity (a CEP) such as a theory can be transitive or intransitive depending upon context prevents the common mistake of supposing that the mere creation or construction (in social constructionist parlance) of a theory means it will have an effect. Whilst there are times when theories impact upon the world, there are also times when they have no effect. The very fact that 'thinking does not make it so' demonstrates this.

Objective and subjective

The terms 'objective' and 'subjective' are often used in confused and confusing ways. In this section, I try to disambiguate these terms by adding a fourth dimension to Sayer's three-fold distinction and identifying 'objective' and 'subjective' 1, 2, 3 and 4.

- Objective$_1$ means value-neutral or impartial as in 'I personally don't stand to gain or lose from this situation, so I can perhaps give a more objective account of it'. Correspondingly, subjective$_1$ means value-laden or partial, as in 'I've known her as a friend for years so my views on her are subjective'.
- Objective$_2$ means something taken to be objectively known or true. Correspondingly subjective$_2$ implies that something is 'not true' or is 'merely a matter of opinion'.
- Objective$_3$ refers to objects, to the nature of things independent of their identification by humans, as in 'the objective properties of capital'. This corresponds to subjective$_3$ which refers to subjects and concerns what we think about something such as the 'subjective experience of class'.
- Although I would never use the terms in this way, it is common to find objective$_4$ referring to material entities and, correspondingly, subjective$_4$, which refers to social or human entities. 'Mountains are objective, whilst working activity is subjective.'

It is not difficult to see how, if these different meanings of objective and subjective are conflated, confusion follows. Let me give one example:

> [B]oth scientific and human relations thinking implicitly relied upon a dualistic ontology which sharply delineated the subjective and objective domains

> of reality. That is they were both grounded in the metaphysical belief that the domain of the human subject and the material environment were both separate and hierarchically ordered.
>
> (Hancock, 1999: 158)

Whilst Hancock is criticising scientific and human relations thinking, and with this I have no quarrel, he uses the terms 'objective' and 'subjective' in a misleading manner. Hancock has a two-fold distinction:

1. The objective domain or 'domain of the material environment' refers to objective phenomena like the commodities produced by this working activity.[14] This equates to the $objective_4$ domain.
2. The subjective domain or 'domain of the human subject' which refers to subjective phenomena like working activity. This equates to the $subjective_4$ domain.

Translating Hancock's ideas into my terminology and describing his two-fold distinction as follows reveals why it is misleading. Hancock's schema has too few categories and so cannot correctly differentiate between different entities. First, it does not take different modes of reality into account. When, quite legitimately, Hancock tries to differentiate between working activity and commodities, he cannot do so on the grounds that working activity is a *social* entity and a commodity is a *material* entity. He has little option but to differentiate them on the grounds that commodities, as material entities, are $objective_4$ (which they are) and working activity is $subjective_4$ (which is misleading) for the next reason. Second, Hancock's schema cannot differentiate between objective and subjective moments of the one entity, in this case, working activity. When we are referring to the nature of things or activities independent of their identification by humans, working activity can be regarded as $objective_3$. Your working activity can, for example, exist without it being identified by certain others. When, by contrast, we are referring to how a worker, a group of workers or a social analyst conceptualises working activity then working activity can be regarded as $subjective_3$.

Human activities and socially real entities

I mentioned above that ideal, artefactual and social (but not material) entities are all *social* in the sense that they are *(human) activity-dependent* – the term 'human' is dropped from now on for ease of exposition. To say, however, that entities are activity-dependent fails to clarify just which humans are and are not involved; which human activities are and are not involved; and when (i.e. the temporal location) these activities occur. The following section draws upon Archer's (1998) work.

Which activities are not involved?

The claim that entities can exist independently of their identification implies that *not all* human activities are required for their existence. Entities such as class structures, patriarchal structures and tacit rules do not have to be identified in order to exist. An individual does not have to identify the constraints that gender places upon them, or others, in order for those constraints to be operational. Entities such as explicit rules and laws, by contrast, do have to be identified in order to exist. To say, of those entities where it is appropriate to do so, that they exist independently of their identification does not mean that such entities are *not* activity-dependent. It merely means that they are not dependent upon the specific activities involved with identification. Not all activities are involved when claiming that entities are activity-dependent.

Which humans are involved?

The term 'our' in the phrase 'entities exist independently of *our* identification' often leads to confusion because we fail to differentiate between 'us' as social analysts and 'us' as those we study, that is human actors (cf. Lewis, 2000: 261):

- An entity may exist independently of its identification by social analysts *and* actors. We (i.e. *all* human beings) may not have discovered it. Institutional racism has only recently been discovered, but clearly it existed prior to its discovery.
- An entity may exist independently of its identification by social analysts, but *not* independently of actors. Actors may have known about institutional racism for many years before social analysts discovered it.
- An entity may exist independently of its identification by actor A but *not* by actors B, C, … Z. Actor A may have just started a new job and is unfamiliar with the *explicit* rules of the workplace, but her workmates are obviously familiar with them.
- An entity may exist independently of its identification by all actors but *not* by social analysts whose research aims precisely to tease these things out. Tacit rules of the workplace are drawn upon in order that action takes place, but the actors involved do not identify these rules.

In short, to recognise that certain entities are activity-dependent does not imply that *all of us* are involved in their reproduction or transformation. When, for example, I am reproducing the structures of Lancaster University Management School, you may not be involved in that reproduction, yet you may still be affected by it when you read this essay.

Which human activities are involved?

In order for social entities to exist, a range of activities is required. These activities are *always* practical and conceptual, and very often (but not always) discursive. For a business organisation to exist, actors must perform a range of activities such as: clocking on and off; carrying out instructions from supervisors; working at an appropriate pace; identifying items; using judgement; engaging in social intercourse with co-workers; and so on.

Whilst entities such as class structures, patriarchal structures and tacit rules exist independently of their identification and explicit rules and laws do not, they all share a common factor. None of them can exist independently of practical and conceptual activity. If, for example, actors ceased to enter into class and patriarchal relations, ceased to draw upon tacit rules, or ceased to follow explicit rules and laws, then class, patriarchy, tacit rules, explicit rules and laws would disappear. Actors must also have some conception about the activities they are engaged in. It is, however, important to avoid two common mistakes.

First, let us recognise that all social entities depend on the concepts agents have of them; they are *concept-dependent* or *concept-mediated.* Second, to say entities do not exist independently of the concepts agents have of them does not mean agents have to have the *correct* conception, or *complete* knowledge, of what they are doing and why they are doing it. It merely means agents have some idea of what they are doing and why they are doing it: agents are purposive. In this sense to say that some social entities can exist 'behind our backs' does not involve reification of these entities. Working-class women do not have to know they are discriminated against in class and patriarchal systems, in order for such discrimination to occur. In fact, they could be discriminated against whilst explicitly denying the existence of such systems. Objecting to this on the grounds that the social analyst claims to know more about the situation than the lay person and is, therefore, a form of cultural imperialism is a red herring. It would be valid only if we were prepared to say that lay persons can never be mistaken, and given that social analysts are also persons, this would be tantamount to saying that analysts can never be mistaken. If we, as analysts, can be mistaken, so too can lay persons and hence we must accept the possibility that social analysts can know things lay persons do not.

In short, to recognise that certain entities are activity-dependent does not imply that *all* humans are involved in the reproduction or transformation of those entities.

At what temporal location are these activities involved?

Whilst some, but not all, humans and some, but not all, activities are involved in the reproduction and transformation of social entities, we need to consider the temporal locations where moments of agency occur. Archer is keen to stress temporality in her own morphogenetic and Bhaskar's transformational approaches. Whilst Archer's sophisticated insights cannot be expanded upon here, I will comment upon a version of the following figure taken from Archer (1998: 376).

Whatever happens, however the interplay between agents and structures takes place, it is important to be clear about one point: action is a continuous, cyclical,

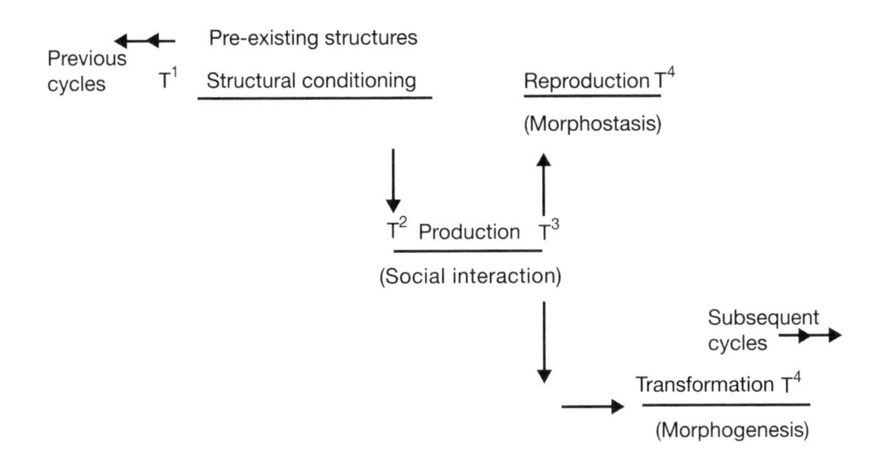

Figure 1.1: Reproduction and transformation of structures

Source*:* Based on Archer's superimposition of the Transformational Model of Social Action and the morphogenetic/static cycle (Archer, 1998: 376).

flow over time: there are no empty spaces where nothing happens and things do not just begin and end. The starting point for an analysis of any cyclical phenomena is always arbitrary: we have to break into the cycle at some point and impose an analytical starting point. The starting point here is some prior cycle.

At T^1 pre-existing structures emerge from a prior cycle and act as pre-existing structures that govern subsequent social interaction.

At T^2 agents find themselves interacting with, and governed by, these (to them) pre-existing structures and a process of production is initiated where these agents do whatever it is they can do given the nature of these pre-existing structures – i.e. they are constrained and enabled by them.

Between T^2 and T^3 the pre-existing structures undergo change, which is completed by T^4 where structures are reproduced (i.e. morphostasis occurs) or transformed (i.e. morphogenesis occurs).

After T^4 a new cycle starts.

Activity, then, is clearly necessary for this cycle to take place. It does not follow, however, that the only activity necessary for reproduction is that taking place between T^2 and T^3. In fact, central to Archer's approach is August Comte's insight that the majority of actors are dead. The past actions of humans interacting with past social structures generated phenomena like the distribution of income, depletion of the ozone layer, libraries full of books and business organisations. These phenomena predate any subsequent activity and exert a causal influence upon subsequent activity.[15] Whilst Archer refers to this as 'structural conditioning', it is distinct from structuralism where the agent is a cultural dope – the 'spoilt brat of history' as Strauss famously put it:

> [S]ocial structures are only efficacious through the activities of human beings, but … only … by allowing that these are the effects of *past actions*, often by long dead people, which survive them (and this temporal escape is precisely what makes them *sui generis*). Thus they continue to exert their effects upon subsequent actors and their activities, as autonomous possessors of causal powers. How they carry over and how they exert their effects is just what the M/M (morphogenetic/static) approach is about.
>
> (Archer, 1998: 368)

This is an important insight because, as Archer notes (1998: 370 and passim), it avoids a problem that arises when voluntaristic concepts such as 'instantiation' are applied. If structural conditioning did not take place, if structures were only present at the moment of their instantiation, that is at the moment when agents act, two bizarre conclusions would follow.

First, structures and structural entities such as business organisations would come and go in virtue of activity. Structures would, for example, come into existence at the point when the workforce arrive in the morning, and they would go out of existence when the workforce go home in the evening. This is counterfactual because the structures that constitute the organisation endure and 'structurally condition' activity in the sense that, for example, they (usually) influence appropriate bedtime.

Second, there would be a kind of 'hole' in history, a space or period where society was un-structured. Imagine trying to construct a sentence, or trying to work at the pace of the workgroup, when just at the moment when we are about to draw upon the structures of grammar or the tacit rules that govern group work pace, these structures and rules momentarily disappear. We would, at that precise moment, be unable to string the words together meaningfully, or gauge the appropriate work pace: we would be unable to act.

In sum, then, whilst social entities are activity-dependent, differentiating between who does and who does not do what, when and how allows a more nuanced understanding of exactly what role human activity plays in the reproduction, or transformation, of these entities. Moreover, it helps identify problems arising when we operate with a repertoire consisting of only one human activity, namely that of socially constructing entities. Recognising only the 'blanket' activity of social construction leaves us with little option but to apply this in an undiscriminating manner, and impedes the development of a more nuanced understanding of the role of human activity in the reproduction or transformation of entities.

Ontological commitments of critical realism: a summary

The following summary indicates how the terminology developed can be used to refer to different modes of reality. Whilst the richness of language implies there are far more permutations than can be sketched here, the summary should give some indication of acceptable phraseology.[16]

Socially real entities are:

- Conceptually *mediated.*
- Irreducible to discourse: there is a remainder and this remainder is non-empty. This remainder is, however, not materially or artefactually real.
- Dependent upon (human) activity.

Ideally real entities:

- May or may not have a referent which may be ideally or *non*-ideally real.
- Are conceptually *mediated.*
- Are reducible to discourse in the sense that they are made from discursive 'stuff'.
- Are always caused by something, even if the cause is a reason.
- Can, but do not always, make a (considerable) difference.
- Are dependent upon (human) activity.

Materially real entities are:

- Not conceptually *mediated* in the sense that they can exist independently of our reflection and hence mediation, although if and when they become the focus of our reflection we can say they are conceptually mediated.
- Irreducible to discourse.
- Are not dependent upon (human) activity.

Artefactually real entities are:

- Conceptually *mediated.*
- Discursive but irreducible to discourse: the remainder is materially real.
- Material but irreducible to material: the remainder is discursive.
- Dependent upon (human) activity.

In sum, then, critical realists are ontologically committed to the existence of an (non-empty) extra discursive, dimension – the prefix '(non-empty)' will be clarified below.

Critical realism and (weak) social constructionism

Now something like these ontological commitments is often accepted by those who are happily associated with postmodernism, post-structuralism or social constructionism. Many aspects of the following comments are perfectly acceptable to a critical realist – although most critical realists would express themselves using different terminology:

- 'This "turn" to language in organization studies can be traced to a heightened awareness of the way linguistic expressions, rules, conventions and practices *shape or affect* organizational practices' (Chia and King, 2001: 311, emphasis added). Notice how the terms 'shape' and 'affect' are used in preference to stronger terms such as constitute and construct.
- 'Symbolic representations, such as theories of organizational functioning, must not be understood as attempts to accurately mirror reality, but must instead be understood as "standing for" the intractable and obdurate experiences of our organizational lifeworlds. … Representation is the quintessential organizing mode through which *our social world is revealed and represented*' (*ibid.*, emphasis added). Notice that theories *represent* or *stand for* what appear to be extra-discursive experiences and an extra-discursive world.
- 'It is the organizational capacity of language to structure our thought-worlds and hence our social worlds through ongoing material acts of punctuating ordering and classification' (*ibid.*: 312). Through language we do things like compile duty rosters and in so doing bring about practical activities such as turning up for work at certain days and times.

What is crucial in these comments is the absence of *ontological exaggeration.* That is, the important role played by discourse is accepted, with no further suggestion that discourse entirely constitutes, or exhausts, the world. Whilst I do not like putting matters like this, another way of saying this is to say that these comments are weakly, but not strongly, social constructionist – with the term 'weak' carrying no pejorative connotations. Those who consider themselves to be postmodernist or post-structuralist, and feel able to accept this ontology, have nothing to fear from critical realist ontology. In a carefully argued paper O'Docherty and Willmott (2001: 464) seek to maintain the insights provided by post-structuralism and postmodernism, in this case in labour process theory, whilst rejecting anti-realist ontology:

> For us it still makes sense to talk, or better, appreciate, that capitalism is something that exists in part outside of language and text, even if it is only through language that this existence is communicated … Instead of the wholesale abandonment of subject/object or structure/agency that an anti-realist approach tends to endorse, we favour a more critical, and we would argue post-structural, as contrasted with 'anti-structural' sensitivity. This involves a self-critical and multi-disciplinary exploration of the complex political, economic, psychological and existential processes that inter-articulate and combine in the practices of the labour process.

Hopefully, this section has clarified some of the ideas, terms and concepts central to the ontology provided by critical realism, demonstrated a high level of ontological sophistication and made it clear that critical realism is not positivism by another name. This has paved the way for the elaboration of a critical realist-orientated ontology of organisation and management, to which I now turn.

Critical realism in action

After discussing some general points, the ontology will be explicated by means of labour process theory.[17] In sketching the ontology, I will refer to configurations of social structures, positioned practices, powers, mechanisms and tendencies.

Structures

According to Porpora 'social structure is a nexus of connections among [agents or actors] causally affecting their actions and in turn causally affected by them' (1989: 344; cf. Lewis, 2000; Scott, 2001). Social structure is relational: it exists in virtue of agents entering into relations. The patriarchal structure is the nexus of (a specific set of) relations between relatively powerful men and relatively powerless women.

The labour process is the location where the specific set of relations between capitalists and workers is produced, reproduced and transformed. In the labour process, workers reproduce themselves as workers and capitalists (create the potential to) reproduce themselves as capitalists. Other structures are, of course, involved in this. The valorisation process cannot work (as it does currently) without the structures of patriarchy locking women into the performance of domestic labour. Capitalists have an overriding interest in generating a sustainable level of profit over an extended period because they enter into relations with other capitalists. For simplicity, however, I leave these other structures out of the discussion and concentrate upon the relation between capitalist and worker.[18]

Positioned practices

If social structures exist, and are relational, then there must exist relata. Agents enter into specific social relations by taking up certain slots or social positions such as landlord and tenant, or capitalist and worker. Attached to any position are a set of practices such as paying wages and turning up for work on time. This combination is referred to as a positoned practice. Social structure consists, then, of a dense web of relations between positioned practices.

The position of capitalist entails practices such as hiring labour power and capital and subsequently producing an appropriate quantity and quality of commodities (goods, services or knowledge) by controlling the transformation of labour power into labour at a rate that generates sufficient profit. Notice, however, that whilst the particular agent could be replaced, the position would still remain, and the practices would still be carried out. This should not be misunderstood to imply the 'death of the subject' or the absence of agency, or some other (post-)structuralist position. The capitalist is free to engage in these practices in various ways and, clearly, to invent new practices – e.g. to implement flexible working practices or partnership agreements with unions. However the practices are undertaken, they must be consistent with the position of capitalist: not any old practices go.

Powers (or capacities or dispositions)

Entities possess powers, that is dispositions, capacities and potentials to do certain things, but not others. Gunpowder has the power to explode, but not to speak a language. Entering into these relations between positioned practices endows agents with a set of causal powers. Agents may, of course, already possess other powers so entering these relations may modify, or even counteract, these prior powers. Causal power lies in the entire web of relations, not in the particular individual or component.

Now powers are rather complex things. Powers may be possessed with or without being exercised and may be exercised with or without being actualised:

- A power is possessed by an entity in virtue of its internal make-up, and this power endures whether or not it is exercised or actualised and, therefore, endures irrespective of any outcomes it generates. When a power endures in this sense, it can be said to act *transfactually*.
- A power exercised is a possessed power that has been triggered, and is generating an effect in an open system. Due to interference from the effects of other exercised powers, however, we can never know *a priori* what the outcome of any particular power will be. An exercised power acts transfactually.
- A power actualised *is* an exercised power generating its effect and not being deflected or counteracted by the effects of other exercised powers. An actualised power does not act transfactually but factually in the sense that the power generates its effect.

To grasp these distinctions more fully, let us consider them via the example of a bicycle:[19]

- When a particular cluster of components such as wheels, frame, saddle and handlebars are combined, we can say the bicycle *possesses* the power to facilitate transportation. This power is transfactual: it endures even if the bicycle remains locked in a garden shed.
- A person may *exercise* the power by bringing the bicycle out of the shed and mounting it – i.e. a person triggers the power. However, due (say) to excessive alcohol consumption, strong head winds or steep gradients, the effect may not be the transportation of a cyclist from A to B. In this situation, the bicycle's exercised power is being deflected or counteracted by interference from other exercised powers.
- A person may *actualise* the power and successfully cycle from A to B. The bicycle's power is not being counteracted by any other powers such as alcohol, strong head winds or steep gradients.

Let us now turn to the social realm and consider the powers possessed by workers. Powers are possessed by workers in virtue of their physiological and social make-up. Unlike most animals, humans do not just execute genetically pre-programmed tasks, they conceive these tasks first – although there may be a complex and recursive process between conception and execution. The power of conception is of crucial importance here because it consists of the powers of *imagination, ingenuity, creativity* that conceived of the Pyramids, the Guggenheim, the cart, the MIR space station, surgical tools – and nuclear weapons. These same powers of *imagination, ingenuity, creativity* are also exercised in the conception of less grandiose endeavours such as finding better ways of producing a rivet, writing a programme or engaging in a telephone conversation. HRM practices such as team working, total quality management, quality circles and especially *kaisen*, along with schemes to increase employee participation and empower employees, are designed to unleash and harness the powers of imagination, ingenuity and creativity that workers bring with them to the workplace. If workers did not have these powers there would be no point whatsoever in even contemplating HRM practices. The fact (and it probably is) that these HRM practices have not succeeded in unlocking workers' powers does not mean they do not exist: something could be counteracting these powers. I will return to this in a moment.

Mechanisms[20]

When we adopt a positioned practice, carrying out the requisite practices usually means engaging with a mechanism or mechanisms. The positioned practice of capitalist brings him/her into contact with mechanisms for recruiting and shedding labour; regulating the rate and mass of profits; regulating skill levels; controlling the workforce;[21] and so on. In virtue of the position a capitalist adopts in the web of class relations s/he, and not the worker, has access to (say) the mechanisms that govern recruitment and redundancy. Agents, holding a range of causal powers engage with these mechanisms. Whilst creating a set of mechanisms to actualise workers' powers for imagination, ingenuity and creativity is the Holy Grail of HRM, it is also possible that the mechanisms available to the HR manager succeed in preventing the actualisation of these powers.

In the past I have used the term 'mechanism' as a label applied to the ensemble of structures and relations, and written that it is the mechanism that has a tendency to x. I now think this is misleading so want to re-work the idea of mechanism in two ways. First I want to avoid thinking of 'mechanism' as a generalising term applied to a set of causal factors and I suggest we treat a mechanism as one component alongside several others. Second I want to avoid conflating tendency with the operation of a mechanism, as if other causal factors play no role in the tendency. Instead I want to equate a tendency with the operation of a *causal configuration.*

Causal configurations

A causal configuration (or just configuration for short) consists of a cluster of causal factors or components, which in this context are, typically, social structures, positioned practices, relations, rules, resources, and so on. Causal configurations are emergent phenomena. That is, when certain components are assembled, they give rise to properties that are not found in any of the components. A bureaucracy has properties for processing information that are not found in the individuals that constitute it. Configurations, then, are emergent from, but irreducible to, the cluster of components that constitute them.

No two configurations will ever be the same (although they can be very similar) because they have different clusters of components that constitute them. Thus, one part of an organisation may differ from another part because they each consist of different structures, positioned practices, powers or mechanisms – or whatever components are relevant.

Depending upon the level of abstraction used, an entity can be conceived of as a particular configuration *sui generis*, or in terms of the sub-configurations that constitute it. The labour process is no exception and can be analysed as a particular configuration, or in terms of any of its sub-processes. We simply zoom in on different sub-configurations depending upon the questions we ask.[22] Whatever the level of abstraction, it is important to note the following: *it is the configuration as a totality, and not any of its individual components, that generates the tendency*.

Tendencies[23]

A tendency is the typical way of acting of a particular *causal configuration*. Now, to write that a configuration has a tendency to x, does not mean that it will x. In an open system, configurations do not exist in isolation from one other; rather there is a multiplicity of such configurations, each with their own tendencies, and these tendencies converge in some space–time location. The sub-configuration that constitutes a workforce with the tendency to resist control co-exists with the sub-configuration that constitutes an employer with the tendency to assert control.

A tendency then, metaphorically speaking, is akin to a force: it drives, propels, pushes, thrusts, asserts pressure, and so on. A tendency relates *not* to any outcome or result of some acting force, such as a regularity or pattern in the resulting flux of events. Rather, a tendency refers to the force itself. The relation between configuration and tendency might be characterised as follows.

- The configuration does not always bring about certain effects, but it *always* tends to. Hence it acts transfactually.
- Configurations continue to causally govern the flux of events, irrespective of the conditions under which they are said to operate. We do not say of a transfactually acting configuration that it would bring about certain events *if* certain conditions prevail, or *ceteris paribus*. Rather, the configuration tends to bring about certain events, period.
- Configurations continue to causally govern the flux of events irrespective of any events that ensue. A transfactually acting configuration does not depend for its action upon the patterns of events that it governs: it continues to govern, whether the ensuing events are constantly or non-constantly conjoined.

When investigating the labour process, we may wish to investigate how the rate and mass of profits is regulated; how skill levels are established; or how the workforce is controlled. Each of these sub-processes is governed by different sub-configurations with their own tendencies. We can, for example, identify various sub-configurations that generate tendencies: to de-skill and to up-skill the workforce; to decrease and to increase the rate of profit; to decrease and to increase the mass of profit; to increase and decrease levels of employment; to increase control of the workforce; and for the workforce to resist control.

These tendencies can counteract, and augment, one another in complex ways. A few examples should suffice:

- Tendencies to de-skill the workforce counteract tendencies to up-skill the workforce, yet both can be going on simultaneously within the same organisation.
- Tendencies to de-skill the work may augment tendencies to increase the rate of profit, yet profit rates could still decline because of the influence of other tendencies.
- Tendencies to increase the rate of profit may be counteracted by tendencies to increase the mass of profit – downsizing and outsourcing means fewer workers to extract profit from.
- Tendencies to increase control of the workforce may augment tendencies to increases in the rate of profit, or may counteract the latter if, for example, the chosen mechanisms of control lead to increased resistance.

Setting out the analysis in terms of tendencies avoids the debilitating (empirical realist) situation where either one thing or the other can be occurring, but not both simultaneously. How much ink has been spilled debating whether organisations de-skill or re-skill their workforce; or whether new forms of control create or negate resistance? For the critical realist, tendency and counter-tendency can be at work simultaneously. It is, then, an empirical (not a philosophical) question to discover which of these tendencies are actualised at any point in time.

Conclusion

Hopefully this chapter has clarified some of the more common comments and objections to critical realism and has gone some way to removing as much misunderstanding as possible. Hopefully, also, it has demonstrated that critical realism can provide a viable ontology of organisations and management, allowing positivism and its empirical realist ontology to be abandoned without having to accept a social constructionist ontology. If, then, you now think critical realism is not what you initially thought it was, if you are persuaded by the ontological arguments, or if you still harbour doubts, then I invite you to peruse some of the chapters that make up this collection to see critical realism in action in organisation and management studies.

Notes

1 For some of the more recent contributions, see especially the collection by Ackroyd and Fleetwood (2000) and also Clark (2000); Delbridge (1998); Easton (1998, 2002); Harisson and Easton (1998, 1999); Kwan and Tsang (2001); Johnson and Duberley (2000); Mingers (1999, 2000a, 2000b, 2001); Mingers and Brocklesby (1997); Mir and Watson (2001); Reed (2000, 2001); Tsang and Kwan (1999).

2 For a critical realist critique of positivism and its empirical realist ontology see Fleetwood (2000) and Sayer (1994, 2000). For a critical realist critique of postmodernism and post-structuralism and its social constructivist ontology in general see Sayer (2000), and in organisation and management studies in particular see Fleetwood (2005). Note well that, throughout this chapter, any critique of postmodernists and post-structuralists is not directed against any particular substantive claims (e.g. an analysis of power) but is restricted to ontological matters. The points of departure come where I suspect postmodernists and post-structuralists (a) misunderstand the nature of critical realism and its ontological commitments; and (b) slip into making ontologically exaggerated claims that amount to denying (or fudging) the existence of an extra-discursive realm.

3 For a good example of how to completely misunderstand critical realism's ontological commitments (e.g. that critical realism is committed to something called a '"real" reality') see Guba and Licoln (1994).

4 Note that nothing turns on the choice of example. If it turns out that fairies are real, then I am simply mistaken: critical realists are fallibilists.

5 Easterby-Smith *et al.* (2002) appear to do the opposite. They place critical realism under the rubric of relativism. Guba and Lincoln (1994) refer to critical realism as 'postpositivist'. Whilst I realise Guba and Lincoln are trying to perform a difficult task, namely presenting a complex taxonomy of paradigms in a concise manner, they manage to (mis)interpret critical realism at almost every turn.

6 It is also associated often with essentialism, and this is not a mistake. Critical realists accept that some entities have essences – which do not have to be fixed but can evolve. A thing (such as an animal, an organisation, or a mode of production) has a set of non-accidental properties that make it the kind of thing it is and not another thing. Many commentators who are now potty-trained to jump at the mention of essence feel they can dismiss the concept without even having to provide an argument – as if 'everyone knows' essentialist thinking is misguided (cf. O'Neill, 1998; Sayer, 2000).

7 Jackson and Carter do not define realism or critical realism and neither of these terms appear in the index or glossary. Alvesson and Skoldberg (2000) make no mention of critical realism, and where they do mention realism, it is to associate it with naïve forms and/or positivism.

8 See Brown *et al.* (2002) and Creaven (2000) on the relation between Marxism and critical realism.

9 Gergen (1998: 150) mentions *critical* realism in one sentence before returning to the unqualified term 'realism'.

10 Because these kinds of elision are common, critical realists should avoid comments such as 'reality hits you in the face' when referring to the social world, because they do nothing to assuage the (mis)interpretion that critical realists treat socially real entities like physically real entities. What is usually meant here is either metaphorical, or that social states, like being unemployed, nevertheless can have physical consequences.

11 Moreover, discourse analysis, as a research technique, is acceptable to critical realists. Fairclough *et al.* (2002) develop contemporary critical realist thought on ideally real entities – in this case semiotised entities (cf. Sayer, 2000; Stones, 1996; O'Neill, 1998).

12 I say 'non-ideal' for simplicity because we can, of course, construe a construal, that is make a mental image of a mental image, or a have a theory of a theory – which I return to below.

13 Discourse, of course, refers to far more than talk, but putting matters like this allows the main point to be made with clarity.

14 I assume commodities are physical entities, and not services, simply for convenience.

15 See Lewis (2000), however, for an argument against the misinterpretation that critical realists treat social structures as efficiently causal entities.

16 The sophisticated ontology developed here should pull the rug from under Potter's (1998: 7) 'furniture argument' whereby the realist critique allegedly turns on realists banging on the table and claiming 'you're not telling me that's a social construction'.

17 Notice that the ontology advanced does not hang on the particular choice of theory: other theories could be used, and the ontology might still be correct even if labour process theory was not

18 I use the terms capitalist and worker for brevity.

19 As will become clear, powers are not restricted to materially or artefactually real entities: human beings can have powers such as powers of communication and imagination. The bicycle example is simple and aids exposition.

20 The term 'mechanism' has unfortunate connotations of 'determinism' and 'mechanistic thinking' but it need not involve these. In fact critical realism sets its face steadfastly against such phenomena. (cf. Lewis, 2000: 266). Further, it is often misunderstood to refer only to 'material' or 'artefactual reality' but again this is not the case – as will become clear. Since the terminology is well established, I (reluctantly) stick with it.

21 Note well that a critical realist can accept control as control over 'labour power and behaviour' or (in Foucauldian mode) as control over 'mind power and subjectivities of employees' (Alvesson and Deetz, 1999: 186).

22 Because configurations are emergent phenomena, tendencies are not mechanistically additive or aggregative.

23 For further elaboration on tendencies, see Chapter 1 in Brown *et al.* (2002).

References

Ackroyd, S. and Fleetwood, S. (2000) *Realist Perspectives on Organisation and Management*, London: Routledge.

Alvesson, M. and Deetz, S. (1999) 'Critical theory and postmodernism: approaches to organizational studies', in S. Clegg and C. Hardy (eds), *Studying Organization: Theory and Method*, London: Sage.

Alvesson, M. and Skoldberg, K. (2000) *Reflexive Methodology: New Vistas for Qualitative Research*, London: Sage.

Archer, M. (1998) 'Realism and morphogenesis', in M. Archer, R. Bhaskar, A. Collier, T. Lawson and A. Norrie (eds), *Critical Realism: Essential Readings*, London: Routledge.

Boje, D., Alvarez, R. and Schooling, B. (2001) 'Reclaiming story in organization: narratologies and action sciences', in R. Westwood and S. Linstead (eds), *The Language of Organizations*, London: Sage.

Brown, A. Fleetwood, S. and Roberts, J. (2002) *Critical Realism and Marxism*, London: Routledge.

Burr V. (1998) 'Overview: realism, relativism and social constructivism and discourse', in I. Parker (ed.), *Social Constructivism, Discourse and Realism*, London: Sage.

Carter, P. and Jackson, N. (2000) *Rethinking Organisational Behaviour*, London: Sage.

Chia, R. (2000) 'Discourse analysis as organizational analysis', *Organization*, 7 (3): 513–18.

Chia, R. and King, I. (2001) 'The language of organization theory', in R. Westwood and S. Linstead (eds), *The Language of Organizations*, London: Financial Times/Prentice-Hall.

Clark, P. (2000) *Organisations in Action*, London: Routledge.

Creaven, S. (2000) *Marxism and Critical Realism*, London: Routledge.

Delbridge, R. (1998) *Life on the Line in Contemporary Manufacturing*, Oxford: Oxford University Press.

Easterby-Smith, M., Thorpe, R. and Lowe, A. (2002) *Management Research: An Introduction*, London: Sage.

Easton, G. (1998) 'Case research as a methodology for industrial networks: a realist apologia', in P. Naude and P. Turnbull (eds), *Network Dynamics in International Marketing*, Oxford: Elsevier Science.

—— (2002) 'Marketing: a critical realist approach', *Journal of Business Research*, 55 (2): 103–9.

Fairclough, N., Jessop, B. and Sayer A. (2002) 'Critical realism and semiosis', *Journal of Critical Realism*, 5 (1): 2–10.

Fleetwood, S. (1995) *Hayek's Political Economy: The Socio-Economics of Order*, London: Routledge.

—— (2000) 'Causal laws, functional relations and tendencies', *Review of Political Economy*, 13 (2): 201–20.

—— (2002) 'An evaluation of causal holism', *Cambridge Journal of Economics*, 26 (1): 27–45.

—— (2005, forthcoming) 'The ontology of organisation and management studies: a critical realist approach', *Organization.*

Gergen, K. (1998) 'Constructionism and realism: how are we to go on?', in I. Parker, *Social Constructivism, Discourse and Realism*, London: Sage.

Guba, E. and Lincoln, Y. (1994) 'Competing paradigms in qualitative research', *Handbook of Qualitative Research*, London: Sage.

Hancock, P. (1999) 'Baudrillard and the metaphysics of motivation: a reappraisal of corporate culturalism in the light of the work and ideas of Jean Baudrillard', *Journal of Management Studies*, 36 (2): 155–75.

Hancock, P. and Tyler, M. (2001) *Work, Postmodernism and Organization: A Critical Introduction*, London: Sage.

Harrison, D. and Easton, G. (1998) 'Temporally embedded case comparison in industrial network research', *Proceedings of the 14th IMP International Conference*, TEBA, Turku, Finland, pp. 241–64.

—— (1999) 'Patterns of net response to environmental change', *Proceedings of the 15th IMP International Conference*, University College Dublin, Dublin, Ireland.

Jackson, N. and Carter P. (2000) *Rethinking Organizational Behaviour*, London: Financial Times/Prentice-Hall.

Johnson, P. and Duberley, J. (2000) *Understanding Management Research*, London: Sage.

Keenoy, T. (1997) 'Review article: HRMism and the languages of representation', *Journal of Management Studies*, 34 (5): 825–41.

Kwan, K.-M. and Tsang, W. (2001) 'Realism and constructivism in strategy research: a critical realist response to Mir and Watson', *Strategic Management Journal*, 22: 1163–8.

Lewis, P. (2000) 'Realism, causality and the problem of social structure', *Journal for the Theory of Social Behaviour*, 30 (3): 249–68.

Linstead, S. (2001) 'Language/organization: introduction', in R. Westwood and S. Linstead (eds), *The Language of Organizations*, London: Sage.

Mingers, J. (1999) 'Synthesising constructivism and critical realism: towards critical pluralism', in E. Mathijs, J. Van der Veken and H. Van Belle (eds), *World Views and the Problem of Synthesis*, Amsterdam: Kluwer Academic, pp. 187–204.
—— (2000a) 'The contribution of critical realism as an underpinning philosophy for OR/MS and systems', *Journal of the Operational Research Society*, 51 (11): 1256–70.
—— (2000b) 'Variety is the spice of life: combining soft and hard OR/MS methods', *International Transactions in Operational Research*, 7: 673–91.
—— (2001) 'Combining IS research methods: towards a pluralist methodology', *Information Systems Research*, 12 (3): 240–59.
Mingers, J. and Brocklesby, J. (1997) 'Multimethodology: towards a framework for mixing methodologies', *Omega*, 25 (5): 489–509.
Mir, R. and Watson, A. (2001) 'Realism and constructivism in strategy research: towards a synthesis', *Strategic Management Journal*, 22: 1169–73.
O'Docherty, D. and Willmott, H. (2001) 'Debating labour process theory: the issue of subjectivity and the relevance of poststructuralism', *Sociology*, 35 (2): 457–76.
O'Neill, J. (1998) 'Rhetoric, science and philosophy' *Philosophy of the Social Sciences*, 28: 205–25.
Porpora, D. (1989) 'Four concepts of social structure', in M. Archer, R. Bhaskar, A. Collier, T. Lawson and A. Norrie (eds), *Critical Realism: Essential Readings*, London: Routledge.
Potter, J. (1998) *Representing Reality: Discourse, Rhetoric and Social Construction*, London: Sage.
Reckwitz, A. (2002) 'The status of the "material" in theories of culture: from "social structure" to "artefacts" ', *Journal for the Theory of Social Behaviour*, 32 (2): 195– 217.
Reed, M. (2000) 'The limits of discourse analysis in organizational analysis, *Organization*, 7 (3): 524–30.
—— (2001) 'Organization, trust and control: a realist analysis, *Organization Studies*, 22 (2): 201–28.
Sayer, A. (1994) *Methodology in Social Science: A Realist Approach*, London: Routledge.
—— (2000) *Realism and Social Science*, London: Sage.
Schmidt, V. (2001) 'Oversocialised epistemology: a critical appraisal of constructivism', *Sociology*, 35 (1): 135–57.
Scott J. (2001) 'Where is social structure?', in J. Lopez and G. Potter (eds), *After Postmodernism: An Introduction to Critical Realism*, London: Athlone.
Shenhav, Y. and Weitz, E. (2000) 'The roots of uncertainty in organization theory: a historical constructivist analysis', *Organization*, 7 (3): 373–401.
Stones, R. (1996) *Sociological Reasoning*, London: Macmillan.
Tsang, E. and Kwan, K.-M. (1999) 'Replication and theory development in organizational science: a critical realist perspective', *Academy of Management Review*, 24: 551–61.

2 Brands, boundaries and bandwagons

A critical reflection on critical management studies

Paul Thompson

> No postmodernist would believe they have the right answers, only that there are subjects whose knowledge and identity have been constituted as privileged in a particular setting.
>
> (Palmer and Hardy, 2000: 281)

Perhaps we can interpret the above as indicating that postmodernists know how to be in the right place at the right time. Certainly, critical management studies has been a major growth area, now with its own conference in the UK and a lively US-based discussion list. While any new forums for radical exploration of management and organisation are welcome, appearances can be deceptive. The diversity of people attending conferences and even contributing to discussions is not entirely indicative of the nature of the beast. For critical management studies is also *C*ritical *M*anagement *S*tudies, and for its adherents a brand of sorts.[1]

This can be seen in the detailed and useful account of the origins and characteristics of CMS by Fournier and Grey (2000). The authors make reference to a plurality of intellectual traditions that include varieties of 'neo-Marxism', psychoanalysis and environmentalism, but that proves ultimately tokenistic. For all their qualifying statements, they state that 'the boundaries are drawn around issues related to performativity, denaturalisation and reflexivity' (2000: 17).[2] There is, thus, no significant difference between claims on behalf of CMS and those made for post-structuralism and postmodernism in general. The reference to 'issues' around the three boundaries is somewhat disingenuous. Though occasionally reference is made to enemies beyond the gate, the debates are overwhelmingly within it – cms becomes CMS the brand.

Given that, what this chapter seeks to do is use Fournier and Grey's framework as a starting point for investigating the CMS phenomenon, whilst attending to some of the variations within and beyond its boundaries. Anyway, let us return to their three boundaries. Reflexivity can be seen as part of the unwillingness to take received wisdoms and practices for granted that constitutes much of the appeal of CMS. As Hardy *et al.* (2002) note, some post-structuralists have gone beyond examining ways in which knowledge is situated within research communities and how research processes shape outcomes, to (over-)emphasising authorial identity and 'confessional melodramas'. But the issue of reflexivity is passed over fairly quickly by Fournier and Grey without trying to give it an explicit or distinctive twist. For this we should be grateful. For even the most enthusiastic adherent of CMS would find it difficult to claim that reflexivity is a specific trait of CMS. Rather it is a shared inheritance of critical approaches to social science in general, including interpretive (such as symbolic interactionist) and critical realist perspectives. For example, reflexivity has been one of the five 'domain assumptions of a critical approach to the study of organisations' in Thompson and McHugh's *Work Organizations* (3rd edition, 2002) for over a decade.[3]

However, the other boundary criteria – non-performativity and de-naturalisation – more explicitly reveal the post-structuralist, postmodern character of the CMS brand. What reflects is a major shift in radical analyses, from ontological to epistemological scepticism.[4] As Epstein (1997: 137) notes, this draws on the general postmodernist attitude of 'radical scepticism towards the truth, or toward claims that there is an objective reality that is to some extent knowable'. The outcome of this shift and the means through which the shift is achieved have deeply negative consequences.

The triumph of epistemological relativism

In Fournier and Grey's words, denaturalisation is about 'deconstructing the reality of organisational life' and 'effacing the process of construction behind the mask of science' (2000: 18). Critiques of the 'naturalistic fallacy' associated with positivism have been prominent in the social sciences and sociology of knowledge since at least the work of Mannheim.[5] As with reflexivity, a type of de-naturalisation is, therefore, part of the shared history of critical social science. A soft postmodern epistemology attracts many to this type of approach to the social sciences – that is a recognition of the socially mediated perceptions of reality and socially constituted character of knowledge, and therefore the difficulty of making truth claims or resolving them. But Founrier and Grey give de-naturalisation a specific imprint that reflects a harder relativist kernel, a strong version, that is the meta-theoretical core of postmodernism and the version of CMS postulated by them. Such a version 'takes the form of an extreme social constructionism, a view that identities, relations and political positions are constructed entirely through interpretation, that there is no identifiable social reality against which interpretations can be judged' (Epstein, 1997: 137). The hard epistemology moves beyond a contingent explanation for being unable to access the real (because it is too fragmented) to an all-purpose one ('truth' is merely the will to power). If it is impossible to adjudicate between 'truth claims', then all we can do is show the construction of a perspective and how it is translated for action (Czarniawska, 1999).

Socially constructing science

Czarniawska is typical of CMS writers in making a critique of scientific orthodoxy – a rejection of what is called the 'logico-scientific mode of knowing' – the prime means to accomplish the shift from ontological to epistemological scepticism. This deserves, therefore, some detailed consideration. In support of her claim that organisation theory can be treated as a literary genre because there is no difference between fiction and any other form of writing, science can be considered as mere 'conversation', whose logic of enquiry is rhetorical (1999: 10). Much of the force of this argument comes from a reading of the philosopher of science, Thomas Kuhn (1962, 1970). Indeed Czarniawska (1999: 18) argues that, 'the insight that scientific knowledge is grounded in metaphorical thinking has been more or less commonly accepted (thanks to writers such as Kuhn 1964/66, McCloskey 1986, Morgan 1986)'.[6]

It seems from this statement that Czarniawska has read Morgan's *Images of Organisation* a lot more closely than she has Thomas Kuhn. So, it's worth recapping Kuhn's argument. He challenged the accepted, positivist view that science was based on the linear, patient, disinterested collection of facts, leading to hypotheses that were then tested or 'falsified' until the truth was discovered. Examining the development of physics and related disciplines, he showed that intellectual development took place within a dominant paradigm, excluding that which challenged its way of thinking. Only occasionally would these periods of puzzle-solving within 'normal science' be disrupted by irresistible forces of change based on the inability of the old paradigm to explain a large number of anomalies, and the existence of an alternative, incommensurable paradigm that would displace the old one. In that struggle, protagonists are not merely comparing findings to the real world, but making judgements about what is acceptable in their own professional domain. Science, then, is not wholly rational, and is shaped by ideologies and power.

Czarniawska is far from alone in her misuse of Kuhn. Post-structuralism in general, and CMS in particular, draw on a woefully partisan and partial reading.[7] Short references to his work seldom mention that it was subject to heavy criticism from within the scientific community, and that Kuhn accepted much of it, drawing back from radical interpretations of paradigm wars (see Caldwell, 1982: 70–8, for a summary). Even more importantly, we should keep in mind that for all the talk of social influences on science, Kuhn did not deny that the outcomes of science were real physical laws, or claim that science is mere discourse. He argued that observation and experiment drastically restrict the range of admissible belief, that progress takes place in the state of knowledge, and that the distinction between the scientific and non-scientific is real. Within his model of 'normal science', there is full recognition that empirical investigation creates 'anomalies' – empirical results that contradict theoretical expectations – and which alter the course of action. As Armstrong (2001: 161) notes, 'Social construction, on the Kuhnian model, is interwoven with impacts against the real, not an alternative to them.' In short, what we can say from Kuhn is that scientific judgements involve both the comparison of paradigms with varying modes of reality and with each other.

Safe in their social constructionist readings, relativists appear to be entirely ignorant of the complexities of such debates. They are also seemingly unconcerned with long-running debate on the left about the nature of science. Re-reading Donald McKenzie's excellent twenty-year old article 'Science and social relations' is to be reminded that the dangers of what Hilary and Steven Rose called 'hyper-reflexivity' have been around a long time, but then were more likely to have their roots in a crude and determinist Marxism that 'reduces science to a mere image of the society in which it develops; destroys the boundary between truth and falsity, science and ideology' (McKenzie 1981: 48).

Given that nobody would leave the house, let alone get on an aeroplane or submit themselves to surgery if science had not discovered truths bounded by the laws of probability, constructionists and deconstructionists are either lying to the world or to themselves. Czarniawska addresses this with a typical pragmatic evasion: 'It is practical to *believe* in the world of causes "out there"; it works most of the time. This does not equal saying that there are ways of describing this world "as it is"' (1999: 10, emphasis in original). But actually it does. Unless processes of scientific discovery had revealed that particular bit of the world as it is, we would not know what works. 'Belief' is antecedent to that fact.

Post-structuralists need their partisan readings of Kuhn because he is a scientist and thus adds legitimacy. Their wilful ignorance and willingness to believe their own rhetoric can, however, be the undoing of epistemological postmodernism. This is nicely illustrated through the Sokal controversy. For the uninitiated, Sokal (1997; Sokal and Bricmont, 1997), a professor of physics, submitted a paper to the leading postmodern US journal *Social Text* purporting to deconstruct accounts of quantum gravity. It was a hoax – containing 'deliciously daft assertions' that crossed 'the boundaries of lunacy' (Sardar, 2000: 7), plus numerous citations of postmodern masters – but was nevertheless accepted and lavishly praised (until, of course, the hoax was revealed in the press and subsequent book).[8]

Beyond the stereotypes

Whether with respect to science, or theoretical knowledge in general, it is perfectly possible to recognise the various forms of social influence on the processes of *discovery*, without accepting the harder relativist baggage concerning *outcomes*. There are three serious bodies of work that critical workplace scholars would find particularly congenial: accounts of the institutional influences upon scientific work, with particular reference to the operation of scientific fields as reputational communities (see Whitley, 2000); the 'strong programme' of the sociology of knowledge originally associated with the Science Studies Unit at Edinburgh University (Barnes, 1974); and the treatment of the work of scientists as a labour process (promoted by the *Radical Science* journal; see McKenzie, 1981).

A failure to draw on any of these streams of the sociology of knowledge is indicative of the way in which CMS ignores any middle-ground positions. Instead, post-structuralists promote a stereotypical opposition between (bad) positivism and (good) social constructionism. As Ackroyd and Fleetwood (2000: 3–4) note:

> Here we arrive at the commonly held position that there are two basic perspectives on offer: either the world is objectively and unproblematically available and capable of being known by the systematic application of the empirical techniques common to positivism, or it is not knowable objectively at all; and in the place of claims to objectivity, we find that what is known is merely the product of discourses.

The language of 'truth claims', 'correspondence theory' and 'essentialism' functions as an intellectual halt sign: signalling that what is in fact merely difficult is in substance impossible. The study of work and organisations, like other social science domains, needed to recover a sense of feasible social science based on a recognition that while we cannot ever wholly know the real, reality can nevertheless bite back. With this in mind, 'reality claim' is more accurate than the pejoratively loaded 'truth claim'. There is an alternative, middle ground between positivism and relativism. As a philosophy of science, *critical realism* accepts that social structures and the meanings actors attribute to their situation have to be recognised in the way we construct explanations (Bhaskar, 1989; Collier, 1994), However, while our knowledge is inherently constrained and shaped by the social process of its production, entities such as labour markets and gender relations exist independently of our perceptions and investigations of them (see Tsoukas, 2000, for a specific application to management and organisation).

As Ackroyd and Fleetwood (2000) argue, the ontological question, 'what exists?' is often confused with the epistemological one, 'how can we know what exists?' Hence, as our knowledge is bound up with our conceptions, the misleading conclusion is drawn that all that exists is our concepts or discourse. The difficulties of establishing absolute certainty should not be used to assert that we can make *no* reality claims. In his defence of postmodern epistemology, Newton asks, 'How can we be sure that we have found "the real"?' (1996: 22). The short answer is that we cannot be totally sure, but that is a far cry from not knowing anything: realists, 'want to hold that better and worse forms of knowledge exist and that there are reliable procedures for producing knowledge of things and events' (Ackroyd and Fleetwood, 2000: 15).

What we know is inherently incomplete, but we require a capacity to generate generalisable knowledge and to identify trends, if not laws. Critical realists eschew the positivist search for laws, preferring to identify tendencies associated with the operation of structural mechanisms in open system conditions (see Fleetwood, 2001). This is not to say that critical realism has solved all epistemological problems and provides a fully formed toolbox for researchers. As with all such frameworks, realists can hide absences and unsolved questions behind formally elegant language. But it is not necessary to fully embrace critical realism in order to accept that while there cannot be an exact correspondence between reality and our representations of it, good research aims to grasp the real with as much accuracy and complexity as is feasible in given conditions. For example, we know that the vast majority of studies of empowerment demonstrate, through a variety of quantitative and qualitative methodologies, a massive gap between managerial claims of delegated decision-making and workplace outcomes. Not only can we attempt to distinguish between particular representations and the socially real, it is fundamental to a healthy social science that we seek to do so. In other words, good empirical work helps us to distinguish between rhetorics of the powerful and the realities of power.

What is the point of all this with respect to critical management studies? Simply this – extreme epistemic suspicion or hyper-reflexivity has been disastrous for the field of study. It has encouraged dumbed down empirical work based on ignorance of or hostility towards the full range of social science methodologies, particularly of a quantitative nature. In addition, we have been either plagued with endless and often obscure meta-theorising, or drawn away from challenging the ontological claims associated with managerialist orthodoxies. When it is fashionable for social science to problematise everything, the focus is always on what we don't know rather than what we do. While there is a role for deconstruction, when it becomes the sole purpose of analysis, the outcomes are ultimately arid and self-defeating. CMS is predisposed to problematise everything and resolve nothing.

Strategies for (non-)explanation – power without responsibility

The argument in this chapter now turns towards the strategies employed in CMS in order to theorise about 'what exists'. It is based on the simple premise that theorising without accessing the real is impossible. If this is the case, what we get from post-structuralists is the worst of both worlds – non-transparent forms of explanation, the power to persuade without the responsibility to account for explanation.

Three overlapping directions can be identified:

1 Retreat wholly into the text

If 'truth claims' are based wholly on the power to persuade, then text itself becomes the only source of legitimacy. Or as Armstrong puts it, 'If all we can know of text is text itself, questions of validity dissolve into rhetorical pragmatics' (2001: 157). The most obvious manifestation of this is quoting your mates, or referring only to those who support your argument. If we go back to Czarniawska's (1999) book, we find that her arguments are justified and legitimated time and again by reference to small number of co-thinkers such as Rorty, Macintyre, Lyotard and Latour. The economist McCloskey is quoted twelve times in the book in support of her relativist claims about the non-scientific nature of economics and other disciplines, yet no other work of economics appears in the index. It is as if this particular claim encompasses the whole discipline, despite, for example, a strong critical realist presence (e.g. Lawson, 1998). Postmodernists are big on hearing alternative voices until any of those voices say anything that disputes their line of thinking. These approaches are given further underpinning by notions of paradigm incommensurability.

Such highly selective readings are not merely examples of 'bad practice'. It is the likely outcome of treating the literature as the sole or main source of authoritative reinforcement/consensus: 'Thus the doctrine of the discursively constituted self encourages the authors to infer the penetration of a discourse from the mere fact of its presence' (Armstrong, 2001: 156).

There is a further dimension to this. Having dismissed any notion of the real and any sense in which research is based on a process of discovery, all references are equal. They need not indicate the status of a work or what empirical evidence it does or does not rest upon. To return to the Czarniawska example, she refers to Kuhn, McCloskey and Morgan as her sources for the view that there is near consensus on the rhetorical nature of science, yet the first is misread (on the basis of a single reference); the second appears to be the only economist in the world who believes that her discipline consists of nothing more than metaphors and stories; and the third writes about the usefulness of metaphors, but *Images of Organisation* does not explicitly discuss the nature of scientific knowledge at all.

2 *Indirect reference to the 'real'*

CMS texts, while denying the possibility of making truth claims, litter their discussions of contemporary organisational life with references to 'new realities', though often with quotation marks to indicate ironic distance. Logically, an approach that rejects narrative and totalising pictures should be hostile to or uninterested in an alternative conception of society, but there is considerable evidence of what Armstrong calls 'the persistence of unreconstructed truth claims within avowedly anti-realist texts' (2001: 7). Even those who have most resolutely avoided any engagement with the empirical cannot resist reference to 'the changing conditions of modern life', to justify their calls for conceptual shifts in the body of organisation theory, or in this case the theory of the organisational body (Dale and Burrell, 2000: 25).

The main example I want to use is Shenhav's study of the 'engineering foundations of the managerial revolution'. He assures us that he does not wish to 'evaluate the ontological status of the propositions and claims presented in the engineering texts' (1999: 135) that he draws on in his fascinating account of the emergence of management systems in the USA. Yet almost every page is replete with description of events that asserts particular interpretation, sometimes of a strong character. For example, we are told that 'The engineering rhetoric is a form of colonizing the mind – the minds of employers and workers as well as of politicians, social scientists and policy-makers. This book explores how this "colonizing of the mind" was realised' (1999: 201). Except that it doesn't. Too often it presents the discourses of *American Machinist* and other journals as if words were deeds. Reality claims are made, but epistemological responsibility evaded.

Finally, in a classic example of having your cake and eating it, Fournier and Grey advance an analysis of the intellectual, political and socio-economic conditions under which the critical and management came together. It is replete with confident claims about agency and context,[9] yet they preface the analysis with the following: 'we should make it clear that we do not see these conditions as having "caused" or determined the emergence of critical management studies' (2000: 10). On what grounds, then, should the reader accept what they say?

3 The discursive production of reality

These two tendencies – to retreat into the text and use it as a source of uncontested authority, and the finding of ways to indirectly refer to the real – come together in a third strategy of creating facts from discourse. As Armstrong observes, qualitative research by post-structuralists in the management field does make substantial reality claims:

> Talk and action are reported as support for the writer's interpretation of them. ... Whilst presenting a surface of empirical engagement, the style actually incorporates a general-purpose interpretative filter through which all possible realities can be assimilated to its theoretical core.
>
> (Armstrong 2001: 162)

He then proceeds to illustrate this primarily through the work of du Gay.

Armstrong's observations parallel a similar exercise carried out by Thompson and Findlay (1999). Their paper seeks to identify strong claims from weak evidence made in CMS studies by, among others, Rose, Grey and McCabe and Knights. For example, it demonstrates that even where qualitative material is collected in case studies, it is often simply attributed to respondents' concerns with identity, concerns which are seen as distinct and discontinuous with traditional terrains of work and management. Ironically, this truly is an example of a way of doing research that is theoretically determined as well as theory-laden.

In conclusion to this section, we would argue that if reality claims are inevitable, we need to have transparent, shared ways of discussing and resolving them – however partial and limited they may be. The enhanced epistemological freedom for the postmodern theorist from anything other than self-referential accountability is secured at the expense of organisational theory in general. Before we get to the third Fournier and Grey boundary, it is worth noting and discussing a fork in the CMS road.

An epistemological escape hatch: multi-paradigm perspectives

Some proponents of CMS/post-structuralism have become unhappy with the consequences of relativism. Unwilling to accept or ignorant that critical realism offers an alternative to positivism and social constructionism, they have to seek other ways out of the relativist *cul-de-sac*, which allow some means of making judgements and making a difference.

The chief escape hatch from pure reliance on deconstruction is development of 'multi-paradigm thinking', under the banner of diversity, dialogue and democracy, so the chapter focuses on a critique of multi-paradigm analysis. Originally promoted by Hassard (1991), who interprets empirical data on the fire service in the UK through the paradigmatic 'eyes' of each of Burrell and Morgan's original quartet, the argument is that the approach reflects the diverse and multi-faceted nature of reality which no single approach can grasp (Schultz and Hatch, 1996).

This has been developed in a number of more recent contributions. For example, Kamoche argues that unless human resource management is analysed from within each paradigm, we may be 'ignoring the insights that other perspectives have been shown to yield' (1991: 13). A 'multi-perspective' approach is also utilised by Daymon (1999), drawing on Martin's (1992) well-known integration, differentiation and fragmentation framework for analysing culture. She asserts that a single analytical lens is insufficient to explain the complex realities of life in new organisational forms such as television stations.

Hassard's argument is superficially attractive. Who, after all, could be against dialogue, or resist the call for greater 'democracy' in organisation theory? (1991: 296). In addition, there is no doubt that such exercises are fruitful individual exercises in collective and individual learning. But, as Parker and McHugh (1991) observed of Hassard's effort, the ability to hop between languages is not the same as demonstrating its analytical usefulness. The practice of multiple paradigm analysis tends to be closure by any other name, for each speaks from behind its own walls. Indeed, Hassard (1988) treats meta-theories as distinct language games in which we can be trained. The normal purpose of dialogue is to resolve issues or move beyond disagreements. This is difficult for postmodernists, given their denial of any grounds against which to make judgements.

It may be true, as Kamoche says, that paradigms generate different insights, but what if those insights are based on competing claims, for instance about the relative weight of hard and soft HRM in contemporary workplace practice? Alternatively, what if the competing insights refer to an entity that is accepted as both entirely discursive and extra-discursive? Similarly, in her previously discussed analysis of competing perspectives on culture in a TV station, Daymon says that an integration lens is useful, because 'commonly held beliefs are found about the need to make profits in order to survive' (1999: 131). But this is not just a belief, it is a real consequence of competitive markets. Other perspectives on culture cannot negate that reality. The relativist twist that everything is of equal value merely adds to the problem and is open to the same objections that were raised by Reed of Morgan's use of metaphors: that we end up taking products down from the shelf as uncritical consumers, rather than promoting rigorous debate and research.

It may well be the case that a single analytical lens is insufficient to explain the complex realities of life in new organisational forms such as television stations. But what if competing claims are being made? For example, integration perspectives are often not just about how things are managed, but are discourses used by management to explain the world in unitary terms. This frequently clashes with how employees (in differentiated or fragmented terms) see and experience the *same* events. Daymon tries to get round this by distinguishing between paradigms and perspectives; the latter being empirically derived without any consistent association with particular methods or epistemologies. The distinction is useful, but the argument, that 'the three separate portrayals of CTV are simultaneously accurate' (1999: 131), is open to the same objections.

Whatever virtues it may have, this mode of analysis reproduces the weaknesses of relativism by other means. There is no solution to the core problem of loss of explanatory power. In addition it draws attention away from a more worthwhile approach – multi-level analysis. It is perfectly legitimate to have a more structural or a more micro emphasis on management or some other aspect of organisational life. Moreover, it is possible to creatively combine micro and macro. The key is not to analytically close off the possibilities of 'seeing' the other dimension, and that observations made about action and structure at different levels – workgroup, organisational, societal – are compatible with one another (Ackroyd, 2000).

To go further, it is even possible to argue that such dimensions are sometimes most effectively addressed by different perspectives. Kellner (1999: 194) says that, 'McDonaldization is a many-sided phenomenon and the more perspectives that we can bring to its analysis the better grasp of the phenomenon one will have.' This 'more the better' outlook may be overdoing it, but Kellner does persuasively argue that postmodern concepts can be successfully deployed to explain a later development of McDonaldization, when a modernist emphasis on mass production was complemented by a set of practices around consumption and management of global identities. Kellner's analysis partly avoids this trap because he utilises different perspectives to explain different things – in his case production and consumption relations – and in different time periods.

Performance

Critical work on management must have 'non-performative intent'. Fournier and Grey (2000: 17) define performativity in a number of ways: part process – 'inscribing knowledge within means–ends calculation' – and part potential outcome – 'the aim is to contribute to the effectiveness of managerial practice'. On this basis they go on to make a distinction between legitimately invoking notions of power, inequality and control; and the illegitimate invocation of efficiency, effectiveness and profitability. So, for example, they criticise harnessing diversity in the name of effectiveness.

It is difficult to find practical or political grounds to sustain such an interpretation. Once again, critical researchers have long questioned the construction of performance categories. The work of Nichols (1986) or Williams *et al.* (1989) are examples of critical scholarship that challenge (and not merely deconstruct) the terms of existing concepts and practices focused on different aspects of performance. But they do not reject making judgements on the basis of performance or outcome (Rosenau, 1992: glossary). After all, what is seen as illegitimately performative – efficiency, effectiveness and profitability – is the terrain through which the capitalist labour process is reproduced and contested. Earlier in their paper, Fournier and Grey themselves (2000: 11) talk of management incompetence and the lack of effectiveness, or is this just discourse? It is certainly difficult to identify the grounds on which they would evaluate the relevant practices.

And why is this terrain illegitimate in itself? In any feasible economic relations some organisations or practices will be more effective and efficient than others, though how this is measured and what action follows from it will always be open to dispute. Productivity matters to employees as well as managers. It is reasonable to argue that HRM or equal opportunity can be positive for efficiency, as long as this is not the only criterion on which progressive practices are advocated. A refusal to engage at this level makes the genuine attempts by CMS to debate grounds for ethical choice or emancipation ultimately hollow. It is also apparent that CMS applies performativity criteria to anyone but academics. Inscribing knowledge within mean–ends calculation sounds pretty much like what we do with our research choices and publishing 'strategies'. It is difficult to see why academic performativity (producing yet another journal article that next to nobody reads) is morally superior or practically more beneficial than, let's say, attempts to improve work design.

CMS is locked into this *cul-de-sac* of non-performativity, not simply because of its location within a business context, but because of the postmodern rejection of the idea of progress or reason in general. Suspicion of performativity can quickly slip into rejection of *any* practice. While the individual politics of postmodernists varies, if there are no grounds for privileging or de-privileging any discourse, the politics in general tends to despair or disengagement. A stance of pure criticism, refusing to assert any values (other than its own relativism), postmodernism cannot provide a basis for a radical alternative, given that 'left politics requires a conception of a better society and an assertion of a better set of values than those that now prevail' (Epstein, 1997: 143).[10]

It is worth noting that aversion to performativity is not characteristic of all in the CMS camp. To illustrate this it is worth quoting Palmer and Hardy's dismissal of 'hard postmodernism' in full:

> Such an approach, or anything close to it, presents difficulties in organisation and management theory because, according to this view 'postmodern organisation' is a contradiction in terms. Not surprisingly the field has proven resistant to such intrusions. Consequently many postmodern writers on organisations have limited their role to one of critique. Rather than abandon modernity and reason altogether, they often advocate a soft or optimistic version of postmodernism, which recognises the ontological existence of the social world, however precarious and fluid, and focuses on the

> location of alternative interpretations, marginalized voices and different readings.
>
> (Palmer and Hardy, 2000: 265)

In seeking to apply the insights of postmodernism to practice, they place themselves in the soft camp, yet their formulation combines both a softer relativism and a desire to shape practice. As we shall see in the next section, both directions are present, in varying degrees and combinations, among CMS writers more generally.

Performativity escape hatches: ethical and managerial enlightenment

With reference to practice, the search for an escape hatch has been more tortuous, but in the absence of any social science criteria to make judgements, the focus has been on normative grounds, notably ethics (Parker, 1998). This has been debated and critiqued elsewhere, the essential point being made that whatever the merits of a critical ethics, if there is no body of meaningful evidence in organisation theory, 'starting with ethics means finishing with nothing to argue about but our own value preferences' (see Thompson *et al.*, 2000: 1156). Fournier and Grey also search for ways 'to sever the logical link between epistemological and moral or political relativism' (2000: 21). But after rehearsing the arguments between hard and soft relativism, they proclaim the debate to have been 'challenging', but reach no conclusions and pass on to the next issue.[11]

There is another, more direct, escape hatch. As Fournier and Grey (2000: 25–6) admit, there is now a small, but flourishing industry of books and consultancy that seeks to use the insights of postmodernism to enlighten management. Palmer and Hardy go explicitly down this line arguing that such insights can help managers encourage multiple stories, diagnose problems, and live with ongoing tensions between the new and old, external and internal, etc. This can promote more successful innovation, learning, change (2000: 283–4). Differences from the humanistic wing of management, or progressive sounding pop management writers, are difficult to spot. Generally, such approaches at least have the virtues of honesty and the modest possibilities for organisational reform. However, the orientation towards management as an agent or alternative consultancy sits rather uneasily with a claim to be within the domain of critical management studies. Or does it?

How not to be critical of management

Ultimately the question is – what is CMS critical of? It is certainly not management itself. When Paul Adler (2000: 3) argued on the American CMS list that 'our critique should be primarily but not exclusively in the name of working people', responses were largely hostile. Such divisions between management and labour were 'dualistic' and had to be 'problematised'.

One critic worried about taking such an oppositional stance towards 'our MBA students and consulting clients'. Treating them as 'other' would be 'subtly and unintentionally hostile towards them' (Chumer, 2000: 7). Palmer and Hardy (2000: 276) reinforce the more general point: 'Postmodern approaches draw our attention to the irrelevance of cutting up the world into distinctions that may no longer be meaningful. One arena where this may be particularly important is the distinction between non-managers and manager.'

While decades of activity on the left has inoculated me against making claims in the name of labour or anyone else, critical workplace researchers cannot ignore the interests of labour and management (albeit fractured in each case). But, for CMS, in the name of fragmented identities and refutation of dualisms, the material reality of divergent interests is set aside, or consigned to the compartment labelled 'out of date and no longer relevant'.

Shorn of such an orientation, the only object left is management theory. In other words, it is the *studies*, not the management, that CMS emphasises. Shut off from performance in the wider world, this kind of CMS can only be concerned with performance in the academic equivalent – in other words with the effectiveness of critique of the mainstream on the one hand, and in the sphere of management education on the other.

This is not a single response. As Fournier and Grey show, there is a continuing divide between purists and pragmatists. The former, whether in the guise of meta-theorists or paradigm warriors, see engagement with management as dilution of the message. The alternative of 'permanent critique' is, however, in itself problematic. For this purpose to be meaningful, it must have orthodoxy to constitute itself against. Yet in many British management schools and some segments of organisation theory, CMS has *become* the orthodoxy.[12] What will it then have to critique? If 'critique has to follow the practices that constitute its target' (Fournier and Grey, 2000: 19), CMS needs the bogeyman.

For some within, or attracted to CMS, it is not enough to leave purely 'textual markers' (Perriton, 2000: 229). Perriton, echoing previous themes from Anthony (1998), goes on to argue that CMS must attend to the diverse performances of management pedagogy and to suggesting alternative management identities. Practical engagement equals management education, or educating management: 'The work of critical educators in this context will be a form of guerrilla warfare on the reproduction of the current managerialist identity of "manager".' While any form of critical practice is welcome, the statement merely draws attention to the limitations of detaching identities from interests.

Having said all that, it is not easy to take a moral high ground. We all have careers to make, reputations to enhance and interests to pursue. Those of us in business schools need to make meaningful to ourselves, to managers and would-be managers what we are teaching. But it still seems legitimate to ask of CMS – is this all there is? Palmer and Hardy refer to postmodern practices 'rattling the cage' (2000: 284), but what cage are we talking about? It certainly doesn't appear to be Weber's iron cage of labour. Their preference for playing devil's advocate, embracing the new or ephemeral, seeing all sides of stories and continually critiquing assumptions is an underwhelming response to the range of intellectual and policy issues facing us. But it is a response that suits the occupational interests of academics, particularly at a time of increased regulation and measurement.

In this sense, the final argument of Fournier and Grey (2000: 27) that the best we can do is ensure that the cacophony of critical voices 'is heard by students of management, "undistorted" by the performative intent (hence the importance of management education for CMS)' is both naive about management and silent about academic performativity. Meanwhile, they are worried that, 'the spectacle of "critical" is being appropriated in ways which are so extensive as to make its meaning indistinguishable from that which was formerly the target of critique' (2000: 27). Well, what a surprise – welcome to the bandwagon effect. In the mid-1980s labour process theory went through the same process. It came out the other side with less adherents and influence, but still with something to say and, in recent years, a determination to connect with public policy and wider constituencies. The choice for CMS is this – does it want to be a (postmodern) brand or a genuine, additional forum for a variety of critical workplace researchers? I have no problem with Fournier and Grey debating or defining the boundaries of a diverse critical community in order to shake some of the bandwagon jumpers off the wagon train. But I do draw the line at locking the enterprise into a brand identity in the name of a broad critical community that far outstrips the sectarian imprint they seek to give it.

Notes

1 I am not assuming that the brand is identical in every context. As in all matters, institutional specificity leaves its mark and, for example, the US-based CMS network appears to be less influenced by postmodernism.
2 How Fournier and Grey arrive at these criteria is not obvious. They say that CMS is 'constituted through a process of inscription within a network of other inscriptions that serve to create obligatory points of passage in terms of work referenced and vocabulary or concepts used for analysis' (2000: 16). What this seems to mean is that you are part of the brand if you quote the right people and use the designated language.
3 For a detailed discussion of issues around reflexivity, see Alvesson and Sköldberg (2000). Interestingly, it has also been argued that contemporary cultures are so knowing that reflexivity has become the norm, and therefore emptied of any radical content (Zizek, 1999)
4 In his review of post-colonial writings and the work of Spivak in particular, Eagleton makes a similar point, that it is 'rather more audacious about epistemology … than about social reconstruction' (1999: 5).
5 I'm grateful to Graham Sewell for enlightening me on this and a number of other points in the chapter.
6 Metaphor itself is not necessarily connected to social constructionism. Lewis (1999) makes a strong case that the use of metaphor performs a useful cognitive role in scientific theorising in that it is part of the linguistic context through which models are suggested and described.
7 Fournier and Grey have a standard one line dismissal of 'the supposed objectivism of natural science' by reference to Kuhn (2000: 13).

8 Sardar is in the broadly postmodern camp, and his excellent pamphlet is recommended reading for those sceptical of just how wrong-headed most social constructionist writing on science actually is.
9 This appears to consist of a kind of elective affinity between the raised but inherently problematic profile of management in the workplace and broader polity, and the increased numbers, better location and enhanced legitimacy of those in a position to critique it from within academia.
10 Disengagement from social change is also reinforced by the tendency of CMS writers to emphasise what Palmer and Hardy refer to as 'constrained actors' (2000: 272). Such constraints derive from concepts of power and identity in which, though resistance if possible, it is ultimately ineffective. As this has been critiqued elsewhere (Thompson and Ackroyd, 1995; Ackroyd and Thompson, 1999), I shall say no more here.
11 For similar inconclusive agonising that eventually settles for 'existential angst', see Newton (1996).
12 This is obviously not the case everywhere, particularly in the USA. But there can be little doubt that, even there, the numerical weight and intellectual confidence of the so-called positivist-functionalist orthodoxy in organisation theory has been severely dented.

References

Ackroyd, S. (2000) 'Connecting organisations and societies: a realist analysis of structures?', in S. Ackroyd and S. Fleetwood (eds), *Realist Perspectives on Management and Organisations*, London: Routledge.

Ackroyd, S. and Fleetwood, S. (2000) 'Realism in contemporary organisation theory and management studies', in S. Ackroyd and S. Fleetwood (eds), *Realist Perspectives on Management and Organisations*, London: Routledge.

Ackroyd, S. and Thompson, P. (1999) *Organizational Misbehaviour*, London: Sage.

Adler, P. (2000) 'Critical in the name of who or what?', Critical Management Studies Workshop Essay. Available at http://www.owner-c-m-workshop@jiscmail.ac.uk (and see comments by Chumer, Kreisher, Willmott and Kaghan).

Alvesson, M. and Sköldberg, K. (2000) *Reflexive Methodology: New Vistas for Qualitative Research*, London: Sage.

Anthony, P. (1998) 'Management education: ethics versus morality', in M. Parker (ed.), *Ethics and Organization*, London: Sage.

Armstrong, P. (2001) 'Styles of illusion', *The Sociological Review*, 49 (2): 155–73.

Barnes, B. (1974) *Scientific Knowledge and Sociological Theory*, London: Routledge and Kegan Paul.

Bhaskar, R. (1989) *Reclaiming Reality*, London: Verso.

Caldwell, B. (1982) *Beyond Positivism: Economic Methodology in the Twentieth Century*, London: Routledge.

Chumer, M. (2000) Comment on Adler, P., 'Critical in the name of who or what?', Critical Management Studies Workshop Essay. Available online at: http://www.owner-c-m-workshop@jiscmail.ac.uk

Coleman, G. (1991) *Investigating Organisations: A Feminist Approach*, Bristol: SAUS Publications.

Collier, A. (1994) *Critical Realism*, London: Verso.

Czarniawska, B. (1999) *Writing Management: Organization Theory as a Literary Genre*, Oxford: Oxford University Press.

Dale, K. and Burrell, G. (2000) 'What shape are we in? Organization theory and the organized body', in J. Hassard, R. Holliday and H. Willmott (eds), *Body and Organization*, London: Sage.

Daymon, C. (1999) 'Tensions in television: quality, profits, and career aspirations', paper for the 17th Annual Labour Process Conference, Royal Holloway.

Eagleton, T. (1999) 'In the gaudy supermarket', *London Review of Books*, 21 (10): 13.

Epstein, B. (1997) 'Postmodernism and the left', *New Politics*, 6 (2): 130–45.

Fleetwood, S. (2001) 'Causal laws, functional relations and tendencies', *Review of Political Economy*, 13 (2): 201–22.

Fournier, V. and Grey, C. (2000) 'At the critical moment: conditions and prospects for critical management studies', *Human Relations*, 53 (1): 7–32.

Hardy, C., Harley, B. and Alvesson, M. (2002) 'Reflexivity in discourse analysis: how far have we come?', paper for EGOS Conference, Barcelona, July.

Hassard, J. (1988) 'Overcoming hermeneutics in organization theory: an alternative to paradigm incommensurability', *Human Relations*, 41 (3): 247–59.

—— (1991) 'Multiple paradigms and organizational analysis: a case study', *Organization Studies*, 12 (2): 275–99.

Kamoche, K. (1991) 'Human resource management: a multiparadigmatic analsyis', *Personnel Review*, 20 (4): 3–14.

Kellner, D. (1999) 'Theorising/resisting McDonaldization: a multiperspectivist approach', in B. Smart (ed.), *Resisting McDonaldization*, London: Sage.

Kuhn, T. (1962, 2nd edition 1970) *The Structure of Scientific Revolutions*, Chicago: University of Chicago Press.

Lawson, T. (1998) *Economics and Reality*, London: Routledge.

Lewis, P. (1999) 'Metaphor and critical realism', in S. Fleetwood (ed.), *Critical Realism in Economics*, London: Routledge.

McKenzie, D. (1981) 'Notes on the science and social relations debate', *Capital and Class*, 14: 47–60.

Martin, J. (1992) *Cultures in Organisations: Three Perspectives*, New York: Oxford University Press.

Newton, T. (1996) 'Postmodernism and action', *Organization*, 3 (1): 7–29.

Nichols, T. (1986) *The British Worker Question*, London: Routledge and Kegan Paul.

Palmer, I. and Hardy, C. (2000) *Thinking About Management*, London: Sage.

Parker, M. (1998) 'Capitalism, subjectivity and ethics: debating labour process analysis', *Organization Studies*, 20 (1): 25–45.

Parker, M. and McHugh, G. (1991) 'Five texts in search of an author: a response to John Hassard's "Multiple Paradigms and Organizational Analysis: A Case Study"', *Organization Studies*, 12 (3): 451–6.

Perriton, L. (2000) 'Verandah discourses: critical management education in organizations', *British Journal of Management*, 11: 227–37.

Rosenau, P.M. (1992) *Postmodernism and the Social Sciences: Insights, Inroads and Intrusions*, Princeton: Princeton University Press.

Sardar, Z. (2000) *Thomas Kuhn and the Science Wars*, Cambridge: Icon Books.

Schultz, M. and Hatch, M.-J. (1996) 'Living with multiple paradigms: the case of paradigm interplay in organizational culture studies', *Academy of Management Review*, 21: 529–57.

Shenhav, Y. (1999) *Manufacturing Rationality: The Engineering Foundations of the Managerial Revolution*, Oxford: Oxford University Press.

Sokal, A. (1997) 'A plea for reason, evidence and logic', *New Politics*, 6 (2): 126–9.

Sokal, A. and Bricmont, J. (1997) *Intellectual Impostures*, London: Profile Books.
Thompson, P. and Ackroyd, S. (1995) 'All quiet on the workplace front? A critique of recent trends in British industrial sociology", *Sociology*, 29 (4): 1–19.
Thompson, P. and Findlay, P. (1999) 'Changing the people: social engineering in the contemporary workplace', in A. Sayer and L. Ray (eds), *Culture and Economy After the Cultural Turn*, London: Sage.
Thompson, P. and McHugh, D. (2002) *Work Organisations*, 3rd edition, London: Palgrave.
Thompson, P., Smith, C. and Ackroyd, S. (2000) 'If ethics is the answer, you've been asking the wrong questions: a reply to Martin Parker', *Organization Studies*, 21 (6): 1149–58.
Tsoukas, H. (2000) 'What is management? An outline of a metatheory', in S. Ackroyd and S. Fleetwood (eds), *Realist Perspectives on Management and Organisations*, London: Routledge.
Whitley, R. (2000) *The Intellectual and Social Organization of the Sciences*, Oxford: Oxford University Press.
Williams, K. *et al.* (1989) 'Do labour costs really matter?', *Work, Employment and Society*, 3 (3): 281–305.
Zizek, S. (1999) 'You may! The post-modern superego', *London Review of Books*, 21 (6).

3 Idealism and ideology

The Caterpillar controversy in critical accounting research

Peter Armstrong

Introduction: idealism and ideology

One of the delights of imaginative writing is the freedom it allows for a parallel world to be created according to the wishes and purposes of the writer. That freedom, paradoxically, depends on the normative constraints involved in the public creation and renewal of language. The evocative power of fiction, that is, is achieved through terms and connectives which depend for their meaning on a constant effort on the part of ordinary users of language to make sense of things which are not language. In this analogue of tendencies in social science, the writers of fiction are the idealists and the public are the realists.

The theme of this chapter can be succinctly stated. Idealism, as a way of doing social science, is not primarily concerned with identifying the terms of its language games with a reality outside of them. In consequence it allows considerable freedom to manipulate the meanings which it draws from the ordinary language use of these terms. It is thus a medium well suited to the writing of ideology. This means that the realist who sets out to critique idealist social science also tends to become embroiled in a critique of ideology. Conversely the critique of ideology often turns on a realist critique of idealism.

An event of this kind happened a few years ago in the literature of critical accounting. This is not the place to say so at length, but it is a literature of vigorous debate and mainstream social scientists would do well to pay attention. The controversy concerned an idealist analysis of the nature and significance of a major company re-organisation. The chapter begins by outlining the thesis and the realist critiques which it provoked. There follows an analysis of the rhetorical devices used in this particular specimen of idealist writing to represent as social science what is really a work of imaginative fiction. Inevitably, in view of what has just been said, this also involves a critique of the ideological nature of its representations.

The Plant With A Future

In 1994, Peter Miller and Ted O'Leary, two of the best-known authors in the critical accounting movement, published a paper on the re-organisation of the

Caterpillar company's plant at Decatur, Illinois (Miller and O'Leary, 1994). The programme was called 'Plant With A Future' (PWAF) and was Caterpillar's response to losses totalling almost US$1 billion in the three years before the inception of the programme in 1986. During these three years the company had closed six US plants, reducing the headcount of hourly paid workers by 44 per cent and that of salaried staffs by 26 per cent. PWAF itself contained an implicit threat of more job losses. In order to avoid identification as a plant *without* a future, Decatur had been required to undertake sub-programmes of product simplification, manufacturing automation and the integration of its information systems around a system of cell manufacture. Materials and components for each cell were delivered via an 'Assembly Highway' to which the completed product was returned for delivery to the next stage of manufacture, or to the paint shop in the case of the final stage. Within the cell teams, flexible working had been introduced, with the teams themselves taking responsibility for quality. In order to ensure this, there was no provision for rectification work outside the cells and no buffer stocks were held. Manufacturing Resource Planning (MRP) software coupled all manufacturing schedules to orders from specific customers, and progress against these schedules was shown on a computer monitor installed in each cell. At the same time, costs and build times were benchmarked against those of Komatsu, then considered a major competitor. Red and green lights in each cell showed whether the process was ahead of its benchmark or behind it. Meanwhile 'non-core' manufacturing processes (generally those which were simple and labour intensive) were outsourced to 'focused, low-cost suppliers'.

All these changes were accompanied by a great deal of managerial communication on the subjects of competitiveness and responsibility to the customer. Wanting Caterpillar employees to experience competition at a personal level, senior executives put it about that 'there's a person at Komatsu who is doing the same job as you are doing at Cat', and it was this message that the red and green lights were intended to convey. Similarly the cell teams were to think of the units on which they worked as having already been sold to identified customers and, in order to encourage this, the customers' details were displayed on the computer monitors alongside the MRP.

This much is fact. The declared object of Miller and O'Leary's paper, however, is to present an *analysis* of these facts, one through which they would be able to offer an understanding of 'the dynamics of a specific attempt to govern the economic and personal dimensions of an enterprise'. They propose to do this by pursuing three distinct levels of analysis: that of the interlinked changes in manufacturing process, management techniques and spatial arrangement at Decatur; that of the general talk of 'advanced manufacturing' as a means through which the USA might compete with Far Eastern imports, and its actualisation at Decatur; and that of the links between the re-organisation and the discourse of 'economic citizenship' which had come to be associated with advanced manufacturing. It is through an exploration of the 'links and relays' between these levels of analysis (which themselves contain linkages between discourses and practices) that the authors seek to understand 'a new mode of seeking to govern economic life', one in which 'a novel type of economic citizen is called upon to play a new set of roles within the enterprise and within the nation'.

Some parts of this thesis, it should be said at once, are convincing. One does not need much persuading that the introduction of cell manufacturing at Decatur, and indeed the re-organisation in general, was influenced by general discourses of advanced manufacturing. Though (oddly) the authors do not stress the fact, they tell us at one point that management consultants were involved, and it would be surprising if these did much else than import the currently accepted success recipes. Similarly, it is not hard to believe that the communications of Caterpillar's management on the subjects of competition and customer focus tapped into wider discourses on these matters, and were indeed behind the design of the information fed to the cell teams by the computer monitor and coloured lights. On these points, the paper is well documented, convincingly argued – and unexciting. They are not, however, its main thrust. What caught the attention of the general reader, and of the critics to be introduced below, was twofold. First, the authors' claim to have demonstrated that the actualisation of new economic citizenship, as an approach to the governance of economic life, was enabled by the managerial re-organisation of Decatur, especially the new plant layout; and second, that reciprocally, the notion of 'new economic citizenship' had been given content by the managerial practices introduced in its name. Though the authors almost qualified their conclusion out of existence by adding that the 'position and meaning of the various components … are mobile and shifting', it nevertheless provoked two substantial critiques, both of which were published in 1998, together with Miller and O'Leary's reply.

Arnold's critique

By the time Miller and O'Leary's paper appeared in print, the Caterpillar company was embroiled in a series of protracted strikes. The occasion of Arnold's critique (Arnold, 1998) was the inconstancy between this turmoil and Miller and O'Leary's contention, however hedged about with qualifications and enclosed in quotation marks, that conditions they had witnessed at Decatur could be described in terms of a new economic citizenship. More broadly, she objected to the implications for the critical accounting project as a whole. At bottom, Miller and O'Leary's conclusions were unitarist. They implied, that is, that there is no long-run incompatibility between the requirements of capital accumulation and the emancipation of the workforce. If such a conclusion from two of the best-known collaborators in critical accounting research was allowed to pass into the literature unchallenged, the effect would be to legitimise forms of 'critical' research which ignored the embedding of management and accounting technique in the struggle between capital and labour. From that point, her procedure was classically realist. In effect she treated Miller and O'Leary's conclusions as hypotheses and took them back to the data. If there was something which might be described as economic citizenship at Decatur, it should have been experienced as such by the workforce. The strike was *prima facie* evidence that there was not. The experiences of trade unionists, as she put it, were asking questions of a theory which portrayed their conditions in terms of a new economic citizenship. She proposed to add to these questions by interviewing members of the United Auto Workers Union Local 751 – the Decatur plant.

Miller and O'Leary, themselves, appear to have interviewed very few workers in the course of their research, and most of those appear to have been shift supervisors. The only quotation from a non-supervisory worker which appears in their paper was obtained not from their interviews but from a local newspaper. Management sources, in contrast, are quoted extensively, sometimes from interviews, but more usually from in-house publications and what appear to be press releases. Miller and O'Leary's account of events at Decatur, in consequence, is actually an account of management accounts. Theirs is an attribution of citizenship which pays no attention to the views of the citizens themselves.

Arnold's interviews revealed a number of discrepancies between the stories of the re-organisation offered by management and the workers' experience of it. For them, the organising theme of the various management initiatives was the loss of jobs. Flexibility meant increased workloads – rather than autonomy – and job losses. Training to do other people's work was challenging and interesting, but it threatened these others' livelihoods. The workers originally co-operated in combating foreign competition by finding more cost-effective ways of doing things and beating production targets. Experience soon showed, however, that this would be followed by the transfer of work to other plants – and job losses. As for cell proprietorship, yes, it gave more control over the actual tasks, but it cost jobs. Such interpretations are scarcely surprising in view of the precipitous decline in employment at Decatur – from 4,600 in 1979 to 1,800 in 1995. The training, the flexibilities, the increased autonomy and responsibility which read as citizenship to Miller and O'Leary added up to increased workloads and insecurity as far as the workers were concerned. Considered as social theory, the management rhetoric which accompanied the changes at Decatur simply failed to account for the data. Expressing the consequent cynicism, the workers began to subvert the managerial acronyms which had accompanied the Plant With A Future programme. When a security perimeter had to be erected around the plant to keep out labour protesters, for example, PWAF began to mean 'Plant With A Fence'.

Arnold also observes that Miller and O'Leary's study took place during an uncharacteristic period of industrial peace, precisely the period during which Caterpillar's management needed the co-operation of the workforce in setting up the new arrangements. Whilst Miller and O'Leary cannot of course be criticised for the timing of their research, subsequent events cast doubt on their benign interpretation of what was going on during this period.

In 1991, the company approached the contract negotiations demanding a reduction of job protection rights. A failure to agree led to a protracted strike which was finally broken by threats to permanently replace the strikers. Following this defeat for the workforce, flexible work schedules were imposed which abrogated the eight-hour day hitherto regarded as a custom-and-practice right. A later strike over unfair labour practices also collapsed whereupon the company imposed a two-tier wage structure with lower pay for new hires, an expansion of part-time and temporary working, greater management control over the content and timing of work, and a further weakening of job protection clauses. Some of the strikers were dismissed whilst others were placed under an order restricting their rights to discuss the strike and to participate in trade union activity. Faced with the fact of this managerial roll-back of the frontier of control, Miller and O'Leary could – and did – argue that they had themselves pointed out the fragile and temporary nature of alignments between ideas and practice. This is quite true, but it is an argument which rather gives away the game. If citizenship rights are as easily retracted as these later events demonstrated, they are not rights at all. Whatever was driving the new hard line in industrial relations – and the critique of Froud *et al.* (1998) is illuminating in this respect – it was certainly not respect for the rights of citizenship.

The critique by Froud *et al.*

Froud *et al.* (1998) also point out that Miller and O'Leary's paper relies almost entirely on management sources. In fact its empirical part largely consists of a translation of management documents into a highly specialised language which has evolved in the dense forests of post-Foucauldian scholarship. Above all, it is a language of 'immunisation'. Accounts written in it are immunised, first from identification with any particular value position, and second from the possibility of contradiction. The first is achieved by presenting socially consequential concepts – such as new economic citizenship – in quotation marks so as to signify that the authors are not to be construed as endorsing them. At the same time they are presented without comment, so as to head off an inference of dissent. Immunisation from consequences is achieved through the employment of a language of mobility and indeterminacy to connect the terms of description. The result has much in common with the prophecies of Nostradamus, in that the meaning of the terms is open, anything is possible and nothing is not foretold.

A second element of Froud *et al.*'s critique concerns the partiality of Miller and O'Leary's treatment of the relevant literatures. The social consequences of advanced manufacturing are what concern us here. Miller and O'Leary represent this as an authoritative consensus on the benign concordances between the requirements of competitiveness, the practices of advanced manufacturing and the new economic citizenship. This is consequential for the structure of their argument. By establishing these connections in advance of the empirics, an impression is created that the authors' interpretation of the Decatur evidence possesses an authority beyond that of the evidence and the interpretation themselves. It appears to be a further illustration of connections which have already been well established by people who know. Against this, Froud *et al.* point out that the representation of a prior consensus is spurious, quite apart from the uses to which it is put. Recent work in the field suggests that advanced manufacturing technology is leading to a new duality of labour markets in which anything which might pass for a new economic citizenship will be restricted to a 'fortunate fifth' of 'symbolic analysts' with the rest abandoned to direct competition with the world's low-wage economies. The relevance to those Caterpillar workers who found re-employment in the companies to which their work had been outsourced is obvious. And so is the relevance to Miller and O'Leary's story.

The third part of Froud *et al.*'s paper uses an analysis of financial and accounting data to situate the actions taken and the stories told by Caterpillar's management against the company's competitive and market situation. In the terms of Bhaskar's realism (1986), the mechanics of product market competition are taken to be a reality which is manifested in the realm of the empirical in the form of management talk and action.

There are two main findings. First that the threat of competition from Komatsu during the early 1980s had more to do with a favourable Dollar–Yen exchange rate than any advantage in productivity, and that the threat had largely evaporated by the late 1980s. Second, the huge investment in automated machinery with which Caterpillar responded to this partly temporary and partly imaginary threat saddled the company with the problem of recovering its costs in a largely static product market. This could only be done by attacking labour costs, and it was this which lay behind the intransigent attitude with which management approached the 1991 and later contract negotiations. In the face of this, Miller and O'Leary could – and did – point out that the indeterminacy of the concept of new economic citizenship allows for just such possibilities of interpretation. This was certainly true of the manner in which they used the term themselves, since they had refrained from defining it. Accepting for the moment that it is variations in interpretation which are at issue, the advantage still lies with the realist approach of Froud *et al.*, since it can explain *why* and *when* hard-line interpretations are likely to be favoured.

Miller and O'Leary's reply

As is the happy norm in academic life, Miller and O'Leary's response (1998) combined a defence of their paper with a somewhat petulant counter-attack on their critics. Far from giving the lie to their account of the Caterpillar re-organisation, the industrial strife which followed it had been allowed for, anticipated even, in their emphasis on the fragility and mutability of the linkages between discourse and practice. The new economic citizenship could just as well 'mean' a hard line in industrial relations as a willingness to bargain for co-operation.

The view of both sets of critics that management talk and action could not be adequately understood apart from the logic of capitalism had about it 'the whiff of the gulag'. The re-organisation of Caterpillar must be understood as a *programme*, and as such its design and re-design are not reducible to the conditions to which they are a response. That was why Miller and O'Leary listened to management, something which their critics had notably failed to do. Arnold had only interviewed union representatives whilst Froud *et al.* had based their analysis entirely on published financial data. Despite this inadequate empirical basis, both were willing to pass judgement on the actions of Caterpillar's management. They believed themselves in a position to do so because, gripped by dogma, they knew the answers in advance. Miller and O'Leary themselves, in contrast, had approached their subject with an open mind. They were interested in finding things out.

Remarkably, for authors heavily influenced by the work of Michel Foucault, this last remark is actually a fair approximation to the positivist credo. As such it cries out for elaboration. It is also, as we shall see, very much at variance with Miller and O'Leary's actual practice. The rest of their response, meanwhile, fails to recognise that the critics were as much concerned to correct imbalances in Miller and O'Leary's work as to offer substitute analyses of their own. The objection was not to Miller and O'Leary's attention to management, but that they *only* attended to management. Similarly, the argument was not that the dynamics of capitalist competition could account for the fine detail of management programmes, but that such programmes can only be adequately understood as responses to these dynamics. Nor was there an objection to Miller and O'Leary's stress on the fluid nature of the links between the discourse and practice. The objection was that instead of exploring the nature and limits of this fluidity, it was functioning at the rhetorical level as a *post hoc* reconciliation of new economic citizenship with whatever took place at Decatur. Links of this character are indeterminate to the point that they tell us nothing about the limits of what can be done in the name of new economic citizenship.

A cell of one's own

This simultaneous stress on the importance of the links between discourse and action as a path to understanding, and on the indeterminacy of these links, raises acute problems with the manner in which Miller and O'Leary read their data. What *are* these 'linkages', 'alignments' and 'congruencies' which figure so prominently in their vocabulary? Are they such that discourse can be demonstrated to influence action or vice versa? And if they are not, how can we know of their existence?

As a preliminary approach to this question, let us examine the author's treatment of the notion of cell proprietorship. Though not co-extensive with the new economic citizenship, it is a key component. Unlike the broader concept, moreover, it was a form of words actually used by Caterpillar management, so we are not troubled with the prior question of why it figures in the analysis at all. What did cell proprietorship mean to Caterpillar's management, and how was it operationalised?

> Individual manufacturing cells or modules were to be understood as 'small businesses', spaces for collective entrepreneurship by the groups of workers within them, the 'cell proprietors'. Each cell would manufacture a sub-product

> from start to finish, with work sequenced in a continuous programmed flow within the cell, and set to performance standards measured against Caterpillar's most demanding foreign competitors.

Here was a small business with flexible working, production schedules and standards all imposed from outside. As we have seen the entrepreneurs were assisted by red and green lights installed in each cell, a green light signifying that the process was on schedule to beat the benchmark time derived from competitor cost analysis, and a red that it was behind. In addition, a computer terminal in each cell called the 'cell proprietor interface' carried details of the specific customer order on which the cell was working, together with the target completion times computed by the MRP software. The declared intention of Caterpillar management was to make competition with Komatsu and the satisfaction of each named customer the business of every individual worker.

Here the connection between management talk and action can be understood as a relatively straightforward operationalisation. Whether these messages were received as intended is another manner. Miller and O'Leary offer no information on reactions to the traffic lights, whilst their single quotation on the matter of customer identification indicates a certain scepticism (factory superintendent – 'a *supposedly* sold unit at the time it was coming down the highway'; emphasis added). What is not clear is how we are to understand the linkage between management's use of the term 'cell proprietorship' and these arrangements. In ordinary language, proprietorship means something like:

> Proprietor: One who holds something as property; one who has the exclusive right or title to the use or disposal of a thing; an owner.
>
> (*Shorter OED*, 1960)

But in the cells of Decatur, there was no ownership of real property, and no exclusive right or title. It was the responsibility for confronting competition and for satisfying customers which was 'owned'. This meaning coincides with what Friedman (1977) called 'responsible autonomy'. But responsible autonomy is a *control strategy*, not a softening of the property rights of the capitalist corporation. The rights are those of flexible working; at a higher level the freedom to find new ways of achieving the objectives of the company, and at a lower level to find new ways of achieving the targets derived from them.

This chewing at the concept of proprietorship so that it becomes amorphous enough to wrap around that of responsible autonomy is, of course, neither new nor innocent. The 'responsible' part of Freidman's couplet implies an internalisation of commitment which cannot be assumed as given. It is something for which management needs to work at the level of ideas – hence Edwards's (1979) alternative term of 'hegemonic control'. Part of that work, into which the localised discourses of Decatur were able to tap, has been a decades-long reworking of the terminology of ownership to cover a devolution of responsibilities which carries with it only a single right – the right to receive blame when things go wrong. This, to be sure, is a 'linkage' between discourse and a concrete situation, but it is a linkage which implies no constraint on the situation. It is misdescription pure and simple, ideology, spin. Insofar as this is the case, and Miller and O'Leary offer no evidence that it is not, the talk of cell proprietorship at Decatur tells us nothing at all about the working arrangements to which it was applied.

A short walk through the quotation marks

Miller and O'Leary do not seem to understand their critics' concerns about their promiscuous use of quotation marks. They use them, they say, 'because we wish to tell the reader what others have said'. The problem is that they rarely tell us *which* others.

A case in point is their persistent enclosure of new economic citizenship within quotation marks. They do not seem to indicate direct speech. As far as can be told from the contexts, the form of words was not in use at Caterpillar. But if this is the case, what do the marks mean? We are left to decide for ourselves. A problem here is that the insertion of quotation marks into indicative sentences, like dripping water onto gremlins, can produce a variety of effects, some of them disconcerting. Consider the following:

> Peter Miller is a professor at the London School of Economics
>
> Peter Miller is a 'professor' at the London School of Economics

This is slightly improper. Two little flicks of the pen and the slight inflection of the reading voice which goes with them, and a distinguished academic finds himself in the company of Punch and Judy men, the old-time brothel pianists of New Orleans and other low-life pretenders. Despite this, the example might still point a way forward. Perhaps the quotation marks signify irony or an implication of falsehood. Perhaps their implication is that something is being passed off as citizenship which would not be described as such if words were used in their normal sense. By now it will be evident that the writer thinks that this is the case, but do Miller and O'Leary? The indications are that they do not. There are no contexts in the paper which contrast conditions in Caterpillar or anywhere else with the meanings which Miller and O'Leary attach to new economic citizenship. Unless we are meant to infer that information on competitor costs and the devolution of responsibilities for production add up to citizenship, in fact, Miller and O'Leary offer little elaboration of what it might mean anywhere in their paper. The mask of irony, if irony it is, is sustained throughout. The second problem with the 'misrepresentation' hypothesis is that no-one is identified as doing it. We are told that beliefs in, or ideals of, new economic citizenship are held, but we are never told by whom. For example:

> A third level of analysis concerns the linkages between the spatial reordering of production processes at Caterpillar's Decatur plant and the claim that the design of advanced manufacturing facilities offers a key opportunity to give shape and form to a 'new economic citizenship' (Dertouzos *et al.*, 1989: 134). This image of a 'new economic citizenship' has been held to consist in a potential empowerment (Johnson, 1992) of shopfloor workers, supervisors and middle managers.

Slippery stuff! Anonymously held images of economic citizenship are held, also anonymously, to consist not of actual but of potential empowerment. There is a problem in tracing responsibilities here, but not irony, so far as can be told, and not an implication of misrepresentation.

A second possibility is that the quotation marks signify that unfamiliar meanings are attached to the words. Normal procedure if this were the case, would be for the phrase to be introduced in quotation marks along with a definition of the particular sense in which it is to be used. The quotation marks would then be dropped in subsequent usages. Arguing against this reading, though not conclusively so, is the fact that Miller and O'Leary persist with the quotations marks *without* clarifying what they mean.

A third possibility is that the use of the quotation marks signifies meanings which *other people* attach to new economic citizenship, with the authors themselves abstaining on the questions of their validity or legitimacy. This reading potentially overlaps the second, since these others may also be using the phrase in an unfamiliar sense. Such a reading, in all its ambiguity, *is* supported by the contexts, the foregoing quotation for one. On the few occasions when new economic citizenship occurs in their paper without quotation marks, moreover, Miller and O'Leary refer to it not directly, but as a claim made by anonymous others, or as an ideal to which they appeal.

Discovering the new economic citizenship

This partial clarification, unfortunately, only confronts us with new problems. For if the meanings attached to new economic citizenship are those of other commentators (probably the MIT Commission and the cited writers of the 'flexible specialisation' school) it is Miller and O'Leary themselves, not these commentators, and not, assuredly, people at Caterpillar, who attach these meanings to intentions, events and objects at Caterpillar. And this occurs precisely at the crux of their paper. Their promise to establish connections between the spatial layout of production and the new economic citizenship is its hook, its McGuffin, its unique selling point. Consider, then, their claims for the introduction of cell manufacturing at Caterpillar, and the physical connection of these cells via an 'Assembly Highway'.

> Practices of synchronous flow manufacture had been deployed. The production process was declared to have been consolidated, simplified,

> modernised, rendered flexible and extensively automated. In making operable these general principles for the design of manufacturing processes, the Assembly Highway gave form to hopes of a new competitiveness and a new mode of economic citizenship in American industry.

Whilst 'hopes of', as a form of words, succeeds in contracting out the conceptualisation of economic citizenship, it is Miller and O'Leary themselves who declare that the Assembly Highway embodied these hopes. But on what basis can they make such a claim and on whose behalf are they making it? Physically speaking, the Assembly Highway was nothing more than a linear space with the manufacture and assembly cells branching off it. Miller and O'Leary's persistent use of the passive voice gives no clue as to who is supposed to have attached to it the significance which they claim; nor do they provide us with evidence that anyone does so. They simply state that it is so. It cannot be the 'commentators' since they are commenting on American industry in general, not Caterpillar in particular. Nor is it anyone at Caterpillar, since the concept was not in use there. We are left with the authors themselves, and, this, we suddenly realise, is why we are presented with no evidence. None is needed, since what better authority could there be on the mental states of the authors than the authors themselves?

In the terms of Habermassian linguistic pragmatics, we are in the presence of truth claims of the third kind, not the first: claims, that is, of sincerity rather than factual accuracy. Assertions of this nature run through the whole of Miller and O'Leary's attempt to link the 'spatial re-ordering of manufacture' and the ideals of new economic citizenship:

> In transforming the relationships between the different stages of the production process, and in envisioning the process as a whole in system terms, the Assembly Highway gave form to the ideals and aspirations contained in a particular notion of the 'customer'. In so doing, the Assembly Highway made possible a temporary and fragile stabilisation of that 'new economic citizenship' appealed to by so many commentators.

Again it is new economic citizenship as imagined by 'commentators' which is at issue. But again it is Miller and O'Leary themselves who declare that the Assembly Highway embodied (for themselves) a particular notion of the customer and thence the commentators' meanings of new economic citizenship. The same trope of unadorned assertion occurs in their interpretation of the manufacturing cells. In these, they tell us:

> all manufacturing work was to be arranged in product and sub-product dedicated 'cells' or modules. The individual's contribution to an overall process or product might be made self-evident in the spatial arrangement and sequencing of manufacturing activities. The ideal of a 'new economic citizenship' could thus be embodied in a distinct spatial arrangement of the factory floor.

Within the critical accounting literature, as elsewhere, spatial arrangements which expose the performances of individuals in this manner are more usually apprehended through the metaphor of the Panopticon rather than one of citizenship. But Miller and O'Leary are in the grip of an idea, and what they are doing is sincerely reporting that fact.

On this point we can see that Miller and O'Leary's reading of their case is quintessentially idealist. Objects and events enter the reading, that is, not as the subject of contingent statements, but as the raw material for feelings of symbolic harmony. Though they feed upon empirical data, such interpretations make no publicly verifiable statements about it. Rather they absorb it, in the manner of a black hole, emitting only a vague radiation. What would it take, for example, for the Assembly Highway *not* to embody the idea of economic citizenship, or for it *not* to embody an ideal of the customer? What, then, does it mean to say that it does? Interestingly, this idealism does not run consistently through the whole of Miller and O'Leary's paper. Their assertion of linkages between competitiveness and the communication of information on competitor costs, like all theorisations, is a mental construct and its application to the empirical data involves interpretations. The crucial difference is that these interpretations allow for the possibility of inconsistency with the mental construct. The traffic lights which measured Caterpillar performance against the Komatsu benchmark were not, by definition, installed with the specific intention of personalising competition. It was the contingent fact that management also spoke of doing so which (more or less) justified that interpretation. This methodological inconsistency raises the interesting possibility that Miller and O'Leary's paper works at the level of rhetoric by a kind of osmosis of credibility. Its relatively mundane excursions into realism may serve to establish a mood of assent which spills over into their more spectacular but less substantial claims.

Enactment and operationalism

Miller and O'Leary are also concerned to trace linkages between the new economic citizenship and other aspects of work at Decatur. Everything which has been said about the significance claimed for the spatial re-organisation of manufacture applies equally here. The claim of linkage is made entirely by assertion and concerns a relationship which exists in the minds of the authors. The difference this time is that the alleged connection is not one of symbolic significance, but that conditions at Decatur constituted an *enactment* of new economic citizenship. This adds a new significance to what they have to say because this involves the attribution of a particular meaning to new economic citizenship. The tactic this time is to leave open the definition of new economic citizenship so that it can be applied by fiat to whatever conditions they observed.

In everyday language, the enactment of a principle or plan refers to a flow of influence running, in the first instance, from ideas to action. There is a mental map which is operationalised in the realm of the real. In practice, to be sure, implementation, like politics, is (sometimes) the art of the possible. There may be a blowback, as it were, in the reverse direction, so that principles and plans are modified in the course of implementation. Enactment, nevertheless, implies that what is done is guided or constrained by that which is to be enacted. Miller and O'Leary's talk of linkages between discourse and practice, indeed, raises expectations that precisely this will be discussed.

In the case of the competitiveness/new manufacturing couplet and the re-organisation at Caterpillar this is exactly what we get. General discussions and previous models of cell manufacture, flexibility and consciousness of the customer and competition are all shown to be articulated by Caterpillar's management and implemented in their re-organisation. But this treatment is not paralleled in the case of the new economic citizenship. Here Miller and O'Leary seem to mean something rather different by enactment. Explaining their reticence on the question of what new economic citizenship might mean, perhaps, they write as if the concept is somehow empty until it is given empirical content:

> It is the novel arrangements of persons and things on the factory floor, the new ways of making calculations of the spaces thus formed, and the distinctive conceptions of the capacities and attributes of individuals who are to occupy such spaces, that gives content to the notion of 'new economic citizenship'.

New economic citizenship here begins to take on the look of a Baudrillardian free-floating signifier. There is no sense of limits to the concrete arrangements to which it can be attached. The 'linkage' between words and action is simply that the former are attached to the latter. Again:

> Experts of varying kinds translate concerns with competitiveness, productivity, flexibility, and cost structures into working arrangements on the factory floor. In the process, they help to constitute and make operable modes of economic citizenship.

Notice that the concerns which are translated in this passage are all about economic performance and the control of labour, not about citizenship. No-one would dispute that Caterpillar's re-organisation was driven by plans and principles which were intended to restore the company's profitability. The point at issue was whether they were also influenced by concerns about citizenship. As has been noted, new economic citizenship as an actual form of words does not seem to have been in use at Caterpillar, but it is still possible that the re-organisation was influenced by concepts which added up to something similar. What were these concepts, we need to know, and is there evidence that they were anything more than an empty rhetoric designed to make the re-organisation more palatable to the workforce, the public and to academic researchers?

Despite Miller and O'Leary's repeated reference to *ideals* of new economic citizenship, the notion that principles gain content only in their practical application is actually the stance of operationalism. Operationalism as a creed is attractive to self-styled practical persons; people, that is, whose practicality consists in running things as they are. This is because it ensures that ideas only count when they are incorporated into concrete social arrangements. The fact that these arrangements are controlled by the aforesaid practical persons means that potentially awkward ideas (such as new economic citizenship) can only influence practice at the price of reduction to a form which can be accommodated within existing systems and priorities (Marcuse, 1991). A perfect example is the operationalisation of economic citizenship (if that is what it is) through the techniques and economic concerns of the managerial specialists at Caterpillar, as described above.

In assimilating the concept of new economic citizenship to the practicalities of the new manufacturing, Miller and O'Leary are following well-established precedents. A case in point is the research of the MIT Commission, their first cited source for the concept. Theoretically modest but practically ambitious, that part of the Commission's objectives which concerns us here was simply to identify 'average' employment practice in America's most competitive manufacturing companies. New economic citizenship were the words chosen as a portmanteau term for these practices. The element of arbitrariness was emphasised in a later publication (Dertouzos, 1997: 212–13) by pointing out international variations in the terms used to describe essentially the same conditions. 'Human Capital' is the accepted term in Sweden, 'Toyotism' in France and 'Human Ware' in Japan (where perhaps they know a little bit more about Toyota than the French). In other words, the Commission attached new economic citizenship as a form of words to conditions which they believed led to competitiveness. It did *not* start from a notion of what constituted citizenship and enquire into the extent to which it existed in successful companies. The result, nevertheless, was an authoritative use of language which identified the new economic citizenship with conditions which actually existed in leading US companies, a kind of backdoor operationalism which deprived the concept of most of its critical edge. Despite its show of theoretical sophistication, Miller and O'Leary's procedure is effectively the same. Having left the definition of new economic citizenship offstage throughout their paper, they are able to use the resulting conceptual space to assert, without arguing the matter point by point, that what they observed in Caterpillar amounted to an enactment of it.

In one respect, indeed, Miller and O'Leary's procedure could be said to be *less* critical than the Commission's, since the very process of averaging ensures that conditions in some companies will fall short of new economic citizenship. The encouragement of reform in such companies, indeed, was the whole point of the Commission's study. Miller and O'Leary's single company study affords no such leverage. What would conditions have had to be like at Caterpillar, one wonders, for Miller and O'Leary to have found them *in*compatible with new economic citizenship? Recall that the story told to Arnold by the workers was one of continuing job losses, increased workloads, deteriorating conditions of employment and the loss of trade union rights. Miller and O'Leary themselves tell us that the PWAF programme was accompanied by 'an aggressive outsourcing programme' in which low-technology labour intensive processes were subcontracted out to 'focused, lower cost suppliers'. How much of this counts as an enactment of new economic citizenship? In order to confront such questions, there would have to be a definition of new economic citizenship, either that of the 'commentators' to which Miller and O'Leary refer, or one of their own. But since they do not offer one, and since they also believe its empirical content to be defined, at least in part, by its enactment at Caterpillar, they would seem to have set an examination which cannot be failed. Let us respond by setting one for their sources.

Citizenship, democracy and newspeak

Miller and O'Leary's primary source for the concept of new economic citizenship is the 1989 report of the MIT Commission on Industrial Productivity. Although Miller and O'Leary persistently refer to the concept as an 'ideal', the commission actually used it as a portmanteau term for employment practices which already existed in the nation's top manufacturing firms. Its elements were a well-educated workforce properly appreciated and rewarded, continuous training, the devolution of responsibility, team working, networking and self-government. Laudable as these may be by the standards of typical UK practice, they are still a long way short of any ordinary language understanding of citizenship.

Sensing an uncertainty of footing perhaps, Miller and O'Leary seek additional provenance for the concept in the literature on flexible specialisation. Inevitably brief, their review is also highly unrepresentative, relying as it does on highly contestable secondary interpretations of the source researches (mainly Sabel, 1991 and Hirst and Zeitlin, 1991). Many of these source researches provide no warrant whatsoever for describing employment conditions in the 'Third Italy' and other industrial districts in terms of economic citizenship. The networks of flexible specialists always depended in part on the exploitation of unofficial labour (Inzerilli, 1990; Blim, 1990: 237), and they often became the exploited subcontractors of larger companies (Blim, 1990: 124). Even when this did not happen, the original pseudo-egalitarian networks of mutual contracting tended, through the mechanics of competition, to degenerate into centrally administered systems of subcontracting, on the model of Benetton (Harrison, 1994). The industries in which the prototypes of flexible specialisation occurred, moreover, served fashion markets such as furniture, footwear, ceramics and clothing, markets in which rapid responses to rapidly changing tastes were more important than the containment of production costs (Amin, 1989). The assumption that product market strategies and employment conditions in such industries, even supposing they could be characterised as flexible specialisation and economic citizenship respectively, have any relevance to cost competition in the market for earth-moving equipment needs justification which Miller and O'Leary do not provide.

It is through the conceptual lens of new economic citizenship, nevertheless, that Miller and O'Leary describe conditions at Caterpillar. The fact that it was not a concept used in the company involves the ethnomethodological sin of description in terms of observer categories. Thoroughgoing ethnomethodologists object to this on the grounds that the resulting descriptions are interpretations, therefore subjective, therefore not reproducible and – again therefore – unscientific. For many of them, it is a logic which drives a retreat into the minutiae of conversational routines. For the rest of us, learning to apply observer categories to external objects and events in a manner acceptable to our speech communities is part of the normal process of language acquisition (Hesse, 1974). Subjectivity, or at least that part of it which is knowable through the manifestations of language, is acquired precisely on terms which allow us to communicate through observer categories. But, and it is an important but, categories may be used persuasively as well as informatively.

In the ordinary language of citizens, the notion of citizenship, economic or otherwise, is not empty of content and is remarkably resilient. It is also full of democracy. Namely:

> Citizen: A member of a state, an enfranchised inhabitant of a country, as opp. to an alien; in U.S. a person, native or naturalized, who has the privilege of voting for public offices, and is entitled to protection in the exercise of private rights.
>
> (*Shorter OED*, 1960)

Once the connection is restored between citizenship and democracy, we can begin to situate contemporary discussions of economic citizenship against the long tradition of social democratic debate on what forms industrial democracy might take in capitalist economies (e.g. Cole, 1917). In the post-war UK and Western Europe these debates have revolved around questions of worker representation on company boards and joint consultative committees, and around the extent to which collective bargaining through elected union representatives can itself function as a form of industrial democracy (Clegg, 1960). Whatever position one takes on these issues, it is clear that the conception of citizenship which can be extracted from the MIT Commission's report falls far short of any of them. So does that which Miller and O'Leary believe to have been implemented in Caterpillar. From this perspective, the work of both can be seen as a continuing project of reworking the language so that *economic* citizenship will come to signify a lesser good even than the mild ameliorations of economic power conveyed by the term citizenship itself. The end point of this operationalisation of the language of critique, like that of Orwellian Newspeak, is a closure of critical thought in which what is possible is contained within what is.

Conclusions: some language games of ideology

So how is the trick accomplished? Froud *et al.* (1998) note the skill with which Miller and O'Leary translate management information into the idiom of post-

Foucauldian scholarship, but only as an explanation of how they are able to inflate it into a paper of almost 13,000 words. In fact their stylistic idiosyncrasies are more consequential than this. Essentially they are ways of writing the data so that their conclusions can be argued without constraint. By these means, the credibility of empirical research ('finding things out') can be attached to what is really imaginative writing. Generally speaking the language forms through which this is achieved work by erasing distinctions which we would normally make in reading everyday situations. In this respect they involve a degradation of commonsense understandings, not a sharpening of them. Some examples are:

Persistent use of the passive

The passive voice is normally used in circumstances where what is done is more important than who does it. Research in the natural sciences is a frequently quoted example. As applied to evaluations of, or reactions to, social situations, however, the passive voice erases some of the most basic data of social science: that of *who* is reacting and making the interpretations. In the case of the changes at Caterpillar, for example, a positive evaluation from a management consultant would mean something very different to a positive evaluation from a worker.

In the uncertainty created by their persistent use of the passive, there is also no way of distinguishing the authors' own interpretations from those which are in the data. In effect, Giddens's double hermeneutic collapses into a confusion in which all we know is that interpretation is taking place. At crucial points in their argument, this confusion allows the authors to read their own interpretations as if they were part of the data, probably without realising they are doing so. It is in this manner that they connect the new economic citizenship, the changes at Caterpillar and the spatial re-ordering of manufacture.

Absent definitions

The number of key concepts and possible modes of connection which are left undefined in Miller and O'Leary's prose is extraordinary, as is their wholesale use of inverted commas to signify that normal meanings are suspended, and suspended without the substitution of others. At the logical limit, of course, this absence of definition allows statements of connection to be made on a whim. If both new economic citizenship and alignment are undefined, for example, I can say that it is aligned with a banana. Later, like invisible ink, the residual meanings re-appear so that something turns out to have been said both about citizenship and bananas.

Hypothetical beings

The prose of 'governmentality' has much to say of hypothetical beings – personifications of the attributes assumed by managers in the design of their control systems. In Miller and O'Leary's case, this stylistic heritage leads to forms of words which make no distinction between these and real people. Since part of the aim of reform programmes is to make people think and behave like imaginary prototypes, the result of this lack of distinction is a tendency to confuse the intentions of these programmes with outcomes. When we are told that 'a new type of economic citizen is called upon to act', for instance, it is not clear whether or not it is being said that these citizens actually exist. If it is, that is an outcome and we are being told something about the way people have been changed. If it is not, that is an intention and we are being told something about the programme. It is a confusion which allows Miller and O'Leary to write about intentions and be read as if they were writing about socially momentous changes.

Postscript

Whilst preparing this chapter, I received an e-mail from Professor Tony Tinker of City University New York. Part of it reads as an appropriate epitaph for the careers of those who co-operated with the 'Plant With A Future' programme.

> Did you know that when Caterpillar finally abandoned Decatur, they insisted on leaving a rusting monument by the highway as a reminder to the unions and the local community not to mess with corporations? I've asked a friend to try to get a photo of it next time he drives through.

References

Amin, Ash (1989) 'A model of the small firm in Italy', in E. Goodman and J. Bamford (eds), *Small Firms and Industrial Districts in Italy*, London: Routledge, pp. 111–20.

Arnold, P.J. (1998) 'The limits of postmodernism in accounting history: the Decatur experience', *Accounting Organizations and Society*, 23 (7): 665–84.

Bhaskar, R. (1986) *Scientific Realism and Human Emancipation*, London: Verso.

Blim, Michael L. (1990) *Made in Italy: Small-scale Industrialization and its Consequences*, New York: Praeger.

Clegg, H.A. (1960) *A New Approach to Industrial Democracy*, London: Blackwell.

Cole, G.D.H. (1917 [1972]) *Self-Government in Industry*, London: Hutchinson.

Dertouzos, M.L., Lester, R.K. and Solow, R.M. (1989) *Made in America: Regaining the Productive Edge*, Cambridge MA: MIT Press.

Dertouzos, Michael L. (1997) *What Will Be: How the New World of Information Will Change Our Lives*, London: Piatkus.

Edwards, R.C. (1979) *Contested Terrain: the Transformation of the Workplace in the Twentieth Century*, London: Basic Books.

Friedman, A (1977) *Industry and Labour: Class Struggle at Work and Monopoly Capitalism*, London: Macmillan

Froud, J., WIlliams, K., Haslam, C., Johal, S. and Williams, J. (1998) 'Caterpillar: two stories and an argument', *Accounting Organizations and Society*, 23 (7): 685–708.

Harrison, Bennett (1994) 'The Italian industrial districts and the crisis of the cooperative form: part II', *European Planning Studies*, 2 (2): 159–73.

Hesse, M. (1974) *The Structure of Scientific Inference*, London: Macmillan.

Hirst, R.P. and Zeitlin, J. (1991) 'Flexible specialisation versus post-Fordism: theory, evidence and policy implications', *Economy and Society*, 20 (1): 1–56.

Inzerilli, Giorgio (1990) 'The Italian alternative: flexible organization and social management', *International Studies of Management and Organization*, 20 (4): 6–21.

Johnson, H.T. (1992) *Relevance Regained: From Top-down Control to Bottom-up Empowerment*, New York: Free Press.

Marcuse, Herbert (1991) *One-Dimensional Man: Studies in the Ideology of Advanced Industrial Society*, 2nd edn, London: Routledge.

Miller, P. and O'Leary, T. (1994) 'Accounting, "economic citizenship" and the spatial reordering of manufacture', *Accounting Organizations and Society*, 19 (1): 15–43.

—— (1998) 'Finding things out', *Accounting Organizations and Society*, 23 (7): 709–14.

Sabel, C. (1991) 'Moebius-strip organizations and open labor markets', in P. Bourdieu and J.S. Coleman (eds), *Social Theory for a Changing Society*, Boulder, CO: Westview.

4 The ontology of work

Social relations and doing in the sphere of necessity[1]

Jan Ch. Karlsson

Introduction

When, about thirty years ago, Richard K. Brown gave a speech to the British Sociological Association on research about working life, he said:

> It never was satisfactory that 'work' should customarily be interpreted as referring solely to gainful employment in the official, formal economy. In the light of the sociological research and writing of the past decade or more such a restriction is completely untenable. In addition it deprives us of a major source of understanding and of explanation. [...] At the present time it is crucially important to maintain research and debate on the widest possible front.
>
> (Brown, 1984: 3–4)

What follows is intended as a contribution to this debate – a debate that I do not think has moved much further forward since this statement was made. I will try to clarify some theoretical problems in the social science theory of work, and suggest solutions to these problems and ideas for further development of fruitful research on work.[2] My argument is basically inspired by two insights from critical realist underlabouring: one is the importance of ontology and ontological reasoning to avoid the epistemic fallacy, the other that social phenomena are relational and that should be reflected in the formulations of concepts and theories.

Whilst I use ontology to evaluate and elaborate the nature of work, not any ontology will suffice. The ontological position adopted here is that sponsored by critical realist philosophy, the basic propositions of which have been dealt with elsewhere (Fleetwood and Ackroyd, and Sayer in this collection) and I will not rehearse them here, but a few words are necessary at the outset on some ontological positions that lead to conclusions I wish to reject.

Work can be considered as a set of activities, or as a set of relations. But some ontologies conceive of activities and relations as nothing more than discourses or social constructs. From this perspective, activities and relations are not extra-discursive phenomena, they are not phenomena that exist independently of our identification of them – they are not objectively real. Activities and relations are entirely discursive phenomena, are dependent upon our identification of them – they are only subjectively real:

> [W]ork cannot have an objective and transcendent meaning. Rather, language and discourse of work are symbolic representations, through which meanings and social interests are constructed, mediated and deployed. In short, the meanings of work do not inhere within the practices of participants but are created, challenged, altered and sustained through contending discourse ... .
>
> (Grint, 1998: 8)

It is not surprising that this ontology leads Grint (1998: 6) to use the whole first chapter of his textbook on the sociology of work to argue the rather pessimistic thesis that 'no unambiguous or objective definition of work is possible'. When (below) I define work as 'activities performed within internal social relations in the sphere of necessity', I do not use the terms 'activities', 'relations' and 'necessity' as mere discourses or social constructs. These terms are used objectively; they have extra-linguistic referents – and that makes debates on conceptual questions possible and meaningful.

I will argue that the debate on the concept of work has come to an impasse in a contradiction between properties of activities versus certain social relations. A second contradiction has been analysed by Karel Kosík (1976) and concerns an empirical versus an ontological conceptual basis – he argues for the latter. My suggestion is an attempt to transcend these contradictions by starting with an ontological concept that makes it possible to specify certain social relations and activities within these as work. But first a brief overview of the general development of definitions of work in social science.

Concepts of work

Human work is as old as humans are – but work as a concept is young. There are still reasons for saying that 'work is well known experientially, yet little understood conceptually' (Cummings and Srivastva, 1977: 5). Paradoxically – or perhaps in consequence thereof – there exist a large number of work concepts; different academic disciplines have diverging perspectives and in many disciplines, perhaps especially in sociology, there is no consensus nowadays in understanding what 'work' is.

In pre-capitalist societies there was no abstract work concept, but with emerging capitalism a – still ongoing – debate was initiated. 'From the Enlightenment to the industrial revolution,' one researcher (Eyerman, 1985: 27) comments, 'Europe was a battleground for competing conceptions of work.' The founder of Physiocracy, François Quesnay (1972 [1759]), still regarded work only as definite activities: the farmer's work, the merchant's work, the entrepreneur's work, etc. But in the continuing development of political economy and its analyses of capitalism's relationships, a real work concept appears – a concept abstracted from the multifarious activities. The first great expression of this is usually said to be Adam Smith's *An Inquiry into the Nature and Causes of the Wealth of Nations* (1976 [1776]) Less than a hundred years later, however, the debate had already become so disparate that the German economist Wilhelm Heinrich Riehl (1862: 5) found himself called upon to complain that the word 'work' covered 'a veritable abyss of concepts'; it is, he said, 'an over-defined word, into which so much meaning has been put that it simply does not have any meaning at all any more'.[3]

Gradually, though, a unitary conception emerged, namely that work refers to the activities that are performed on the market – and thereby wage labour became the prototype for the concept. In the middle of the previous century, mainstream work research was characterised by the fact that its central concept was not made explicit and hardly even discussed. The meaning of the concept was self-evident and research on work usually withdrew from the theoretical problems and the complexity of the concept by – mainly tacitly – accepting the easy formula 'work = wage labour'. In the same way as a non-decision is a form of decision, a non-definition functioned as the definition of work.

So far, in this brief story of the work concept in social science, it has moved from an undefined to an over-defined and finally to a non-defined concept. Then came a strong reaction to what was regarded as a narrow economic conception, i.e. activities on the market. And that is where we still are today. The critics' basic idea is that the work concept must be widened, so that other activities may also be included. Often this more inclusive concept is built up by adding activities around wage work and with a starting point in this conception (see, for example, Daniels, 1987; Horn, 1981). Primarily, however, it does not seem to be a result of a theoretical discussion to develop a better work concept; rather, it appears as part of a wish to give certain activities a higher level of visibility and status. 'Work' is an important ideological concept in capitalist society (Accornero, 1980; Anthony, 1977; Krämer-Badoni, 1978) and, by taking advantage of this, these critics try to achieve such aims. But this is seldom stated explicitly. One exception is the Norwegian sociologist Cato Wadel (1984: 23), who says that his main objective is to mark the importance of certain activities. He says that there is no theoretical motivation for using the term, but that 'it upgrades an activity if it is called work'.

The problem with this perspective is that the work concept once again tends to be over-defined, but in a different way from the one that Riehl meant: the 'widening' of the concept makes it so inclusive that it becomes meaningless. If, for example, one includes in the concept of work everything that a person does in 'securing identity, status and structure' or meeting role obligations (Wallman, 1985: 52 and 1984: 52, respectively), then there is very little that is not work. A concept that in this way includes almost everything loses its meaning.[4] Not surprisingly, there is also a reaction to this 'totalising' turn of the debate; it leads to the standpoint that work in fact *is* a meaningless concept (see, for example, Höfener, 1977).

One type of limitation is, however, fairly common: the work concept should not include anything that can be regarded as morally bad or damaging, rather only that which is good. This train of thought all too easily leads to the more or less explicit position that everything that is good is work. The argument is, however, usually limited to the character of the product, for example arms ('activities that produce canons cannot be work'); it does not refer to the social relations within which the activities are performed. If the argument's moral principle were to be followed consequently, every activity in exploitative work forms would not be work; they can hardly be deemed as belonging to what is morally good.

The short history of work concepts in social science is varied and often confusing. The reference list in this essay can be regarded as a small example: there are quite a few texts in several languages and from several disciplines with titles on the theme 'what is work?' But the question seems to me to be far from answered in a satisfactory way. Therefore I think that we who are conducting research on work organisations and working life should use some of our efforts to continue discussing definitions of work.

As I have tried to show through this overview of the shifts in the debate on the work concept in social sciences, the core of the theoretical dilemma is this: the established formula 'work = wage labour' is inadequate; but the proposed solutions tend to make the concept limitless and thereby fruitless.

Analyses of the way in which the concept of work has been used in the social sciences are rare. Those that exist mainly use a traditional approach: they posit a number of research traditions against each other. This approach has as its rationale the idea that the work concept should be regarded as part of a wider social theory or of a specific discipline. There are several such suggestions for dividing lines, usually put forward with a synthesising (or sometimes an eclectic) aim or as a contrast to the author's own conceptual suggestion (e.g. Cohen 1953; Friedmann, 1961; Gross, 1958; Lufft, 1925; Moser, 1964; Nowak, 1929; Ruyer, 1948; Scheler, 1971; Shimmin, 1966; Tellegen, 1957; von Weiszäcker, 1948). But I will diverge from them. My starting point is that there is a contradiction between whether work should be regarded as a set of activities *per se* or as those activities that are performed within certain social relationships. In the first case work activities tend to be seen as historical constants and as applicable to every member of a given society; these activities are work whenever, wherever and within whatever social relations they occur. In the second case, an activity that is work during a given historical period, or in connection with a specific social category, can be non-work during another period or in connection with another social category; it all depends on the social relations. When one wishes to analyse work, one can in the first case immediately look for the specified activities; in the second case one must first find the specified social relations.

Work as activities

The analysis of scientific work concepts by Karl Elster at the beginning of the previous century seems to be one of the most cited. His sources are almost exclusively encyclopaedias of the social sciences and his main conclusion is: 'The different definitions agree on one point. They recognise that "work" always is an activity' (1919: 621). And this is still the case – all definitions that I have found have this reference to work as having to do with activity.

However, modern authors differ from the older ones: none of them mentions the toil of an activity as a criterion for work, but in Elster's review it has a prominent place. Thus, one author (Rosher, cited in Elster, 1919: 617–18) says that 'the attribute of toil always belongs to the concept of work'. Nevertheless, Elster does not accept this idea and his primary argument against it is that the drudgery of an activity cannot in itself specify it as work. Effort is part of all activities in the sense that the agent expends energy – activities are toil. Further, there are many physical and psychological activities that require much more effort than those which are usually called work, among them mountain climbing and chess playing. Elster's objections might seem a bit simple, but at the same time satisfactory enough – especially as 'toil' has virtually disappeared from the conceptual discussion.

Once it is established that work is an activity, some further kind of delimitation is made, so that certain activities are to be regarded as work and others are not. Often the criterion for an activity to be work is that it is directed towards a goal. Here, many authors refer to a well-known passage of *Capital*:

> A spider conducts operations that resemble those of a weaver, and a bee puts to shame many an architect in the construction of her cells. But what distinguishes the worst architect from the best of bees is this, that the architect raises his structure in imagination before he erects it in reality. At the end of every labour process, we get a result that already existed in the imagination of the labourer at its commencement. He not only effects a change of form in the material on which he works, but he also realizes a purpose of his own that gives the law to his modus operandi, and to which he must subordinate his will.
>
> (Marx, 1970: 178)

This is an ontological conceptualisation in that it specifies a difference between human beings and other animals. But when it comes to distinguishing work from other human activities it seems wanting,[5] which can perhaps be most clearly seen in the foremost elaboration of this theme – the one by Georg Lukács (1973, see also 1948: 431–63). The basis of his argument is that work is 'telos realisation', i.e. to reach a goal formulated in advance of performing the activity. 'Teleological positioning' (*teleologische Setzung*) is the essence of work. When the goal is formulated, the agent triggers a chain of causal determinants that – in their turn – lead to the goal being reached.

Lukács's development of Marx's reasoning has, however, been heavily criticised. Agnes Heller (1981) reminds us that all actions are teleological; Lukács simply regards them as modified versions of work activities. And work is in his interpretation a 'one man show', which only has to do with the goal of the agent.

Therefore all social actions have to be explained by an analogy with the individual agent's actions.

A different kind of critique has been delivered by Peter Ruben and Camilla Warnke (1979). In opposition to teleological positioning they stress the tool as the core of human work. It is through using tools that human beings have won the power to formulate goals; the tool is the ontological precondition for teleological positioning, not the other way around (1979: 23): 'Teleological positionings are expressions of the consciousness that have been generated in and through work, i.e. not simply as preconditions for work, but rather its ideational element!' Further, they say that it is seldom possible to understand in advance and predict all preconditions for the course of a work process. In reality, work is always richer than the posited goal (including the instruments of work and their use). Therefore it is quite unrealistic to reduce work to what is teleologically posited.

In a similar way, Jürgen Habermas (especially 1968 and 1976) has delimited the work concept to 'instrumental action', but now in opposition to 'communicative action'. The criticism against him therefore follows somewhat different lines and mainly points to his marginalisation of the concept by allowing traits of work in capitalism to be the model of its total conceptualisation. Thus Eyerman and Shipway say:

> Habermas takes *absolutely* for granted what is but a tendency under the capitalist mode of production; i.e., work for Habermas is only, has only ever been, and will always be, purely instrumental activity. The tendency towards instrumentality in the labor–nature process which reaches its greatest distortion under capitalism thus becomes absolutized for *all* historical periods and all social formations.
>
> (Eyerman and Shipway, 1981: 559)

The characteristic that work is a goal-directed activity gives us, however, an opportunity to place work in relation to some types of non-work. The dimensions that we can use are, then, activity versus non-activity and goal-direction versus non-goal-direction. A non-goal-directed activity is play – and there is a strong tradition of trying to define the characteristics of work by contrasting it with what denotes play (e.g. Marcuse, 1973 [1933]), by, for instance, placing 'playing man' – *homo ludens* – as an ideal against, or at least a complement to, 'working man' (for example, Huizinga, 1955 [1938]).[6] Also the opposite of activity, passivity, can be goal-directed: rest, necessary in order to be active later. A non-goal-directed passivity, finally, is idleness. Even here there is a tradition of positing idleness as an ideal that is the opposite of work; among the most famous texts in this tradition is Paul Lafargue's *The Right to Idleness* (1972 [1883]) – written in opposition to the parole 'the right to work' – and Bertrand Russell's *In Praise of Idleness* (1960 [1932]).

If Lukács took the extreme position that goal-direction is a sufficient criterion for an activity to be work, Wadel is at the other extreme. He explicitly rejects the aim of the activity as a relevant characteristic for the concept of work; instead he directs his attention towards the function of the activity: 'Work is human activity which can be shown to maintain, establish or change commonly valued social institutions, *whether these activities have this as a goal or not*' (1977: 407, emphasis added). But Wadel is an exception. Most other authors use goal-direction as a part of their definitions of work.

It should be noted, however, that a negative conceptualisation is an enormously influential line of thought: work is defined by what is *not* the aim of the activity. This is the perspective of classical economics, where work is primarily regarded as a sacrifice (cf. Macpherson, 1985: 241). The most widely cited formulation comes from Alfred Marshall, although it originates from Jevons. Work, Marshall says, is 'any exertion of mind or body undergone partly or wholly with a view to some good *other than* the pleasure derived directly from the work' (1907 [1890]: 65, emphasis added). A problem is that most activities have more than one goal – few activities are not at least partly performed for reasons other than the pleasure of performing them. Many difficulties therefore arise in drawing even a rough line between work and other activities.

Sometimes the reasoning is driven a few steps further, so that work by definition must be unpleasant. An example can be found in Richard B. Lee's well-known study of !Kung San, a hunter-gatherer people in Botswana. Lee defines his work concept by listing a number of activities. Thereafter he asks (1979: 252): 'When a hunter consults the oracle discs, is that work? When he spends the evening in camp listening to reports of game sightings on the eve of a hunt, is he working?' And the answer is: 'Because these activities are carried out in a socially pleasurable context, I have not considered them as work.' Part of the planning, the teleological positioning of the activity, is excluded simply because it takes place in a pleasant situation.

This reasoning has deep historical roots – going back at least to Greek Antiquity and the distinction between activity and contemplation, and the evaluation of what these concepts stand for. The clearest connection with this idea in recent times can, as far as I know, be found in Yves Simon (1936). Human life contains, he says, two opposites: manual work and contemplation. In between these extremes we find spiritual work, which is nobler and work to a lesser degree than the manual type. There are, further, two kinds of spiritual work, namely that which prepares manual work (i.e. positioning of telos) and that which prepares contemplation; here the latter is nobler and work to a lesser degree than the former.[7]

It seems that it is untenable to base a fruitful social scientific definition of work on the properties of activities as such. This is not surprising if we consider that the objects of social science are relational. So, let us turn to the other side of the contradiction between activities and social relations.

Work as social relations

A number of authors restrict the application of their work concept to a specific type of society or even more limited contexts. Of course, this is a result of their research interests: Lee (1979) analyses a hunter-gatherer society and has no immediate reason to develop a more general definition; Dubin (1965) writes a textbook on work in North American private enterprises (although he calls it *The World of Work*), and so on. At the same time, there are authors who are trying to find a concept in order to make it possible to compare societies and cultures, for example Udy (1970) and Lewenhak (1980).

Independent of scope in this regard, many arguments are built around the social relations with which the activities are associated. One possibility is, of course, to establish the social nature of work at a general level. The most cited example is probably this: work is 'an activity that produces something of value for other people' (*Work in America*, 1973: 3). The explicit aim with this formulation is to be able to include the housewife's activities in the concept of work.[8] Cases in which people 'are productive only for themselves' is regarded as a possible definition of leisure activities. This might, however, turn out to be a bit confusing, because the authors do not clarify whether they regard the relationship between work and leisure as contrary or contradictory: is leisure a surplus category – everything that is not work – or are there actions that fall outside the two categories? Are there, in other words, activities that do not produce anything of value to anyone? Another – and even more serious – problem is that all consumption in a market society will be work, as that is of value to the seller of the goods. The formulation does not provide a discrimination that holds.

There is, further, a strong idealistic trait in this kind of reasoning (perhaps most marked in Novarra, 1980: 17ff.): Only 'good' activities can be included in the work concept. A simple example will illustrate the misleading consequences thereof: the Swedish company Bofors produces arms; for a number of years it also made toothpaste. If we regard arms as something bad and toothpaste as something good, only the Bofors' employees making toothpaste were working during this period – not those making cannons and ammunition. And today, when the company has stopped making toothpaste, none of the employees work. Even though it is a laudable aim to struggle for human work to produce only good things, I am afraid that such a concept cannot be used to analyse work historically or today. And it is hardly fruitful to regard wage labour as non-work.

Often the social relations are made more precise than in the definitions that I have discussed so far – especially when a sociological perspective is contrasted to an economic view. Edward Gross, for example, says that

> the sociologist is interested in work insofar as it involves some form of social organization. The focus is therefore on what are called *work relationships*. A work relationship is one in which persons perform activities which are designed to achieve objectives usually defined by others. The activities that they perform are called 'work'.
>
> (Gross, 1958: 11)

He gives an example of a factory work crew: the workers' objectives are set by foremen, the boards of directors and, indirectly, by society at large through customers' demand on the market.

Here, then, all leading functions in a work organisation are excluded from the work concept, a view that can be traced back to Max Weber's (1978: 114) analysis. He distinguishes between those economic activities that are managerial (*disponierende*) and those that are oriented towards managerial instructions; only the latter are regarded as work. Compared to Lukács's reasoning, we find here that the unity between telos and its realisation is transformed into an absolute opposition, where only the moment of realisation is allowed to be part of the work concept. One consequence of this argument is that it will be difficult in concrete research to deal with people who have both leading and telos-realising functions. The problem is a major one as all hierarchical work organisations have such groups; some of their tasks are made up of telos-positioning for the work of people below them, others of realising telos posited by people above them in the hierarchy. One example would be the foreman that Gross mentions. When does he work and when does he manage? There are also historical examples, among which the most obvious ones are the slave overseers of the ancient world – often slaves themselves – and the bailiffs of the Middle Ages.

Against Lukács I have argued that there are cases when one person formulates telos and another person realises it, and this can be work; against Gross (and Weber) the objection is the opposite one – there are also cases when one and the same person fulfils both functions and this can be work.

Further, Gross comments on his use of the word 'usually' in the definition, saying that two exceptions may be considered. First, there are cases in which one or more agents themselves formulate goals for their actions. But such situations are, he argues, only brief and rather unimportant. Second, it is the social culture that determines people's goals. But culture operates through people, Gross says, and thereby this objection is supposed to be of no consequence either. His conclusion is that none of the exceptions are of any practical importance. His defence against the exceptions does, however, lead to some dubious points. As regards the first exception, I do not at all find it without importance. All peasants who own their land and do not produce for a market – and they make up a large and important social category in history – would, for example, not be working. In this respect the definition seems to be too narrow. The argument about the second exception has the opposite consequence: it is difficult to find actions that do *not* have culturally influenced goals (apart from purely biological reflexes). Here we must ask whether there are any interesting activities that are *not* work according to Gross.

In a similar way, one can object to Lee Braude's (1963: 347 and, somewhat modified, 1975: 12–13) formulation that says that work covers all actions that the agent undertakes in order to survive socially; this includes all activities that the agent performs in order to enhance his or her position in the different status hierarchies of society. But are there not aspects of social survival – in Braude's meaning – in everything we do? This criterion hardly specifies a certain category of actions. He also – as, for example, Sylvia Shimmin (1966: 197) – lets the views of the agent be partly decisive for the definition. This is acceptable as a starting point for social scientific concept building, but not as an end point. Scientific concepts are, or should be, different from everyday concepts.

In the few explicit definitions of what I have termed the non-defined work concept – according to 'work = wage labour' – we find the clearest specified social relationship. 'By work,' Dubin (1965: 4) says, 'we mean continuous employment, in the production of goods and services, for remuneration' – and he makes clear that by remuneration he means a wage in a modern exchange economy.

The main problem with the social relations approach to definitions of work is that it is unclear what types of social relations are to be taken into account and what they are to be about. What kind of social relation of what? We need a principle for this to be able to solve the contradiction between activities and social relations as a basis for the concept. Otherwise it becomes all too easy to neglect the contradiction as such.

As an example thereof, we might consider the following quotation from a well-known analysis of women's work. The authors, Louise Tilly and Joan W. Scott, explain the way they use the work concept as follows:

> Work is defined as productive activity for household use or for exchange. The meaning, location, and nature of work, of course, have changed over time. During the nineteenth century what we have termed work usually meant wage earning, as it does today. But in earlier centuries the jobs women performed to help support their families did not always or necessarily bring in money. Growing vegetables, raising animals, preparing food, making clothing, and helping with farm or craft work served household needs. These activities had economic value, but it was more often what economists call 'use value' than 'exchange value.' Furthermore, this kind of work merged imperceptibly with women's household or domestic chores. As a result our use of the term *work* for the early modern period of the seventeenth and eighteenth centuries encompasses all of these activities. For the period of industrialization, however, work denotes only market-oriented, or wage-earning jobs. This definition is somewhat arbitrary, for it excludes domestic activity, the useful, economically valuable housework that women perform for their families. We do not deny that unpaid household labor is work. Indeed, we suggest that its value to families was often seen as greater than the value of women's wage labor. To avoid confusion, however, we have found it useful to refer to housework as domestic activity in order to distinguish it from wage-earning or 'productive' activity. Similarly, reproduction – the bearing and raising of children – is a kind of 'work' with economic value to society and to the family. Nonetheless, it is not included in our use of the term *work.*
>
> (Tilly and Scott, 1978: 3)

The first problem with this form of reasoning is that it creates confusion in spite of the terms being chosen to avoid just that: household work is work, but to make things clear we do not call it work; bearing and raising of children is also work, but in order not to mix things up we will not call that work either. Clearly this is suggestive of the – often unreflected – resistance that many researchers have against using more than a single work concept. Instead of discussing things in terms of *different* social work forms, Tilly and Scott prefer to sometimes avoid the work concept.

There is, however, also an inconsistency in the conceptual basis. The authors, in fact, discuss at least three types of work: household work, reproduction and wage labour. But only the first two phenomena are *activities* in themselves; they can be defined by enumerating the activities that make up the concept. The third phenomenon – wage labour – is, however, not an activity, but a *social relation*. It cannot be defined through a list of activities; it must be defined by substantial social relationships, within which any number or kind of activities can be performed.

The problem is, then, that a definition of work according to properties of activities is wanting. But so is the formula 'work = wage labour', although that is the least ambiguous definition not depending on activities but on a social relation. But, as I mentioned at the beginning of this essay, there is also another conceptual contradiction concerning work. That may perhaps provide inspiration for a solution.

Doing in the sphere of necessity

In a philosophical critique of the work concept in the social sciences, Karel Kosík (1976: 118ff.) says: social scientists express a very limited view on human work, as they discuss the work concept from a starting point in an analysis of work activities – work in its empirical forms; thereby they miss the whole point, they do not even touch upon the problem of work. Their reasoning expresses theoretical confusion, uncritical empiricism and sociologism. The question of what work is is a question for philosophers – social scientists are not equipped to deal with it; 'work' is an ontological concept, not an empirical one.[9] Hard words – but worth listening to and reflecting upon.

A common trait in social scientific definitions of work is, as I have noted, that it is an activity. But Kosík directs his critique against what he considers to be a limitation in this idea; hereby he is building on – apart from Hegel and Marx – an early article by Marcuse (1973 [1933]). Kosík's point of departure is Hegel's emphasis on work not being an activity like any other activity; it is a *doing* (*Tun*), something that permeates human life and history. In general outline, Hegel's view may be summarised thus: it is in work that human beings differ from animals. The latter satisfy their needs through directly consuming what nature provides, but humans transcend this level – even though we too have a biological, instinctively grounded side; through work we transform natural materials in accordance with our intentions. We thereby gain knowledge about the characteristics of the objects and we learn the laws that govern our beings. Then we use this knowledge in the processes of work, which in its turn further develops the transformation of natural objects that we can accomplish. Work means, then, that our theoretical knowledge of the world develops and we move away from the purely instinctive stage. 'The role of labour,' a commentator (Plant, 1977: 84) on Hegel's view says, 'is crucial; it inaugurates human history, the record of man's transformation of his environment, and distinguishes man from animal and the evolution of merely natural forms.'

The idea that humans create themselves and their world through work is the basis of this ontological concept of work.[10] The question 'what is work?' is an aspect of the question 'what are human beings?' The idea that work is a specifically human activity is, however, not limited to the Marxist tradition. It is, thus, very strongly expressed by Schrecker (who explicitly distances himself from Hegel as well as Marx). Only humans create civilisation and make history; the activities accomplishing this are work.[11] Without this specific character of work, he says (1967 [1948]: 140), society is 'transformed into a natural association comparable to an ant hill or beehive, and ultimately to a machinery which, once put into action, has no further history'.

When Marcuse (1973 [1933]) discusses the work concept, he too takes his point of departure in the notion that humans thereby actively and consciously create themselves; at the same time he emphasises another side of work. He devotes the main part of his analysis to what he terms the 'burdensome character' (*Lastcharakter*) of work. This exists independently of the way in which the process of work is organised, other working conditions and the experiences of the worker. The *Lastcharakter* lies in the fact that the worker is subjected to the laws of things in work. And further (1973 [1933]: 17): 'In labor it is always primarily a question of the thing itself and not of the laborer. [...] In labor one is always distanced from one's self-being and directed toward something else: one is always with others and for others.' To some extent this analysis is due to the fact that at this time Marcuse was influenced by Martin Heidegger (cf. Kellner, 1973; Moser, 1964). And Kosík (1976: 130f) criticises Marcuse for, among other things, the emphasis on the development of the individual and for not distinguishing between, on the one hand, the fact that humans create things and, on the other, that social institutions can appear as though they were things.

But Kosík makes use of the perspective of the two sides of work. In the continued philosophical investigation, he develops the argument in the following way: what constitutes work is its objectivity – a concept that contains two phenomena: first that the result of work is a durable product – the activity is objectified; and, second, that work is an instance of human beings as objective subject – as practical beings. The objectified creations exist independently of the consciousness of the individual and they are a precondition for the continuity of human existence.

Kosík summarises what is specific to work: it is there that human beings humanise nature and objectify their intentions; we thereby live in a world that we create ourselves – in opposition to the (other) animals, who are tied to naturally given conditions. So far, however, we have mainly been concerned with human doing at a general level. When Kosík goes on to further specify the work concept, he refers to the following quotation from Marx:

> *Labour-time*, even if exchange-value is eliminated, always remains the creative substance of wealth and the measure of the *cost* of its production. But free time, *disposable time*, is wealth itself, partly for the enjoyment of the product, partly for the free activity which – unlike labour – is not dominated by the pressure of extraneous purpose which must be fulfilled, and the fulfilment of which is regarded as a natural necessity or a social duty, according to one's inclinations.
>
> (Marx, 1972: 257)

Whilst Marx's builder and bee definition deals with telos positioning as a specifically human characteristic, this definition is ontological at another level: it specifies what work is among humans, in human societies. Kosík's conclusion is that *work is the doing of human beings in the sphere of necessity*.[12] We work when what we do is based on an external necessity to which we must submit in order to secure our existence. (However, Kosík says, the sphere of necessity cannot be counterposed in any simple way to an independent sphere of freedom; this is an important philosophical insight, but I cannot enter this discussion here.) The conclusion implies that a specific activity can be work or non-work depending on whether it is performed as a necessary precondition for existence. To exemplify the point, Kosík (1976: 124) says: Aristotle did not work when writing his *oeuvre* – his existence was secured anyway; but the modern professor of philosophy works when translating Aristotle, as this activity is performed as part of an occupation – it is a socially determined necessity for him or her to earn an income.[13]

A conclusion that we can draw from the argument that I have reviewed is that what I have spoken of so far as the basis for an ontological work concept must now be reconsidered. According to this concept, human work creates human beings. It can probably be considered as historically correct – at least after the so-called original affluent societies (Lee, 1979; Sahlins, 1972) – as human doing is and has been work to such a high degree.[14] It is, however, a theoretically insufficient formulation and instead it should read: human doing creates human beings. The concept 'doing' is broader than the concept 'work'. Work is doing in the sphere of necessity; doing can in principle – as opposed to work – exist also in the sphere of freedom.

Kosík poses this concept of work against what he regards as the concept in social science: empirical activities. As we have seen, this is only one side of a conceptual contradiction, in which social relations is the other. Even though Kosík's picture of the debate in the social sciences seems incomplete, I think he provides us with the key to solving the conceptual problems. The formulation 'doing in the sphere of necessity' can be seen as an overriding definition of work. For social scientific research, however, this is not enough. Our task is to analyse the specific and substantial historical and social forms of work. The ontological work concept indicates a roughly delimited area of analysis for social science studies. These studies cannot, consequently, be based on an activities approach to the concept of work. We need a whole set of concepts to cover different types of social relations within the 'sphere of necessity'. The often-heard claim that we must widen the work concept can thereby be dispensed with – and thus also the risk of turning work into a meaningless concept for the social sciences. The idea of widening *the* work concept is replaced by the ambition of developing work concept*s*. Thereby we can avoid the impasse of realising that a particular phenomenon probably is work, but not being able to analyse it as such, due to a poor and rigid terminology.

But there are many types of relations and we need some type of distinction here. A basic distinction is made by Roy Bhaskar (1989: 42): 'A relation R_{AB} may be defined as *internal* if and only if A would not be what it *essentially* is unless B is related to it in the way that it is.' Internal social relations are distinguished from *external* ones, i.e. relations that are possible but not necessary for the existence of A; and an internal social relation makes up a social structure (Danermark *et al.*, 2002; Sayer, 1992). Whether an activity is to be regarded as belonging to the category work depends on the social relations within which it is performed. The critique against the formula 'work = wage labour' has been extremely important, but it has missed the decisive theoretical point that this formulation contains. It indicates a specific *work form*, a specific internal social relation, a social structure – the one involving capitalists and wage labourers: none of them would be what they are without the relationship between them. Instead of adding a number of activities to wage work, we can now try to also delimit *other such relations*, developing a terminology that covers a whole set of work forms – i.e. internal social relations structuring the sphere of necessity.

The definition of work that I suggest is therefore: *work is activities performed within internal social relations structuring the sphere of necessity*.

Work forms

It lies outside the scope and ambition of this essay to try to present a full typology of work forms. I will, however, discuss two existing typologies that I regard as non-starters; then I will outline some work forms that I suggest as starters for such an analysis.

Let me first note that there is in the relevant literature what can be called a conventional model of work throughout history, based on social forms of work defined through internal relations. The model says that there are four types of social work forms in human history, namely slavery, serfdom, wage labour and independent work. Often, however, the latter form is excluded and the model is reduced to three work forms. M.I. Finley (1981: 142) reacts strongly against this model, saying: 'We are in thrall to a very primitive sociology which assumes that there are only three kinds of labour-status: the free, contractual wage-earner, the serf, and the slave. Everyone must somehow be fitted into one of these categories.' The conventional model probably has its strongest hold in Marxist tradition (e.g. Cohen, 1978: 63ff.), but it also exists more or less explicitly in several non-Marxist theories of societies and work throughout history.

Self-employment, which is a very old work form, still exists in modern capitalist societies, where wage labour is, of course, the dominant work form. And thereby the potential of the model is emptied, as neither slavery nor serfdom are present. This seems a bit thin, however, especially as several current typologies are richer. Therefore I want to discuss two such typologies, namely those proposed by Enzo Mingione and Ray Pahl, respectively. I choose them as they are well known, and they also touch on the theoretical principle that I have suggested: work forms are internal social relations that structure the sphere of necessity.

Mingione (1985, 1991) defines work as those activities that contribute to material survival. His definition is, then, not built on social relations, but the typology of work forms that he suggests is still construed in such a way that social relations (although not always internal ones) are the basis of its dimensions. He uses four dimensions: (a) if the activity is formal or informal; (b) if it is legal, illegal or not provided for by law; (c) if money is involved or not; and (d) if it is public or private. This makes up rather a complicated model. All formal work forms are legal, monetary and public; the informal ones can be illegal as well as not provided for by law, monetary as well as non-monetary, public as well as private. Put together, the dimensions would logically result in sixty-four work forms, but Mingione limits his discussion to eight forms: (1) purely formal activities; (2) mixed formal/informal activities; (3) activities that elude fiscal, social security or labour legislation; (4) criminal activities; (5) paid activities or transactions not provided for by law; (6) reciprocal or voluntary unpaid activities; (7) self-provision in the household; and (8) normal domestic work.

Now, it seems to me that Mingione's typology is an example of a 'chaotic conceptualisation'. A chaotic concept 'arbitrarily divides the indivisible and/or lumps together the unrelated and the inessential, thereby "carving up" the object of study with little or no regard for its structure and form' (Sayer, 1992: 138). Above all, chaotic concepts neglect the distinctions between formal and substantial, external and internal relations. It would be very hard to perceive Mingione's eight work forms as social structures. Further, some of the types of work – such as self-provision in the household and normal domestic work – are discussed in terms of activities *per se* rather than social relations. Let me therefore turn to Pahl's typology.

Pahl's (1984: 123ff; 1988; 1997) concept of work has the meaning of 'getting by', which might be regarded as a version of the idea of doing in the sphere of necessity. He also emphasises that the important analysis concerns the social relations in which the tasks are embedded. Throughout, he uses the example of a woman ironing and we recognise two of the work forms from the conventional model: wage work and self-employment. In the first case, the woman is an employee whose task it is to iron shirts; in the second case, she has a small business in which she performs this service. The other work forms are new ones. In symbolic work the activity is performed out of love; the woman irons her lover's shirt, thinking about him while she does so. Patriarchal work is different: here she does the same thing, but not for love; instead she is dominated by her husband. Another category is work related to, but not part of, employment; for example, if the woman irons her own blouse because her wage work requires that she looks neat. Unpaid community work is the case when she irons an older relative's clothes if this relative is not able to take care of the task. Reciprocal work, finally, is performed with the idea of getting a comparable favour in return some other time.

Pahl makes an important point in stressing social relations: the same activity – ironing – can be performed within quite different relations and thereby different work forms. This could also be taken as implying that this activity can actually be non-work, which in Pahl's argument is play. The typology seems to me to be much clearer than the one suggested by Mingione. But it still contains problematic traits. The most important one is that Pahl does not make a distinction between external and internal social relations. The typology is not as 'chaotic' as Mingione's typology, but the concept 'getting by' must be given an immensely wide interpretation to be applicable. If, for example, symbolic work (activity for love) is to be regarded as a *work* form, 'getting by' loses any distinct meaning. We are back to the problems involved in the tradition of widening the concept of work: it becomes so wide that it loses all meaning. Further, Pahl does not follow his own principle in a consistent way. Regarding one of his ironing scenes he says (1988: 747): 'The activity is genuinely a pleasure and would not, therefore, be classed as work.' In this case, it is not the type of social relation that is decisive, but the feelings of the worker – and he falls back on the idea that work cannot be pleasurable.

These two 'richer' typologies do not, it seems to me, lead us anywhere but into cul-de-sacs, so we have to start again with wage work and self-employment. In the debate on the concept of work, wage work is usually taken as a given; it is seldom problematised as a work form. In labour market theory and class theory, however, different forms of wage work are discussed (see, for example, Højrup, 1996; Karlsson, 1995; McRae, 1986). On this basis I suggest that we distinguish at least two types of wage work: proletarian and career wage work. Both are, of course, situated in the labour market, but there the similarity ends. In proletarian wage work what is sold on the labour market is the right to control one's labour power during a specified period of time. The buyer of labour power is responsible for the use of it, i.e. what the worker is to do. The basic trait is then time: the wage worker sells labour power per time unit. In career work, on the other hand, time is not the 'goods' on the labour market, but expertise, for example competence in handling functions such as marketing, product development, research or management. To a large extent it is the career worker's responsibility to take care of these functions, even if it requires activities outside 'normal' working hours.

Further, the position in the hierarchy of work organisations is subordinate in proletarian wage work and superordinate in career wage work. In the first case there are no career ladders to climb; the workers can, of course, change jobs, but such changes do not give them more power or a 'higher' position. In the second case, the labour market is structured as career ladders; the workers start at a low level but by achieving good results, showing ambition and loyalty, and gaining educational credentials they can obtain promotions.

Self-employment is a third work form. Here, the social relation is not that of the labour market, but that of the market for products or services. The workers do not primarily sell their labour power, but the results of their work. Usually three criteria are mentioned for this work form (Bechhofer and Elliott, 1981: 138): the self-employed control their own labour power and they own some kind of production instruments; the labour power of the family is part of the production process;[15] and if there are employees, their labour power is to be regarded as an extension of that of the family.

There is also the work form of investors – or capitalists. In Marxist, as well as Weberian social theory, the activities of investors are usually not regarded as work. Following the concept that I suggest, they are. The defining social relationship for this work form is neither primarily the labour market nor the market for goods and services, but the stock market.

Regarding these four work forms one might ask: what about the criticism in the debate on the concept of work that says that (women's) household activities are being excluded? Where is child-care, cleaning the house, washing up? First of all, in my perspective these are activities, not social relations and thereby not work in themselves. When child-care is carried out within the social relations of a work form it is work; when it is not, it belongs to some other category. On the other hand, I want to suggest that there are a number of work forms that empirically are virtually women-specific. Each one of them is structurally coupled to one of the four work forms that I have mentioned so far. It should, however, be noted that a theory of work cannot *explain* why these work forms are women-specific. A theory of patriarchy that is not based on or does not involve the concept of work is necessary for such an explanation.[16]

The housewife work form is connected with that of proletarian wage work, and the back-up woman work form to that of career work. This means that they are quite different (Jakobsen and Karlsson, 1993; Christensen, 1987). The housewife's activities are directed towards the home and the family. But she cannot influence that on which her livelihood is based, namely her husband's wage, which is set in negotiations over which she has no influence at all. The back-up woman's activities, on the other hand, are directed towards her husband's career, which she can influence to some extent. His success is not only dependent on his performance directly in work, but also on his showing the 'correct' lifestyle – and it is the back-up woman who produces this lifestyle.

Theoretically there are reasons to believe that there are women-specific work forms connected with independent work and investor work respectively. However, very little is known about them. Concerning investors Daniel Bertaux (1983: 79) has remarked that they 'certainly are among the least known of all social categories'; although this seems correct, it could be added that the investor's wife is even less known to social science – and that goes perhaps also for the independent worker's wife.

Conclusion

A number of demands on a definition of work have been expressed more or less explicitly in this essay. I now want to state them explicitly. First, such a definition should at least roughly be able to delimit work from other social phenomena; it should demarcate a category of phenomena as work unlike other phenomena that are not work. Second, the delimitation should be done objectively, that is independent of everyday conceptualisations of work and the emotions of workers connected with the activities. Everyday concepts and social science ones are usually rivals, as the latter aim at going beyond the surface of the former to the mechanisms behind our way of thinking in ordinary life. If, further, the definition ties work to a specific feeling, for example dislike or lack of pleasure, many opportunities for making concrete studies of people's emotions connected to work are closed – and that is done literally by definition. Finally, it must be possible to include what exists on the labour market in the concept of work.

There are two contradictions in the ongoing debate on the concept of work in the social sciences: one concerns whether work is, on the one hand, activities or properties of activities, or, on the other, social relations; the second, whether the conceptual basis should be empirical or ontological. Regarding the first contradiction I have found that an activities approach does not produce demarcation lines that hold; in practical social scientific use it cannot sort out what is work and what is not. The consequences are much the same with most definitions of the social relations type, mainly because there is no clear answer to the question of what kind of social relations are involved. There are also conceptual suggestions that mix the two principles, which of course leads to confusion.

One specific variant of the social relations approach has, however, a clear conceptual advantage, namely wage labour. It points out a specific work form, structured by the relation between capitalist and worker. Any activity performed within this relation is undoubtedly work. But, as the criticism of the formula 'work = wage labour' indicates, this does not make it possible to say whether all activities outside this relation are non-work or if there are other work forms as well.

One argument against the activity approach is at the same time directed towards an empirical base in the second contradiction. We need to go beyond what can be observed. An ontologically based – and admittedly rough – delimitation is that work is doing in the sphere of necessity. But what this sphere contains varies historically and in different contemporary social contexts, which makes it necessary for social science to be able to make further distinctions. And by now the pieces for doing this are in place. The distinctions must be built on social relations – but of a specific kind; here the concept wage labour shows the way by being based on internal relations. Social science needs to develop concepts for further work forms on the same basis – and I have tentatively given some examples.

My suggestion is, then, that the concept of work in social science can most fruitfully be defined as activities performed within internal social relations structuring the sphere of necessity. This does not mean that I regard it as the definitive statement on the matter. All knowledge in social science is fallible – and thereby possible to improve upon. For the time being, I think that the formulation can at least meet the demands I have put forward for a definition of work. It can delimit work in an overriding way, which means that a given activity can be work or non-work, but which also makes it possible to distinguish between different work forms. Further, there are no references to everyday conceptualisations or to the feeling states of workers, which means that all roads to concrete studies of emotions and work are open. Finally, it follows that all activities that are performed on the labour market are work – but that there are a number of other work forms that must also be taken into account in social scientific analysis of work.

Notes

1 I want to thank Henrietta Huzell, Patrik Larsson, Kathleen Lynch and Andrew Sayer for very helpful comments on an earlier version of this essay.
2 My aim is, then, different from Paul Ransome's excellent *The Work Paradigm* (1996), as he is concerned with the everyday concept of work.
3 Quotations from other languages than English are translated by me.
4 For a critique of this type of 'widening' of the concept of work, see Karlsson (1995).
5 Marx also defines work at this ontological level, which I will take up later.
6 For analyses where work and play are not entirely regarded as antonyms, see Burke (1971) and d'Epinay (1992).
7 Possibly Hannah Arendt's (1958) discussion of *vita activa* will also come to the reader's mind. Her line of reasoning is, however, quite different from that of Simon.
8 It is thus part of an effort to transcend the formula 'work = wage labour'. Just how deeply rooted this idea is, and how difficult it is to abandon it, is illustrated a bit further on in the same book. Concerning politics in relation to women's choice between being housewives and working on the labour market, it is said: 'Government is quite appropriately reluctant to intervene in matters involving family life. Consequently, those responsible for public policy have often shied away from taking a stand on the pros and cons of women *working*' (*Work in America*, 1973: 63, emphasis added). Suddenly the activities of housewives are no longer work.
9 A similar standpoint, though stated in different terms, can be found in Kwant (1969: 122f).
10 There are two main lines of argument against this idea. The first says that there is certainly such a difference between humans and (other) animals, but this has a supernatural origin – we have not created ourselves, we are created by God (e.g. Crosby, 1976). The second maintains that the difference does not exist, at least not in such a marked way (e.g. Ingold, 1983). It would, however, lead too far to go into this critique here. (For a defence of the idea, see Cornell, 1986: 18ff. and Woolfson, 1982.)
11 An almost literal formulation can be found in an article by Jean Lacroix (1952: 21): 'to work is to have an history, it is to make history.'
12 Sometimes the sphere of necessity is regarded as simply material production – or the core of such production (e.g. Ganßmann, 1994: 75) – but that is too restricted an interpretation.
13 Perhaps it was not an entirely successful choice by Kosík to take Aristotle as his example. According to what we know about Aristotle's biography, parts of his philosophical activities were probably work in Kosík's meaning. I refer to it anyway, as it illustrates his argument so well.

14 An often-quoted analysis of the history of ideas on work is, for example, introduced by this sentence (Febvre, 1948: 19): 'As long as there have been Men, work has not ceased to fill life for the majority of them.'

15 In a wider perspective self-employment is a type within a much larger work form that can be called *family work*. Historically family work is a very important work form, and it has often been combined with several forms of forced work, such as conscription and tenantship (Karlsson, 1986: 64ff.).

16 Recent feminist research argues that the 'totalisation of "work"' (Jónasdóttir, 1994: 69ff.) in explanations of sex/gender relations has led to a theoretical impasse. Liselotte Jakobsen and I (Jakobsen and Karlsson, 1993) have tried to combine the notion of work presented here and Jónasdóttir's notion of 'love power' in her theory of patriarchy to an analysis of the social structures of everyday life. But in the present context I limit the discussion to the concept of work.

References

Accornero, A. (1980) *Il lavoro come ideologia*, Bologna: Il Mulino.

Anthony, P.D. (1977) *The Ideology of Work*, London: Tavistock.

Arendt, H. (1958) *The Human Condition*, Chicago, IL: Chicago University Press.

Bechhofer, F. and Elliott, B. (1981) 'Petty property: the survival of a moral economy', in F. Bechhofer and B. Elliott (eds), *The Petite Bourgeoisie: Comparative Studies in the Uneasy Stratum*, London: Macmillan.

Bertaux, D. (1983) 'Vie quotidienne ou modes de vie?', *Schweizerische Zeitschrift für Soziologie*, 9: 67–83.

Bhaskar, R. (1989) *The Possibility of Naturalism: A Philosophical Critique of the Contemporary Human Sciences*, Hassocks: Harvester.

Braude, L. (1963) 'Work: a theoretical clarification', *The Sociological Quarterly*, 4: 344–8.

—— (1975) *Work and Workers*, New York: Praeger.

Brown, R.K. (1984) 'Working on work', *Sociology*, 18: 311–23.

Burke, R. (1971) '"Work" and "play"', *Ethics*, 82: 31–47.

Christensen, L.R. (1987) *Hver vore veje*, Copenhagen: Etnologisk Forum.

Cohen, G.A. (1978) *Karl Marx's Theory of History: A Defence*, Princeton, PA: Princeton University Press.

Cohen, J. (1953) 'The ideas of work and play', *British Journal of Sociology*, 4: 312–22.

Cornell, L. (1986) *Arbete och arbetsformernas utveckling*, Gothenburg: Göteborg University.

Crosby, J.F. (1976) 'Evolutionism and the ontology of the human person: critique of the Marxist theory of the emergence of man', *The Review of Politics*, 38: 208–43.

Cummings, T.G. and Srivastva, S. (1977) *Management of Work: A Socio-Technical Systems Approach*, Kent, OH: Kent State University Press.

d'Epinay, C.L. (1992) 'Beyond the antinomy: work versus leisure? The process of cultural mutation in industrial societies during the twentieth century', *International Sociology*, 7: 408–23.

Danermark, B., Ekström, M., Jakobsen, L. and Karlsson, J. Ch. (2002) *Explaining Society: Critical Realism in the Social Sciences*, London: Routledge.

Daniels, A. Kaplan (1987) 'Invisible work', *Social Problems*, 34: 403–15.

Dubin, R. (1965) *The World of Work*, Englewood Cliffs, NJ: Prentice-Hall.

Elster, K. (1919) 'Was ist Arbeit?', *Jahrbücher für Nationalökonomie und Statistik*, 112: 609–27.

Eyerman, R. (1985) 'Work – a contested concept', in B.O. Gustavsson, J. Ch. Karlsson and C. Räftegård (eds), *Work in the 1980s: Emancipation and Derogation*, Aldershot: Gower.

Eyerman, R. and Shipway, D. (1981) 'Habermas on work and culture', *Theory and Society*, 10: 547–66.
Febvre, L. (1948) 'Travail: évolution d'un mot et d'une idée', *Journal de psychologie normale et pathologique*, 41: 19–28.
Finley, M.I. (1981) *Economy and Society in Ancient Greece*, Oxford: Basil Blackwell.
Friedmann, G. (1961) 'Qu'est-ce que le travail?', in G. Friedmann and P. Naville (eds), *Traité de sociologie du travail*, Paris: Armand Collin.
Ganßmann, Heiner (1994): 'Labour and emancipation', *Economy and Society*, 23: 66–92
Grint, K. (1998) *The Sociology of Work: An Introduction*, Cambridge: Polity.
Gross, E. (1958) *Work and Society*, New York: Thomas Y. Crowell.
Habermas, J. (1968) *Technik und Wissenschaft als 'Ideologie'*, Frankfurt/Main: Suhrkamp.
—— (1976) *Zur Rekonstruktion des Historischen Materialismus*, Frankfurt/Main: Suhrkamp.
Heller, A. (1981) 'Paradigm of production: paradigm of work', *Dialectical Anthropology*, 6: 71–9.
Höfener, H. (1977) 'Versuch über die Arbeit. Kritische Anmerkungen zu einer vernachlässigten Kategorie der Ökonomie', in M. Hereth (ed.), *Grundprobleme der politischen Ökonomie*, Munich: Piper.
Højrup, T. (1996) *Omkring livsformsanalysens udvikling*, Copenhagen: Museum Tusculanum.
Horn, R.V. (1981) 'Workers and work: an activities approach', *Labour and Society*, 6: 111–25.
Huizinga, J. (1955 [1938]) *Homo Ludens*, Boston, MA: Beacon Press.
Ingold, T. (1983) 'The architect and the bee: reflections on the work of animals and men', *Man*, 18: 1–20.
Jakobsen, L. and Karlsson, J. Ch. (1993) *Arbete och kärlek. En utveckling av livsformsanalys*, Lund: Arkiv.
Jónasdóttir, A.G. (1994) *Why Women Are Oppressed*, Philadelphia, PA: Temple University Press.
Karlsson, J. Ch. (1986) *Begreppet arbete. Definitioner, ideologier och social former*, Lund: Arkiv.
—— (1995) 'The concept of work on the rack: critique and suggestions', in R.L. Simpson and I. Harper Simpson (eds), *Research in the Sociology of Work, Volume 5: The Meaning of Work*, Greenwich, CT: JAI Press.
Kellner, D. (1973) 'Introduction to "On the philosophical formation of the concept of Labor"', *Telos*, 16: 2–8.
Kosík, K. (1976) *Dialectics of the Concrete*, Dordrecht: D. Riedel.
Krämer-Badoni, T. (1978) *Zur Legitimität der bürgerlichen Gesellschaft. Eine Untersuchung des Arbeitsbegriffs in den Theorien von Locke, Smith, Ricardo, Hegel und Marx*, Frankfurt/Main: Campus.
Kwant, R.C. (1969) *Philosophy of Labor*, Pittsburgh, PA: Duquesne Studies.
Lacroix, J. (1952) 'La notion de travail', *La vie intellectuelle*, 32: 4–31.
Lafargue, P. (1972 [1883]) *Le droit a la paresse*, Paris: François Maspero.
Lee, R.B. (1979) *The !Kung San: Men, Women and Work in a Foraging Society*, Cambridge: Cambridge University Press.
Lewenhak, S. (1980) *Women and Work*, New York: St. Martin's Press.
Lufft, H. (1925) 'Der Begriff der Arbeit', *Jahrbücher für Nationalökonomie und Statistik*, 123: 1–13.
Lukács, G. (1948) *Der junge Hegel*, Zurich: Europa Verlag.
—— (1973) *Zur Ontologie des gesellschaftlichen Seins. Die Arbeit*, Darmstadt: Luchterhand.
Macpherson, C.B. (1985) 'Notes on work and power', in B.O. Gustavsson, J. Ch. Karlsson and C. Räftegård (eds), *Work in the 1980s: Emancipation and Derogation*, Aldershot: Gower.

McRae, S. (1986) *Cross-Class Families: A Study of Wives' Occupational Superiority*, Oxford: Clarendon Press.
Marcuse, H. (1973 [1933]) 'On the philosophical foundation of the concept of labor in economics', *Telos*, 16: 9–37.
Marshall, A. (1907 [1890]) *Principles of Economics*, London: Macmillan.
Marx, K. (1970) *Capital I*, London: Lawrence and Wishart.
—— (1972) *Theories of Surplus Value, Volume III*, London: Lawrence and Wishart.
Maslow, A. (1970 [1954]) *Motivation and Personality*, New York: Harper and Row.
Mingione, E. (1985) 'Social reproduction of the surplus labour force: the case of Southern Italy', in E. Mingione and N. Redclift (eds), *Beyond Employment*, Oxford: Basil Blackwell.
—— (1991) 'A preliminary discussion of the concepts of work and social reproduction oriented to the interpretation of the Post-Fordist transition', in A. Enander, B.O Gustavsson, J. Ch. Karlsson and B. Starrin (eds), *Work and Welfare: Papers from the Second Karlstad Symposium on Work*, Karlstad: University of Karlstad.
Moser, S. (1964) 'Zum philosophischen und sozialwissenschaftlichen Begriff der Arbeit', *Archiv für Rechts- und Sozialphilosophie*, 50: 87–103.
Novarra, V. (1980) *Women's Work, Men's Work*, London: Marion Boyars.
Nowak, H. (1929) 'Der Arbeitsbegriff der Wirtschaftswissenschaft', *Jahrbücher für Nationalökonomie und Statistik*, 131: 513–39.
Pahl, R.E. (1984) *Divisions of Labour*, London: Basil Blackwell.
—— (1988) 'Epilogue: on work', in R.E. Pahl (ed.), *On Work: Historical, Comparative and Theoretical Approaches*, London: Basil Blackwell.
—— (1997) 'Bringing work to life', in J. Holmer and J. Ch. Karlsson (eds), *Work – Quo Vadis?*, Aldershot: Ashgate.
Plant, R. (1977) 'Hegel and political economy', *New Left Review*, 103: 79–92.
Quesnay, F. (1972 [1759]) *Tableau Économique*, ed. M. Kuzcynski and R.L. Meek, London: Macmillan.
Ransome, Paul (1996) *The Work Paradigm: A Theoretical Investigation of Concepts of Work*, Aldershot: Avebury.
Riehl, W.H. (1862) *Die deutsche Arbeit*, Stuttgart: Cottasscher.
Ruben, P. and Warnke, C. (1979) 'Arbeit – Telosrealisation oder Selbsterzeugung der menschlichen Gattung?', *Deutsche Zeitschrift für Philosophie*, 27: 20–31.
Russell, B. (1960 [1932]) *In Praise of Idleness and Other Essays*, London: Allen and Unwin.
Ruyer, R. (1948) 'Métaphysique du travail', *Revue de métaphysique et de morale*, 53: 26–54, 190–215.
Sahlins, M. (1972) *Stone Age Economics*, New York: Aldine Atherton.
Sayer, A. (1992) *Method in Social Science: A Realist Approach*, London: Routledge.
Scheler, M.F. (1971 [1899]) 'Arbeit und Ethik', in *Gesammelte Werke. Bd 1. Frühe Schriften*, Bern: Francke.
Schrecker, P. (1967 [1948]) *Work and History: An Essay on the Structure of Civilization*, Gloucester, MA: Peter Smith.
Shimmin, S. (1966) 'Concepts of work', *Occupational Psychology*, 40: 195–201.
Simon, Y. (1936) 'La définition du travail', *Revue de philosophie*, 36: 426–41.
Smith, A. (1976 [1776]) *An Inquiry into the Nature and Causes of the Wealth of Nations*, Oxford: Clarendon Press.
Tellegen, F. (1957) 'Wat is arbeid?', *Annalen Tijmgenotshap*, 45: 228–46.
Tilly, L. and Scott, J.W. (1978) *Women, Work and Family*, New York: Holt, Rinehart and Winston.

Udy, S.H. (1970) *Work in Traditional and Modern Society*, Englewood Cliffs, NJ: Prentice-Hall.

von Weizsäcker, V. (1948) 'Zum Begriffe der Arbeit. Eine Habeas Corpus-Akte der Medizin?', in E. Sahlin (ed.), *Synopsis. Festgabe für Alfred Weber*, Heidelberg: Lambert Schneider.

Wadel, C. (1977) 'Hva er arbeid?', *Tidskrift for samfunnsforskning*, 18: 387–411.

—— (1984) *Det skjulte arbeid. En argumentation for et utvidet arbeidsbegrep*, Oslo: Universitetsforlaget.

Wallman, S. (1984) *Eight London Households*, London: Tavistock.

—— (1985) 'Employment, livelihood and the organisation of resources: what is work really about?', in B.O. Gustavsson, J. Ch. Karlsson and C. Räftegård (eds), *Work in the 1980s: Emancipation and Derogation*, Aldershot: Gower.

Weber, M. (1978) *Economy and Society: An Outline of Interpretive Sociology*, Berkeley, CA: University of California Press.

Woolfson, C. (1982) *The Labour Theory of Culture: A Re-Examination of Engels's Theory of Human Origins*, London: Routledge and Kegan Paul.

Work in America (1973) Cambridge, MA: MIT Press.

5 Human resource management and realism

A morphogenetic approach

Denise Thursfield and John Hamblett

Introduction

The purpose of this chapter is to set before the reader a realist framework through which to explore the nature and development of human resource management (HRM). We do not offer an all-embracing analysis of the rise of HRM. Rather we endeavour, through a focus on the experience of one organisation, to provide a rudimentary framework through which such an analysis might be conducted in the future. We claim no novelty for the tools we employ here; these are taken from the work of Margaret Archer, and her 'morphogenetic approach' (Archer, 1995). In this regard, the concepts most significant for our endeavours will be 'stratification', 'analytical dualism' and 'emergence'.

In sum this is what our chapter will look like. The first section has been written in order to achieve three tasks. First, we want to locate our work within an existing critical discourse. Second, we want to offer the rudiments of an argument, which suggests that the inconsistencies and contradictions that characterise HRM are best understood through a stratified, realist ontology. Third, we want to offer a defence, necessarily schematic, of our placing of 'flexibility' at the heart of our analysis. Such being the case, although it is not our intention to replicate existing critical accounts, we begin our exposition with a summation of the orthodox and critical approaches to HRM (see, for example, Blyton and Turnbull, 1992; Legge, 1995; Storey, 1995). Following this we offer a brief methodological excursus that includes a description of the location of our empirical investigation and the means by which data was generated. We conclude this section with some remarks on the concept of 'flexibility' and its relation to the discourse of HRM.

Following this we begin the task of applying Archer's morphogenetic model. This major section falls into two rough halves. We begin with an account of the morphogenetic model. Our comments will be primarily, though not exclusively, expositional, for in addition to offering an outline of the model it is our intention, also, to demonstrate its efficacy as a means by which to interpret the theory and practice of HRM. We carry this second goal over to the concluding half of this section. Here, through reference to our empirical work, we offer a practical demonstration of its explanatory power in relation to the emergence of 'flexibility' in one organisation. We bring our chapter to a close with a brief summation of the points made.

Orthodox and critical HRM: some notes on method, and the idea of 'flexibility'

HRM and its critics

The orthodox approach to the development of HRM, as summed up by Sparrow and Hiltrop (1994), views HRM as evolving in linear fashion from the 1970s. Its antecedents are to be found in the human relations theories of the 1950s, the behavioural sciences of the 1960s, in particular the motivation theories of Maslow (1954) and Herzberg (1968), and the human capital theories of the 1960s and 1970s (for example, Schultz, 1961). The accent at this stage was on the human aspect of human resources as exemplified by the so-called 'soft' model of HRM. This model emphasises the importance of treating employees as valuable assets, and lays stress on the development of skills and commitment. Central to the discourse of the soft model are such terms as 'collaboration', 'participation' and 'trust' (Legge, 1995: 35). In recent years a strong-sounding argument suggests that the focus has shifted towards the 'hard' model. Here, the emphasis falls on the integration of people management and corporate business strategy (see, for example, Purcell, 1995; Budhwar, 2000). Such integration is deemed necessary due to increasing competition and economic uncertainty. As a result, so the argument runs, the focus of HRM has changed from 'human' to 'resources', where employees become factors of production comparable to machinery and land, and the aim of the firm is to acquire them as cheaply as possible. The keywords of the hard model are 'flexibility', 'quality' and 'commitment' (Legge, 1995: 35).

Within the orthodox discourse HRM is presented as a normative model that provides optimistic possibilities for future people management practice (e.g. Sparrow and Pettigrew, 1988). This normative approach is characteristic of the various textbooks that provide prescriptive guides for a variety of personnel practices (e.g. Bratton and Gold, 1999; Foot and Hook, 1999). By contrast, critical commentators have identified a number of significant inconsistencies and apparent contradictions within the orthodox approach to HRM. Within the critical discourse, broadly defined, a line of what we would refer to as *idealist* critique has developed. Roughly speaking this work may be defined by its use of hermeneutics and a focus, consequent on this, on the medium of language. This perspective is exemplified by the work of Keenoy and Anthony (1992), who view HRM as a cultural construction that is made up of a number of metaphors and myths.

Closer to, and more compatible with, our own concerns, a brand of materialist criticism has emerged. From this perspective, a number of fundamental flaws are offered for scrutiny. It is suggested, for example, that HRM represents nothing more transformative than a simple re-branding of 'personnel management'. Arguments of a similar kind suggest that while HRM flourishes at the level of rhetoric, workplace reality remains largely undisturbed by the new broom. Serious questions have been raised, also, about the ways in which and the degree to which various stakeholders of HRM have contributed to its propagation (Legge, 1995). Legge demonstrates that the elision of flexibility, commitment and quality results in contradictions that cannot be resolved from within orthodox HRM. She also argues that it is the soft model rather than the hard model that differs from personnel management, but it is the hard model that is practiced more widely.

Further disagreements of a theoretical kind surrounding the meaning of HRM open up the concept to a plethora of definitions, none of which seem satisfactory. Noon (1992), for example, questions whether it is a map, a model or a theory. He argues that HRM cannot be regarded as a theory due to its inherent internal inconsistencies and a shortage of supporting empirical evidence. He suggests that belief in HRM is based not on 'deconstructing theory or looking for proof', but on faith in the message (1992: 29). We want to say that the arguments proffered by Legge and others are amenable to the application of the realist, morphogenetic model. We also suggest that by performing such a synthesis, the nature of HRM *vis-à-vis* the stratified and dualistic nature of the social world can be fruitfully articulated. We want to strengthen that claim, now, by means of methodological excursus .

Methodology, real things and 'flexibility'

We take as our methodological starting point Sayer's view of method as covering 'the clarification of modes of explanation and understanding, the nature of abstraction, as well as familiar subjects of research design and methods of analysis' (Sayer, 1992: 3). The realist mode of explanation, understanding and abstraction is rooted in principles that provide the fundamentals of social enquiry. First, realist social theory aspires to identify and explain the causal mechanisms that link events (Keat and Urry, 1982; Pawson, 1989). Second is a concern to demonstrate the stratified nature of the social world and to show how causal mechanisms can, and do, operate on these various levels. Third, social reality is context-dependent, and causal mechanisms are contingent on time and location.

In this context, our aim is to explain the nature of functional flexibility in one organisation and to identify the causal mechanisms that gave rise to it. The application of Archer's morphogenetic model allows us to demonstrate the stratified, multi-level nature of these mechanisms. In keeping with the third principle, we utilise empirical evidence of functional flexibility from a precise historical and spatial location to illustrate the superiority of the morphogenetic approach in relation to HRM. We make no claims to predict the nature and course of functional flexibility elsewhere. Despite being grounded in rigorous philosophical principles, realist methodology does not countenance what Sayer terms the methodological imperialism of the scientistic and interpretative paradigms.

Thus, 'Methods must be appropriate to the nature of the object we study and the purpose and expectations of our inquiry. [...] The variety of possible objects of study in social science stretches beyond the scope of a single model of research' (Sayer, 1992: 4).

The object of our research, the nature of functional flexibility and the underlying causal mechanisms that engender it within a precise organisational context, is investigated using qualitative methods. The organisation, Chemicals UK, is a chemical processing plant that manufactures chemical intermediates for a variety of consumer products. Primary research took place on three production plants and the craft maintenance workshop. The first production plant mass manufactures one standardised product. The second produces niche-market goods for individual customers, whilst the third manufactures pharmaceutical intermediates. Maintenance of these plants is the responsibility of technicians based in the craft maintenance workshop. Semi-structured interviews were carried out with twenty-eight process workers of varying grades, ten craft technicians (electricians, fitters and welders), nine middle (production and maintenance) managers, four senior production managers and the personnel officer. Documentary evidence relating to recruitment and selection, training, job specification and production schedules was also accessed.

Before quitting this section we should offer some kind of warrant for our specific focus on 'flexibility'. We want to say that 'flexibility' can be seen as a natural choice rather than as a contrivance we have developed for our own purposes. We offer two major supports for this case. First, flexibility is argued to have become the 'driving concept behind the restructuring of work in recent years' (Bradley *et al.*, 2000: 31). Second, flexibility is central to HRM (e.g. Legge, 1995; Blyton and Morris, 1992), both in terms of practice and theory. It is, moreover, an ideological construct of a very robust kind.

Although marked by the same definitional confusions, inconsistencies and contradictions as HRM, it is possible to draw out the major points of distinction. At the concrete level, flexibility is defined as a normative set of practices adopted by firms, for example the numerical and functional flexibility proposed by Atkinson (Atkinson, 1984; Atkinson and Meager, 1986) and the flexible specialisation thesis put forward by Piore and Sabel (1984). At the theoretical or ideational level, numerical flexibility is associated with the 'hard' HRM model whilst functional flexibility is associated with the 'soft' model (Blyton and Morris, 1992). This soft model assumes that functional flexibility embodies a deepening and widening of employees' skills, and a key role for workers in the new flexible production process (Pollert, 1991).

There can be few concepts within the HRM canon that have attracted more systematic critical attention than 'flexibility'. Critics of the concept question, for example, the degree to which flexibility represents a real break with past organisational forms, and the extent of flexibility in practice (Pollert, 1991; Casey, 1991). Elger (1991) suggests that the incidence of multi-skilling amongst the workforce in general is negligible, and functional flexibility consists of simple task rotation and job enlargement. Such criticisms, as powerful and well-argued as they are, however, have done little to diminish either the theoretical, or practical import of this notion within the orthodox discourse.

Applying Archer: HRM and the morphogenetic model

The model and its workings

Our aim now is to show how realist social theory in the form of Archer's morphogenetic model can help to illuminate the factors and processes underpinning the development of HRM. The morphogenetic model incorporates four definitive propositions concerning stratification, analytical dualism, temporality and mediation. The social world comprises both structure and agency, or parts and people. These elements of society are discrete entities that engender their own distinct emergent properties. Social analysis requires that these entities are analysed independently and that the interaction between them is exposed and explained. This form of scrutiny involves a rejection of conflationary theories that disregard either structure or agency, or that resort to notions of duality of structure. A short digression to relate these conflationary approaches, and their inappropriateness to HR research, will help reinforce our argument in favour of analytical dualism.

Archer identifies three forms of conflation: downward, upward and central. Downwards conflation adopts an ontological position that reifies structure and takes it as the focus for social research. From this position, structure determines the behaviour of people. Human action is viewed as marginal, and the capacity for human autonomy and agency in engendering social change is disregarded. Archer argues that structuralist ontology promotes an over-socialised or over-determined portrayal of people. Consequently, it fails, also, to explain social change in an adequate fashion. Transformation must necessarily occur at the structural level, for example through systematic adaptation to existent features, because of impersonal forces or factors (Archer, 1995). This form of conflation is characteristic of orthodox accounts of the development of HRM. HR practices are viewed as systemic adaptations to 'globalisation' and 'economic uncertainty'. The role of agency, especially the agency of those subordinate groups on the receiving end of HR practice, is disregarded (e.g. Budhwar, 2000).

The second form of conflation identified by Archer, upward conflation, is associated with methodological individualism. Structure is viewed as little more than the outcome of the beliefs and actions of individuals who make up present-day society. The focus for social research is, therefore, everyday life, and the ways in which individuals construct their own reality through daily interaction with others. From this ontological position structure is no more than the outcome of current human agency (Archer, 1995). Archer's critique of methodological individualism bears some similarity to Keenoy and Anthony's analysis of HRM, informed as it is by the post-structuralist fascination for language. They argue that, from the post-structuralist paradigm, 'The "Real" is a condition we can envisage (or fantasise) as impossible to reach, while at the same time it represents an absolute abstraction which, through our actions, we aim to approach' (Keenoy and Anthony, 1992: 248).

Archer argues that structuralism and methodological individualism are both guilty of epiphenomenalism. Structuralism marginalises the individual while methodological individualism marginalises structure. Both ontological positions present an incomplete and partial view of society in that they attend to only one stratum of reality.

The third form of conflation criticised by Archer is central conflation. A singularly influential example of this is offered by Giddens's structuration theory (Giddens, 1994). This form of conflation differs from the first two in that it gives equal weight to structure and agency. According to Giddens, the two are mutually constituted, that is they form two elements of one whole (1994). For realist analytical dualism, however, agents and structures, or people and parts, are radically different entities possessing different emergent properties (Bhaskar, 1989; Archer, 1995). A further area of disagreement concerns the concept of temporality. For structuration theorists, structural properties become real when, and only when, instantiated by the activities of current actors. For realists, structures both precede human activities and are the emergent outcome of activity. A third dispute concerns the concept-dependent nature of social reality, that is the idea that social structures do not exist independently of agents' ideas about them. Giddens argues that 'Structure has no existence independent of the knowledge that agents have about what they do in their day-to-day activity' (Giddens, 1994: 87–8).

Bhaskar counters this assertion by arguing that the existence of social structures may, in reality, depend on their inappropriate conceptualisation: that there may be a causal relationship between the mistaken beliefs of agents and the continuance of social structures (Bhaskar, 1979 quoted in Archer, 1995).

The superiority of realism's explanatory power is illustrated by a comparison between structuration theory and realism. Taking the third point of dispute first, the use of structuration theory to explain the contradictory and fragmented nature of HRM would be highly problematic. To argue that the various ideas and practices that constitute HRM are concept-dependent would entail either a privileging of certain concepts over others (and therefore admitting that some conceptualisations are inappropriate) or an acceptance of relativism.

Let us take, as an illustrative example, the practice whereby firms subcontract aspects of business to individuals operating on a self-employed basis. For management theorists such as Handy (1994) this practice is conceptualised as 'portfolio' working, and is infused with notions of personal choice, freedom and independence (Bradley *et al.*, 2000). For others, however, self-employed subcontactors are, in reality, a particularly exploited group of wage labourers (Bradley *et al.*, 2000; Rainbird, 1991). If we are to accept that objects of inquiry really are concept-dependent, some means of adjudicating between these various conceptualisations is necessary. Either that or we agree that the nature of the practice is dependent on individual interpretations. In contrast, the stratified and dualistic realist approach provides a means of separating out the concrete practices of various forms of numerical flexibility and the causal mechanisms that engender them, and the various idealistic interpretations put forward to explain the practice.

With respect to the first and second points, the notions of instantiation and duality assume that structure and agency exist co-terminously. Such an assumption renders it impossible to draw out the separate effects of structural and agential generative mechanisms over time. The result is an elision of the paradoxical ideas and practices of HRM. A further practice relating to the notion of numerical flexibility, temporary short-term employment contracts, provides us with illustration of this point. The notion of instantiation suggests that this practice as a feature of the occupational structure is instantiated each time an employer hires a casual or temporary worker, and each time an individual engages in this type of employment. To understand and explain the phenomena of numerical flexibility, however, we need to identify the causal mechanisms that engendered its emergence. This would involve exploration of the economic circumstances and policies of the 1980s that resulted in a pool of numerically flexible workers willing to accept such contracts. It would also involve identification of the primary agency of those promoting numerical flexibility, in the past and present, as both an idea and a practice. Finally, the secondary agency of those individuals who find themselves caught up in an economic system of which numerical flexibility is a component would require explication. Such an analysis facilitates an explanation that does not conflate or ignore the paradoxical aspects of numerical flexibility. For example, the distinction between numerical flexibility as a normative model (Atkinson, 1984; Atkinson and Meager, 1986) and numerical flexibility as an intensification of capitalist exploitation (Pollert, 1991).

The dualistic approach, which gives equal weight to the separate strata of structure and agency, gives prominence to notions of emergence, interplay and temporality. Although the emergent properties of structures and cultures do not determine agency, they constrain or enable the possibilities open to agents. Archer (1995) gives, as an example, the forms of conversation possible in a primitive society. Structures in existence at any one point in time are emergent, necessarily, from the agency of past generations of actors, who were themselves constrained and/or enabled by prior structures. Agency cannot construct new structures autonomously of those that exist already, it can only transform or reproduce existing structures and cultures. It is via interplay between structural and/or cultural emergent properties and people's emergent properties at any one time that social forms are transformed or reproduced. Archer terms these processes of transformation and reproduction morphogenesis and morphostasis.

The point of contact between structure and agency is the location or domain in which morphogenesis or morphostasis takes place. Bhaskar terms this the mediating system, which consists of positions (filled by individuals) and practices (activities). Archer calls this mediating system the position practice system: where position refers not only to roles occupied by individuals, but also the situations and contexts in which they find themselves.

We have now reached a point where we can say something about how a realist mophogenetic approach to HRM might be applied in practice. Such an approach would take ontological stratification as its starting point. It would then need to abstract the relevant generative mechanisms on each stratum, and the structural, cultural and people's emergent properties. It is these properties belonging to various strata that allow for separation and differentiation. Emergence occurs when properties of one stratum engender, through interaction with other properties, properties on a different stratum. In addition, following completion of emergence, the properties that distinguish various strata have relative autonomy from one another and possess their own causal powers (Archer, 1995: 14). A morphogenetic approach also requires a demonstration of how interplay or mediation between structure and agency leads to morphogenesis or morphostatis. Finally, a truly morphogenetic theory of HRM would need to adopt a historical approach.

Chemical UK: morphogenesis and flexibility

Orthodox accounts of flexibility contain strong similarities to the downward conflation identified by Archer. Flexibility is seen to have grown in response to a variety of factors. Examples include the strength of the Japanese economy and the corresponding need to import Japanese methods such as core and peripheral employment practices and just-in-time production methods. Another example concerns the extent to which changes in consumer demand patterns have led to flexible production methods that enable an effortless shift between products, or which can accommodate flexible consumer demand in service industries. In addition, technological development has resulted in new machinery that has transformed the nature of work from Fordism to post-Fordism (Piore and Sabel, 1984). Flexibility is portrayed accordingly as a systemic adaptation to developing economic and technological conditions. Flexible work practices are an impersonal and automatic response by sections of the economy to trends in capitalism. The inadequacies of this approach are that it fails to account for the contradictions between the rhetoric of flexibility and its exercise in practice. It also ignores the role played by human agency in the emergence of flexibility, both as an idea and in practice (for example, the extent to which the ideas surrounding flexibility are shaped by academic discourse and the variety of ways in which corporate agents may implement these ideas).

If we view flexibility in terms of ontological stratification we can overcome these problems and provide a more satisfactory account. Explanation of the ideas surrounding the concept would be conducted through an investigation of their emergence from the socio-political system. Such an investigation would take as its foci such states of affairs as 'Thatcherite anti-collectivism', deregulation of the employment relationship and, more controversially perhaps, management education. The emergent properties of the socio-political system would then be explained by generative mechanisms pertaining to relations of production which are themselves emergent from the state of productive forces.

Examples would include changes in labour supply, the effects of labour market conditions and new technologies (Blyton and Morris, 1992) conceived as emergent from intensified competition, recessions and volatile product markets. The identification and isolation of structural, cultural and agential mechanisms would allow for a deeper understanding of the contradictions that lie at the heart of the concept of flexibility.

To illustrate how this investigation might be conducted in practice we explore the introduction of functional flexibility as part of a general HR strategy at Chemicals UK (Thursfield, 2000). During the 1980s, a number of emergent properties at the level of productive forces, and the firm's relation to productive forces, led to the conditions from which flexibility emerged. These were an increase in competition from developing countries, the early 1980s recession and Chemicals UK's position in the production chain.[1] The outcome of these emergent properties of both capitalism and Chemicals UK's position in relation to capitalist competition was a sharp decline in the firm's profits: a fall of 59 per cent between 1994 and 1995. Efforts to reverse this decline included the introduction of a HR strategy of which flexibility was the cornerstone.

Management at Chemicals UK attempted to impose three types of functional flexibility. First, functional flexibility between production workers through what the firm termed 'empowered team working'. Second, functional flexibility between production and maintenance workers whereby production workers carried out minor maintenance tasks on the plant. Third, flexibility between different production plants whereby workers on one plant could cover for absent employees on a different plant. We shall demonstrate that the types of flexibility described above have been mediated by the agency of employees. The forms of flexibility in operation at Chemicals UK are the result of interaction between structural, cultural and people's emergent properties.

Flexibility as a structural emergent property

We begin our task with an analysis of flexibility as a structural emergent property (SEP) of the organisation of production at Chemicals UK. Archer tells us that SEPs are an outcome of material resources, either physical or human. SEPs are not aggregate institutional patterns, social organisations or socio-economic groupings. Such phenomena are heterogeneous categories of events, which may or may not be imposed by researchers, and which are characterised by contingent regularities. SEPs are, in contrast, the result of natural and necessary internal relations. Flexibility as an SEP could not be what it is without its constituent elements and the relations between those elements. Emergent properties are, furthermore, more than a combination of particular elements, rather they have the generative power to modify those elements. This, Archer argues, sets emergence apart from aggregation. For example, the demographic structure is not only an aggregate of people, but can modify the power of people to change it by defining the population of child-bearing age (Archer, 1995).

Orthodox accounts of the development of HRM are an example of seemingly regular contingent relations (e.g. Budhwar, 2000). The various ideas and practices that constitute HRM do not depend on each other for existence and meaning. Changes at the strata of the economic base and relations of production are related contingently to the shifts in the employment relationship associated with HRM. Similarly, orthodox accounts of flexibility are often guilty of confusing contingency for necessity. Numerical flexibility is contingent on changing patterns of consumer demand rather than a natural and necessary outcome. Similarly, the flexible organisation of work is contingent on the type and organisation of technology rather than a natural and necessary outcome. Archer points out that this is not to argue that contingent relations cannot influence each other; rather it is to argue that an understanding of emergence requires the identification of natural and necessary internal relations.

What, then, are the natural and necessary relations between the elements constituting flexibility at Chemicals UK? First is the working time and shift pattern arrangement. This pattern ensures that the plant is in continual operation and that overtime is unnecessary. The workforce is divided into four shift groups and employees work a twelve-hour shift pattern, with four days 'on' and four days 'off'. This pattern is broken by three eighteen-day holiday periods. The second constitutive element is 'empowered team working'. Empowered teams consist of four men and each team is responsible for one particular production plant. Membership of each team is constant and teams have no supervisor. Rather, a senior manager provides line management and support. The benefits of team working to employees are, supposedly, to give them greater control and discretion over their work and thus enhance job satisfaction. The introduction of team working in the early to mid-1990s coincided with a fall in the number of employees, from around 1,100 to 750, a fall made possible by the introduction of the twelve-hour shift pattern and empowered team working.

The third element of flexibility at Chemicals UK is the multi-skill training given to all new and existing employees. This training has two aspects. First process production workers are trained, within the team, to perform all tasks on a plant. This is in contrast to the days before teamwork where each operative had his/her own job to perform and did not stray beyond this. The second aspect of multi-skill training concerns process operatives learning basic craft maintenance skills in order that minor problems on the plant can be dealt with quickly. Managers argue that interruptions in production, caused by minor breakdowns and the unavailability of a craft maintenance technician, are unnecessarily costly.

An initial glance at the above elements suggests that the relations between them, and between elements and flexibility, are merely contingent. On closer inspection, however, we want to say that natural and necessary relations become identifiable. First, the rigidity of working time arrangements and the eradication of overtime render the covering of absenteeism imperative. Under the old, pre-1994, individuated organisation of work, absent employees could not be covered, leading to possible interruptions in production. The introduction of empowered team working ensures that team members can cover any absenteeism. It also ensures that team members will bring pressure to bear on anyone with a poor attendance record. Second, the teamwork system requires that team membership remains constant. This constancy is made possible by the working time arrangements that ensure that teams are kept together over a lengthy period.

There is a point to be made, too, concerning relations between team working and multi-skill training. For without training, the interchangeability of people and tasks would not be possible (this is especially true of a hazardous environment such as a chemical plant). Multi-skill training ensures, also, that following the shift change-over (where there is a complete replacement of one group of personnel for another), there will be employees available with the skills to deal with an ongoing situation or problem. In terms of the natural and necessary relations between flexibility and its constituent elements, the form of flexibility in operation would not be possible without the precise mix of constituent elements, and their internal relations.

If flexibility is an SEP of production at Chemicals UK, it must possess the power to modify the constituents of which it comprises, whether activated or not. A number of modifications are discernible, even though the system has been in place for only six years. So, for example, the occurrence of functional flexibility within the team, that of task rotation between members, is variable. Within some teams task rotation is the norm whilst others have settled into a pattern of individuals taking major responsibility for particular tasks. Discretion within the team has been used to keep things much as they were prior to the introduction of flexibility. Consequently, the extent of multi-skill training taking place within the team is limited and basic. This is particularly true of flexibility between craft maintenance workers and between process and maintenance workers. Evidence of this kind offers further support to those authors mentioned earlier who argue that the general incidence of flexibility in practice is minimal (e.g. Casey, 1991; Elger, 1991).

Flexibility as a cultural emergent property

Our second task is to explore the nature of flexibility as a cultural emergent property (CEP). CEPs belong to the strata of ideas, theories and beliefs, and are independent of cultural agents (people). Relations between cultural agents are causal and may be contingent. So, for example, X may or may not persuade Y of the truth of X's beliefs, or X may or may not succeed in manipulating Y. However, relations constitutive of CEPs are logical, natural and necessary. CEPs are objective and are the product of previous generations of thinkers and the causal relations pertaining to those thinkers. Following their emergence, CEPs have a life of their own in that they exist regardless of whether current agents comprehend them or not.

Flexibility as a CEP at Chemicals UK comprises three distinct elements, all of which are associated with the soft HRM model (Blyton and Morris, 1992; Legge, 1995). The first is what Legge terms development humanism and is embedded in human capital theory. It is the notion, articulated by the Human Resource Manager and a Production Manager, that employees benefit from having their capabilities developed through flexible working. Not only do they increase their skills, they are more fulfilled and satisfied with their work. Thus:

> We are keen to promote flexibility at Chemicals UK. It is better for us and for them. If people are learning more skills and using them, they will get more job satisfaction and fulfilment.
>
> (Human Resource Manager)

> I think process operatives enjoy their work more if they are given the opportunity to do a variety of jobs. It makes things more interesting.
>
> (Production Manager)

The second element, related to the first, is a belief in the need for an adaptable and responsive workforce, and the ability of humans to provide this. Changes in the economic environment in which Chemicals UK operate have resulted not only in a need for task flexibility, but also a flexibility of attitude. That is, a willingness to accept changes in the organisation of work as serving the interests of the firm and its employees. In the opinion of the Senior Production Manager:

> In the present climate people have to be prepared to adopt flexible working. Having demarcation lines is no longer an option. It's not good for the company if people will only carry out a narrow range of tasks. They must be willing to learn and be flexible in their approach. Our better operatives understand this, but some are stuck in the past and we need to change that.
>
> (Senior Production Manager)

The third element concerns a belief in the harmonisation of employment relations, and is evidenced by the delayering of the organisation. In particular, the conflation of supervisor and process operative grades to create three process operative levels. These elements are integral to the ideas surrounding functional flexibility that characterise the organisational culture at Chemicals UK. Although these ideas are the product of previous thinkers, for example academics, new senior managers, whose backgrounds are, primarily, in business education rather than chemistry, introduced them to the firm in the early 1990s. An example of this phenomenon is the Senior Production Manager referred to above. This manager recently completed an MBA and displayed an eagerness to put to use his new found expertise in flexibility:

> I actually wrote my MBA thesis on the introduction of flexibility into a chemical company such as this. It was very useful and I developed some good ideas for the future.
>
> (Senior Production Manager)

Once introduced, however, the theory of functional flexibility became an objective emergent property of the organisation's culture. So although, as we shall demonstrate below, the form of flexibility realised at Chemicals UK is clearly modified by the agency of employees, the concept has gained some currency in the organisation. Posters extolling the virtues of flexible working are found in social areas of the plant and articles on flexibility appear regularly in the firm's staff newsletter. Whilst shopfloor workers may complain that certain aspects of flexibility are unworkable, and resist engaging in certain practices, there is a broad, if weak, acceptance of the idea:

> We all have to be flexible now, learn to do each other's jobs and swap around.
>
> (Process Operative)

> Flexibility is the big thing nowadays.
>
> (Process Operative)

Flexibility and the emergent properties of people

As yet we have said little about the role of people in the introduction and development of flexibility at Chemicals UK, an omission that requires rectification. As Archer explains: 'the exercise of socio-cultural powers is dependent *inter alia* upon their reception and realisation by people: their effect is not direct but mediated, for there are no other ways in which it could be exercised' (Archer, 1995: 195). She goes on to say that: 'all structural influences (i.e. the generative powers of SEPs and CEPs) are mediated to people shaping the situations in which they find themselves' (1995: 196).

The generative powers of structures in which people find themselves depend, for their reproduction or transformation, on the powers of people who act as mediators. Like structures and cultures, people are stratified, with the different strata of persons, agents and actors pertaining to different functions. The person corresponds with the individual human being. Agency refers to the various collectivities to which individual human beings belong. The actor refers to the social self of an individual that emerges from the person's social interaction as an agent. Thus, agency is emergent from persons, for example as persons reposition themselves between different collectivities. This is termed by Archer the double morphogenesis. Social actors are emergent from agents through a process whereby social identities are shaped by agential collectivities. Actors may, for example, obtain their social identity from a role that they invest in and come to personify (Archer, 1995). Archer defines this as the triple morphogenesis.

To fully appreciate the morphogenesis of agency it is necessary to take a closer look at the agential stratum. Agents are members of collectivities who share the same life chances and interests. Collectivities are not made up of statistical artefacts, they are characterised by internal and necessary relations. Membership of a particular collectivity depends, for example, on the person finding him or herself (through birth or other means) in a position where he or she shares the same life chances as other members of the group. Archer also distinguishes between primary and corporate agency. Beginning with primary agency, each person has an agential effect on the environment of which they are a part by virtue of their existence. They may not be involved in active attempts to reproduce or transform that situation, but they have effects nonetheless. As Archer states; 'no being without doing, no doing without consequences' (Archer, 1995: 259). Thus, whilst agents may not be overtly involved in the transformation or reproduction of systemic organisation, we cannot say that they have no effect on it; the effects are, however, unarticulated, uncoordinated and unstated in aim.

In contrast to primary agency, corporate agency is characterised by causal powers that are overt and clearly stated: for example, the articulation of shared interests, organising for collective action and the exercising of corporate influence over decision making. The actions and interactions of corporate agents are calculated and represent more than the sum of particular individuals' interests. Corporate agency is active rather than passive. It is conducted in relation to reasons, and shapes the context in which all actors act. Primary agency takes place within this environmental context and, by responding to corporate agency, transforms or reproduces that environment.

To understand how the emergent structural and cultural properties of flexibility at Chemicals UK are transformed and/or reproduced we begin by identifying the corporate and primary agents. At Chemicals UK, corporate agency in relation to flexibility consists of senior line managers, in particular operational managers rather than HR managers. Legge (1995) suggests a number of reasons why line managers have a vested interest in the introduction of HR initiatives such as flexibility. Examples are a desire to enhance career prospects and a need for line managers to demonstrate a proactive approach rather than a reactive response to environmental conditions (Legge, 1995). Both the above reasons are detectable in the actions of corporate agents at Chemicals UK. The shared interests of this group relate to their position on the front line of the company's attempts to increase profitability. Over the past ten years profits at Chemicals UK have suffered a sharp decrease and the firm is under constant threat of closure. In addition, individual plants are also threatened if productivity continues to decline. Pressure from city shareholders led to the replacement of one set of managers with another, and these managers are charged with the task of turning the company around. Whilst operations managers have backgrounds in chemical engineering, a number have a more recent history of business education, and it is this group that constitute corporate agents. Like the examples given by Legge, this group of managers are keen to show that they are proactive in dealing with the fall in profitability. One aspect of their joint generative powers is to influence decision making in the organisation, and the means of dealing with the situation in which they find themselves and the company is through the introduction of functional flexibility.

Primary agency at Chemicals UK concerns the collectivity of process workers and craft maintenance technicians. The shared interests that bind this group relate to the firm's opportunities for cutting staffing levels and intensifying the pace of work provided by the working time arrangements and teamwork now in operation. The total number of employees could, for example, be reduced even further if teams consisted of multi-skilled individuals capable of process and maintenance work. Such a development would also cut out any remaining slack in the system and thus intensify the pace of work. The response of this group is not, however, articulated resistance. The economic climate and fears over job losses render such an option difficult. The voice of the union is muted and union officials, in fact, signed the flexibility agreement ten years prior to this research. The response of individual actors to certain forms of flexibility at chemicals UK has been simple non-compliance. Process operatives rarely perform minor maintenance work and there is no flexibility between individual plants. Operatives argue that they are not competent to carry out maintenance work in such a dangerous environment and that they lack the knowledge to shift between plants. Hence:

> I'm a process operative not a fitter. I'm not going to start breaking into them pipes with the stuff we make here – it's too dangerous. Just because I've had a few days training in fitting doesn't mean I would know what to do if anything went wrong. I wouldn't know how to put it right if I made a mistake.
>
> (Process Operative)

> It takes a long time to get to know a plant. You can't let someone loose on a job until he's got that knowledge of the plant. It's not safe.
>
> (Process Operative)

And from the Shift Production Manager:

> We still do not get flexibility between plants. You can have a plant that is seriously understaffed and another that is fully staffed, but there is no flexibility between them.
>
> (Shift Production Manager)

A further unintended consequence of the teamwork system has been the emergence of a strong sense of solidarity amongst team members. An effect of this solidarity appears to have been to reinforce the reluctance of process operatives to move between individual plants. A number opine that the team is the basic work unit and that employees should not be required to operate outside their own group. Managers are attempting to overcome this reluctance by promoting the idea of adaptability discussed earlier, for example through items in the newsletter. They are also attempting to break down the sense of team solidarity through the introduction of peer group appraisals.

Conclusion

The contribution of this chapter has been to demonstrate how human resource management is most gainfully understood and described from a stratified-realist ontology. We have argued that the ideas and practices of HRM are fragmented and contradictory, and, therefore, that HRM should not be regarded as a unitary concept. Rather, it is best conceived as a disparate set of practices and ideas that exist on vertical social strata. We have also argued that these practices and ideas are the emergent properties of vertical generative mechanisms operating on each stratum. The lower level social strata of productive forces and relations to productive forces are inclusive of the socio-political system that includes HRM practices. The socio-political system is, in turn, inclusive of the ideas surrounding HRM, although the latter can alter the former over time through morphogenesis.

A second contribution has been to demonstrate how the development of HRM is emergent from causal processes operating at the levels of structure, culture and agency. We have argued that the orthodox approach tends towards downward conflation, the elision of contradictory theories and practices, and a neglect of the role of agency in the introduction and development of HR practice. To support our argument we have employed empirical evidence of the introduction of flexibility in one organisation.

The hybrid form of functional flexibility found at Chemicals UK is emergent from relations between generative mechanisms at the level of structural, cultural and people's emergent properties. At the level of structure the shift system, empowered team working and multi-skill training interact to generate a particular form of flexibility. These structural properties are also an outcome of the ideas surrounding flexibility that were introduced to the firm by past and current senior managers. The nature of flexibility in practice is mediated by the position-practice system through the agency of corporate and primary agents. Corporate agents, in the form of operational managers, promote flexibility in order to advance their collective interests. Primary agents, whilst not articulating clear aims, have, nonetheless, had a clear impact on the emergent form of flexibility at Chemicals UK. Flexibility between team members is now generally accepted in practice and as an idea (despite concerns about cuts in the numbers of employees and the subsequent intensification of work since the introduction of team working). Flexibility between process and maintenance employees and between plants is, in contrast, far from established. It is evident that, at this early stage in the cycle, the issue of whether flexibility at Chemicals UK will be subject to morphogenesis or morphostasis is uncertain.

Note

1 Chemicals UK manufactures intermediate goods that form the raw materials of other companies' production processes; for example, optical brightening agents that are used in soap powders and chemical dyes used in ink. Because of this position they can be unaware of changes in the demand for their product, and senior managers argue that the firm needs to respond more quickly to unexpected changes in the product market.

References

Archer, M. (1995) *Realist Social Theory: The Morphogenetic Approach*, Cambridge: Cambridge University Press.

Atkinson, J. (1984) 'Manpower strategies for the flexible organisation', *Personnel Management*, August: 28–31.

Atkinson, J. and Meager, N. (1986) *Changing Work Patterns: How Firms Achieve Flexibility to Meet New Needs*, London: NEDO.

Bhaskar, R. (1979) *The Possibility of Naturalism*, Hemel Hempstead: Harvester.

Bhaskar, R. (1989) *Reclaiming Reality*, London: Verso.

—— (1998) 'Societies', in M. Archer, R. Bhaskar, A. Collier, T. Lawson and A. Norrie (eds), *Critical Realism: Essential Readings*, London: Routledge.

Blyton, P. and Morris, J. (1992) 'HRM and the limits of flexibility', in P. Blyton and P. Turnbull (eds), *Reassessing Human Resource Management*, London: Sage.

Blyton, P. and Turnbull, P. (eds) (1992) *Reassessing Human Resource Management*, London: Sage.

Bradley, H., Erickson, M., Stephenson, C. and Williams, S. (2000) *Myths at Work*, Cambridge: Polity.

Bratton, J. and Gold, J. (1999) *Human Resource Management: Theory and Practice*, Basingstoke: Macmillan.

Budhwar, P.S. (2000) 'Evaluating levels of strategic integration and development in human resource management in the UK', *Personnel Review*, 29 (2): 141–61.

Casey, B. (1991) 'Survey trends in "non-standard employment"', in A. Pollert (ed.), *Farewell to Flexibility*, Oxford: Blackwell.

Collier, A. (1994) *Critical Realism: An Introduction to Roy Bhaskar's Philosophy*, London: Verso.

—— (1998) 'Stratified explanation and Marx's conception of history', in M. Archer, R. Bhaskar, A. Collier, T. Lawson and A. Norrie (eds), *Critical Realism: Essential Readings*, London: Routledge.

Elger, T. (1991) 'Task flexibility and the intensification of labour in UK manufacturing in the 1980s', in A. Pollert (ed.), *Farewell to Flexibility*, Oxford: Blackwell.

Foot, M. and Hook, C. (1999) *Introducing Human Resource Management*, Harlow: Longman.

Giddens, A. (1994) 'Elements of the theory of structuration', in *The Polity Reader in Social Theory*, Cambridge: Polity.

Gramsci, A. (1971) *Selections from the Prison Notebooks*, ed. and trans. Q. Hoare and G. Nowell-Smith, London: Lawrence and Wishart.

Hamblett, J., Holden, R. and Thursfield, D. (2002) 'The tools of freedom and the sources of indignity', in J. McGoldrick, J. Stewart and S. Watson (eds), *Understanding Human Resource Development: A Research Based Approach*, London: Routledge.

Handy, C. (1994) *The Empty Raincoat: Making Sense of the Future*, London: Hutchinson.

Herzberg, F. (1968) *Work and the Nature of Man*, London: Staples Press.

Keenoy, T. and Anthony, P. (1992) 'HRM: metaphor, meaning and morality', in P. Blyton and P. Turnbull (eds), *Reassessing Human Resource Management*, London: Sage.

Keat, R. and Urry, J. (1982) *Socal Theory as Science*, London: Routledge and Kegan Paul.

Legge, K. (1995) 'HRM: rhetoric, reality and hidden agendas', in J. Storey (ed.), *Human Resource Management: A Critical Text*, London: International Thompson Business Press.

Marx, K. (1967) 'Letter to P.V. Annenkov', in D. Caute (ed.), *Essential Writings of Marx*, New York: Macmillan.

Maslow, A.H. (1954) *Motivation and Personality*, New York: Harper and Row.

Noon, M. (1992) 'HRM: a map, model or theory?', in P. Blyton and P. Turnbull (eds), *Reassessing Human Resource Management*, London: Sage.

Piore, M. and Sabel, C. (1984) *The Second Industrial Divide: Possibilities for Prosperity*, New York: Basic Books.

Pollert, A. (ed.) (1991) *Farewell to Flexibility*, Oxford: Blackwell.

Purcell, J. (1995) 'Corporate strategy and its link with human resource management strategy', in J. Storey (ed), *Human Resource Management: A Critical Text*, London: International Thompson Business Press.

Rainbird, H. (1991) 'The self-employed: small entrepreneurs or disguised wage labourers', in A. Pollert (ed.), *Farewell to Flexibility*, Oxford: Blackwell.

Sayer, A. (1992) *Method in Science: A Realist Approach*, London: Routledge.

Schultz, T.W. (1961) 'Investment in human capital', *American Economic Review*, 51: 2: 1–17

Sparrow, P. and Hiltrop, J.M. (1994) *European Human Resource Management in Transition*, London: Prentice-Hall.

Sparrow, P. and Pettigrew, A. (1988) 'How Halfords put HRM into top gear', *Personnel Management*, 20 (6): 30–4.

Storey, J. (ed.) (1995) *Human Resource Management: A Critical Text*, London: International Thompson Business Press.

Thursfield, D. (2000) *Post-Fordism and Skill: Theories and Perceptions*, Aldershot: Ashgate.

Part II

Methodology

Critique and development

Critical realism has a good deal to say about methodology, and this is an area of academic work in which realism is beginning to make a considerable impact. Potentially, as Andrew Sayer pointed out in the first edition of his path-breaking book on methodology twenty years ago (Sayer, 1984), realism can and should revolutionise practice in social science.

Among other things, critical realism suggests that both qualitative and quantitative methods are relevant to the adequate explanation of events; and this alone is a considerable challenge to much orthodox thinking in methodology. The basic reason why realists think both quantitative and qualitative information will be required is not difficult to state in a summary way. The key point, as is also argued in the first chapter of this section, is that realist ideas about explanation hold that researchers should postulate generative mechanisms which cause events to occur. It follows that in human activities, and organisation and management studies (O&MS) is a good example of a discipline that deals with these, complete explanations will implicate both the context in which events take place and the meanings attributed to events by key actors and groups of actors. To simplify drastically, the context of events is often best accounted for by summarising or by description, and by establishing how widespread particular contextual features are. This points to the relevance of certain kinds of quantitative data, especially descriptive statistics. In addition, however, the meaning attributed to things by actors will also be important, especially at key junctures in causal processes, and this points to the need for interpretation and the collection of qualitative information. Critical realists' desire to reject empiricism does not mean they reject all forms of empirical data – although they accept, along with post-modernist and post-structuralist ideas, that it must be treated with caution.

Because both qualitative and quantitative information are likely to be important in explanations, realists reject the fashionable idea, widely believed by writers in the field of O&MS, that qualitative and quantitative approaches are necessarily incompatible. They reject as particularly wrong and pernicious the view that qualitative and quantitative data necessarily support alternative approaches to and views of the world. In the realist view it is possible and indeed necessary to produce theoretically based accounts of generative mechanisms that are true. In short, realists are seeking to rewrite the approach to methodology that, until recently, was becoming the orthodoxy in O&MS. Unpacking the implications of the idea that both qualitative and quantitative insights are relevant to effective research designs is a new and demanding agenda. But without this it is difficult to see how the realist goal of revealing the mechanisms causing events to occur will be realised. This goal is likely to demand a good deal of innovation in the methodology of O&MS, and it is no surprise to find realist writers exploring the implications of this agenda.

It is interesting to speculate why methodology has not been of more interest to social scientists before this, and this applies as much to realists as to others. For reasons that merit consideration as a research topic in their own right, methodology has been persistently devalued and neglected in many areas of social science in the latter half of the last century. The founding fathers of the first really viable approaches to social science, produced at the beginning of the last century, clearly regarded general methodology as being of supreme importance, as is indicated, for example, by the methodological essays of sociologists such as Durkheim or Weber and the innovative work of economists such as Veblen, Commons or Keynes. In the writings of these progenitors, moreover, it is clear that they were developing what we would recognise today as realist ideas. Although they differed somewhat in the level of generality at which they sought explanations, all had similar ideas about the nature of satisfactory explanations. Like contemporary realists, they suggested that the point of empirical investigations is to bring to light the causal mechanisms, which, when set out fully, account for events. True, there was not universal acceptance of this emerging realist view amongst all practitioners and in all fields of social science. There was a tendency for specialist areas of social science to develop specialist methods; and, in some areas, there was clearly the strong development of positivist approaches to method (in clinical psychology, for example) as well as, more rarely, strongly anti-positivist movements (in ethnomethodological studies, for instance). In these specialist areas either positivist or anti-positivist ideas tended to dominate the teaching of methodology.

Yet, if we put to one side the functionalist studies which predominated in North American O&MS, the methods in use in the mainstream of the field of O&MS in Europe, especially in the post-World War II period, were anything but methodologically positivist. In practice, in European O&MS, research seldom stuck with one type of research method, and often used a variety of data collection techniques in the context of the same research project, much as realists now advocate. The use of data in O&MS research was usually broad, drawing on history, as well as being frequently innovatory, including reference to and use of diverse empirical materials. Institutional writers, for example, ranged across historical studies, archive work and social surveys. Whilst some institutionalists used social surveys, they seldom relied on the data from them exclusively. Famously, the 'Columbia school', represented by the work of such luminaries as Peter Blau, Amatai Etzioni and Alvin Gouldner, pioneered the organisational case study and produced some of the most compelling accounts of organisations in the genre. More recently, labour process analysts have also used diverse kinds of data. Few of them eschewed historical data, and many also drew on archive materials as well as undertaking surveys and focused case study work. Case studies are, of course, inherently multi-method in their design. Case studies incorporate diverse kinds of data and combine them to show how complex generative processes work themselves out in particular situations. Also, it was O&MS that kept alive the tentative experiments involving research with active interventions aimed at changing organisations that had originated in the action research of the 1930s.

However, there was in actuality little attempt to systematise this varied research practice in O&MS or to develop methodological teaching based on it. Only a few writers had strong convictions about the importance of research methodology to developing knowledge in O&MS. However, the methodological challenge was not satisfactorily met. Indeed, so far as the teaching of research methodology was concerned, it tended to be provided by people who had a special interest in the technicalities of research, and who therefore tended to take strongly positivist or, more rarely, strongly anti-positivist positions. Indeed, one area that did tend to support the views of the recent radical critics of social science in O&MS, who took the view that the field was strongly dominated by positivism, was teaching in research methodology. In the area of methodology teaching, there was often some substance to the view that positivism was significant since the most developed accounts of research methodology involved the teaching of quantitative methods. These derived their claims to legitimacy directly or indirectly from ideas about experiments which are firmly rooted in positivist ideas.

The perceived domination of research methodology by positivists undoubtedly did give credence to the idea of the real importance of positivism in O&MS. So much so that when people sought to reject these methods to develop alternative approaches to developing knowledge, they tended to propose not just alternative notions to the positivist way of studying events, but methods that were, as far as possible, the diametric opposite of positivist ideas. Certainly, the kind of information sought in research and the sort of techniques of data collection used by qualitative researchers often involved the inversion of the criteria of relevance proposed by positivists. The qualitative methodologies that were developed involved a fundamentally different basic conception of the subject matter for research, and what its basic substance is, but in other ways, there were compelling similarities. While the methodological approach of qualitative research aims at recovering actors' meanings (which can only be recognised, understood and appreciated) and is, thereby, very different from that of positivism, qualitative research imported many of the formal attributes of its quantitative counterpart. For example, research must be scrupulously undertaken observing methodological rules and protocols of procedure similar to those laid down in manuals of positivist research. Also the researcher should beware of possible interactive effects between the investigator and the subjects of research similar to the 'experimenter effects' that threaten positivist research designs.

The end of this development was a situation where it was widely believed that qualitative and quantitative research procedures offered fundamentally different approaches to research, and the knowledge produced by them contributed to quite distinct and incompatible forms. The limitations of this 'alternative paradigm' conception of research and the role of methodology are considerable and need to be overcome. This view implies that there will always be competing accounts of things and events in the world and there is no possibility of developing more adequate knowledge from research projects, or combining different kinds of insights. Critical realists, however, do not accept this view of what research can achieve. As this section of the present volume suggests, critical realists are taking steps towards developing more inclusive research designs and refining those multi-method designs such as the case study that are already in use.

In the first chapter of this section, Stephen Ackroyd considers the development of social science and its relation to the philosophy of science initially from a historical point of view. He argues that the historical preoccupation of the philosophy with natural science was the source of considerable problems for social science in that there was a tendency to assume that social science must be made like natural science. Ackroyd argues that this was a substantial mistake, and that, actually, the development of workable social science depended on assimilation by social science of lessons from the powerful anti-positivist critique developed by humanist scholars in the late nineteenth and early twentieth centuries. In this view, the first viable social science was recognisably realist, based on a recognition of the capacity of people to construct their own social institutions, but was also theoretically structuralist. Structures are an emergent property of action, which, nonetheless, provide the context for further action. If this is correct, to claim, as some contemporary analysts do, that a focus on meaning is necessarily to reject structuralism (and to be post-structuralist) is highly questionable. Ackroyd goes on to argue that realist explanation necessarily invokes different kinds of data, and ends the chapter by elaborating the principles that underwrite realist research. At the end of the chapter, by way of conclusion, a set of general characteristics of realist-inspired research are set out.

There follow several chapters that argue for the limitations of the existing research methods in use in particular branches of O&MS, and how they can sensibly be changed and developed. All these chapters, in their different ways, argue for a broadening of the scope of the methods employed in the branches of O&MS with which they are concerned. If more adequate research is to be developed, these writers argue, then there must be a broadening of scope, sometimes in several directions simultaneously. In Chapter 7, the first in this series, John Mingers argues that the positivist assumptions unthinkingly brought to research practice in operational research have artificially limited success in this field. He argues that the quantitative methods in use in this field do not simply require supplementation, but the positivist framework that shapes research needs to be fundamentally recast. Illustrating his argument by research undertaken by leading researchers in the field of forecasting, Mingers develops a devastating critique of the limitations of the knowledge generated in this field. He argues that knowledge in this field is limited in the conclusions it can draw and these limitations follow from, among other things, the reliance on quantitative data and the failure to develop theory in appropriate ways. Mingers suggests that researchers could transform knowledge in the field by drawing on different kinds of data. He recommends the analytical framework suggested by the sociologist Jürgen Habermas, and argues for the addition of data relating to the choices between actors, which, potentially, can illuminate the characteristic choices made by actors and lead to more accurate and reliable forecasts.

There follow two chapters that argue for refining the research methods in use in the area of marketing within O&MS. In Chapter 8, Debbie Harrison and Geoff Easton suggest some refinements to the case study methods. Case studies, of course, have been used in marketing research perhaps more effectively than in any other area in the field of O&MS. In this area more than some others, the importance of case studies has been more adequately realised than elsewhere, where the procedure has been assessed by reference to positivist assumptions. A key realisation with this research design is of course that if the selection of the case itself, and the decisions about the kinds of data selected for consideration within the case, are informed by theory, it is possible to make generalisations based on findings. This overcomes what is taken to be a key limitation of case study designs, that they do not allow generalisations to be made. However, the selection of cases and data on the basis of theoretical relevance gets around this limitation. There is also, of course, the possibility of comparing similar cases, again selected on the basis of theoretical relevance. This will contribute some understanding of the role that differences in the configuration of cases make to the outcome of common causal processes. Harrison and Easton's chapter refines the logic of case study design by arguing that if investigators divide up (or, to use their term, periodise) the temporal dimension in which the cases are located, more precise comparisons can be made using similar cases than would otherwise be possible. The device of periodisation is, of course, a conceptual matter; as the basic idea is not to treat time as measured time periods, but to consider it as a process in which related events follow each other in logical sequence. The suggestion of Harrison and Easton is, therefore, another proposal to increase the theoretical basis of research design.

Chapter 9, by Alex Faria, is a contribution which also suggests some theoretically relevant amendments to a research focus popular in marketing. Faria reports on some of his research in which he has undertaken network analysis. Network analysis is becoming increasingly popular in diverse fields within O&MS, so this argument is more generally relevant than might be initially thought. Faria contributes an essay which suggests that assumptions commonly brought to research into networks, in particular that they do not centrally involve power or coercive relations of any kind, may have systematically coloured the findings of research in this field. The idea that networks are inherently co-operative derives from the perception that they are unlike other forms of relationship operative in the economy. On the one side we have hierarchies, whose organising principle is authority, and on the other we have markets, where relationships are backed by contracts and ultimately by the sanction of courts of law. By contrast with both of these, networks seem voluntary, based on trust and free from compulsion. Faria argues that this conception of networks does not bear either theoretical or close empirical scrutiny. In realist understanding, networks are emergent phenomena, and while we may expect the possibility that these are quite different from existing patterns of relationships, it is necessary for methods of investigation to be sufficiently sensitive to clarify their actual characteristics. Institutional theory, for example, suggests that there are likely to be considerable forces inducing similarity in relationships. From the findings of his comparative research into industrial networks in Britain and Brazil, Faria shows that considerations of power, often masked by the failure of actors to acknowledge their existence, are in fact relevant to understanding the operation and functioning of these structures, when it is commonly assumed that they are not.

In Chapter 10, the last essay of this section, by Clive Lawson, the author deals with some similar theoretical and methodological issues in the field of economics. Lawson argues that, if it is possible to conceive of organisations as bundles of competences as some institutional economists do, then the same idea can be attributed to larger economic entities such as industries and regions. This insight also fits with the realist conviction that there are emergent properties of institutions. It is argued by Lawson that, as economists develop an interest in understanding the emergent properties of firms, industries and regions, research techniques will have to be developed that are sensitive enough to bring their properties to light and to get an accurate picture of them. In some ways the points made by Lawson are similar to Faria's; and, in this chapter too, we have an argument that suggests that methods that are appropriate to the situation under investigation must be developed. But, unlike Faria's argument, Lawson's account is not about what has actually been found and what is now known about firms and their relationship to industries and regions. Unlike Faria, Lawson is not arguing what research suggests after the investigation of firms and groups. His point is that the choice of quantitative methods is not likely to be helpful in studying the phenomena he wishes to study, given what competence theory, informed by critical realism, suggests about them. In Lawson's view case studies and qualitative investigations using participation are what are required. Hence Lawson, like Mingers, also produces an argument in favour of the use of qualitative methods in a field traditionally dominated by the exclusive use of quantitative methods and overly influenced by positivist philosophy.

In conclusion, the points these critical realist authors make about research are not simply that research should not rely exclusively on single sources of data or privilege particular research designs. Consistent themes are that theory is relevant to research, and it is this that directs the researcher's attention away from too much reliance on traditional kinds of data. There is considerable scope for creativity in seeking out and utilising different kinds of data. In this judgement lies the realisation that the way theory relates to data is not prescriptive, and the interpretation and use of data certainly cannot be reduced to a set of rules about how to proceed. The relationship between data and what it describes is problematic and unpredictable in a way that existing research paradigms fail to acknowledge. The process of research both involves the exercise of more discretion than is often thought to be required and also necessarily implicates theoretical ideas as a basis for ways to think about what is being investigated and found. Existing approaches to research, whether qualitative or quantitative, tend to put methods and theory into separate, watertight compartments; but realist research suggests this is neither necessary nor desirable.

Reference

Sayer, A. (1984) Method in Social Science: A Realist Approach, London: Hutchinson.

6 Methodology for management and organisation studies

Some implications of critical realism

Stephen Ackroyd

Consideration of research methodology is often shaped by the assumption that particular approaches to research are superior and ought to be followed invariably. In one form, this view is that methods of investigation ought to be scientific; in another form, that studies of human beings must necessarily employ only qualitative techniques that are true to the nature of their subjects. Accordingly, many textbooks on method can be classified into those which recommend quantitative techniques exclusively, and are preoccupied with measurement (Marsh, 1988; Moser and Kalton, 1984), and those which propose qualitative techniques, and are preoccupied by meaning (Denzin and Lincoln, 1994; Silverman, 2000). In this chapter, the idea that there are some inherently superior methods of study which, if competently utilised, can secure superior knowledge, is rejected. Instead it is argued that both quantitative and qualitative techniques are valuable.

Although realists are often found arguing against particular methods for certain purposes (see, for example, the contribution of Mingers to this volume) and in favour of particular applications for others (as in Harrison and Easton's and Delbridge's contributions), in general, for reasons that will be discussed, realism licenses a wide variety of research procedures. Realist authors can be found advocating both qualitative (Miles and Huberman, 1994) and quantitative (Byrne, 2002) methods. It will be argued here that realism does not support one or other of these particular kinds of research technique exclusively, but allows researchers to be selective in their choice of investigatory tools. Insightful empirical research is a creative activity in which valuable insights cannot be produced by the routine use of particular research techniques. There are some methods textbooks these days that see no distinction of principle between qualitative and quantitative methods, but, with some honourable exceptions (Bryman, 1988; May, 1997), few are able to provide a rationale for this that is convincing. It will be argued that critical realism provides a strong and effective defence of this kind of methodological pluralism.

It is, certainly, difficult to identify common features in research (other than of a very general nature) between subjects within the area of the natural sciences (such as physics and biochemistry or engineering), not to mention between these and the various branches of social study (such as economics, psychology and management studies). Despite this, much effort has been expended on trying to stipulate which research practices are most valid in an unqualified way. For British and American scholars, the debate is often cast in terms of distinguishing which branches of study can be truly scientific, and hence are to be preferred, from those that cannot be. Alternatively, there is the argument that studies of human behaviour must consider the self-reflective and evaluative capacities of human subjects. Such arguments entail different kinds of methodological imperialism both share the conviction that particular methods should be applied everywhere.

Cultural biases in the definition of science

It is helpful to be aware that there is as much cultural bias in thinking about methodology as there is in other areas of thought. For example, a position which suggests that only certain research techniques and procedures are properly scientific is, in large part, a culturally specific view and a product of particular assumptions. In German-speaking areas of Europe, the proliferation of higher education in universities and the systematisation of knowledge predated the rise of natural science. Partly for this reason, the term for learning or knowledge in German, *wissenschaft*, means all learning or knowledge generally, and takes in most branches of disciplined enquiry. When suitably qualified, *wissenschaft* can be applied to most branches of human enquiry. What English speakers label sciences are, to German speakers, merely *exakte-wissenschaften,* while historically orientated studies are *historischewissenschaften* and the cultural studies and humanities are *geisteswissenchaften.* As well as natural science, then, *wissenschaft* includes the humanities, which, in the English-speaking world, are not regarded as having any kind of fundamental kinship with scientific knowledge.

For reasons to do with British and American history and culture, in these societies, science is regarded as not only distinct, but also an achievement which eclipses other forms of knowledge. For English speakers, science is essentially natural science and there is an associated tendency to endow that kind of knowledge with special (and, usually also, vastly superior) authority. One interesting result of this is that some translations of German academic disciplines are incongruous to English ears. German historical investigations are sometimes translated into English as 'historical science' or speculative study of human behaviour as 'human science' (Ricouer, 1982; Anderson *et al.*, 1986). In British and American thinking, all areas of social studies are likely to be thought of as outside the pale of what is said to be truly rigorous study. As such, subjects such as organisation and management studies are held to be suspect unless they show they are adopting the character and using the methods of the 'true sciences'. In German and other European thought, it is not that no distinction is drawn between the natural sciences and other 'sciences', but they do tend to be thought of simply as being different. For many European thinkers, if anything, it is the natural sciences that are the poor relations. For Wilhelm Dilthey (1910), for example, human sciences make use of subjective and objective understanding (what he called inner and outer experience); as such, they preserve a direct link with our basic human understanding of life and help to define the historical situated world. For Dilthey, these additional features are obviously valuable and the natural sciences manifestly lack them.

A very wide variety of research practices have been developed and used in different branches of study at different times and places and it is unhelpful to think that some of these are inherently more effective than others. It is more useful to think in terms of different areas of intellectual activity and knowledge construction embodying differences of emphasis in research practices at different times and places. Research procedures and practices will vary in a number of ways, not only in terms of the overall research design (its methodology) and the techniques utilised (its research methods) but also in other dimensions: the extent to which designs and methods allow the development of formally codified knowledge, for example, or, most significant of all, the extent to which they allow disciplines to contribute to the general culture. Viewed from a wider perspective, then, it can be argued more generally that it is really not helpful to suppose that there are particular research practices that can be relied on always to secure knowledge once systematically applied. It will be argued instead that research should not feature prior commitment to the use of particular methods. Methods are means of accomplishing things and should be thought of as being like tools. It all depends what kind of tasks there are to do and what is being sought to be accomplished what tool should be used. To borrow an analogy from Lawson (1994: 258), a big stick may be useful for cleaning a dusty old mat but it is not useful for cleaning a dirty window. True, we may become much more skilled in the use of some tools, and spend much more time using them, but there is no point in thinking our favourite tool is the only one that is essential or valuable. Only a child takes the hammer from the toolbox every time.

Often, however, this is not accepted and, for a variety of reasons, particular views of appropriate research methods are staunchly defended. Among the defences in use are tradition (these techniques have been found successful in the past) and utility (these methods bring results). But in arguments of this sort, the ultimate line of defence is to hold that different approaches to study are rooted in different philosophical positions; that is, in different conceptions of the world (ontology) and how to achieve knowledge of it (epistemology). In such debates, it is further assumed that, because philosophy deals with fundamental questions, philosophical ideas must be the foundation of all knowledge. The reasoning is logically unassailable but it nonetheless is potentially very misleading in practice. It should be remembered that philosophy is also an area of study and, as with all other forms of knowledge, its character and content are shaped by processes of cultural development.

Positivism as a cultural development

Whatever else it may be, positivism is a cultural reflection on science and scientific achievements. As is suggested by Table 6.1, positivism was first elaborated as

Table 6.1 Development of approaches to philosophy of social science

	Pre-history and enlightenment	*19th century*	*Early 20th century*	*Later 20th century*	*Today*
Positivism	Emergence of rational scepticism	Development of positivist philosophy in branches of social science	Further development of positivism (logical positivism, etc.)	Concerted application of positivism to many social sciences: • psychology • management science • economics	Embattled status of positivism in many branches of social science and *some* branches of natural science
	Beginnings of natural science	Elaboration of natural science	Further elaboration of natural science		
					Polarisation of views
Anti-naturalism	Emergence of rigorous study of human products	Increasingly defensive, posture of humanities	Determined rejection of positivism	Application of anti-naturalism to social studies	Elaboration of anti-naturalist positions: e.g. post modernism, post-structuralism
	The development of hermeneutics	Emergence of idealist philosophy	Development of phenomological philosophy	Development of ethnomethodology	
Realism		Common sense realism	Creation of a workable social realism by social science founding fathers: Weber, Durkheim, Simmel	Consolidation of realist social science Development of critical realism as an articulated philosophy	Development of the critical realist approach as a research paradigm applicable in many areas: e.g. management/ organisation studies

a definite philosophical position in the late eighteenth and early nineteenth centuries (shortly after natural science had itself begun to develop) and was progressively refined during the twentieth century. It has always had the tendency to be greatly concerned with what was taken to be the leading edge of science. For this reason, much positivist philosophy of science is accurately viewed as extended discussion of the implications of physics. The leading philosophers of science are much concerned with this discipline (Braithwaite, 1967; Popper, 1959). Positivists either argue overtly, or their work is taken to imply, that because the 'leading' branches of science proceed in particular ways, and use particular methods, all branches of science must do the same, or approximate these methods as best they can. Followers of positivism in the social sciences take the view, referred to by critics as 'scientism', that the methods found successful in the leading areas of science should be applied to all branches of disciplined enquiry. As suggested by Table 6.1, positivism was applied in an increasingly concerted way to the social sciences in the twentieth century. It seems clear in retrospect that, as long as philosophers promoting positivism remained authoritative, many practitioners in social science felt constrained to attempt to make their practice approximate a particular view of what scientific knowledge should be.

Following the model of physics, positivists suggest that, to be scientific, social science must stick closely to empirical observations that are measurable at high levels. Indeed, positivist philosophy indicates that much time and effort should be devoted to developing measurement scales, by reference to which behaviour might be objectively measured and compared (Fleetwood, 2001a, 2001b). In addition to test theories concerning behaviour, precise predictions derived from theories should be experimentally tested. This overlooks the fact that in some branches of science experimental techniques are not important. Despite this, in positivist-inspired social science, much effort was put into developing scaling techniques; positivists also tried to test hypotheses by the use of experimental methods or methods that were in some ways approximations to these study designs. Unfortunately, very often, the importance of thinking about the subject under study (considering what might be salient) tended to take a back seat to consideration of the merely technical problem of how to measure things that might be important and how to test their effects.

Thus, for example, in behaviourism, a positivist movement in psychology that was influential in that subject from the 1930s on, researchers sought to treat the mind itself as a 'black box', the working of which could only be inferred indirectly from observable phenomena. Behaviourist psychologists argued that the scientist may only (a) observe the inputs (stimuli) to which experimental subjects are exposed and (b) then carefully measure the behavioural outcomes after exposure. This is not in itself problematic, but this determined empiricism came along with a failure to realise the importance of thinking about the complex mechanisms that connect inputs and outputs; in short, to make a theory of mental processes central to their project. In effect, behaviourists, accepting the prescriptions of positivism, turned their attention away from considering the way the mind actually works; which, though undoubtedly a knotty problem, might reasonably be thought a basic requirement of any valuable knowledge of human psychology.

Positivism is ill-equipped to recognise some basic human attributes (such as self-reflection and evaluation) and is hard put to develop techniques sensitive enough to recognise the more developed human tendencies which arise from these capacities (such as reasoning and learning), not to mention key collective accomplishments that are built on these capacities (such as developing unique institutions which shape and channel behaviour). Hence, the impulse to reject positivism is not at all unreasonable in that it marginalises (when it does not entirely devalue) accounts of humanity that begin from and feature what is unique and distinctive about human capabilities. For example, many positivist studies have looked for an association between job satisfaction and attendance at work (i.e. low absenteeism) on the grounds that a satisfied person will be highly motivated to attend work (and disinclined to be absent). But what if the employee assumes (not unrealistically for many ordinary employees) that all work is likely to be unfulfilling and so the opportunity for absence is an attractive feature of a particular job? In such cases, satisfaction with work is likely highly correlated with absence. Similarly, positivist-orientated approaches to investigating unemployment often seek to distinguish between cases in which separation from employment is voluntary or involuntary, arguing that insecurity is an outcome from rather than a cause of unemployment. But a person who apparently volunteers for unemployment may nonetheless be seeking separation from employment on the grounds that their current job is too insecure and so they are seeking something better. (See Fleetwood, 2001a: 61.)

Understanding behaviour depends on appreciating its meaning, but this is not all that is needed for explaining it in many circumstances. Judging how significant behaviour is brings other considerations of relevance to bear, not only its meaning. Knowing how general something is (and so having recourse to counting the numbers of instances of it) is often valuable. To show how frequently different kinds of acts are associated may be important too. There are many situations where such quantitative research is a useful corrective to received opinion. In management studies, for example, it might be thought that absence from work is associated with lost production but it is often important to look at what evidence there is. While the supposed connections may be quite firm in the popular imagination, actually measuring these things has shown that they are often not directly associated. Thus, it is often useful, as a first stage of analysis, to show how much absence there is recorded at a particular plant, and to what extent it can be shown to be associated with lost production and other things. Among the things that may be found to be useful following such purely quantitative studies is to consider the way figures like this are constructed and for what purposes they are used.

In sum, it seems clear that when positivism is relied on as an exclusive model for social science practice, it causes social scientific practice to be bent and distorted in particular directions. At best, positivism has led many practitioners to focus on developing research procedures (scaling and other kinds of instrumentation) and contrived research designs (attempts to approximate the experiment by showing associations between measured variables taken with the use of scaling procedures) which recognise key human attributes. At worst, positivist emphasis on developing tools and techniques of study generally takes attention from what were actually more basic problems for social science, concerned with adequate description, explanation and, particularly, the development of adequate theory.

Anti-positivism: reclaiming human powers

The requirements of positivism concerning how to develop knowledge are in many ways so inappropriate that it led many to question and to reject any use of these methods for the study of human affairs. In so doing there was a return to long-established traditions of study.

Because they predate the rise of science, traditional approaches to the study of human activities do not share the assumptions and outlook of positivism. Of most importance here is hermeneutics. Hermeneutics has its roots in the problem of interpretation of biblical and other sacred texts. In the world before printing, copies of sacred books were made through the process of copying by hand an original (or what was taken to be an original) version of a text. Inevitably, this gave rise to multiple versions of the text, and the very considerable problem of knowing which was the original, authentic and 'correct' version. Hermeneutics arose as the development of techniques to solve these problems of meaning and interpretation. But a decisive step away from the examination of texts was taken in the Enlightenment (roughly speaking the early eighteenth century) when scholars began to ask difficult questions about the nature of historical knowledge as such. The basis of practice remained a concern for texts, but interest gradually shifted to a consideration of the motives and contributions of the author in the production of works of art and literature.

To understand a work of art, for example, is in good part to recover the artist's objectives; and, by extension, to interpret any human act is to re-create the actor's web of motivations. Both cases require, above all, the empathetic identification with the situation of another human being – something which positivism denies as necessary or appropriate. The aim of this approach to study gradually became the interpretation of meaning as the basis for understanding human activities. In this pursuit, the consideration of purpose and intention emerged as being fundamental. Without understanding how people conceive their situation, there is no possibility of understanding their actions. This can be seen, not only as something that links the individual character of a person with their activities and products, but also as the basis for understanding the activities and products of a community or nation as well. Thus, in Hegel's idealist philosophy formulated at the turn into the nineteenth century, the consciousness of a whole historical era is thought of as a stage in the progress of society coming to know itself. History and the understanding and interpretation of it become essentially the same processes.

As suggested by Table 6.1, in the early twentieth century, humanistic studies adopted an increasingly defensive posture as positivism was more stridently asserted and applied to more areas of application. It was not, however, until the early years of the twentieth century that there was the determined rejection of positivism and the elaboration of a philosophy of knowledge that was not only anti-positivist, but against the idea that any techniques drawn from natural science are applicable to human affairs (complete anti-naturalism). Key to this movement was the attempt to elaborate a human-centred philosophy through a sustained consideration of the processes within conscious life. The most concerted and significant development here is known as the phenomenological movement, usually identified as beginning with the work of Edmund Husserl (1859–1938). Husserl's mature work was published when he was in his late sixties and early seventies in the late 1920s and early 1930s. Also important was some of the early work of Martin Heidegger (1889–1976) which appeared at about the same time. This work helped to stimulate a remarkable flowering of anti-naturalistic philosophy in the work of a large number of European intellectuals including Max Scheler, H.G. Gadamer, Paul Ricouer, Hannah Arendt, Simone de Beauvoir, Alfred Schutz, Maurice Merleau-Ponty and Jean-Paul Sartre.

In the course of these developments certain elements of phenomenological ideas were forged into a systematic approach to social studies, particularly by some of the writers listed above, of whom Alfred Schutz (1964, 1966, 1967) is pre-eminent. From the work of Schutz, the contemporary approach to social study known as ethnomethodology has been developed. (For a summary of this development see Benson and Hughes, 1983.) In more recent years, several anti-naturalistic approaches to social subjects have been elaborated. Much postmodernist and supposedly 'post-structuralist' writing shares similar assumptions to the roots of this tradition of thought, in being intensely concerned with human ability to construct meaning. The common point of doctrine is that, because our knowledge of the external world is mediated by concepts, the actual nature of this is not merely subordinate to our comprehension of it, but is actually unknowable independently of our concepts. (For a critique, see Fleetwood's contribution to this collection and Fleetwood, 2005.) Also, human behaviour, it is reasoned, is self-conscious and reflective and, because of this, the relationship between the social scientist and his subjects is quite unlike that found in science. The subject matter of social studies, it is argued, is constructed in particular ways; as such it is not objectively knowable, but is only knowable through its distinctive constructions. This gives rise to some distinctive emphases in method: there are those wishing to understand the ways people create meaningful worlds and what these contain, and those who wish to reverse the process, looking to deconstruct knowledge. (For a critical realist take on objectivity and subjectivity see Sayer, 2000: 58–62.)

Be that as it may, there is one basic similarity in the use made of both positivism and phenomenology; followers of both think there are particular observations that give privileged access to knowledge. Consistently, if ironically, with this too, post-structuralists also have a similar conception. Observing discourse (or language, semiotic activity, or texts), as a precondition of and precursor to deconstructing that discourse, is thought to give privileged access to knowledge (see Fleetwood, Chapter 1 in this volume). In all these cases, focused attention on observed events is required: on the one hand there is focus on measurement; on the other hand there is focus on specific events in everyday life. In the language of philosophy, both these give a primary role to epistemology, suggesting that how knowledge can be obtained from observation is a key issue. It is for this reason too that these very different doctrines share an insistence on the use of particular techniques, and make this central to their idea of what constitutes effective study. Exponents of these points of view suggest that particular kinds of techniques of study are the key to developing knowledge and understanding, and so the recommendation of *specific* techniques of study is very important to them. On the one hand, positivism insists that things should be measured and compared quantitatively, if possible using experimental research designs; on the other hand, phenomenology suggests that the point is to uncover the basic properties of the human experience, to use Husserl's terms, to uncover the attributes of the human 'life world', and this must be studied by immersion in it. To the positivist and the phenomenologist alike, their projects move from epistemology to the consideration of techniques of study and each approach has highly distinctive methods (ideas about the way knowledge should be developed) associated with them.

Philosophy as the art of the insoluble

The issues with which philosophy deals are indeed basic questions, but they are also extremely difficult to solve. Hence, philosophy is not to be thought about, as it sometimes is, as a kind of very general or inclusive theory that works in the same way as the theories and ideas that inform research. Philosophy does not offer a set of postulates from which many conclusions can reliably be drawn. There is not a philosophical postulate that is generally accepted as correct and which cannot plausibly be denied on the basis of alternative assumptions. Thus, philosophy is a field of human enquiry in which basic questions are asked but where there are actually few definitely reliable and generally accepted answers. Indeed, the fundamentally contested nature of philosophy has become more and more central over time, and today may be thought of as constitutive of the subject. Peter Medawar, a scientist who also turned to the consideration of issues in the philosophy of science, has argued that science may be thought of as 'the art of the soluble' (1970), because it proceeds by formulating questions about the world to which there are particular and reliable kinds of solutions to be discovered. Turning this idea around, and using the standards of science to evaluate philosophy, the subject may be considered to be the art of the insoluble, because it deals with the fundamental question that empirical disciplines cannot answer.

Considered in this way, philosophy is not the most promising basis on which to found empirical studies. Clearly, however, since in this book a particular philosophical doctrine is being consistently advocated, our scepticism about the value of philosophy is not total. The philosophy of social science can be an illuminating area of study, but care must be taken to understand what is likely to be achieved by looking into it and in attempting to use it to inform empirical study. The view adopted here is that the nature of philosophy is not the only problem and is certainly not the major one. There is, for example, a tendency for academic practitioners, in one way or another, to be over-impressed by the importance of philosophical doctrines, sometimes without realising it. Also, practitioners often use philosophy prescriptively, that is to follow it as a set of principles and procedures about how study should be conducted, when it either was not devised to do this and/or there are obvious limits to the value of its use as a set of prescriptions.

And so to realism

If the above is persuasive, the most that may be claimed for philosophy is that it has some relevance to empirical studies, but what this may be is, at best, unclear. Any studies of organisation and management we undertake will have philosophical presuppositions and implications in addition to whatever substantive value they have; and, though we may choose to pay attention to these, there is really no necessity to do so. If this is so, however, why make such a song and dance about critical realism and its contemporary relevance? Realism, after all, is just another set of philosophical precepts. Thus, why should we assert in this book and elsewhere that these doctrines are extremely valuable to the practitioner in our academic field?

The basic reason is that critical realism, as a philosophy of science, offers a series of valuable insights into the practice of social science and particularly into the place and role of methodology. One reason realism can do this should now be apparent from the discussion of the alternative positions as summarised in Table 6.1. Whereas the positivist and phenomenological approaches to social studies were largely built up following the development of the abstract philosophy of positivism on the one hand and phenomenology on the other, this is not the case for realism. The work of many key, founding contributors to social science, such people as Max Weber, Emile Durkheim and Georg Simmel, for example (not to mention many more recent writers and researchers), made their contributions to social science at the beginning of the twentieth century. An awareness of the limitations of positivism and knowledge of the significance of the hermeneutic tradition were background considerations of those who initially contributed to the new area of study. Bauman (1978), for example, writes at length on the contribution of hermeneutics to the writing of key figures in the founding of social science including Marx, Weber, Mannheim and Parsons.

All these theorists acknowledged that the social world is basically an interpreted world, and that relationships between people, institutions and structures are produced by people; that is, they are socially constructed. But they also believed two other things as well. First, that the constructed world is not *merely* socially constructed, but acquires an independence from individual people and groups. The institutional structure manifestly has independent effects on behaviour whatever the constructors think about the matter. In Fleetwood's terms (see Chapter 1 of this volume) structures are socially real and not reducible to their conceptualisations, that is to discourse. Second, and following on from this, it is possible to contrive a theoretically grounded account of institutions, society and social processes, despite their origins as social constructions. Thus it is wrong to claim that constructionist social science is post-structural. It is more accurate to say that realist social science was, from its inception, post-constructionist.

The realist view of social science accounts for the sense people have of being constrained or enabled by their circumstances in terms of the structures in which they are located. These are held to be not simply a product of the discourses with which people engage, but have their own distinctive real properties. Even the simplest of relationships considered in structural terms, let us say an ephemeral relationship between two people waiting at a bus stop, has a structure reproduced by the participants. Georg Simmel analysed some of the general properties of the elementary social form involved here as 'the dyad'. Once specific forms of dyad (the parent/child; the wife/husband) are institutionalised and embedded and their forms supported by larger structures (civil society, community and the law) they become yet more formative and obligatory and likely to be reproduced in roughly the same form over considerable tracts of time. Nevertheless, it is also a distinguishing feature of dyads that they can easily be dissolved (other things being equal) because their reproduction depends only on the mutually supportive actions of just two parties: indeed, without external support, dyads can be unilaterally dissolved by the action of one member.

By contrast with this, more complex forms or sets of relationships involving more participants cannot be unilaterally dissolved, and this simple fact explains much, though by no means all, about the obligatory properties of collective social forms. Institutions, which we may understand as complex sets of relationships that have become traditional, are correspondingly even more difficult to dissolve, in that to break them down requires the agreement of several parties to act against their habitual practices. In addition, we must note that all structures – it becomes obvious when we consider institutions and other large collectivities – embody power. Power ensures the perpetuation of existing patterns of advantage and disadvantage. For these reasons, institutions tend to persist despite the views and intentions of many – and perhaps most – of the participants in them. None of this requires that critical realists are committed to the naive conceptions of sovereign power and some (but by no means all) points of the Foucauldian view of power are well taken.

So it is that the structures can produce outcomes that few really approve or desire. For example, the economy can produce persistently high levels of unemployment despite the wishes and intentions of many employers, all government representatives, most members of political parties and relevant pressure groups, and the unemployed themselves. Yet the reasons why there is this sort of effect cannot be adequately accounted for without understanding the extra-discursive qualities of politico-economic structures. Until it is recognised that there are extra-discursive (i.e. structural) properties of sets of relationships, and investigating these properties becomes an object of research, understanding of what is happening in social collectivities is likely to take the form of mutual scapegoating. In the case of structural unemployment this would involve people choosing which group of the set of groups involved to blame for the performance of the set: either it is the fault of the employers, the government or (most implausibly of all) the unemployed themselves. The set of relationships as a whole, and how this is reproduced by the actions, motivations and beliefs of the participating groups, must become the object of study. The aim of such study is not, however, to implicate all groups equally, but to analyse the way outcomes are the consequence of particular causal processes, in which some actions and contributions will undoubtedly be more salient than others.

The development of an empirically grounded and policy-relevant form of knowledge of this kind has been undertaken by realist social science since the turn of the twentieth century. The founding fathers of realist social scientists – and several generations of followers – met with considerable success. The work of founding theorists provided the base on which social science could be elaborated, and the new knowledge was also sought in a large number of specialist areas where formerly positivism had been dominant.

Organisation and management studies are but two of a long line of areas of knowledge to which realist social science has contributed. Given the above description, the applicability of realism to organisation and management studies is in principle fairly obvious: organisations are structures that are reproduced by the participants in them, but they have emergent properties that bind participants into a particular pattern of relationships. To be sure, different groups of participants have differential room for manoeuvre, for securing outcomes in their favour and for shaping the attributes of the broader pattern of relationships. Very crudely expressed, managers as a group are distinguished by the power (backed by the board of directors, the shareholders and the framework of law) to redesign the organisational structure itself: to decide how a company will be organised, what activities will be undertaken and how many people will be employed. Nevertheless the structure of an organisation will not be precisely as one group decrees that it will be. There is the countervailing and resisting action of other groups within the organisation to be considered, as well as the effects of external agencies. Even in this case, however, where the organisation is so much a product of rational design, the way in which the organisation actually functions is not available to the casual observer or the ordinary participant. Realist analysis of organisations (and the role of management) which considers how they actually work, rather than how they are supposed to function, has been developed in the thirty years after World War II.

The abstract philosophy of realism, however, did not achieve much formal expression until well after the World War II. Only in the last three decades has a sophisticated or 'critical' realism been elaborated with the works of Rom Harré (1970, 1972) and Roy Bhaskar (1979; see also Keat and Urry, 1974). Indeed, critical realism, as the most recent of the formally articulated philosophies of science, was developed in the knowledge of the achievements of social science, which the other philosophies – postivitism and phenomenology – were not. Rom Harré and most of the recent generation of contributors to the critical realist account of social science, of course, are also social scientists in their own right. The same cannot be said for other traditions of thought. This is important because there are many pitfalls in trying to transfer ideas from one field (or epoch), where they seem to apply, to others where they may not. However, the achievements and potential of realist social science have come under challenge in recent years. Part of the reason, as we argued in the introduction to our last book about realism and management studies (Ackroyd and Fleetwood, 2000), is that many recent writers, especially in relatively new fields of study, clearly do not understand realism appropriately and wish to bundle it in with positivism, suggesting that it has similarities of outlook. Some writers seek to bundle realism in with positivism and suggest that because it is content to use the term science as a label, it must be like positivism. This is a surprising and very serious mistake.

Realism is a distinct philosophical position, which begins from a conception of the subject matter of social science (like phenomenology but unlike positivism), rather than from views about the form that knowledge of the world should take. In philosophical language, realism gives prominence to ontology rather than epistemology. The realist view of how things and events in the world may be explained is also very distinct from positivism, owing much to the ideas that originated in an appreciation of the hermeneutic tradition. There is a good deal of writing that deals with the ontology and epistemology of critical realism, by setting out the philosophical character of the realism, in particular its ontology and epistemology. (See, for example, Sayer, 2000; Ackroyd and Fleetwood, 2000; and Fleetwood's and Sayer's contributions to this volume.)

The intention in the remainder of this chapter is, however, to concentrate on the realist conception of explanation and to relate this to the kinds of uses that realists have for techniques of research. The aim here is to summarise these differences and to focus the discussion on realist ideas about explanation. Table 6.2 provides a very condensed summary of the characteristics of realism (as compared to the two other approaches to knowledge discussed in this chapter). It suggests that the realist account of explanation is distinctive, but logically related to the broader ontological and epistemological commitments of realism. Of course ideas about research methods are closely related to ideas about explanation. Hence, this approach will take the discussion more quickly to the consideration of the place of different techniques and methods in realist research, and the reasons why realist social science utilises and seeks both qualitative and quantitative data.

Realist explanation

Something is explained when placed in a causal sequence, and the (perhaps various) antecedent causes of that event are identified. There is no implication

Table 6.2 Comparison of the characteristics of positivism, hermeneutics/ phenomenology and critical realism

Ontology	*Epistemology*	*Basic ideas*
Positivism	Naive realism: what can be observed is real; status of the non-observable is doubtful. Reductionism: no orders or levels in the world; 'flat' or 'fused' reality.	Unified science: physical, life and social sciences are basically the same kind of activity. 'Sense data' is the crucial basis of knowledge. Hence, to find measurable events and variables is crucial. Knowledge is nomothetic.
Hermeneutics/ phenomenology	Idealism: what exists is primarily a property of perception, an expression of mind. In human studies the concern is with social experience: with common or collective objectifications.	The subject matter of human studies, '*geisteswissenschaften*', should be studied in terms of the unique properties of social experience, both individual and collective. Knowledge is ideographic.
Critical realism	What is real is not given. The world has structure (there are levels of reality) and emergent structures. The engagement of people with structures is transformational.	Subject matter has to reflect both its meaningfulness to actors and their location in a given network of relationships and structures. Knowledge is 'dualistic'.

Place and role of theory	*Nature of explanation*	*Methods of study*
Ideal of theory is a set of laws (or approximations to them in the form of well-founded generalisations) from which conclusions can be deduced. Where theory is not law-like, precise hypotheses should nonetheless be derived for testing.	Something is explained when shown to be invariably related to something else, as suggested by theory and tested by experiments. Strong statistical relationships are acceptable as an approximation to invariance.	High-level measurement and use of scaling are basic techniques of study. The aim is to use measures to test hypotheses. The ideal method is the clinical experiment. Controlled experiment and statistical control and probability testing are acceptable approximations.
If used, this idea has a general meaning as 'perspective', genre or approach. Alternatively it refers to very low level or 'local' generalisations.	Something is explained if it is shown to have properties unique to its 'essential' qualities and particular situation. It may also display recurrent aspects making it part of a specific cultural pattern.	A focus on the meaning attributed to things and events by specific groups. Immersion in the subject matter with the objective of understanding it. Extended and accurate description is required.
Theory is a conjecture about the connectedness of events and the causal sequences produced by generative mechanisms.	Something is explained if it is allocated a place at the end of a causal sequence. There may be multiple causes of a single event, co-variation and feedback.	The aim is to produce a good theory which accurately identifies causal mechanisms. The ways these work themselves out in given cases will be complicated. Multiple data is required.

here that explanation is understood in terms of event regularity or can be complete or definitive. However, this proposition can be elaborated by thinking in terms of (a) causal mechanisms and (b) the particular contexts in which they work themselves out. An example may help: a disease that is caused by an infective agent has a particular effect on the cells of the body, causing specific symptoms such as fever, disorientation, a rash on the abdomen, and so on. We can think in terms of the generative process of the disease (that gives rise to the bodily symptoms of any infected person) involving the interaction of the infective agent and the reaction of the body. In this case, it is problematic to separate the generative mechanism from relevant aspects of the context (the body), but our theory of the disease suggests that the infective agent is the cause and the context the body. Hence, specifying the context appropriately, and establishing the character of causal mechanisms are key problems of realist research. There are, in many cases, differences of outcome that can only be explained by context and which are not attributable to the character of the generative mechanism involved. Thus, if a patient is physically very robust, their body may resist the processes of the disease more effectively than someone who is weak. Alternatively, a medicine or treatment, which mitigates the mechanism of the disease, may also change the outcome. In sum, explanation is accounting for specific outcomes through the consideration of causal mechanisms at work in particular contexts (Pawson and Tilley, 1997: 57–9). A version of Pawson and Tilley's diagram, which they use to depict realist explanation, is given in Figure 6.1.

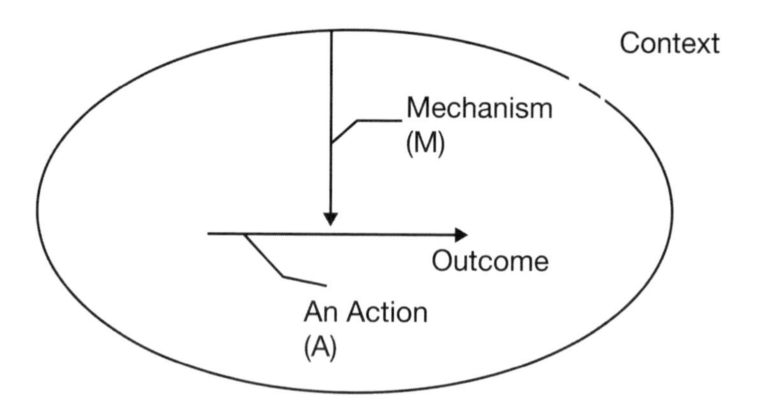

Figure 6.1 Realist explanation

Note: An action (A) is said to be causal if its outcome is produced by a mechanism operative in a given context.

Source: Based on Figure 3.1, 'Generative causation', in R. Pawson and N. Tilley, *Realistic Evaluation* (Sage, 2000), p. 58.

In this way, from a realist point of view, research can equally well be theoretical as well as directly empirical: concerned with considering generative mechanisms, and just how specific elements and their associated capabilities feature in these; as well as empirical, that is exploring the character of causal processes in particular cases or considering evidence about the extent of such processes in the world at large. It is seldom that empirical research can be thought of as testing the validity of ideas about causal mechanisms – at least not in a direct or definitive way. This is because a failure to show an association between an effect and an outcome may be attributable to peculiarities of the context. In short, because the mechanism does not exist in a closed system, the predictive capacity of theory (on which positivism rests) is potentially lost. On the other hand, if empirical indicators do not, with reasonable consistency, suggest that a mechanism is operative, then we have grounds for seeking an alternative theoretical account of what is going on, as our theoretical account does not relate to many observed features of the world. It is potentially a damaging criticism of realist explanation that it is irrefutable: if no evidence for a causal mechanism is found, then it is easily accounted for as attributable to peculiarities of the context. For this reason, it is incumbent on realists to focus on and attempt to specify circumstances in which particular research techniques are likely to find conclusive evidence of the existence of theoretically postulated causal mechanisms. It has to be acknowledged, however, that particular telling or conclusive research is likely to be quite rare.

In this approach, however, research is necessarily a collective activity. To revert again to the medical comparison: before the search for a specific infective agent can take place, some understanding of the physiological processes that the agent disrupts is necessary. In the absence of both of these, however, there could be some knowledge of the disease and even of how to treat it effectively: the symptoms of the disease and the sequence of presentation could be known, as could specific remedies that seem to have some effect. However, such knowledge would be incomplete, and in a much less satisfactory form, than that available after the physiology of the body and the generative mechanism of the disease has been specified. Until the normal processes of the human body are sufficiently known, the likely mechanism of a disease, including the likely existence of a specific infective agent, cannot be postulated. From this it is clear that the results of any one piece of research are unlikely to be conclusive, although there can be breakthrough projects, such as research that identifies the particular germ or virus, for example. Any given piece of research contributes to an ongoing stream of work which makes a contribution within the context of a given body of existing knowledge. Research is not only dependent on similar understandings, but on a background of existing knowledge and a network of actual and potential relationships between researchers. Notice that realism embraces the role of shared understandings, background knowledge and networks, without collapsing the finding of research into these phenomena as many post-structuralists do.

The specific mechanisms in which realist social researchers are interested typically involve the interactions between individuals and groups considered as agents and their interaction with other groups in the context of larger collectivities. A recurrent concern is the extent to which these groups reproduce and/or transform the collectivities in which they are engaged. Thus the context of interest here is also very much bound up with developing an understanding of generative processes, and separating them conceptually from the particular contexts in which they will operate. In her discussion of realist social theory, Archer draws a distinction between 'corporate' and 'primary' agents (Archer, 1995: 258). By 'corporate agents' she means that some groups are constituted so that they are capable of acting in a unified or 'corporate' way in pursuit of their interests. Citing Bentley's dictum 'when the groups are stated, everything is stated' (Bentley, 1967: 200) with qualified approval, Archer goes on to point out the different powers of groups. Corporate agents, with the capacity to alter the terms of interaction, are different from 'primary agents' or groups distinguished by the lack of much capacity to induce change in their circumstances, but who nonetheless continue to constitute themselves and in this and other ways contribute to reproducing their own circumstances. An inability to effect change is best understood in terms of limitations on the agency of groups, which is restricted to the ability to reproduce the context in which they find themselves. Archer writes (1995: 258):

> in short, the prior social context delineates collectivities in the same position … and within this context they have to carry on. … Those in this category are termed 'Primary Agents'. They are distinguished from 'Corporate Agents' at any given time by lacking a say in structural or cultural modelling. At that time they neither express interests nor organise for their strategic pursuit.

In short, individuals vary in the extent to which they are merely complicit in social reproduction, or whether they are capable of producing change to their benefit as well.

The action of all groups of agents will be to produce and reproduce institutions and other structures that will have a formative effect on the attitudes and behaviour of all the participants in them; though, as we have seen, some will be empowered and some dis-empowered by their position within collective structures. In this sense the structures in which individuals and groups are implicated are to a considerable extent beyond their direct control. Thus, in realist research, interest extends beyond the consideration of the experiences and beliefs of groups and their particular conceptions of the world, to a consideration of the socially constructed phenomena to illuminate the causal configurations that are often unobservable and which operate 'behind the backs' of actors and help to shape their discourses. The object of research is to identify the causal processes that link and articulate structures, that are to some extent known by participants in them and partially (and often implicitly) acknowledged in reflective commentary on their circumstances. The target of research activity may be either the patterns of relationships which constitute the building blocks of structure (and which lend themselves to objective assessment) or the reflective views that participants have on their circumstances. In addition it may involve putting together both sorts of data to identify or exemplify the patterns of relationships in which groups of actors are implicated in particular ways.

Realist research summarised

Three points concerning general methodology

First, realists propose that causal processes are chains of connected events in which the capacities of objects are activated sequentially. In other words, causal processes are constituted by chains of causal mechanisms interacting to produce the events we observe. In the social realm, individuals and social groups have powers or capacities and, when they interact, they give rise to connected social processes in which events are caused. Human collectivities, the groups, institutions and organisations (managed and unmanaged) which make up societies, are not reducible to the content of the subjectivity of groups. They have properties that emerge from interaction and are often involved in the causal mechanisms affecting people. These emergent properties and the causal mechanisms in which they are implicated are not directly available to observation but can be apprehended indirectly. They are usually only painstakingly reconstructed by iterative empirical research guided by theory.

Second, general research methodology has *two* indispensable aspects: conceptualisation/theory construction and empirical investigation. Of these, conceptualisation must come first, for without concepts even perception is problematic; but it is also true that research is important because we cannot read off the world from the concepts we have of it. Things and events have a capacity to contradict our expectations, and our theories are therefore corrigible through observation. Research is undertaken to test theories and to develop accounts of events based on theory. Data is seen to a considerable degree to transcend the theoretical analysis brought to it, inviting alternative interpretations and the amendment of theory. Considered in this way most attempts to study something usually involve some approximation to both theory and investigation. Even the humble student essay, which is usually not based on any original theory or data collection, nonetheless considers (a) the ideas that are used in particular areas of work and (b) how these ideas relate to or account for things and events. Viewed in this way, essay writing is research.

Third, theory, however, is the most important activity in research. Without adequate conceptualisation it is impossible to make observations (never mind discriminate between significant and less significant observations). In more developed forms, theory offers conjectures about generative mechanisms; and, if they are appropriately conceived, theories will provide an explanation featuring the causes lying behind observed events. Theory is, ideally, both abstract and general. The development of knowledge through research is therefore, in a fundamental sense, conceptually driven. But theory is only important in research because it embodies an account of the causal processes possibly active in a given situation. A realist-orientated theory, which considers the tendencies and powers of the institutions and groups it describes, can be a reliable guide to what happens, but need not be so in every case. Its efficacy resides in the identification of causal configurations/powers, and it does not stand or fall by being able to predict the ensuing patterns of events.

Ten implications for research practice

1 *Theory is indispensable.* All research is necessarily theoretical even if only in the minimal sense that it is guided by prior conceptualisations of some sort. Also, however, research may be mainly conceptual in that primary attention is given to ideas: to the conceptualisation of things and events and to ideas about what is causing what. In practical terms this may mean that existing literature and research related to a particular subject area are sifted, evaluated and considered in order to understand and to gain some critical purchase on existing knowledge or to clarify ideas. Finally, research may be primarily theoretical, in that active consideration is given to the concepts and ideas that might be useful in understanding a given subject area. In theoretical research, attention is given to making a better causal account than is provided by existing knowledge.

2 *Findings/data are to some extent independent of theory.* What is regarded as relevant to a particular research question is not uninfluenced by prior conceptions an investigator has, but neither do those conceptions determine what is seen and taken to be significant. Observations can challenge our preconception of what is occurring. The difference between research observations and the everyday sort is that, in research, data are systematically constructed and collected, and the nature of observations made is checked out against theoretical expectation. Undoubtedly, a key source of data is direct observation of the ways that groups of people assimilate their experience and react to being in particular situations. Hence qualitative data in relation to such situations is often valuable. However, it is also important to find out how extensive evidence is for a particular construction of experience or events amongst similar groups or any research population. Hence economical ways of collecting such evidence, such as social surveys using questionnaires, are also potentially a useful way of constructing data. Pawson (1996) has recently argued for a particular way of thinking about (in his term 'theorising') the social process of the interview as the basis for reliable inferences. The use of inductive statistics, say to estimate the generality of the relationships depicted, is to be thought of as an extension of the use of descriptive statistics, rather than a way of definitely proving the existence of particular causal relations.

3 *Taken together, theory construction and data collection (research activity) establish the operation of mechanisms.* In order to develop ideas about mechanisms it is often

essential not to focus too strongly on particular phenomena or isolate them for study. Indeed, in order to clarify the nature of a mechanism, it has to be examined in a context. Using the language of systems, such things as work processes or management systems are open to their environment, and this will affect the way they work. In practice, study designs which identify a context or contexts (within which frame causal processes work themselves out) are indispensable to the identification of mechanisms. In such studies, research information will therefore necessarily have to be related to both the context in which a mechanism may be operative or describe the causal mechanism itself; that is, it may be centrally implicated in an explanation or contextualisation of it. Thus, realist research is, in many branches of study, including the fields of management and organisation, holistic, and often takes the form of case studies. Critics of case studies, who focus on the possibility that untypical attributes of particular organisations (or other contexts) may render the results from the research ungeneralisable, overlook two points. First, in realist case study research, the aim is to generalise about mechanisms, and so the procedure recognises and accepts that the contexts in which they work themselves out may indeed be partly contingent. Second, however, the basis for believing in the possibility of generalisation is theoretical rather than empirical. Realist case studies seek to show how mechanisms work themselves out in a particular instance. Because research is theoretically based, realists reject the notion that case studies cannot be the basis for generalisations, as is now becoming more widely recognised (Yin, 1989; Easton, 1992). There is also the possibility of undertaking comparative case studies, in which two or more examples are considered that differ little except in theoretically significant aspects. These are particularly relevant for illuminating the characteristics of generative mechanisms.

4 *Research does not privilege particular kinds of data.* The approach to research does not privilege particular kinds of observations or data as giving rise to knowledge, as both positivism and some forms of anti-naturalism do. Reasons may be causes, and so individual reasoning may affect outcomes. Equally, however, institutions will be causes, and established ways of doing things may inhibit motivation from taking new forms. There is no prior commitment to the importance or causal priority of data relating to ideas or acts, or the ideas or behaviour of individuals, groups or institutions. On the contrary, a causal account identifying a mechanism will link events in a sequence, and will often implicate data relating to both ideas and acts, either individual or collective, which may be relevant to a satisfactory explanation. Thus the realist typically accepts the position of Thomas and Znanieki (1927) to paraphrase them: 'If people believe their situations to be real, they are real in their consequences.' This is helpful but insufficient. Clarifying the thinking of individuals and groups suggests the applicability of qualitative methods, as these are indispensable for illuminating motives, intentions and reasons. The capacity to formulate and express reasons is a human power, and potentially therefore may feature as a link in a generative mechanism.

In the realist view, the reasons, motives or intentions of individuals and groups can be causes and feature in generative mechanisms; but the point is not to stop with the clarification of such things, but to see them as being operative within particular generative mechanisms.

5 *Research is interpretive and creative.* There are no procedures or routines that can guarantee that a better understanding of the causes of events will arise from data collection. For example, the discovery of statistical associations between 'variables', as happens when the data from a social survey is analysed, cannot be taken as having established causal relationships. Unless there is some theoretical basis for thinking that observed events are connected by particular mechanisms, there is little reason to think of associated variables as anything other than chance events. For the realist, what recommends the use of social surveys as a source of data is a principle of economy. It is a way of obtaining at least some data relating to general features of situations: some aspects of the context in which more salient events occur perhaps. Other data collection techniques recommend themselves as ways of gaining insight into causal mechanisms: the experiences of groups and their characteristic way of thinking give direct insight into causal relationships. Realists have clarified particular uses of ethnographic research designs (Porter, 1993), for example. Direct observation of particular situations (participant observation), allowing groups of actors to reveal their characteristic ways of behaving, is a more likely candidate as the key research method. Here the aim is to bring to light evidence of the way people – especially groups – understand their situation and act on these understandings. For some avowedly realist writers on methodology, their theorisation of the research relationship must inevitably lead to the predominant use of qualitative research techniques (Miles and Huberman, 1994). But the basic point to make is that data alone are not enough, it is the sense made of data, as illustrating the operation of mechanisms, that is important.

6 *Research is iterative and ongoing.* The validity of particular generative mechanisms is seldom established once and for all. Clearly there can be decisive research programmes which offer new findings which change perceptions about situations, and there are new interpretations of existing data which change our views of likely causes. On the other hand, because the real world is highly complex and subject to change, research is likely to be ongoing. From this account it is clear that research is likely to involve a division of labour between theorists and empirical researchers. Where there are no general accounts of mechanisms, there can be the production of simplified models or accounts of general relationships that are exemplary or typical, that point to the existence of mechanisms and suggest new lines of thinking and empirical research. The construction of an abstract or 'ideal typical' model of institutions or processes is not an end in itself, but a legitimate stage in the process of research and in the development of knowledge.

7 *Data and knowledge are things made by people.* As something made, data are, in some respects, little different from any other cultural creation. All data are

constructed for particular purposes and with particular ends in view. To claim to have knowledge (systematically assembled from data or not) is indubitably to make a particular claim to power. Thus it is open to study the ways in which data are constructed by different groups and how they use it, which is, when narrowly conceived, called secondary data analysis. But data are not purely and simply made in the form that suits its creators. Reality bites back as it were, disciplining and shaping our understanding. The key point to make is that we need to develop more fully a reflective understanding of the extent to which our knowledge is limited by being self-serving. More broadly understood, we can think of a social science understanding of knowledge production. Such approaches to data and knowledge construction are often highly revelatory of the assumptions that groups bring to their situation, and how they attempt to enhance their standing and resources. But knowledge from research makes claims to be different to other kinds of knowledge and so will often be in tension with common sense and other authoritative ways of describing and explaining things. What data are (in terms of quality and validity) can vary, as can the plausibility of the general accounts of reality developed through the interpretation of survey data. For these reasons, if scrupulously undertaken, academic research can claim differences from, and, in some respects, superiority to, other accounts of events and forms of knowledge.

8 *Critique is a legitimate goal of research.* Criticism of existing knowledge or 'received wisdom' can and should be undertaken by social science and management studies. If it is true that all knowledge is a claim to power, it is also true that some knowledge is specifically developed and held by those in authority and exercising power. This is obviously true of management theory and thought more generally. The value biases of management ideas are often very clear. The views of managers (including not a few supposedly supported by research findings) are often apparently simply descriptive, while they are actually prescriptive. The realist view of research suggests that much knowledge (and data derived from research) is flawed because it is under-theorised or otherwise ill-founded and inadequate, often coming to conclusions that serve the interests of the powerful. Critical realism suggests reasons why this is so, and ideas about the ways in which more adequate forms of knowledge might be achieved.

9 *Knowledge of causal mechanisms makes research potentially policy relevant.* Understanding the mechanisms that give rise to particular forms of behaviour makes realist research particularly relevant to policy applications. Pawson and Tilly (1997) have recently made a powerful case for this. Among the arguments developed by these authors is the proposition that much existing policy-related research is handicapped by its positivist design, seeking to clarify which variables are associated with (and so may be assumed to cause) the undesired behaviour that policy seeks to correct. The usual prescription for this is to look for associations between, say, the levels of reported crime and the policy interventions designed to curb it using

quasi-experimental methods of research (Campbell and Stanley, 1966). The problem with this is that it does not lead to any effective knowledge of what to do, as there is a substantial flaw in both the implicit theory of criminal behaviour and the methodology used to study it. If, on the other hand, research is aimed at clarifying the mechanisms which produce given outcomes, this can yield an understanding that can explain why and in what circumstances policies are likely to be effective.

10 *Events can be changed by intervention.* Realists take the view that all collectivities (from social groups to multi-national corporations) are actively constructed and reconstructed by the people that make them up, though they are not entirely in their control. If this is so, it can be argued that the place of research is not simply to interpret the meaning of data, and say what the likely outcomes of causal processes will be, but to try to intervene and actively find out the limits of the powers of groups. But the search can change things directly. It can be argued that a research design that merely interprets data will never effectively test sets of propositions about generative mechanisms. Only an approach which actively tries to redirect the typical pattern of outcomes arising from generative mechanisms, by direct intervention, can do this. Research which attempts to change situations by the positive action of the people in them is called action research. Realist action research will involve not simply attempting to change situations within limits set by a preset desired outcome, but testing the extent that typical generative mechanisms can be changed by re-engineering the outlook, beliefs and attitudes of participants.

Concluding comments

The range of techniques that might be employed in a realist-orientated research project is actually very wide. Some of the procedures available to the student of management and organisation have been mentioned in the above summary, but nothing like the complete range has been specified. There is much to be gained by thinking creatively about the utilisation of research techniques, rather than simply applying them as others have done in the past. Hopefully, however, enough has been said to suggest that the data collection techniques available range across the alleged divide between qualitative and quantitative methods. Many realist researchers, as illustrated by this account and others in this volume, prefer qualitative techniques, but still think their aim to be the creation of objective knowledge. However, perhaps the most important point to note is that the views elaborated here could hardly be more different from the conception of realism held by some, according to which realists believe that the world has a straightforward correspondence with the ideas we have of it, and therefore can be studied empirically without undue difficulty.

On the contrary, it has been argued here that although it is believed that there is a world independent of our identification of it, obtaining access to it is not straightforward. To make the point that constructionists and relativists rightly stress, it is impossible for us to gain access to the world in a way that is not mediated by our conceptions. For the realist-orientated researcher, however, it is possible to gain access *not only to the way the world appears, but also to the way the world actually is in some of its salient aspects*. This project is made more difficult because the way the world is in some of its aspects is indistinguishable from the way the world is thought to be. The realist, however, holds, against the trend of popular thought, that in its most important aspects, the world is usually not as we think it is. Obtaining an accurate perception of the way the world is, therefore, can only come from modifying our conceptions of it in relation to better-founded observations of the way it is. Research is an indispensable facilitator of this process.

To express the matter in a condensed and metaphorical way, and so run the risk of over-simplification, it is as if the mechanisms we seek to discover are mostly hidden from observers most of the time. It is as if we are trying to guess at the working of a clock, only being able to observe some of the face, some of the hands and almost nothing of the mechanism, and having little idea of its purpose. If we can only see part of the mechanism, there are two ways in which we might improve our knowledge. One is to make guesses about the nature of the thing we can only partly see (to make a theory of it), the other is to try to improve what we see (to collect precisely targeted observations/specific data). In this conception, research in effect has the purpose of obtaining some evidence that hidden mechanisms may take a particular form. But research is not and cannot be naive, disinterested or innocent. The evidence itself has to be organised and construed conceptually. This is why effective conceptualisation and theory construction is so basic to the realist conception of the way knowledge can be developed (Fleetwood, 2002: 37–9).

References

Ackroyd, S. and Fleetwood, S. (2000) *Realist Perspectives in Management and Organisation Studies*, London: Routledge.

Anderson, R., Hughes, J. and Sharrock, W. (1986) *Philosophy and the Human Sciences*, London: Routledge.

Archer, M.S. (1995) *Realist Social Theory: The Morphogenetic Approach*, Cambridge: Cambridge University Press.

Bauman, Z. (1978) *Hermeneutics and Social Science: Approaches to Understanding*, London: Hutchinson.

Benson, J. and Hughes, D. (1983) *The Perspective of Ethnomethodology*, London: Longman.

Bentley, A.F. (1967) *The Process of Government*, Cambridge, MA: Harvard University Press.

Bhaskar, R. (1978) *A Realist Theory of Science*, Brighton: Harvester.

—— (1979) *The Possibility of Naturalism*, Hemel Hempstead: Harvester.

Braithwaite, R.B. (1967) *Scientific Explanation: A Study of the Function of Theory, Probability and Law in Science*, Cambridge: Cambridge University Press.

Bryman, A. (1988) *Quantity and Quality in Social Research*, London: Routledge.

Byrne, D. (2002) *Interpreting Quantitative Data*, London: Sage.

Campbell, D.T. and Stanley, J. (1966) *Experimental and Quasi-experimental Designs for Research*, Chicago, IL: Rand McNally.

Delbridge, R (2002) 'Working in teams: ethnographic evidence from two "high performance" workplaces', in S. Fleetwood and S. Ackroyd (eds), *Realism in Action in Management and Organisation Studies*, London: Routledge.
Denzin, N. and Lincoln, Y. (1994) *Handbook of Qualitative Research*, London: Sage.
Dilthey, W. (1910) *The Formation of the Historical World in the Human Sciences*, trans. Makkreel and Rodi, Princeton, NJ: Princeton University Press.
Easton, G. (1992) *Learning from Case Studies*, 2nd edn, London: Prentice-Hall.
Fleetwood, S. (2001a) 'Conceptualising unemployment in a period of atypical employment: a critical realist analysis', *Review of Social Economics*, 59: 211–20.
—— (2001b) 'Causal laws, functional relations and tendencies', *Review of Political Economy*, 13: 201–20.
—— (2002) 'The Ontology of Organisation and Management Studies', in S. Fleetwood and S. Ackroyd (eds), *Realism in Action in Management and Organisation Studies*, London: Routledge.
—— (2005, forthcoming) 'The ontology of organisation and management studies: a critical realist approach', *Organization.*
Harré, R. (1970) *The Principles of Scientific Thinking*, London: Macmillan.
—— (1972) *The Philosophies of Science*, Oxford: Oxford University Press.
Harré, R. and Secord, P.F. (1972) *The Explanation of Social Behaviour*, Oxford: Blackwell.
Harrison, D. and Easton, G. (2002) 'Temporally embedded case comparison in industrial marketing research', in S. Fleetwood and S. Ackroyd (eds), *Realism in Action in Management and Organisation Studies*, London: Routledge.
Keat, R. and Urry, J. (1974) *Social Theory as Science*, London: Routledge.
Kowalczyk, R (2002) 'Tracing the effects of a hospital merger', in S. Fleetwood and S. Ackroyd (eds), *Realism in Action in Management and Organisation Studies*, London: Routledge.
Lawson, A. (1994) 'A Realist Theory for Economics' in R. Backhouse (ed.), *New Directions in Economic Methodology*, London: Routledge.
Marsh, C. (1988) *Exploring Data: An Introduction to Data Analysis for Social Scientists*, London: Macmillan.
May, T. (1997) *Social Research: Issues, Methods and Process*, Buckingham: Open University Press.
Medawar, P. (1970) *The Art of the Soluble*, London: Macmillan.
Miles, M. and Huberman, A.M. (1994) *Qualitative Data Analysis*, Beverley Hills, CA: Sage.
Mingers, J. (2002) 'Future directions in management science modelling', in S. Fleetwood and S. Ackroyd (eds), *Realism in Action in Management and Organisation Studies*, London: Routledge.
Moser, C. and Kalton, G. (1984) *Survey Methods of Social Investigation*, London: Heinemann.
Pawson, R. (1996) 'Theorising the interview', *British Journal of Sociology*, 47: 295–314.
Pawson, R. and Tilly, N. (1997) *Realistic Evaluation*, London: Sage.
Popper, K.R. (1959) *The Logic of Scientific Discovery*, London: Hutchinson.
Porter, S. (1993) 'Critical realist ethnography', *Sociology*, 27: 591–609.
Ricouer, P. (1982) *Hermeneutics and the Social Sciences*, trans. J.D. Thompson, Cambridge: Cambridge University Press.
Sayer, A. (2000) *Realism and Social Science*, London: Sage.
—— (2004) 'Why critical realism?', in S. Fleetwood and S. Ackroyd (eds), *Critical Realist Applications in Organisation and Management Studies*, London: Routledge.
Schutz, A. (1964) *Collected Papers*, vol. II, The Hague: M. Nijhoff
—— (1966) *Collected Papers*, vol. III, The Hague: M. Nijhoff

—— (1967) *Collected Papers*, vol. I, 2nd edn, The Hague: M. Nijhoff.
Silverman, D. (2000) *Doing Qualitative Research: A Practical Handbook*, London: Sage.
Thomas, W. and Znanieki, F. (1927) *The Polish Peasant in Europe and America*, New York: Alfred Knopf.
Yin, R.K. (1989) *Case Study Research: Design and Methods*, London: Sage.

7 Future directions in management science modelling

Critical realism and multimethodology

John Mingers

Introduction

This chapter argues for a re-orientation of the fundamentals of management science[1] in terms of both underlying philosophy and related methodology. In particular, it suggests that critical realism provides an underpinning which resolves many divisive issues as well as fitting in with management science's distinctive approach. It further argues that multimethodology (the use of a plurality of intervention or research methods) is an appropriate and complementary methodology.

The relevance and importance of critical realism for management science was highlighted in my earlier articles (Mingers, 1984, 1992a, 1999) and was developed most fully in my article of 2000 (Mingers, 2000a). The history of management science was shown to embody both the empiricist view of philosophy of science (what is often known as 'hard operational research') with its emphasis on observation, data collection, mathematical modelling, and prediction and control, as well as the conventionalist, primarily interpretive, view ('soft operations research') emphasising subjective viewpoints, problem structuring rather than solving, and learning rather than prediction. This split has contributed to several ongoing debates within management science:

- Is management science best viewed as science or technology? Clearly the early pioneers were scientists who saw their work as doing science (Blackett, 1962; Waddington, 1973; Larnder, 1984), a view supported by Miser (1991b, 1993). However, more recent opinion has been in favour of operational research (OR) as technology (Keys, 1989, 1998; Ormerod, 1996a).
- Assuming that management science is at least related to science, should it be seen as natural science, social science (Checkland, 1981; Jackson, 1991a, 1993; Checkland and Haynes, 1994; Tsoukas and Papoulias, 1996), or indeed critical science (Mingers, 1980, 1984, 1992b; Jackson, 1991b, 1999).
- What is an appropriate philosophy of science, whether it is natural or social? Proponents argued for the traditional positivist or empiricist viewpoint with various flavours – inductivist, deductivist, falsificationist (Dery *et al.*, 1993); a wider view of science as craft, developed by Ravetz (1971) and contested by

Miser (1991a, 1996), Keys (1991), and Ormerod (Ormerod, 1996a, 1996b); various types of constructivist, interpretive or postmodern stances that to a greater or lesser extent deny the possibility of an observer-independent reality (Bryant, 1993; White, 1994; Brocklesby and Cummings, 1996; Tsoukas and Papoulias, 1996; White and Taket, 1996; Brocklesby, 1997); or the social studies of science argument that successful science is actually the result of a political and social process (Keys, 1997, 1998).

Mingers (2000a) suggested that the adoption of critical realism could to some extent alleviate all these disputes, as well as fitting in with the generally realist nature of management scientists and the approach of practitioners. This was done, in part, by considering three common methods – system dynamics, statistics and forecasting, and soft systems methodology (SSM). Whilst the former was shown to be highly compatible with the basic critical realist retroductive methodology, statistics was overly empiricist and SSM was overly interpretivist. Suggestions were made as to how they could suitably be re-interpreted in a critical realist manner.

This chapter develops the theme by discussing the nature and role of mathematical modelling from a critical realist perspective. It takes as the main exemplar statistical forecasting, and in particular econometric-type modelling, but much of the evaluation would apply to other types of statistical analysis as well as mathematical programming. The final section discusses the role of quantitative modelling within a multimethodological approach based on critical realism.

Critical realism and management science: some general issues

In very broad terms, the main tenets of critical realism that are of importance for management science are: to re-establish a realist view of *being* in the ontological domain, whilst accepting the relativism of knowledge as socially and historically conditioned in the epistemological domain (Bhaskar, 1978); and to argue for a critical naturalism in social science (Bhaskar, 1979). More specifically, this involves:

- Ontologically, the existence of a domain of structures and mechanisms, events, and experiences (the Real). The structures have causal powers or tendencies the interplay of which leads to the occurrence (or absence) of particular events (the Actual). These structures may be physical, social, or conceptual, and may well be unobservable except through their effects. Some, but not all, of the events will be observed or experienced by people and thus become Empirical. Events and experiences themselves have causal properties.
- Epistemologically, the recognition that our knowledge is always provisional, and historically and culturally relative – we do not have observer-independent access to the world – but that this does not make all theories or beliefs equally valid.

- Methodologically, the view that science is not essentially about discovering universal laws, purely predictive ability, or the simple description of meanings and beliefs. Rather, it is centrally concerned with *explanation, understanding* and *interpretation.* It moves from some phenomenon (or its absence) that has been observed or experienced, to the postulation of some underlying mechanism(s) or structure(s) which, *if they existed*, would causally generate the phenomena. Efforts are then made to confirm or refute the proposed mechanisms. It is accepted from the outset that science, especially social science, is inherently transformative so that, for example, an understanding of the causes of some unwanted circumstances can inevitably lead to attempts to remove or change them (Bhaskar, 1994: 109).

How does this fit with the approach of management science in general? Unfortunately this is difficult to answer since management science is such a diverse field with many competing viewpoints. The following very general statements might perhaps be uncontentious:

- Management science is essentially concerned with bringing about change to real world situations perceived as problematic by at least some of their stakeholders. It is thus primarily a practical and applied subject.
- Its *raison d'être* is to apply some kind of scientific or analytic approach to such situations, although there will be significantly different views as to what constitutes such an approach.
- The contexts, usually organisational, within which it has to work are at least in part social and political. They are thus open rather than closed systems, and not easily susceptible to laboratory experimentation. This means that a common characteristic of management science is the use of *models* and *modelling* whether they be mathematical, computer-based, pictorial, or linguistic.

Modelling in management science: prediction or explanation

A good generic definition of a model within management science is that given by Pidd (1996: 15): 'a model is an external and explicit representation of part of reality as seen by the people who wish to use that model to understand, to change, to manage and to control that part of reality.' Whilst this certainly captures many elements of modelling it is, in a sense, too general – it obscures significantly different approaches to models and modelling. These can be seen more clearly in Mitchell (1993: 113) who distinguishes broadly two types:

1 The model simply as a device for predicting outputs from inputs. There being no need for the model to *represent* the real system in any particular form.

2 The model as a statement of beliefs held about the world by some of those involved. Such a model will generally involve some sort of knowledge or at least beliefs about significant aspects of the real system.

He goes on to suggest several dimensions for describing models. The most relevant is that of *black box versus structural*. Black box models simply link inputs with outputs, or seek patterns within particular data sets without any concern for the underlying causal mechanisms or relations. Structural models, on the other hand, explicitly embody relationships or theories and only use the data to estimate parameters or validate theories. Related dimensions are: *predictive/exploratory* – in order to be exploratory in any more than a very limited sense a model would have to be structural in order to be able to explore a wide range of different possibilities; and *instrumental/realistic* – generally instrumental models will be black box (and vice versa) but it is possible to mistake an instrumental model based on an analogy or metaphor for a genuinely structural one.

Rivett (1994: 28) makes a similar distinction between models that *explain* and models that simply *describe*. He illustrates this with the difference between Babylonian and Greek astronomical models. The Babylonians collected meticulous observations of planetary movements over many years and, simply from the data, were able to calculate and predict future movements quite accurately. The Greeks, on the other hand, developed a theory or model about *how* the planetary system worked, based on fifty-two concentric rotating spheres, and were also able to make reasonable predictions. Rivett (1994: 30) argues for the superiority of explanatory models:

> [There was now] an explanatory model which was then used to go beyond the limits of experience and observation. ... This is the power of an explanatory model, and is why one should always start modelling by listening to people, by reading about the problem area, and by thinking. Modellers should start by trying to think of explanations that make sense ... even when we have a descriptive model we still have to explain why it makes sense.

It is clear from a critical realist perspective that the role of modelling should definitely be that of explanation and understanding rather than prediction. The argument can be made from two directions. On the one hand the inevitable limitations of data-only models, as in econometrics (Lawson, 1997), means that their predictive accuracy will always be very poor in anything other than a very well-defined and largely closed (perhaps mechanical or physical) system. More positively, trying to gain some understanding of the underlying causal mechanisms, no matter how difficult this is, will potentially provide: a much richer understanding of the situation; the ability to consider possible changes that are outside of available or actual conditions; and ideas or theories that are potentially transferable to other situations, or can be built on cumulatively. This use of modelling fits in well with critical realist retroductive methodology. The hypothesised mechanisms can be explicitly represented via models, such as those of system dynamics, discrete event simulation or even soft systems methodology (SSM), and the consequences of their operation can be studied.

The chapter will now move on to a more detailed consideration of statistical models, mainly econometric forecasting models, in management science.

Statistical modelling in management science

Statistical analysis is a form of modelling that explicitly recognises the existence of uncertainty in a set of data. It is conventionally seen as having two possible roles – descriptive and inferential. Descriptive statistics are simply concerned with summarising the main characteristics of a dataset, particularly highlighting any patterns (and anomalies) that may not immediately be obvious. Inferential statistics goes beyond the data as given, recognising that it is likely to be only a sample of all possible values (the population), to draw inferences from the sample to its underlying population.

From a critical realist perspective, descriptive statistics is unobjectionable and, indeed, very useful. If patterns exist within some set of observations (be they quantitative or qualitative) then there must be some underlying structures, mechanisms or constraints generating them, and this may prove a good starting point for a critical realist investigation. We must be aware, of course, that the patterns in the data cannot be assumed simply to reflect an underlying reality. Critical realism recognises that the *process* of observation or, as we would call it, data *production* inevitably imposes itself on the results. This is especially so, we would argue (Mingers, 1989), within management science (as opposed to a pure research situation) where much of the data we work with is produced on a routine basis within an organisation, often for purposes different to the actual study, and with highly variable (and uncertain) levels of quality.

The critical realist critique

At first sight, inferential statistics would also appear to be compatible with critical realism in moving from actual observations to something underlying them, even if it is populations rather than mechanisms or structures. However, when we look at what is actually meant by this within statistics we find a very impoverished and empiricist viewpoint. We have taken an informal sample of 'business statistics' textbooks typical of those used on both undergraduate and postgraduate courses in business studies and management science to see what view was portrayed of the purpose (and limitations) of statistical modelling.[2]

A standard definition of the purpose of inferential statistics is '[t]he objective of statistics is to make inferences (predictions, decisions) about certain characteristics of the population based on information contained in a sample' (Mendenhall *et al.*, 1986: 7), where a sample is 'a subset of measurements selected from the population of interest'. This is already quite a limited aspiration – concentrating on making *predictions* about a defined *population* based only on *measured* data. However, it becomes even more so when we look at the definition of the underlying 'population'. Here there is a significant split between textbooks: several define a population as a collection of *objects of interest* whose characteristics can be measured (Ehrenberg, 1982; Anderson *et al.*, 1993; Picconi *et al.*, 1993), but several others (Mendenhall *et al.*, 1986; Kvanli *et al.*, 1989; McClave and Benson, 1989; Mendenhall and Sincich, 1989) actually limit the population itself to *data* rather than objects – 'a population is the set representing all measurements of interest to the sample collector' (Mendenhall *et al.*, 1986: 4). The real world seems to have been lost altogether in favour of merely that which can be measured, with no attempt at *explanation* at all.

Most of these textbooks have no discussion about the relationship between data analysis and wider questions of science, explanation and knowledge. One exception is Ehrenberg (1982) whose approach resonates quite well with critical realism. He distinguishes clearly between description and explanation. Much of science, he says, is a process of using data to build up more and more generalised law-like relationships. Patterns within data are tested to see if they hold under other conditions, and the result may be wider generalisations. However, he recognises that these are never universal and that they are usually purely *descriptive* (of the data) rather than being directly causal or theoretical. They do not, of themselves, enable us to identify the underlying mechanisms causing the relationship.

> Statistical hypotheses are … narrowly descriptive and differ from those of normal science, which tend to be explanatory or causal. … Explanations and theories imply causal mechanisms. But these are difficult to pin down. … The method is … seeing whether we can eliminate some of the possible explanations.
>
> (Ehrenberg, 1982: 254–6)

Statistics can play an important role here – both in identifying patterns to begin with, and in systematically eliminating potential causal mechanisms – although only to the extent that the relevant factors can be quantified.

Moving now to the practice of statistical modelling in management science, we shall consider in detail two papers (Fildes, 1985; Allen and Fildes, 2000) that set out to document the 'state of the art', at least in econometric-type forecasting. These sources have been chosen for several reasons: they are comprehensive and up-to-date surveys of econometric practice; they are written from a management science perspective; and they show some implicit sympathy for a critical realist perspective. Not all the criticisms of econometrics made in this chapter should therefore be assumed to apply to Fildes and Allen in particular.

To begin with, we can summarise the main criticisms of statistical modelling, particularly forecasting, that have been made from a critical realist perspective by a variety of authors (Sayer, 1992; Lawson, 1997; Pawson and Tilley, 1997; Porpora, 1998; Olsen, 1999; Ron, 1999; Mingers, 2000a; Fleetwood, 2001a):

1 The implicit philosophy of statistical modelling is inherently empiricist. It embodies a view of causation that is successionist rather than generative. It is based on the Humean conception of constant conjunctions of events. It is assumed that events occur in regular sequences and that these can effectively be quantified yielding a set of related variables, often over time. From these data mathematical equations can be generated that represent semi-universal laws. No other form of causation can be inferred from statistically significant results – they only imply association (Abbott, 1998). In contrast, critical realism emphasises the importance of generative causation – i.e. moving from observed data associations to the interacting causal mechanisms that underlie them, rather than simply a wider population of unobserved data.

2 Major assumptions have to be made about the closure and stability of the system under study. Extrinsic closure is the assumption that those factors not included in the model will not change, or will not have a substantive effect on the model if they do. In practice, there will be many variables excluded from the analysis for a variety of reasons. It could be because data is not available, or because the factors are not measurable; or because a factor is not operative at that point but could become so; or because the investigators are ignorant of it. These may well have significant effects on the phenomena being analysed (Liu, 1960). Moreover, social systems are never closed but always open to historical change and accident (what is sometimes called 'path dependence' (David, 1986)). This is a generalisation of the Lucas critique (Lucas, 1976; Hoover, 1988) that econometric models cannot be used for evaluating policy change since such changes will inevitably undermine the model by changing people's economic behaviour. Intrinsic closure is the aggregating assumption that economically active individuals are inherently identical, rational and linearly additive, with no emergent properties or non-linear dynamics. A further point here is that the data themselves are often extremely unreliable, as much a reflection of its process of production as some real factor.

3 Any model is always under-determined by the data. Partly because of the previous point, many different sets of variables, subject to different sets of relationships, will be compatible with the data. It is generally not possible to choose between them *on purely statistical grounds* and so all kinds of other, judgemental, factors come into play – *ad hoc* criteria, personal belief or intuition, 'experience', potential usefulness, robustness, etc. These undermine the supposedly 'scientific', observer-independent approach. Often the form of the model is chosen more for its mathematical properties, i.e. its tractability, than its realism.

4 Much statistical modelling is highly a-theoretic. That is, it does not draw on already available theory, even in disciplines such as economics where much is available, but instead restricts itself to simply describing or summarising the data in a concise way (Cooley and LeRoy, 1985).

5 The prevailing approach to statistical analysis – the null-hypothesis significance-test procedure (NHSTP) – is open to many criticisms (Chow, 1996):

- The null hypothesis (H_0), that which is assumed to be the case, could almost never be true.
- The null hypothesis (H_0) also includes the many assumptions of the model which are also highly unlikely (especially in the case of regression).
- The alternative hypothesis gives no specific information about the situation. In reality there are many possible hypotheses and the choice of H_0 and H_1 are essentially arbitrary.
- The chosen significance level is essentially arbitrary and therefore so is the likelihood of a significant result. The same is true of sample size.
- The results do not give the probability of H_1 being true, nor do they relate in any way to practical importance or significance.
- In practice, results tend to be either obviously significant, or not, and thus not requiring a test. Or, if they are in the grey area a larger sample is needed.

6 The final problem, a result of the above, is the pure lack of empirical success of econometric forecasting in practice.

Fildes' papers are useful in that they provide a comprehensive overview of econometric forecasting with an awareness of some of the above issues, guidelines for practitioners, and reference to many actual studies. The first paper (Fildes, 1985) summarises up to 1985 and the second (Allen and Fildes, 2000) updates this with new technical developments to 2000. We shall generally use the 1985 paper except where the later one is significantly different. The following sections discuss these points in turn.

1 Empiricism and causation

In the 1985 paper Fildes outlines what he considers a comprehensive approach to model building recognising immediately that this is often not followed in practice, or even in textbooks. This is, in outline:

(a) Define the system and theoretical model
(b) Convert the theoretical model to a data model
(c) Specify and test the model

  (i) Collect and refine data
  (ii) Specify functional form and estimation method
  (iii) Test assumptions
  (iv) Select variables and final model
  (v) Sensitivity tests for uncertain variables

(d) Compare with baseline forecasts
(e) Use model

One of the main general points that he makes is the importance of the early stages of model building, especially in terms of building on previous research and developing a theoretical model before going on to a data model. In this he is following the arguments of Hendry *et al.* (1990) that much econometric practice has been a-theoretical in developing empirical models independently of theory and using *ad hoc* criteria to choose between the many competing models. Fildes suggests that a theoretical model can be developed from a wide range of sources – what has been done before, theoretical work, prior research, unexplained findings or discussions with experts. This approach would certainly be applauded by critical realists, particularly against the alternative of an entirely data-driven approach such as that of Box-Jenkins.

However, the applause must be tempered when we see that the main purpose of this stage is not the identification of possible underlying structures or generating mechanisms, but simply large numbers of potential (theoretical) variables:

> On completing this stage … the modeller should be left with a number of competing theoretical models of the system, each model supplemented with additional ad hoc variables. The variables can be categorized into those core variables the modeller would like to include and those that are merely doubtful possibilities.
>
> (Fildes, 1985: 553)

The next stage, discussed below, is attempting to measure the variables.

This whole approach only makes sense with a particular view of causality. Fildes does discuss the issue of causality:

> Despite disclaimers to the contrary, economic model-building aims to identify causal models … [c]orrelation, or more precisely an appropriately specified econometric model of a system with stable predictive power to describe behaviour in that system, is as rigorous a definition of 'causality' as any experimental science can specify.
>
> (Fildes, 1985: 553)

The main position that Fildes is here defending against is that of a positivistic view of science that only accepts the results of experiments with strong controls over all relevant factors. In this we would agree but from a critical realist perspective the problem(s) with this particular view of causality are rather different.

First, the model will inevitably lack ontological depth. All the variables, and the factors they represent, must occur at essentially the same level of aggregation – organisation, industry, economy – whereas the actual world is a complex interweaving of different structures at many different levels (Fleetwood, 2001b). Second, despite Fildes' protestations, regression does only rely on *association* between variables. Such association could be the result of a genuine causal relation, but could equally stem from a mutual relation with a third, underlying, variable; a causal relation in the wrong direction; or indeed sheer coincidence. Third, the underlying assumption is one of stable event regularities (Humean causation). Although seldom explicitly discussed, Hendry (Hendry *et al.*, 1990: 184) accepts that 'I am a Humean in that I believe we cannot perceive necessary connections in reality. All we can do is set up a theoretical model in which we define the word "causality" precisely, as economists do with y=f(x).'

These abstract ideas can be illustrated by a project described by Ackoff (1978). A large American oil company owned hundreds of petrol stations but was concerned that many seemed unprofitable. It commissioned market researchers to investigate factors that influenced profitability. They talked to many experts and came up with over 100 potential variables. From these they eventually developed a regression model with thirty-five independents to predict the potential sales of a particular station. This model was used but did not perform well. Ackoff became involved and argued that the equation might *describe* behaviour in a predictive way but did not *explain* it. Why do drivers choose particular stations? It was found that most gas stations were sited at four-way intersections. Thus, for each incoming road there were four possible exits (including turning round after filling up) – sixteen routes in all. Ackoff found by observation that, for any particular station, just four routes yielded the majority of customers. Combining this information with the traffic densities at particular intersections provided a more accurate model to predict station performance.

But Ackoff was able to go further and understand, explain, and interpret these observations in turn. He hypothesised that drivers were concerned about how much time was lost in getting petrol and was able to show that the time lost as perceived by drivers generated the same ordering of routes as that which was actually observed. With this rich causal model, which only involved a couple of explanatory factors, it was possible to redesign and re-site petrol stations and significantly improve profitability. This example provides an excellent illustration of the difference between a successionist and a generative causal model.

2 *Stability and closure*

We can begin with Fildes' definition of an econometric model:

> Econometric models are just one of a number of different ways of characterizing an economic or behavioural system. They contrast with 'systems models' in that they are typically aggregative linear or almost linear models with a well-defined stochastic structure. Model parameters are estimated from the data using well understood and statistically 'optimal' techniques based on these stochastic assumptions. The variables modelled (or their proxies) are typically measurable.
>
> (Fildes, 1985: 550)[3]

We can see immediately the assumptions outlined above concerning stability and closure. It is a given of the whole approach that it makes atomistic and linear aggregating assumptions, and accepts that anything of relevance will be (reliably) measurable. Fildes recognises that this does cause problems for the modeller at stage A, systems definition:

> the level of aggregation in a model, the number of hierarchies to be included ... are not so self-apparent. ... Nor is the choice of causal framework straightforward. ... To complicate matters further, systems-based arguments suggest the possibility of higher aggregate-level characteristics'
>
> (Fildes, 1985: 552)

Unfortunately, 'it seems that little guidance is to be found in either the systems or the econometrics literature with regard to systems definition' (1985: 553).

The next move is from the theoretical model, such as it is, to the data model, and here more major problems occur. The theoretical variables will have to be measured in some way and those that have not been thought of, or cannot be measured, will have to be excluded. The model itself will have to be constructed on the assumptions of *closure* – that the excluded variables will together form relatively small random errors, and *stability* – that the relations underlying the data will remain constant. Little is said by Fildes about these major difficulties other than 'a modeller should attempt to include difficult-to-measure variables' (1985: 555) and, on stability, 'On the face of it a prime requirement for effective forecasting is stability of the model over time' (1985: 559). Some of the many problems with regard to measurement, generally acknowledged by Fildes, are: factors that are important but cannot be measured in principle; factors that cannot be measured directly, but for which there may be proxies; factors that can be measured but for which the measurements may be unreliable, or have missing data; factors for which there may not be sufficient data; factors that may be measured differently across observations; factors that are themselves difficult to forecast; data rarely conforms to the statistical assumptions underlying the methods.

3 Ad hoc nature of modelling

Having arrived at a set of data, often based on what is available as much as anything else, the next stage is the building of the model itself. Many decisions have to be made in developing a model: its functional form (e.g. linear or non-linear, absolute, differenced, transformed); single equation, structural equations, or vector autoregressive (VAR); what lag structure to use if any; which outliers to delete; what to do with missing data; and which variables to include or exclude.

Here, the major critique is that the model is always under-determined by the data and therefore choices are made in an *ad hoc* way, often based neither on sound statistical theory nor on domain-specific theory. That this is the case is amply demonstrated by several quotations from Fildes:

> [where data does not conform to assumptions this] will lead the modeller … to propose a more general model. … The generalization chosen will usually be *ad hoc*.
>
> (1985: 557)

> The phrase 'specification search' has been appropriated … to describe the *ad hoc* process by which a modeller shifts through the data in search of a model.
>
> (1985: 560)

> [The] recommendation to 'use one of the Stein rules …' seems unlikely to be followed until evidence accrues that these offer an improvement over current *ad hoc* procedures.
>
> (1985: 562)

> [T]here is no evidence to suggest that straightforward (but *ad hoc*) procedures for dealing with the problem are inadequate.
>
> (1985: 562)

> [T]he *ad hoc* rules such as 'choose the model with minimum standard error' can be used, for there is no evidence that they perform any worse
>
> (1985: 562)

He does give a general modelling strategy, but it is clearly the case that experienced modellers could easily come up with significantly different models based on the same set of data, thus undermining claims to researcher-independent objectivity. This has been demonstrated empirically by Magnus and Morgan (1999) who conducted an experiment in which an apprentice had to try to replicate the analysis of a dataset that might have been carried out by three different experts (Leamer, Sims and Hendry) following their published guidance. In all cases the results were different from each other, and different from that which would have been produced by the expert, thus demonstrating the importance of tacit knowledge in statistical analysis.

Magnus and Morgan conducted a further experiment which involved eight expert teams, from different universities, analysing the same sets of data, each using their own particular methodology. The data concerned the demand for food in the USA and in the Netherlands, and was based on a classic study by Tobin (1950) augmented with more recent data. The teams were asked to estimate the income elasticity of food demand and to forecast per capita food consumption. In terms of elasticities, the lowest estimates were around 0.38 whilst the highest were around 0.74 – clearly vastly different especially when remembering that these were based on *the same sets of data*. The forecasts were perhaps even more extreme – from a base of around 4,000 in 1989, the lowest forecast for the year 2000 was 4,130, while the highest was nearly 18,000 (see Magnus and Morgan, 1999: 297, Figure 4)!

A further area of significant judgemental adjustment is after forecasts have been made. It is commonplace, particularly among economic forecasters, to adjust forecasts to reflect aspects of the situation not contained in the model, for example unusual data, particular out-of-the-ordinary events, or simply the fact that recent forecasts have under- or over-estimated the trend (Fildes and Stekler, 2000). Such *ad hoc* changes do significantly improve at least short-term accuracy, but, equally, simply illustrate the points made above about model closure, and do little to help longer-term forecasts.

4 Statistical modelling as a-theoretical

Much statistical/econometric modelling is a-theoretic in two senses. First, there is the question of statistical theory. There is much available, and it is certainly covered extensively in textbooks, but as Fildes demonstrates, it is often ignored in practice and there is little empirical evidence of its actual value in forecasting. Second, and more important from a critical realist perspective, is that substantive or domain theory may be relevant to the situation. Here, Fildes identifies two different approaches to modelling – specific to general and general to specific (although they could more typically be called extrapolative and causal respectively). In the former, typified by the Box-Jenkins procedure, the main emphasis is on modelling a variable purely in terms of its own past history (autocorrelations). Occasionally, one or two other 'explanatory' or dummy variables may be added. This gives a conceptually simple model and a well-defined modelling process but, as Fildes points out, 'Little attention is given to the specification of the system in which the variables are defined and measured. Even less attention is given to earlier work, empirical or theoretical' (1985: 566).

The approach Fildes recommends, general to specific, does attempt to draw on previous work, although it is usually previous empirical studies rather than theory directly. But he recognises that there is a strong tendency to concentrate attention on the data that are available, perhaps using a variety of techniques, rather than trying the harder task of generating new data on the basis of available theories. However, several econometricians are much more critical arguing that econometrics is, in general, profoundly a-theoretical (Koopmans, 1947; Cooley and LeRoy, 1985; Hoover, 1988; Hendry *et al.*, 1990). One of the comments made by the assessors of the Magnus and Morgan experiment was: '{a}nother worrying aspect is the shift towards a more inductive approach, a shift away from the economic underpinning in favour of more elaborate statistical methodology' (Barten *et al.*, 1999).

One unusual reaction to the problem of basing data analysis on theory is that of Sims (1980), who developed one of the currently fashionable modelling approaches – vector autoregressive (VAR) models (Allen and Fildes, 2000). In order to avoid the problems of having to distinguish between exogenous and endogenous variables, of having to forecast the exogenous ones, and of having to specify some sort of theoretically appropriate model, VAR begins with a totally general specification in which *all* selected variables become endogenous and each is specified as a function of lagged values of all the other variables. Thus, if there are six variables there will be six equations to be estimated, each containing several lags (up to twelve or thirteen for monthly data) of the other five variables.

From a critical realist perspective this seems entirely the wrong response in that it is virtually completely data-driven and abdicates almost any role for economic theory or judgement. Whilst it appears to remove the need to make boundary judgements about different classes of variable, in reality it doesn't – it simply extends the boundary outwards to the variables included in the model as opposed to those which are ignored. This, as demonstrated above, is the main problem anyway – the assumptions of closure and stationary random residual variation. The idea that it somehow avoids having to forecast the independent variables also seems misplaced – they are still forecast, perhaps with no greater degree of accuracy, but it just becomes an automatic part of the process rather than a separate one. Finally, one is left with an enormous estimation problem given the vast number of parameters in the system. The whole traditional thrust of regression modelling has been to construct a parsimonious model, with as few variables as possible, in order to avoid spurious correlations or fits specific to the original dataset. With a VAR model we have to estimate large numbers of parameters,[4] many of which will in fact be statistically insignificant. Any attempt to reduce this number becomes almost impossible because of the vast set of possible combinations and the dangers of spurious significance when carrying out a sequence of significance tests (Allen and Fildes, 2000). Even Allen and Fildes, who discuss VAR extensively, recommend that 'If possible, use a single equation to make forecasts rather than a system of equations' (2000: 111).

5 *Significance testing*

The many serious problems with the whole significance testing approach have been outlined above and I will not go into more detail here. An important alternative to this – Bayesian modelling – is discussed below.

6 *Forecasting accuracy*

At a general level there is some agreement that econometric models do very poorly in *ex ante* forecasting (Leamer, 1983; Rosenberg, 1992; Hutchison, 1994; Kay, 1995; Smith, 1995), that is forecasts made before the event, using, where necessary, forecasts of the independent variables, as opposed to *ex post* forecasts using the actual values of the independent variables. Even in the latter case performance on holdout samples is much worse than within the sample on which the model was estimated. Indeed, Kay says about forecasts of the UK economy:

> Economic forecasters do not speak with discordant voices … they all say more or less the same thing at the same time. And what they say is almost

> always wrong. The differences between forecasts are trivial relative to the differences between all forecasts and what happens.
>
> (Kay, 1995: 19)

An article in the *Financial Times* on 30 January 2002 discussed forecasts, based on econometric models, for growth in GDP in the British economy during 2002. The forecasts ranged from 0.4 to 2.6 per cent, the highest being 650 per cent of the lowest! Mills and Pepper (1999) analysed the forecasting performance of the main UK forecasters – the Treasury, LBS and the National Institute – between 1970 and 1995. Their overall conclusion was that 'Major economic events tend to be poorly forecasted, with both serious bouts of inflation and deep recessions being underpredicted. … Forecasters do have a tendency to be incorrect in the same direction and to underestimate actual changes' (Mills and Pepper, 1999: 256). Sherden (1998: ii), in a provocative book about the difficulty of predicting the future, has documented how poorly forecasters in a whole variety of fields perform: 'Of these sixteen types of forecasts, only two – one-day-ahead weather forecasts and the aging of the population – can be counted on. The rest are about as reliable as the fifty-fifty odds in flipping a coin.' Even Fildes (2000), in a partly critical review of the book, accepts that much of the criticism of economic forecasters is justified.

Fildes has carried out three major reviews of the accuracy of model-based forecasting. His first 1985 paper summarised all the comparative literature that could be found up to that point. It compared forecast accuracy for 'causal', i.e. regression models against two other approaches – simple extrapolative and judgemental. In the comparison with extrapolative, eighty papers were examined. The conclusions were fairly clear and depended on whether the forecasts were *ex post* or *ex ante*. With *ex post* forecasts, where all the independent variables were known, results generally favoured modelling rather than extrapolative. However, with *ex ante* forecasts (the actual situation in practice) results were more mixed with the models often performing less well despite sometimes having judgemental 'corrections' made to the actual forecasts to reflect developments not currently in the model. The results on judgemental forecasting (from only a few comparisons) were even less clear with no particular advantage to modelling emerging.

Allen and Fildes' (2000) paper synthesised these studies together with a major comparison of Armstrong (1985) and post-1985 studies. The results, if anything, are even less clear. With regard to extrapolative models, Armstrong claims that they are better than model-based in the short term, but Fildes argues the relative performance is similar regardless of time horizon. In terms of *ex post* and *ex ante* the later evidence seems to contradict the earlier, but this depends very much on which studies are included. With regard to judgemental forecasting, the results suggest that causal methods will *only* be superior where there are many observations available and large changes in the environment are likely. Again, however, the results can be interpreted in different ways.

Fildes and Stekler (2000) provide a detailed consideration of the accuracy of macroeconomic forecasting in the USA and the UK. Their review is best summarised in their own words:

> We have found that most forecasters fail to predict recessions in advance and sometimes fail to recognise them contemporaneously. Forecasters also seem to make systematic errors such as underestimating growth during periods of economic expansion, overestimating it during declines, under-predicting inflation when it is accelerating and overpredicting when it is decelerating. Despite the *relatively large errors observed*, almost all forecasts are superior to the predictions that could have been obtained from naive models and *often* better than those generated by time series models. … In addition, there is little evidence that forecasts have improved over time.
>
> (Fildes and Stekler 2000: 29–30, emphasis added)

Unfortunately, these studies do not generally discuss the *absolute* accuracy of any of the forecasting methods[5] nor which methods may be appropriate in which circumstances. There is some evidence on this in a study by Makridakis *et al.* (1998), which also summarises the results of many comparisons including a special issue of *International Journal of Forecasting* (October 1990) that looked at the accuracy of major macroeconomic models, and other studies by Fildes (Fildes and Makridakis, 1995; Fildes *et al.*, 1997). The general conclusions are: (1) that simple methods, e.g. naive trend extrapolation generally, do as well as more complex models (e.g. Box-Jenkins or regression) including complex econometric models; (2) that there is some evidence that particular models may be more appropriate for particular forecasting horizons; (3) that there is little evidence that the quality of forecasting is improving over time; and (4) that *combining* forecasts from different methods, even in a fairly *ad hoc* way, often considerably improves forecast accuracy.

In a later paper describing a forecasting competition between different forecasting techniques, Makridakis and Hibon (2000: 459) again show that complex methods are no better than simple ones and suggest that this may be because 'real life time-series are not stationary while many of them also contain structural changes as fads and fashions can change established patterns and affect existing relationships'. In other words, the social and economic world is not a closed system as econometric modelling would presume.

We can perhaps summarise the state of play with Allen and Fildes' (2000) conclusion: '*A well specified econometric model should forecast at least as well as the naïve no-change method*' (p. xxx). Given the problems, outlined above, of the availability and reliability of data, the difficulty of developing a 'well-specified' model, and the significant costs in time and expertise involved, then this is surely damning with faint praise.

Bayesian modelling

As a slight digression, I want to consider briefly an approach to statistical modelling which is an alternative to the traditional one discussed above. Although it often ends up in the same place, it approaches from an interestingly different starting point and seems to have a greater affinity with the critical realist approach.

In contrast to the traditional approach, Bayesian modelling is characterised by the following (West and Harrison, 1989; French and Smith, 1997):

1. An interest in the subjective knowledge, beliefs and judgements of those concerned with a particular situation or decision. These beliefs, which will generally be uncertain, can be represented by *subjective* probabilities.
2. An explicit approach to modelling such beliefs that allows both changes in belief in the light of new information, and the combining together of information from different sources.
3. A focus on *causal structures* and particularly the updating of beliefs about underlying causes in response to the occurrence (or non-occurrence) of particular events.

Technically, this approach stems from a well-accepted mathematical result called Bayes' theorem which is used to adjust probabilities in the light of new data.[6] Suppose we have a die but are not sure if it is biased towards a six or not. Our *prior* probabilities are, say, fifty-fifty that it is unbiased. We throw it four times and get three sixes. This outcome or event can be used to adjust our view about the die. We calculate the *likelihood* of this outcome given the two possible situations or causes. It is clearly more likely to have occurred if the die is biased, and we can use Bayes' theorem to update the prior probabilities into *posterior* ones – say 60/40 in favour of a biased die. This process could be continued with more data generating more certainty about the situation.

There is no debate about this procedure from a technical point of view – Bayes' theorem follows from the laws of probability and is accepted by traditionalists. The dispute comes in terms of the source of the probabilities. Traditional statisticians generally take a 'frequentist' view that valid probabilities can only come from the objective observation of relative frequencies, and deny the legitimacy of subjective probabilities. Bayesians, in contrast, are very happy to use subjective judgement and expert knowledge along with empirical data where it is available.

> Knowledge is available in several forms, a useful classification being into historical information and professional wisdom or advice. From analysis of historical information we may derive a model … [b]ut other knowledge that is not – cannot be – part of such a formal model may also be valuable. … The Bayesian paradigm provides a rational, coherent, formal framework for combining information.
>
> (Pole *et al.*, 1994: 9)

The approach begins by eliciting the beliefs of a decision maker or expert in terms of causal structures relevant to the situation and the prior probabilities of the various outcomes. This is by no means a simple process and much of the learning goes on at this stage. These can be represented in a variety of forms – decision trees, belief nets, influence diagrams, and probability distributions.

They can include values and preferences as well as probabilities. The next stage is to obtain further information with which to update these prior views. This could involve collecting quantitative data, undertaking specific tests or even experiments, or obtaining particular knowledge or expertise not currently available. The final stage (although the whole process is ongoing and iterative) is to generate the posterior probabilities and distributions in the light of the extra information. Bayesian modelling has a very wide range of potential application areas – decision analysis and decision making in general (French and Smith, 1997), forecasting (Pole *et al.*, 1994), traditional statistics (Berry, 1996) and belief networks (Oliver and Smith, 1990).

Belief networks are particularly interesting from a critical realist point of view, as they can be seen as a way of operationalising critical realism's retroductive methodology. We will illustrate this with an example from McNaught (2001). Suppose you are walking along and see a youth disappearing into the window of a house. Two possible explanations occur to you – it could be a burglary, or it could be that the person has locked themselves out. You decide to do something to help decide between the two and knock at the door, reasoning that a burglar is unlikely to answer but a legitimate occupant would. If you don't receive a reply it is not absolutely conclusive since the person may not have heard, but your (posterior) belief in the burglar theory rises and that of the lock-out falls. You could also find out more information that might affect your prior beliefs. For instance, is this an area with a high burglary rate? If so, the prior probability of a burglary may be high. Or, can you find out if a youth lives in the house or not? If not, then clearly one explanation falls straight away. This system of causal links can be represented in a belief network, and the various probabilities can be added to it. As particular events do or do not occur, Bayes' theorem can be used to update the relevant probabilities, and these in turn can be propagated throughout the network. This type of approach can be very useful in many forms of diagnosis, such as medical or mechanical fault finding.

The critical realist approach: multimethodology

The preceding sections have essentially been a critique of the traditional, empiricist approach to quantitative modelling. This section addresses the question of what role modelling, especially quantitative modelling, plays in a critical realist view of management science. This will be done by locating it within a wider context, that of a general methodology for management science interventions. The particular approach advocated here, *multimethodology*, has been developed at least in part with critical realism in mind. As such, it can also provide a contribution to critical realism itself, particularly in terms of action-oriented research.

Multimethodology

The fundamental tenet of multimethodology is the importance of combining together techniques or methods[7] in dealing with real-world situations whether the purpose is pure research or a practical intervention.[8] More specifically, the combination should involve both hard/soft, qualitative/quantitative methods.

The multi-dimensional world

Using a particular method or methodology is like viewing the world through a specific instrument such as a telescope, an X-ray machine, or an electron microscope. Each reveals certain aspects but is blind to others. Although they may be pointing at the same place, each instrument produces a different, and sometimes seemingly incompatible, representation. Thus, in adopting only one method, one is often gaining only a limited view of a particular research situation, for example attending only to that which may be measured or quantified; or only to individuals' subjective meanings and thus ignoring the wider social and political context. This argument is a strong one in support of multimethod research suggesting that it is always wise to utilise a variety of approaches.

A framework has been developed (Mingers and Brocklesby, 1997) from Habermas's (1979, 1984, 1987, 1993) theory of communicative action and is shown in Figure 7.1. His more recent work has concerned itself with the pragmatics of human communication and its implications for ethics. Habermas (1984: Chapter 3) argues that the distinctive nature of humans is their ability to communicate and debate through language, and he calls this activity commu-

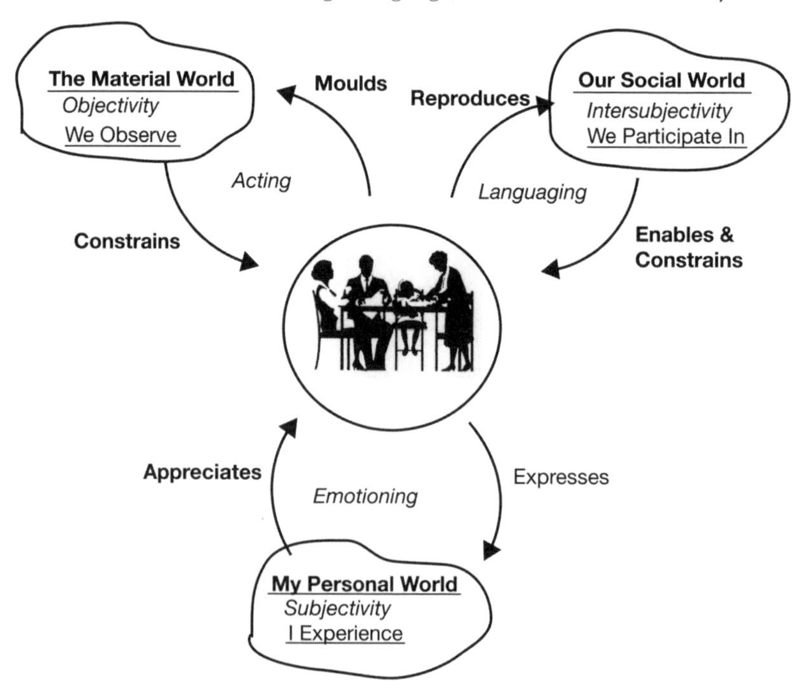

Figure 7.1 Habermas's three worlds

nicative action. Its fundamental purpose is achieving and maintaining understanding amongst those involved. There are, of course, other types of action – instrumental (aimed at achieving personal goals in a non-social way), strategic (aimed at influencing other actors to achieve one's goals) and discursive (aimed at re-establishing agreement after a breakdown).

Habermas (1984: 75–101) analyses communicative action not abstractly in terms of syntax or semantics, but as real, purposeful, pragmatic interaction between social subjects. He is concerned with actual utterances made by speakers engaged in a social process, and argues that such utterances implicitly raise or embody particular validity claims. These claims can always be challenged or questioned and the speaker must be prepared and able to justify them for the utterance to be acceptable. Four validity claims are distinguished: comprehensibility, truth, rightness and sincerity. Comprehensibility simply means that the utterance should be understandable to a competent speaker of the language. The other three refer to relations between the utterance and three different worlds – the objective world of actual and possible states of affairs; the social world of normatively regulated social relations; and the subjective world of personal experiences and beliefs.[9]

Thus, an acceptable utterance must be understandable; it must be true with respect to an external world; be based on valid social norms that are considered right; and be meant sincerely in reflecting the speaker's beliefs. A listener may question any of these claims leading to further utterances aimed at justifying them that may, themselves, be questioned. The process as a whole is seen as an ideal-type for rational communication in which the 'force of the better argument' (Habermas, 1990: 159) should eventually hold sway.

If we broaden Habermas's theory from considering only utterances towards research and intervention in general, then we can categorise methods in terms of their relationship with the three worlds – the material world, the social world and the personal world. Each domain has different modes of existence and different epistemological possibilities. The material world is outside and independent of human beings. It existed before us and would exist whether or not we did. We can shape it through our actions, but are subject to its constraints. Our relationship to this world is one of observation (rather than participation or experience), but such observations are always theory- and subject-dependent. We can characterise this world as objective in the sense that it is independent of the observer, although clearly our observations and descriptions of it are not.

From this material world, through processes of evolution, linguistically endowed humans have developed, capable of communication and self-reflection. This has led to the social and personal worlds. The personal world is the world of our own individual thoughts, emotions, experiences and belief. We do not observe it, but experience it. This world is subjective in that it is generated by, and only accessible to, the individual subject. We can aim to express our subjectivity to others and, in turn, appreciate theirs.

Finally there is the social world that we (as members of particular social systems) share. Our relation to it is one of intersubjectivity since it is, on the one hand, a human construction, and yet, on the other, it goes beyond and pre-exists any particular individual. It consists of a complex multi-layering of language, meaning, social practices, rules and resources that both enables and constrains our actions and is reproduced through them. One of its primary dimensions is that of power (Mingers, 1992b).

Research intervention as a process

The second argument for combining methods is that research and intervention are not discrete events but a process that has phases or, rather, different types of activities that will predominate at different times. Particular methodologies and techniques are more useful for some functions than others, and so a combination of approaches may be necessary to provide a more comprehensive outcome. To help do this in practice some categorisation of the phases of an intervention would be useful, against which could be mapped the strengths and weaknesses of various methods. Producing such a classification is difficult because research and intervention in general are so diverse – from library-based literature reviews, through experimentation, surveys and ethnography, to action research or critical intervention in real-world organisations. So, any such typography needs to be very abstract.

An analysis of the general process of research and intervention, based on the work of Bhaskar (1979: 144), Maturana (1990: 18), and Tashakkori and Teddlie (1998), led to the identification of the following four phases:

Appreciation of the research situation, as experienced by the researchers involved and expressed by any actors in the situation, and prior literature and theories. This will involve the identification of the experience or phenomena to be explained, initial conceptualisation and design of the study, and the production of basic data using methods such as observation, interviews, experiments, surveys, or qualitative approaches. ... Note that this cannot be an 'observer-independent' view of the situation 'as it really is'. It will be conditioned by the researcher's previous experience and their access to the situation.

Analysis of the data produced so as to understand the history that has generated it, and the particular structure of relations and constraints that maintain it. This will involve analysis methods appropriate to the methodology of the study and the data produced in the first stage. Explanation will be in terms of possible hypothetical mechanisms or structures that, if they existed, would produce the phenomenon that has been observed, measured, or experienced.

Assessment of the postulated explanation(s) in terms of other predicted effects, alternative possible explanations and, within action research, consideration of ways in which the situation could be other than it is. Interpretation of the results, and inference to other situations.

Action to bring about changes if necessary or desired, or to report on and disseminate the research results.

Put crudely, these phases cover: What is happening? Why is it happening? How could the situation or explanation be different? And so what? We should emphasise immediately that these activities are not seen as discrete stages that are enacted one by one. Rather, they are aspects of the intervention that need to be considered throughout, although their relative importance will differ as the project progresses. Equally, different studies will place their emphasis at some stages rather than others.

The context of a research intervention

Developing work of Checkland (1981) we can conceptualise a research intervention in terms of three notional systems: an *intervention system (IS)*, a *problem content system (PCS)* and an *intellectual resources system (IRS)* as shown in Figure 7.2.

The PCS is the part of the world within which the problem or research opportunity exists. It could be one or a number of organisations, or part of an organisation; a particular country or industry; or some area of academic discourse. It will include the clients of the intervention or funding bodies for the research. It will generally be a complex interaction of people, social practices, ideas and knowledge, and technology. The IS are the particular agents or practitioners engaged within the situation (some of whom, particularly in action research, may ordinarily be involved in the situation). The IRS consists of those frameworks of theories, methodologies and techniques that could potentially be

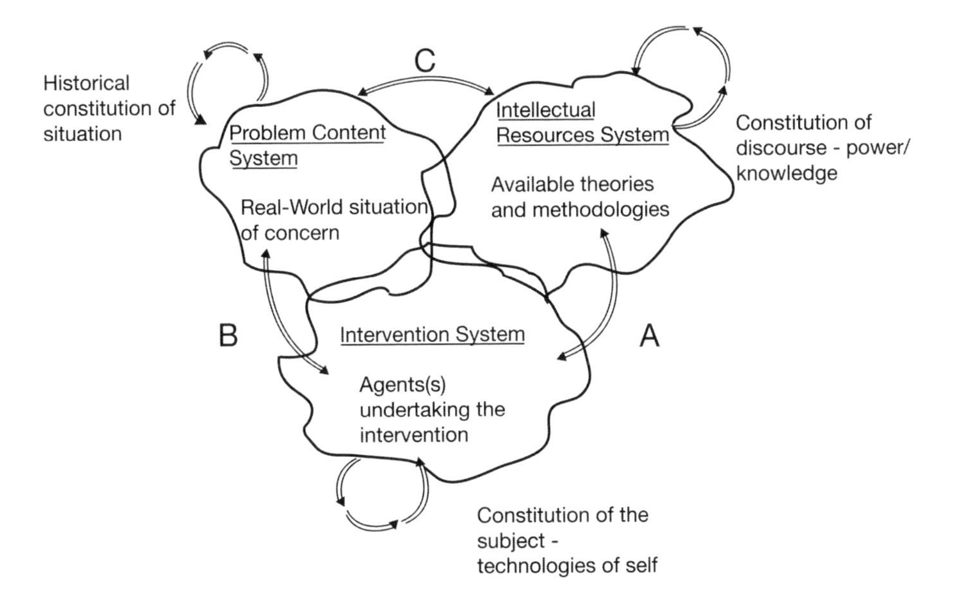

Figure 7.2 The context of interventions

relevant to the situation, although not necessarily within the agent's current repertoire. There are self-referential relations of each system with its own past history that leads it to be the way that it is. It is one of the contentions of this approach that, in the development of management science methodologies, too little attention has been paid to the nature and role of the agent or practitioner involved in interventions in terms of their relationships to both the situation and to the intellectual frameworks available to them. In some ways this is ironic – the development of soft and then critical methodologies focused attention on the human actors in the problem situation but generally remained silent about the users of such methodologies.

These three domains and their relations constitute the context at the point of engagement in a research situation. Consideration of these sorts of issues will determine both the initial actions taken and the planning or design of the research intervention (Ormerod, 1996b) as a whole. During an intervention they both condition, and change in response to, what happens. Thus they serve as continual reference points for the process of critical reflection that is necessary to structure the research choices made during the process.

A framework for mapping methodologies

In the section above on the desirability of multimethodology, two important features of research interventions were described – their multidimensionality and the different types of activity that need to be undertaken. By combining these two factors, a grid is produced (see Table 7.1) that can be used to map the characteristics of different research methodologies to help in linking them together.

Table 7.1 Framework for mapping methodologies

	Appreciation of	*Analysis of*	*Assessment of*	*Action to*
Social	social practices, power relations	distortions, conflicts, interests	ways of altering existing structures	generate empowerment and enlightenment
Personal	individual beliefs, meanings, emotions	differing perceptions and personal rationality	alternative conceptualisations and constructions	generate accommodation and consensus
Material	physical circumstances	underlying causal structure	alternative physical and structural arrangements	select and implement best alternatives

The logic of this framework is that a fully comprehensive research intervention needs to be concerned with the three different worlds – material, personal and social – and the four different phases. Thus each box generates questions about particular aspects of the research situation that need to be addressed.[10] The framework can then be used in two ways: either considering the questions and asking what research methods may be useful in addressing them; or looking at a research method(ology) and mapping it on to the framework to see which areas it addresses, and appraising its relative strength in each box. Examples of using the framework for both direct intervention and research can be found in other works of mine (Mingers, 1997, 2000b, 2001).

Quantitative modelling within multimethodology

This section will discuss a putative role for quantitative modelling within management science interventions from the critical realist and multimethodology perspective.

With reference to Table 7.1, where might mathematical or statistical modelling be valuable? In terms of the three worlds, the main consideration is that any form of quantitative modelling, by definition, can only deal with factors or processes that can be measured or counted in a reliable way. Generally these will be aspects of a problem situation that relate to the material world rather than the social, concerned with norms, power and communication, or the personal, concerned with values, meanings and beliefs, and thereby involving interpretation and understanding.

In terms of the phases of an intervention, quantitative modelling can be potentially useful at all of them but especially so in *appreciation* and *assessment*. At the beginning of a project the main effort is in finding out about the nature of the situation you are dealing with. Clearly, producing and analysing data will be valuable in gaining a general appreciation. Such analysis can begin to identify the major relationships and constraints that will be of importance, but can only ever give a partial picture. More specifically, some statistical techniques are very good at identifying patterns in large sets of data. For instance, supermarkets have vast stores of data about our shopping habits but uncovering unexpected relationships requires sophisticated data mining or multivariate statistical techniques.

Such modelling is what was described above as descriptive rather than explanatory. That is, its aim is to generate a compact representation of the patterns and relationships of the data themselves, without going beyond that to try to explain the underlying causal mechanisms at play. This is essentially the second phase, *analysis* – which is really the main plank of critical realism's retroductive methodology. Generally, this phase requires theoretical understanding and imagination to come up with potential explanations rather than detailed modelling. But there are modelling techniques that can be valuable. Within statistics, methods such as factor analysis and path analysis do aim to go beneath the surface to draw out latent variables or causal connections. Whilst, more generally, simulation methods such as system dynamics or discrete events can be used to build models of possible causal mechanisms to see if they can replicate the behaviour of interest, the goal of this form of modelling would not be prediction so much as learning.

The third stage is one of *assessment*, either of competing causal explanations, or of potential changes to the situation that may be desirable or feasible. Here again modelling can be useful. Statistical methods such as analysis of variance or covariance, or correspondence analysis can be used to test for the effects of hypothesised structures (or demi-regs as Lawson (1997) calls them). Whilst we do not expect to find universal regularities with the social and economic world, nevertheless underlying causal structures may well give rise to differences or contrasts that are relatively enduring over space or time. Such differences could relate to ways of structuring organisations; ways of producing goods or services; different types or sources of raw materials; and so on. Statistical tests can be used to detect the existence of such contrasts or to check the efficacy of possible changes. Equally, OR techniques such as mathematical programming or simulation could be used to generate and test various alternative options, at least in terms of the factors which can be quantified.

The fundamental point of this discussion is that quantitative modelling does have a serious role to play within research interventions but, theoretically at least, that role should always be seen as one of assisting the general critical realist approach of better explanation and learning, rather than simply description or prediction. And the inevitable limitations of such models to that which may be quantified means that they can only ever be part of the whole project plan.

Having said that, we also have to recognise that, in the end, management science interventions are primarily practical exercises, driven by the needs of the clients who are sponsoring and often paying for the work, and limited by time and resource constraints (as indicated in Figure 7.2). This means that there will also be occasions when only a 'quick and dirty' data-driven approach is feasible. To take a simple example, a very common requirement is forecasting short-term sales for a large number of items. This could occur in a large garage which keeps perhaps 5,000 different spare parts. The garage will need a system for forecasting demand for each part over the next two months. Ideally, each part should be investigated to discover the factors underlying demand in order to build an explanatory model. In practice, this would be quite infeasible, and the costs could never be justified. The only viable approach is to identify (by Pareto analysis) the small number of parts that account for most of the turnover and study them in detail, but, for the large number of parts that contribute little, to use a crude, data-driven, extrapolative method such as exponential smoothing.

Conclusions

This chapter has been primarily concerned with the nature and role of quantitative modelling within management science. It may seem as though it has largely been negative and critical, but we would like to make it clear that our concerns are not so much with mathematical modelling itself, but with the predominantly empiricist understanding of the modelling process. From a critical realist perspective quantitative modelling[11] can be very useful as a way of discovering patterns of events that reveal the presence of underlying structures; conceptualising and exploring the behaviour of possible generative mechanisms; and conducting analyses to test out possible explanations. It should not, generally, be seen as simply driven by or descriptive of available sets of data, and should be part of wider investigations that include the softer, qualitative, aspects of problematic situations.

Notes

1 This term should be taken to include operational research (OR), systems thinking and information systems insofar as they adopt an approach towards investigating and intervening in the organisational world based on explicit modelling.
2 We choose textbooks not to try to prove our contentions about statistical modelling but because we are concerned with management science *practice*, and it is from textbooks that practitioners will have learnt their craft.
3 An example of a stochastic assumption is that the forecast errors are independent, identically normally distributed, random variables. This implies homoscedasticity, i.e. that the error variance is constant across the range of values of the dependent variable. Other assumptions typically made in regression are that all relationships are linear, that the explanatory variables are all normally distributed and independent of each other.
4 With six variables, and therefore equations, each using twelve lags, we need to estimate seventy-three parameters per equation!
5 There is an excellent example in Rosenhead and Mingers (2001: 185) of the difficulty of forecasting a major economic series – the world demand for oil. The graph shows forecasts made at various times since 1955 in comparison with the actual outcomes which were always highly divergent.
6 Formally, if C1 and C2 are the two possible causes (biased or unbiased), and E is the event or outcome (three heads out of four), then

$$Pr(C1|E) = Pr(E|C1)xPr(C1) / (Pr(E|C1)xPr(C1) + Pr(E|C2)xPr(C2))$$

7 Clarification of terms such as 'technique', 'method' and 'methodology' can be found in Mingers (2001).
8 In fact this is not a dichotomy but the ends of a dimension. All research involves some form of intervention or effect, and all interventions involve research. In this section I shall generally refer to a 'research intervention' to cover both aspects.
9 These three worlds are related to Popper's worlds 1, 2, 3. The differences are discussed in Habermas (1984: 76).
10 These questions should not be interpreted objectivistically, that is capable of answers independent of the agents involved. Rather they will involve ongoing debate, construction and reflection amongst the agents and actors involved.
11 Including in that term approaches such as simulation, mathematical programming, system dynamics and combinatorial heuristics as well as the statistical approaches discussed in the chapter.

References

Abbott, A. (1998) 'The causal devolution', *Sociological Methods and Research*, 27 (2): 148–81.
Ackoff, R. (1978) *The Art of Problem Solving*, New York: Wiley.

Allen, G.P. and Fildes, R. (2000) 'Econometric forecasting', in J.S. Armstrong (ed.), *Principles of Forecasting: A Handbook for Researchers and Practitioners*, Norwell, MA: Kluwer.
Anderson, D., Sweeney, D. and Williams, T. (1993) *Statistics for Business and Economics*, New York: West Publishing.
Armstrong, J.S. (1985) *Long Range Forecasting: From Crystal Ball to Computer*, New York: Wiley.
Barten, A., Cramer, J., Hashem Pesaran, M., Schmidt, P. and Wickens, M. (1999) 'Comparative assessments of the field trial experiment', in J. Magnus and M. Morgan (eds), *Methodology and Tacit Knowledge: Two Experiments in Econometrics*, New York: Wiley, pp. 269–83.
Berry, D. (1996) *Statistics: a Bayesian Perspective*, Belmont, CA: Duxbury Press.
Bhaskar, R. (1978) *A Realist Theory of Science*, Hemel Hempstead: Harvester.
—— (1979) *The Possibility of Naturalism*, Sussex: Harvester.
—— (1994) *Plato Etc*, London: Verso.
Blackett, P. (1962) *Studies of War*, New York: Hill and Wang.
Brocklesby, J. (1997) 'Becoming multimethodology literature: an assessment of the cognitive difficulties of working across paradigms', in J. Mingers and A. Gill (eds), *Multimethodology: The Theory and Practice of Combining Management Science Methodologies*, Chichester: Wiley, pp. 189–216.
Brocklesby, J. and Cummings, S. (1996) 'Foucault plays Habermas: an alternative philosophical underpinning for critical systems thinking', *Journal of the Operational Research Society*, 47 (6): 741–54.
Bryant, J. (1993) 'OR enactment: the theatrical metaphor as an analytic framework', *Journal of the Operational Research Society*, 44 (6): 551–61.
Checkland, P. (1981) *Systems Thinking, Systems Practice*, Chichester: Wiley.
Checkland, P.B. and Haynes, M.G. (1994) 'Varieties of systems thinking – the case of soft systems methodology', *System Dynamics Review*, 10 (2–3): 189–97.
Chow, S. (1996) *Statistical Significance: Rationale, Validity and Utility*, New York: Sage.
Cooley, T. and LeRoy, S. (1985) 'Atheoretical macroeconomics: a critique', *Journal of Monetary Economics*, 16 (3).
David, P. (1986) 'Understanding the economics of QWERTY', in W. Parker (ed.), *Economic History and the Modern Economist*, Oxford: Blackwell, pp. 30–49.
Dery, R., Landry, M. and Banville, C. (1993) 'Revisiting the issue of model validation in OR: an epistemological view', *EJOR*, 66: 168–83.
Ehrenberg, A. (1982) *A Primer in Data Reduction*, Chichester: Wiley.
Fildes, R. (1985) 'Quantitative forecasting – the state of the art: econometric models', *Journal of the Operational Research Society*, 36 (7): 549–80.
—— (2000) 'Book review', *International Journal of Forecasting*, 16 (1): 132–3.
Fildes, R. and Makridakis, S. (1995) 'The impact of empirical accuracy studies on time series analysis and forecasting', *International Statistical Review*, 63: 289–308.
Fildes, R. and Stekler, H. (2000) 'The state of macroeconomic forecasting', *Discussion Paper*, 99–104, Lancaster: Lancaster University.
Fildes, R., Hibon, S. and Makridakis, S. (1997) 'Generalising about univariate forecasting methods: further empirical evidence', *International Journal of Forecasting*, 14 (3): 339–58.
Fleetwood, S. (2001a) 'Causal laws, functional relations and tendencies', *Review of Political Economy*, 13 (2): 201–20.
—— (2001b) 'Conceptualizing *un*employment in a period of atypical *em*ployment: a critical realist perspective', *Review of Social Economy*, LIX (1): 45–69.
French, S. and Smith, J. (eds) (1997) *The Practice of Bayesian Analysis*, London: Arnold.
Habermas, J. (1979) *Communication and the Evolution of Society*, London: Heinemann.

—— (1984) *The Theory of Communicative Action Vol. 1: Reason and the Rationalization of Society*, London: Heinemann.

—— (1987) *The Theory of Communicative Action Vol. 2: Lifeworld and System: A Critique of Functionalist Reason*, Oxford: Polity Press.

—— (1990) *Moral Consciousness and Communicative Action*, Cambridge: Polity Press.

—— (1993) 'On the pragmatic, the ethical, and the moral employments of practical reason', in J. Habermas (ed.), *Justification and Application*, Cambridge: Polity Press, pp. 1–17.

Hendry, D., Leamer, E. and Poirier, D. (1990) 'The ET dialogue: a conversation on econometric methodology', *Econometric Theory*, 6: 171–261.

Hoover, K. (1988) *The New Classical Macroeconomics: a Sceptical Enquiry*, Oxford: Blackwell.

Hutchison, T. (1994) 'Ends and means in the methodology of economics', in R. Backhouse (ed.), *New Directions in Economic Methodology*, London: Routledge.

Jackson, M. (1991a) 'The origins and nature of critical systems thinking', *Systems Practice*, 4 (2): 131–49.

—— (1991b) *Systems Methodology for the Management Sciences*, New York: Plenum Press.

—— (1993) 'Social theory and operational research practice', *Journal of the Operational Research Society*, 44 (6): 563–77.

—— (1999) 'Towards coherent pluralism in management science', *Journal of the Operational Research Society*, 50 (1): 12–22.

Kay, J. (1995) 'Cracks in the crystal ball', *Financial Times*, 29 September.

Keys, P. (1989) 'OR as technology: some issues and implications', *Journal of the Operational Research Society*, 40 (9): 753–59.

—— (1991) 'A technologist's response to Miser', *Journal of the Operational Research Society*, 42 (5): 431–3.

—— (1997) 'Approaches to understanding the process of OR: review, critique and extension', *Omega-International Journal of Management Science*, 25 (1): 1–13.

—— (1998) 'OR as technology revisited', *Journal of the Operational Research Society*, 49 (2): 99–108.

Koopmans, T. (1947) 'Measurement without theory', *Review of Economics and Statistics*, 29 (2): 161–72.

Kvanli, A., Guynes, S. and Pavur, R. (1989) *Introduction to Business Statistics*, New York: West Publishing.

Larnder, H. (1984) 'The origin of operational research', *Operations Research*, 32: 465–75.

Lawson, T. (1997) *Economics and Reality*, London: Routledge.

Leamer, E. (1983) 'Let's take the con out of econometrics', *American Economic Review*, 73 (1): 31–43.

Liu, T. (1960) 'Under-identification, structural estimation, and forecasting', *Econometrica*, 28: 855–65.

Lucas, R. (1976) 'Econometric policy evaluation: a critique', in K. Briunner and A. Meltzer (eds), *The Phillips Curve and Labour Markets*, Amsterdam: North-Holland, pp. 19–46.

McClave, J. and Benson, G. (1989) *A First Course in Business Statistics*, San Francisco, CA: Dellen.

McNaught, K. (2001) *An Introduction to Bayesian Belief Networks*, OR 43, Bath: OR Society.

Magnus, J. and Morgan, M. (eds) (1999) *Methodology and Tacit Knowledge: Two Experiments in Econometrics*, New York: Wiley.

Makridakis, S. and Hibon, M. (2000) 'The M3-competition: results, conclusions and implications', *International Journal of Forecasting*, 16: 451–76.

Makridakis, S., Wheelwright, S. and Hyndman, R. (1998) *Forecasting: Methods and Applications*, Wiley: New York.

Maturana, H. (1990) ' Science and daily life: the ontology of scientific explanations', in W. Krohn, G. Kuers and H. Nowotny (eds), *Selforganization: Portrait of a Scientific Revolution*, Dordrecht: Kluwer Academic Publishers, pp. 12–35.

Mendenhall, W., Reinmuth, J., Beaver, R. and Duhan, D. (1986) *Statistics for Management and Economics*, Boston, MA: Duxbury Press.

Mendenhall, W. and Sincich, T. (1989) *A Second Course in Business Statistics: Regression Analysis*, San Francisco, CA: Dellen.

Mills, T. and Pepper, G. (1999) 'Assessing the forecasters: an analysis of the forecasting records of the Treasury, the London Business School, and the National Institute', *International Journal of Forecasting*, 15: 247–57.

Mingers, J. (1980) 'Towards an appropriate social theory for applied systems thinking: critical theory and soft systems methodology', *Journal of Applied Systems Analysis*, 7 (April): 41–50.

—— (1984) 'Subjectivism and soft systems methodology – a critique', *Journal of Applied Systems Analysis*, 11: 85–103.

—— (1989) 'Problems of measurement', in M. Jackson, P. Keys and S. Cropper (eds), *Operational Research and the Social Sciences*, New York: Plenum Press, pp. 471–7.

—— (1992a) 'Criticizing the phenomenological critique – autopoiesis and critical realism', *Systems Practice*, 5 (2): 173–80.

—— (1992b) 'Recent developments in critical management science', *Journal of the Operational Research Society*, 43 (1): 1–10.

—— (1997) 'Towards critical pluralism', in J. Mingers and A. Gill (eds), *Multimethodology: Theory and Practice of Combining Management Science Methodologies*, Chichester: Wiley, pp. 407–40.

—— (1999) 'Synthesising constructivism and critical realism: towards critical pluralism', in E. Mathijs, J. Van der Veken and H. Van Belle (eds), *World Views and the Problem of Synthesis*, Amsterdam: Kluwer Academic, pp. 187–204.

—— (2000a) 'The contribution of critical realism as an underpinning philosophy for OR/MS and systems', *Journal of the Operational Research Society*, 51 (11): 1256–70.

—— (2000b) 'Variety is the spice of life: combining soft and hard OR/MS methods', *International Transactions in Operational Research*, 7: 673–91.

—— (2001) 'Combining IS research methods: towards a pluralist methodology', *Information Systems Research*, 12 (3): 240–59.

Mingers, J. and Brocklesby, J. (1997) 'Multimethodology: towards a framework for mixing methodologies', *Omega*, 25 (5): 489–509.

Miser, H. (1991a) 'Comments on "OR as technology" ', *Journal of the Operational Research Society*, 42 (5): 429–33.

—— (1991b) 'Toward a philosophy of operational research', *INFOR*, 29 (1): 4–13.

—— (1993) 'A foundational concept of science appropriate for validation in operational-research', *European Journal of Operational Research*, 66 (2): 204–15.

—— (1996) 'Comments prompted by "On the nature of OR – entering the fray" ', *Journal of the Operational Research Society*, 47: 1322–3.

Mitchell, G. (1993) *The Practice of Operational Research*, Chichester: Wiley.

Oliver, R. and Smith, J. (eds) (1990) *Influence Diagrams, Belief Nets, and Decision Analysis*, Chichester: Wiley.

Olsen, W. (1999) *Developing Open-systems Interpretations of Path Analysis: Fragility Analysis Using Farm Data from India*, Critical Realism: Implications for Practice, Örebro University Sweden, Centre for Critical Realism.

Ormerod, R. (1996a) 'On the nature of OR – entering the fray', *Journal of the Operational Research Society*, 47 (1): 1–17.

—— (1996b) 'Response to Miser: the objects and objectives of operational research', *Journal of the Operational Research Society*, 47: 1323–6.

Pawson, R. and Tilley, N. (1997) *Realistic Evaluation*, London: Sage.

Picconi, M., Romano, A. and Olson, C. (1993) *Business Statistics: Elements and Applications*, New York: HarperCollins.

Pidd, M. (1996) *Tools for Thinking: Modelling in Management Science*, Chichester: Wiley.

Pole, A., West, M. and Harrison, J. (1994) *Applied Bayesian Forecasting and Time Series Analysis*, London: Chapman Hall.

Porpora, D. (1998) *Do Realists Run Regressions?*, 2nd International Centre for Critical Realism Conference, University of Essex.

Ravetz, G. (1971) *Scientific Knowledge and its Social Problems*, Oxford: Oxford University Press.

Rivett, P. (1994) *The Craft of Decision Modelling*, Chichester: Wiley.

Ron, A. (1999) *Regression Analysis and the Philosophy of Social Sciences: A Critical Realist View*, Critical Realism: Implications for Practice, Örebro University Sweden, Centre for Critical Realism.

Rosenberg, A. (1992) *Economics: Mathematical Politics or Science of Diminishing Returns*, Chicago, IL: University of Chicago Press.

Rosenhead, J. and Mingers, J. (eds) (2001) *Rational Analysis for a Problematic World Revisited*, Chichester: Wiley.

Sayer, A. (1992) *Method in Social Science*, London: Routledge.

Sherden, W. (1998) *The Fortune Sellers: The Big Business of Buying and Selling Predictions*, New York: Wiley.

Sims, C. (1980) 'Macroeconomics and reality', *Econometrica*, 48: 1–48.

Smith, D. (1995) 'Tables turn on Britain's leading forecasters', *Sunday Times*, 24 December.

Tashakkori, A. and Teddlie, C. (1998) *Mixed Methodology: Combining Qualitative and Quantitative Approaches*, London: Sage.

Tobin, J. (1950) 'A statistical demand function for food in the USA', *Journal of the Royal Statistical Society A* 113 (II): 113–49.

Tsoukas, H. and Papoulias, D. (1996) 'Creativity in OR/MS: from technique to epistemology', *Interfaces*, 26 (2): 73–9.

Waddington, C. (1973) *OR in World War 2: Operational Research against the U-Boat*, London: Elek Science.

West, M. and Harrison, J. (1989) *Bayesian Forecasting and Dynamic Models*, New York: Springer-Verlag.

White, L. (1994) 'The death of the expert', *Journal of the Operational Research Society*, 45 (7): 733–48.

White, L. and Taket, A. (1996) 'The end of theory?', *Omega, International Journal of Management Science*, 24 (1): 47–56.

8 Temporally embedded case comparison in industrial marketing research

Debbie Harrison and Geoff Easton

Introduction

In this chapter we specifically address the issue of multiple case studies and offer a new basis for case embeddedness: time. The approach combines the concept of periodisation (Jessop, 1990) with the work of Pawson and Tilley (1997) which offers a practical realist approach to evaluation based on context–mechanism–outcome (CMO) configurations. A number of methodological benefits are identified including increasing the number of cases available and providing the possibility to explore the role of different contexts on the outcomes of the processes involved. The approach is demonstrated using case studies from a study of the impact across different industries of the banning of chlorofluorocarbons (CFCs).

Case methodology and epistemology

The value of the case study research method has long been recognised in the management literature (e.g. Bourgeois and Eisenhardt, 1988). However, until recently it has largely been regarded as a useful adjunct to or precursor of more traditional positivistic, large-scale data collection methods, or only appropriate in situations which are 'interesting' and/or unique. What has changed is the recognition that the case study methodology is consistent with a different ontology and epistemology from that of other research methodologies, specifically a critical realist approach (Easton, 1995; Tsoukas, 1989).

Two important issues in the use of the case method are those of generalisation and explanation. It is often argued that one cannot generalise from a single case. Therefore case studies can only ever be used as a preparation for a piece of large-scale (meaning large numbers and not greater effort) positivist research. From the latter, results can be generalised either because they exhaust the population of events (e.g. in national accounting econometric studies) or to populations via random sampling techniques and statistical inference.

From a critical realist approach, any event is the outcome of a number of deep structures or processes (e.g. economies of scale) working together and influenced by contingencies (e.g. markets, products, countries). Causality is assumed to be an attribute of the entities being researched; people make things happen, networks coordinate resource flows, gravity causes objects to fall (Sayer, 1984). Explanation involves (a) identifying the causal processes and the contingencies; and (b) discovering the mechanisms by which they determine observable outcomes. The outcomes may be a single event (the decision of a firm not to use CFCs from the end of 1989) or regularity (the almost constant nature of frequency of brand purchases in a product field, despite major differences in brand penetration).

The role of the researcher is to keep in mind the question 'why?' when working with the data. The use of case studies allows a researcher to attempt to tease out ever-deepening layers of reality in the search for generative mechanisms and influential contingencies. This process creates the depth and detail supportive of capturing the 'hows' and 'whys' rather than only the 'whats'. The metaphor of peeling layers of an onion comes to mind. The ability to return to the case situation and collect more data time after time is one of its great strengths. The process is also different because it is driven by a multitude of different hypotheses, each of which may require new, substantiating data to be collected. Pawson and Tilley (1997), for example, suggest eight different ways in which placing CCTV cameras in a car park might lead to a reduction in car thefts. The onion may require peeling in a number of different ways before a satisfactory explanation emerges.

Further, since case studies are, by definition, longitudinal in nature they provide the ability to examine evolutionary processes, historically or in real time. This is a crucial advantage in being able to assign causality, a central tenet of the critical realist approach. In addition a longitudinal approach is desirable in that lags occur in the interplay of empirically observed events and mechanisms underlying these. This further facilitates a focus upon processual aspects of the object.

Moreover the concept of generalisation differs radically from that espoused by positivists. Realists believe that identifying a plausible, defensible 'deep' explanation in one instance can be a major contribution to theory. The question of whether this theory, or any of its components, applies elsewhere then becomes an empirical one. It may be widely applicable or it may be narrowly applicable. By contrast, positivists accept that constant conjunction is the best 'indicator' of causality though it cannot guarantee it. This view leads to the assumption that one theory, in the sense of the same set of empirical regularities, will fit all situations. For this to be the case a model built around a set of variables must be assumed to 'capture' the underlying dynamics of the phenomena in question.

Realists work incrementally, researching new contexts to see whether and how the same deep processes are present, and how they are influenced by particular contexts. Which research method should be employed depends not only upon the research problem/context but also the values of the researcher. The former determines the 'effectiveness' of each research approach. The latter will influence the choice in terms of whether the researcher values theory comprising 'deep' explanations across a narrow range of contexts or 'shallower' explanations across a wider range of contexts.

Multiple case comparisons

The arguments put forward in the previous section lead to the conclusion that one case is enough. As Tsoukas (1989: 556) states, within the realist paradigm case studies are not concerned with empirical regularities: 'explanatory idiographic studies are epistemologically valid because they are concerned with the clarification of structures and their associated generative mechanisms, which have been contingently capable of producing the observed phenomena.' Indeed, it would be near impossible to study sufficient numbers of cases in order to satisfy statistical requirements because of time and resource constraints. Rather, each case is an example of some phenomenon.

The number of cases to use has always proved to be a contentious issue. Some researchers, notably Eisenhardt (1989) suggest a specific and arbitrary number, one that, presumably, makes them feel that they have comfortably 'covered the field'. Yet this approach is, implicitly, positivist. Large numbers of cases imply a sampling, statistical inference mode that is wholly inappropriate if one adopts a realist approach. The nature of the phenomena to be studied, the importance of contexts, and the research questions should determine the number of cases and no universal prescription can be valid.

It is true that a single case will be a sensible choice in many circumstances where there are, for example, many contingencies operating and where the deep processes work in complex ways. However, it is often the situation that more than one case study is written as part of a research project. We would argue that the use of multiple cases more often results from the nervousness of the researcher than from any profound concerns about epistemology or methodology. The decision to use multiple cases should not be taken lightly since how many and which cases are to be investigated will fundamentally affect the outcome of the research.

From a critical realist perspective these choices depend upon the expected nature of the contingencies and deep processes present in different situations. When working in a completely new domain, it will probably be sensible to research a single case, then to decide if more than one case is necessary and, if so, what kind of context would best help in theory development. When the research follows up previous work it might be expected that a range of case study contexts might be planned in advance. Yin (1994), despite not explicitly adopting a realist approach, has some useful advice on these issues.

There are two kinds of multiple cases, independent and embedded. In the latter, multiple case studies are carried out within a closely similar context. For example, a case context could be a particular industrial network and the embedded cases could be individual actors within the network. The actors form a part of the network and help create its emergent properties. The similarity of context in the embedded cases approach should, in principle, allow for more detailed understanding of the deep processes involved since the context is, in some senses, controlled. Independent cases might most sensibly be used where it is expected that the context is crucially important in determining the way in which deep processes lead to the observed outcomes.

The analysis of multiple cases can be carried out in a number of different ways (Yin, 1994; Eisenhardt, 1989; Ragin, 1987; Ragin and Becker, 1992; Tsoukas, 1989). Tsoukas (1989) discusses a three-stage process of explanation using an explicitly realist, although somewhat under-specified, approach. The key question is that of 'what is responsible for the observed patterns?' Yin (1994) advocates a pattern matching method, between a prior theoretical framework and the findings of a case. The necessity of a replication strategy for multiple cases is emphasised. Eisenhardt (1989) provides a cradle-to-grave inductive template for the application of the case methodology in management. In the search for cross-case patterns, she advocates the familiarisation of the researcher with each individual case. The next stage is to search for and identify similarities and differences in the combined empirical data. This *contrastive explanation* leads to the grouping together of multiple cases.

Ragin (1987) has developed a comparative approach method based upon Boolean logic principles. Conceptual characteristics present and absent in multiple case studies are coded into binary digits. Each case is then moulded into what is termed a 'truth table'. The truth table codes the presence and absence of particular characteristics. The aim of the approach is to reduce a case to a logical statement that contains several characteristics. Each case statement – representing an explanation – can then be used for purposes of comparison. Each statement would be expected to contain several characteristics, and hence the approach is underpinned by the idea of multiple conjunctoral causation. In other words, a case explanation centres upon a group of characteristics that interact at a given point in time. As Ragin states, 'cases [should be] … examined as wholes – as combinations of characteristics' (1987: 16).

Each of these articles offers useful advice but a number of issues remain unresolved. The grouping together of multiple cases based on similarity and difference is problematic. Contexts and mechanisms operating (or not) in various combinations may feasibly produce similar or different outcomes and this may not be captured. Other advice offers more epistemological/theoretical underpinning yet is vague as to the realities of the 'how to'. Ragin's method emphasises the crucial point that multiple contingencies operate to produce particular outcomes. This method works best when operating with a large number of similar cases, yet much of the detail of any given case is lost. Issues of comparability of analysis in the multiple case scenarios are especially pertinent.

Temporally embedded case analysis

Case studies are typically embedded cross-sectionally or 'vertically'. In other words, the embedded cases are situated at lower hierarchical levels within the overall case and are described within the same time period. For example, a case study of an industry sector might have several 'mini' cases within it of, say, customer, supplier, competitor and institutional organisations. The case is treated as a whole entity when analysing the case data.

For this essay we have adopted an alternative embedded form: *embeddedness of cases in time*. A temporally embedded case study is considered to be a series of multiple, mini-case studies in single time periods or a within-case period. A cross-sectionally embedded case becomes a series of interrelated mini-cases (Griffin, 1993). For this research, temporally embedded case analysis is based on a combination of the idea of periodisation (e.g. Jessop, 1990; Lester, 1997; Norcliffe and Bartschat, 1994; Phillips, 1994) coupled with context–mechanism–outcome (CMO) configurations (Pawson and Tilley, 1997).

The technique of periodisation increases the number of cases available, yet simultaneously facilitates analysis by maintaining the embeddedness of the cases created. One other important benefit is that, by homogenising multiple cases into periods, there is some consistency in order that comparisons can be made across multiple cases. The concept of CMO configurations described by Pawson and Tilley (1997) is best considered as a way of operationalising critical realism. The use of CMO configurations in research can result in a less abstract and thus more concrete analysis (e.g. Sayer, 1984). It would, of course, be possible to conduct case analysis using only periodisation or CMO configurations. What is interesting is that each approach brings particular benefits for case analysis when combined together. A critical realist explanation involves a search for generative causality in particular contexts in speculating upon the unobservable underlying forces operating within an object. By combining periodisation with CMO configurations, there are several benefits for the analyst of the single case.

By beginning with the observable outcomes or events for a particular period, a researcher is able to track contextual changes and their impacts on the outcomes over time. It is possible to investigate which contextual features are important in different time periods. Some contexts may only be present in certain time periods. Indeed, multiple contexts may operate in different ways in different time periods.

Checks on the stability of mechanisms over time can be made. What mechanisms are operating in what ways via interaction with contextual features? Are some mechanisms more important than others? Some may be present or absent in different time periods and this may have a crucial impact. 'Depending on conditions, the operation of the same mechanism can produce quite different results and, alternatively, different mechanisms may produce the same empirical result' (Sayer, 1984: 108). Overall, a researcher is able to assess the impact of contexts and mechanisms in a relatively systematic way both within and across time periods within the case.

For multiple case study analysis a researcher is able to ensure some comparability of analysis if the same periods are used across cases. It is then possible to check in a systematic way whether and how certain contextual characteristics and mechanisms are influential or not in different cases in the same period and in different periods. Which contextual features are important in what cases in a particular period? How do multiple contextual features operate in a given period in different cases? This allows many more comparisons to be made of the influence of outcomes, contexts and mechanisms, and their relationships across cases.

Overall, the use of the analysis potentially increases the depth of an explanation from one case or a set of cases. The uniqueness of a given case can be maintained, coupled with a more standardised comparison of multiple cases.

Periodisation

In an extensive review paper Jessop (1990) discusses the technique of periodisation for regulation theory. This requires a researcher to develop a series of stages or phases or periods that relate to a research object. Many researchers have sub-divided single cases into distinct yet related periods of time for analysis purposes. For example, a set of research studies from the McGill stable has empirically demonstrated the configuration school of thought (e.g. Mintzberg and Waters, 1982; Mintzberg and McHugh, 1985). Each case has a common methodology for the study of strategy formation, as 'strategic periods' are used to sub-divide retrospective accounts in order to operationalise questions about strategy formation within organisations. Of course, any single period has overlap with other periods. There are two general approaches to how periodisation can be determined in embedding a case in time.

The first is the use of a context that is external to a case study or to a set of cases to create a series of periods (Jessop, 1990; Norcliffe and Bartschat, 1994; Phillips, 1994). We term this as 'periodisation by context'. For some research studies periodisation will be appropriate because a standard set of phases makes sense for all of the cases. The detail of a case is related to the context that frames that case. A division is likely to draw upon some combination of: the incorporation of key events reported by interviewees; secondary sources tracing the history of a particular context; set blocks of time which are equal in length; or some prior, theoretically derived breakpoints. One feature similar to all of the cases in a study is then standardised.

There are many examples of studies in the management literature where there is some relatively standardised, external context, operating outside of a single organisation; for instance, the de-regulation of the energy market, environmental changes that affect many if not all organisations within an industry and the ending of a patent protection within the pharmaceutical industry. A number of issues are raised by the use of a 'periodisation by context' technique. The major benefit is the comparability of multiple cases through the standardisation of some common vector. Further, there is shorthand for data presentation in that the detail of the development of some shared context does not need to be repeated within each case. The two main concerns are first that the periodisation represents a researcher imposition. Second, there is always some fluidity across the periods rather than each representing some clear and distinct phase of time.

The second approach is when periodisation is based more upon the internal process or narrative of a case and becomes more inductive (Lester, 1997). The context of a case varies rather than being fixed over multiple cases, and thus it becomes more difficult to use for the purposes of more general explanation (though it needs to be incorporated). One difficulty is that the appropriate period divisions may be relatively arbitrary when the processes of a narrative are gradual over time. This is exacerbated when multiple cases are to be analysed, as it is less clear as to whether or not the cases are comparable.

One possible way of sub-dividing cases when the context is not standardised might be to adopt the 'episode' notion from the industrial networks literature. A case could be broken down into a sequence of episodes so that periods have a more theoretical rather than a primarily contextual bases. Particular episodes or a series of episodes could then be compared both within a case and across multiple cases. A case study of the development of an innovation over time is one possible example. In Leminen's (1999) study one case was sub-divided into four periods: 'negotiation', 'feasibility', 'execution' and 'conclusion'. If multiple cases were broken down into similar sequences, some comparability would be possible.

Context–mechanism–outcome configurations

Pawson and Tilley (1997), as evaluation researchers, try to emphasise *why*, rather than whether, a policy intervention works. A 'realist formula' is introduced as mechanism + context = outcome, or '*casual outcomes follow from mechanisms acting in contexts*' (1997: 58, italics in original). The authors state that social programs produce changes because of the operation of particular mechanisms. In other words, 'programs work (have successful "outcomes") only in so far as they introduce the appropriate ideas and opportunities ("mechanisms") to groups in the appropriate social and cultural conditions ("contexts")' (1997: 57). Pawson and Tilley provide an example from criminology research that they term a realistic theory of repeat victimisation (1997: 139). This example is illustrated in Table 8.1 (see Kaneko, 1999 for an application of the CMO framework to the evaluation of smoking cessation programmes).

The outcome represents the 'raw material' of the realist research task. For Pawson and Tilley, researchers operating within a realist epistemology have 'the task of modelling the different ways in which the Ms, Cs and Os come together

Table 8.1 Context–mechanism–outcome

Context	+	*Mechanism*	=	*Outcome*
Repeated co-presence of particular motivated offender and suitable victim in the absence of guardian		Offender believes that risks are low, rewards are enough and crime is easy		High rate of repeat offences, with short-term heightened vulnerability of victim

... [in] *context–mechanism–outcome pattern configurations*' (1997: 77, italics in original). The relationship among the parts of the matrix, and the different combinations of a matrix, are of interest to the researcher. Different patterns of contexts–mechanisms may be responsible for producing a variety of causal outcomes. For instance, different context–mechanism configurations may produce the same outcome, i.e. $C_1 + M_1 = O_1$ and $C_2 + M_2 = O_1$. Conversely, the same context–mechanism configurations may produce different outcomes, i.e. $C_1 + M_1 = O_1$ and $C_1 + M_1 = O_2$. However, '[it is] impossible to reach a complete statement of all the permutations of mechanisms and contexts upon which invariable outcome patterns depend' (1997: 119).

By using CMO configurations in an analysis, theory is formed from the interrelationships of the three elements of a realist explanation. A focus on the 'outcomes' level of analysis acts as the starting point for a deeper analysis of the phenomenon in question. The similarity and difference technique advocated by authors such as Eisenhardt becomes messier, because the central issue is to investigate the similar and different Cs and Ms involved in the causal generation of observable outcomes. It is 'families of configurations' (Pawson and Tilley, 1997: 123) that can be compared with each other in building theory. For case analysis, the aim would be to generate a 'series of context–mechanism–outcome pattern configurations, which explain how particular outcomes may have been produced' (1997: 134). It is probable that there would be multiple CMO pattern configurations, both between periods within a case and within periods across multiple cases. Thus 'progress in theory development occurs by explicating the mechanisms and contexts ... of regularities' (1997: 63).

One central issue in adopting the Pawson and Tilley framework as a way to operationalise critical realism is that these authors discuss CMO configurations as a data analysis *method* with little reference to ontology. This is a somewhat 'cut-down version of realist models of explanation. This acknowledges the way in which the activation of mechanisms depends on context, but not the dependence of the mechanisms on structures which might themselves be removed or changed' (Sayer, 1998: 166). Indeed, the M + C = O format is somewhat mechanistic.

Table 8.2 A revised CMO configuration

Outcomes	*Contexts*		*Mechanisms*
	External	Internal	

Further, the term 'context' is ambiguous because this implicitly subsumes both necessary and contingent conditions (Sayer, 1984). Pawson and Tilley do not provide clear definitions in illustrating the nature of contexts and mechanisms. In this essay, the work of Pawson and Tilley and that of Sayer has been used in tandem (see Table 8.2). The outcome is one aspect of the response process for a given case at a particular point in time. 'Internal context' is a reference to what Sayer would term the necessary or internal relations of an object. The label 'external context' approximates to Sayer's external or contingent relations of an object. This division requires an interpretation to be made on the part of the researcher. Mechanisms are a deeper explanation of the ways of acting of internal relations, or internal contexts, and again require interpretation on the part of the researcher.

Pawson and Tilley offer little advice for the situation where it is necessary to combine multiple configurations when building an explanation for a particular outcome within a case. This issue is exacerbated when multiple cases are incorporated within the same research study. The authors do not fully discuss how a set of combined contingencies and mechanisms from several cases are combined into a broader, more generalisable mid-range theory. Nor do they state that what is needed is theoretical comparability rather than attempting to replicate empirical situations.

Finally, the authors are concerned with evaluating the effectiveness of a particular intervention in the field of criminology. The process implications of this are important because of differences in the substantive content of studying social science settings more generally.

Some empirical examples

The data used below are taken from a comparative study of the response of multiple industry sectors to the phasing out of CFCs (Harrison, 1999). These chemicals were banned under the Montreal Protocol framework because they deplete the ozone layer. The major benefit of adopting periodisation is the comparability of multiple cases through the standardisation of the political–scientific story (sub-divided into eight periods).

In brief, period one covers the 1960s to 1974, when the scientific community was concerned with the impact of the space shuttle and supersonic transport. Period two (1974–80) marks the beginning of the debate as to the impact of CFCs. Period three (1980–5) is a lull period in the story, when scientific and political interest in CFCs waned. Periods four and five contain some hugely significant scientific and legislative events over the timespans 1985–7 and 1987–9 respectively. Period six (1989–1992) covers some substantial revisions to the Protocol agreement, for both CFCs and hydrochlorofluorocarbons (HCFCs). Period seven (1992–5) marks the passing of the CFC ban along with tighter restrictions around HCFCs. Finally, period eight (1995–2015) covers the schedule of supply limits for HCFCs.

By tracking contextual changes and checking the stability of mechanisms over time, we make a comparison of several periods within a single case. A comparison of the detail of the 'same' period across two case studies is then undertaken. There is a subtle shift in emphasis in the analysis because the first is concerned with both the periods and the linkages between those periods, and the second with the periods themselves. Overall, the aim is to provide a clearer explanation of when and how particular contexts and mechanisms impact upon and change outcomes over time.

Multiple periods within a single case

This section discusses an analysis of one case by considering and comparing CMO configurations across four time periods. For this analysis the Pawson and Tilley formula should perhaps be contexts–mechanisms–outcomes, in that we are presenting bundles of contextual variables and mechanisms interacting to generate certain outcomes. The bundles are then presented in a tabular format by period for ease of comparison. The analysis proceeds in a number of stages. First, the sequence of the outcomes over the multiple periods of the case is presented. The task is then to consider, for each of the periods or mini-cases, how the contexts and mechanisms interact.

Outcomes for four periods: the aerosol case

The single case is that of a UK aerosol manufacturer. When combined across the four periods, the outcomes of the case represent the actions and behaviours of the organisation in response to the regulation of CFCs.

In the first period, a preliminary search for possible alternative routes took place. This involved a parallel investigation of two not-in-kind (NIK) technology[1] routes in-house. In the second period there was a requirement, as a result of an EEC directive, for a 30 per cent reduction in the use of CFCs in aerosols. There was an initial incorporation of butane into propellants that represented a partial response. While the technical demands involved were 'minimal', research and development activity continued. In the third period the discovery of the ozone hole in 1985 marked the beginning of the intense response period where most activity took place. The nature of retailer customer demands dramatically shortened the time scales available for response. What followed was a difficult period of technical development as the pace was forced and very fast. A complete reformulation of some products was required. In the fourth period, following the agreement of the Montreal Protocol, the focal actor had already completed a significant proportion of the required changes.

C-M analysis

Table 8.3 presents the bundle of contexts and mechanisms for four periods in a single case. Each context and mechanism represents some theoretical theme derived from a literature review or from the data (or some mixture of these). By referring to Table 8.3, it is possible to assess that some of the contextual characteristics have an influence (present) yet others do not (absent). Both of these

Table 8.3 Multiple periods for one case

CMO configuration: period one

Outcomes	*External contexts*	*Internal contexts*	*Mechanisms*
Search for other routes	Links between aerosols and ozone made in the USA	Experience of some alternatives Some ability to use alternatives in place No pressure from customers	Precautionary approach CFCs used for all personal care products US issue Requirement to maintain aerosol format

CMO configuration: period two

Outcomes	*External contexts*	*Internal contexts*	*Mechanisms*
Initial use of other route within the product range	Scientific debate intensifies EEC demands	Experience of some alternatives Some ability to use alternatives in place No pressure from customers	A more reactive approach CFCs used for all personal care products No ban expected Requirement to maintain aerosol format

CMO configuration: period three

Outcomes	*External contexts*	*Internal contexts*	*Mechanisms*
Rapid and intense developing of revised product	Discovery of the ozone hole	Experience of some alternatives	A more reactive approach
	High product–issue association	Some ability to use alternatives in place	CFCs used for all personal care products
		Relationships with 'new' suppliers in place	A ban inevitable
			Requirement to maintain aerosol format
		Huge pressure from customers	

CMO configuration: period four

Outcomes	*External contexts*	*Internal contexts*	*Mechanisms*
Most activities completed	Agreement of the Montreal Protocol	Experience of some alternatives	A more reactive approach
	High product–issue association	Some ability to use alternatives in place	CFCs largely eliminated from production
		Relationships with 'new' suppliers in place	Ban, but not before 2000
		Huge pressure from customers	Requirement to maintain aerosol format

states may be causal. The crucial point to bear in mind is that the influence (or not) of the particular contexts is in itself dependent on, or embedded within, combined interaction with other contextual characteristics.

From periods one to two the context bundle changes in terms of the type and nature of external contexts. For example, no legal requirements are in place during period one, yet there are some demands within period two. For period three, the inclusion of intense customer pressure has the effect of intensifying the need to act (outcome). Hence, across the periods we are able to systematically track and compare contextual changes.

Some of the contexts are always present. These include the ability to use some alternative routes. Some contexts are only important later, e.g. the level of product–issue association. In other words, certain contexts are only present in some time periods. Further, the nature of contextual features may be stable or can change over time. The nature of customer pressure changes in nature across the four time periods. Thus different contextual features, when combined, are important in different time periods. In fact, contexts 'absent' in earlier periods can have a critical impact on the outcome in a later period, perhaps if there is some change in the nature of another contextual characteristic.

In terms of mechanisms, the initial assessment can be made in terms of when a particular mechanism is interacting with other contexts–mechanisms and when it is not. Across each of the periods all of the mechanisms are present. What is interesting are the shifts in the nature of these mechanisms over time. For example, opinion as to whether a ban will occur is different in nature in each of the four periods. The mechanisms do not have fixed ways of interacting across the periods; some are stable yet others change in nature. The crucial point is that the influence of mechanisms has to be considered in conjunction with the set of contexts operating in that period.

One period for multiple cases

This part of the chapter presents an analysis of two cases. We provide a comparison of different CMO configurations for the *same* period – period five (1987–9) as part of a wider response. The outcomes for the same period in both cases are presented. These represent the response to the CFC regulation at a certain period of time. The bundles of contexts–mechanisms are then presented for both cases in a tabular format for ease of comparison. The task is then to consider, for the same period of time in both cases, the two issues that were discussed earlier in the chapter: surfacing the similarities and differences in the role of certain contexts and mechanisms, and relating the combinations of contexts and mechanisms to outcomes.

A comparison of outcomes for one period: the response of the dry cleaning and aerosols cases in period five

The outcome of case one (a dry-cleaning firm) was that a 'wait-and-see' approach was adopted following a scenario-planning exercise. A response time frame was set for action to begin in 1991 when it was convenient for the actor. The situation became one of business as usual with a plan in place. The outcome of case two (an aerosol manufacturer) was that the change-over began following an industry-wide announcement for the phasing out of CFCs. This occurred just one year after the agreement of the Montreal Protocol. There was sector-wide imitation in order to remain competitive or even survive. CFCs were removed from all products and replaced with hydrocarbons.

C-M analysis

Table 8.4 presents the CMO configuration for the one period for each of the two cases. In referring to the table, it is possible to see clearly that some of the contexts have an influence (present) yet others do not (absent). In addition the influence of contexts that are present can vary across the cases.

It is possible to compare the roles of external contexts such as 'CFCs cited as ozone depleters' and 'agreement of the Montreal Protocol'. Further, for case two the presence of the external context of 'aerosols blamed for the ozone hole' had an important impact upon the outcome when combined with the set of internal contexts within the case. This external context is present in both cases, yet is operating in a different way within case one. There are then contrasts in the response context as the analysis continues. There are some similarities in the internal contexts present in each case, e.g. experience and current use of alternative resources. The key context is the difference across the cases in the nature and extent of customer pressure for change. The presence of this key context in the latter case strongly impacts upon the outcome of response in representing particular conditions for mechanisms to be 'activated' within.

Table 8.4 also presents the bundle of mechanisms for each of the two cases. For example, in both cases a ban on the use of CFCs is considered by managers to be inevitable. By contrast, the likelihood of adopting a fluorocarbon alternative is very different. This is influenced by interaction with the extent of resource centrality across the two cases. For case one, CFCs were not a dominant technology; the 'alternative route' of perchloroethylene was more heavily used. For the aerosol manufacturer, CFCs were used across the product range.

Conclusions

One of the problems for researchers wishing to research in a way that is consistent with a critical realist ontology has been bridging the gaps between philosophy, epistemology and research methods. By combining the epistemologically positioned CMO framework and the periodised case research method we hoped to demonstrate, in practical terms, one way of achieving this goal.

There are also benefits to this approach for case analysis. First, there is an improved depth of analysis. The analysis moves beyond a superficial search of similarities and differences. This is an especially pertinent remark with regard to comparative analysis of multiple cases. Both contexts and mechanisms are

Table 8.4 A single period for two cases

CMO configuration: case one

Outcomes	*External contexts*	*Internal contexts*	*Mechanisms*
Identification of alternatives	CFCs cited as ozone depleters Agreement of the Montreal Protocol No product–issue association	Vast experience of alternative Use of alternative in place Relationships with suppliers in place No pressure from customers	Wait and see Relatively low centrality of CFCs A ban is inevitable Low requirements to remain with fluorocarbons

CMO configuration: case two

Outcomes	*External Contexts*	*Internal Contexts*	*Mechanisms*
Clear need to switch to hydrocarbons	CFCs cited as ozone depleters Agreement of the Montreal Protocol Aerosols blamed for the ozone hole	Experience of some alternatives Some ability to use alternatives in place Customers demand CFC-free aerosols	A relatively reactive stance High centrality of CFCs A ban is inevitable High requirement to maintain some product dimensions

considered in multiple in a systematic way over time, and as bases of comparison across cases. Second, the analysis allows a researcher to track changes over time carefully and thoroughly.

There are several limitations of this essay. First, there are issues concerning periodisation in general. There are difficulties of comparison when periodisation is not as dependent upon context. Should the basis of comparison be turning points or cumulation? Even when the case periodisation *is* based more on context, the periods are largely arbitrary on the part of the researcher (Phillips, 1994). In a cross-case comparison at least some extent of standardisation is necessary, which may not be palatable to some. However, this does then allow 'clean' comparison across multiple cases that is tied to an epistemological standpoint.

Note

1 In this case a not-in-kind technology refers to a substitute other than HCFCs or HFCs.

References

Bourgeois, L.J. and Eisenhardt, K.M. (1988) 'Strategic decision processes in high-velocity environments: four cases in the microcomputer industry', *Management Science*, 34 (7): 816–35.

Easton, G. (1995) 'Case methodology for industrial network research: a realist epistemology apologia', *Proceedings of the 11th IMP International Conference*, Manchester University.

Eisenhardt, K.M. (1989) 'Building theories from case study research', *Academy of Management Review*, 14 (4): 532–50.

Griffin, L.J. (1993) 'Narrative, event-structure analysis, and causal interpretation in historical sociology', *American Journal of Sociology*, 98 (5): 1094–133.

Harrison, D.J. (1999) 'Strategic responses to predicted events: the case of the banning of CFCs', unpublished doctoral dissertation, University of Lancaster.

Jessop, B. (1990) 'Regulation theory in retrospective and perspective', *Economy and Society*, 19 (2): 153–216.

Kaneko, M. (1999) 'A methodological inquiry into the evaluation of smoking cessation programmes', *Health Education Research*, 14 (3): 433–41.

Lemminen, S. (1999) 'Mapping dynamics of buyer–seller relationships', Proceedings of the 15th Annual IMP Conference, edited by D. McLoughlin and C. Horan, 2–4 September 1999, University College Dublin.

Lester, A. (1997) 'The margins of order: strategies of segregation on the Eastern Cape frontier, 1806–*c.*1850', *Journal of Southern African Studies*, 23 (4): 635–53.

Mintzberg, H. and McHugh, A. (1985) 'Strategy formation in an adhocracy', *Administrative Science Quarterly*, 30: 160–97.

Mintzberg, H. and Waters, J.A. (1982) 'Tracking strategy in an entrepreneurial firm', *Academy of Management Journal*, 25: 465–99.

Norcliffe, C. and Bartschat, T.Z. (1994) 'Locational avoidance by non-metropolitan industry', *Environment and Planning*, 26 (7): 1123–45.

Pawson, R. and Tilley, N. (1997) *Realistic Evaluation*, London: Sage.

Phillips, D. (1994) 'Periodisation in historical approaches to comparative education: some considerations from the examples of Germany and England and Wales', *British Journal of Educational Studies*, 42 (3): 261–72.

Ragin, C.C. (1987) *The Comparative Method: Moving Beyond Qualitative and Quantitative Strategies*, Berkeley, CA: University of California Press.

Ragin, C.C. and Becker, H.S. (eds) (1992) *What is a Case? Exploring the Foundations of Social Inquiry*, Cambridge: Cambridge University Press.

Sayer, A. (1984) *Method in Social Science: A Realist Approach*, London and New York: Routledge.

—— (1998) 'Realistic evaluation', *Sociological Review*, 46 (1): 164–6.

Tsoukas, H. (1989) 'The validity of idiographic research explanations', *Academy of Management Review*, 14 (4): 555–61.

Yin, R.K. (1994) *Case Study Research: Design and Methods*, London: Sage.

9 Theorising networks from a critical realist standpoint

The discovery of power and contextual issues within and outside 'networks'

Alex Faria

Introduction

In spite of several obstacles to gaining legitimacy within academic circles, networks were taken as a new development paradigm in the late 1980s and early 1990s. Authors of different nationalities challenged the established views based on hierarchy, market and rivalry by recognising the causal importance of relations between entities 'rather than the entities themselves' (Easton, 1996: 291). Among other causes such recognition was triggered by the successful attack of Japanese organisations, which were taken as 'network organisations' by analysts (see Dore, 1983), and their triumph over large Western organisations and markets (Saunders, 1994: 12). As the Japanese success was assessed as extremely costly, not only to large organisations but also to national governments, a new international view came to be accepted, led by the USA and Europe. This was the view that economic development required proactive and more socially driven business systems capable of anticipating market needs (Piore and Sabel, 1984).

Supply networks in particular soon became a major representation of networks (Johnsen *et al.*, 2000) within business and academic circuits. Within the business circuit it happened as important automobile makers, mainly Americans, inspired by the success of the Japanese *keiretsu*, constituted vertical co-operative arrangements in diverse parts of the world. Within the academic circuit it happened as expensive and extensive international empirical research (Womack *et al.*, 1990: 9) established world-wide understanding that this type of network was more effective than other governance modes for being based on inter-firm co-operation and continuous improvement. In line with practices undertaken by automakers, the study also established the understanding that supply network was 'applicable anywhere by anyone'.

Accordingly, several researchers in business took supply networks as a governance mode capable of accelerating product development, enhancing collective learning, increasing flexibility, and enlarging innovation capabilities (see Wynstra *et al.*, 1999). In parallel to the world-wide diffusion and reproduction of the ideas developed by Womack and associates, researchers of other disciplines concerned with development set up the understanding that networks could bring industrial, regional and national development (Sternberg, 2000; Young and Francis, 1994), and dissolve certain conceptual controversies in the field (Waarden, 1992). Their argument was that networks were more effective than industrial policies led by the state (Larry, 1994) for being not based on command and direction 'but rather on negotiation and bargaining' (Kenis, 1991: 299) between private and public actors. As a result business organisations, politicians and academics, in developed and developing countries, agreed in the end on the new paradigm.

Nevertheless, despite the production and world-wide transfer of academic frameworks grounded on the expensive work of Womack and associates, supply networks became a potential new fad in the 1990s. Indeed, serious problems in different countries and industrial sectors made organisations and researchers realise that it was one thing to design and another to manage those networks.

These problems led some to understand that the industrial networks framework, built and tested empirically by European researchers since the early 1980s but largely ignored by mainstream scholars and journals in the USA, was more realistic than the centralised model adopted by automakers. The key argument of this school of thought is that the network is more effective than other governance modes because of its decentralised and more loosely coupled structure (see Hakansson and Johanson, 1993). In response, automakers and researchers pointed out that problems would disappear if first-tier suppliers effectively played the role of managers in those networks. Among certain key tasks these manager firms should participate actively in the processes of strategic alignment with the automobile makers (D'Cruz and Rugman, 1992) and get the commitment of lower-level suppliers in order to make effective collaborators of them (Bertodo, 1991). However, researchers disregarded the corresponding power issues related to such a role being attributed to first-tier suppliers.

Moreover, at the time, some other researchers challenged those who prescribed networks as a universal panacea (Nohria, 1992: 1). They argued that regional or national contexts in which business and managerial activities are accomplished and gain meaning should be recognised. Nevertheless, most researchers in the field also disregarded this important argument.

This chapter argues, and demonstrates, that the dismissal of power and contextual issues in the field of networks is a central obstacle to the development of realistic and relevant frameworks. The construction and use of proper research guidelines grounded on critical realism are then shown to be important, to avoid the possibility that networks, and the relations between entities, are taken as merely 'metaphorical' (Salancik, 1995) and prematurely dismissed.

This chapter demonstrates that current academic knowledge on networks, comprising schools of thought and corresponding research methods, fails to problematise the power and influence of the global supra-network, led mainly by transnational corporations (TNCs), within and outside 'networks' of firms. This discovery, based on the use of critical realism and mainly on the accounts of managers, puts into question the type of effectiveness or development that 'networks' and academic knowledge can produce. It also leads to the proposal that academics and governments should manage more realistically the increasing commodification, diffusion and internationalisation of management knowledge (Chumer *et al.*, 2000).

Grounded on these discoveries, the author argues that reflexivity is a key issue to critical realists: first, because of the influences that TNCs and the transnational capitalist class (Sklair, 2001) have been exerting on the academy and on its practitioners, practices and products; and second, because they tend to take managers as lay actors rather than as competent practitioners and citizens as critical realism, although positioning itself as 'under-labourer' for science struggles to be taken as a credible philosophy and methodology of social science and as an 'emancipatory' project within the academic circuit (Baehr, 1990). Actually, the critical consciousness of managers on the power of the global supra-network detected in this investigation challenges a problematic feature that tends to be attributed by academics and corresponding institutions in search of legitimacy: the transfer of knowledge from the academy toward practitioners. By challenging such Western representation of science (Deetz, 1996: 194) critical realists could help liberate managers and citizens from the increasing commodification, diffusion and internationalisation of management knowledge. Besides, such a posture may give an important direction to the more recent concern with dialectics, and in particular the theory–practice dichotomy, expressed by critical realists (see Bhaskar and Norrie, 1998).

The literature on networks: dismissal of power and contextual issues

Management researchers have serious difficulties in investigating and theorising networks because of the variety of meanings mobilised by different disciplines and authors (Harland, 1996). The field has been correctly portrayed as 'a terminological jungle in which any newcomer may plant a tree' (Nohria, 1992: 3); accordingly it can be argued that such diversity (Araujo and Easton, 1996) has been creating more confusion than clarity to researchers, practitioners and other users of knowledge on networks.

An important source of confusion in the field has been the opposition between two schools, namely supply chain management (Lamming, 1993) and industrial networks (Axelsson and Easton, 1992). Supply chain management researchers, who represent the Anglo-American tradition, became more popular than their European opponents. Although they disclaim hierarchy governance, they represent strategic action in networks as 'pure deliberate strategy' (Mintzberg and Waters, 1985). They reproduce the understanding that strategy is the result of precise intentions articulated in such a way that desired outcomes are clearly understood before actions are taken.

This happens because supply chain management draws upon the assumption that structure follows strategy and on a particular theory of collective strategy (Astley and Fombrun, 1983). Such theory represents formulation and implementation of strategies as jointly undertaken by members of the network and led by the central strategist. Decisions made by any supplier are portrayed as subordinated to the collective strategy and unambiguous. From such a standpoint the key customer and any supplier are expected to agree upon the best alternative before actions are undertaken.

Such discourse is contradictory since it was supply chain management researchers who argued that the centralised structure of supply networks that work out in Japan would not be effective in the West for cultural and institutional reasons (Lamming, 1996). In spite of this important argument they seem not to notice that the supply chain management school sets up a hierarchical division of labour, responsibilities and rewards between the key customer firm and its suppliers. The key customer firm is taken as the captain of the network and suppliers are taken as those who should cope with challenges posed by the competitive market. Accordingly they fail to build a non-centralised representation of supply networks. They argue, for instance, that first-tier suppliers' strategies and decisions should be grounded on three guidelines: continuous adaptation to the key customer needs; upgrade of its capabilities; and increase of added value through collaboration with the key customer firm and lower-tier suppliers (Lamming, 1993: 226). They also argue that first-tier suppliers who fail to meet such requirements would be left with an operational role within networks, and that they could then become second-tier suppliers or even be removed from the network.

Inspired by the well-known work of Mintzberg, which showed that strategy follows structure rather than the other way round, and by other socio-democratic influences in Europe (Wensley, 1995), industrial network researchers disclaim the principles of centralisation and hierarchy put forward by supply chain management researchers.

Centrality is disclaimed through the argument that a network consists of several actors who 'pursue their own interests when acting' (Hakånsson and Johanson, 1993: 44). Control of one party over another is disclaimed on the grounds that, because actors have limited resources and reduced capacity to predict which relationships will become relevant in the future, it would be too risky and potentially ineffective for them to build dependence on the resources of a central actor. Moreover, they take so seriously the representations of embeddedness (Granovetter, 1985) in general and of connectedness in particular (Mattsson, 1989; Easton, 1996) that the dyadic level and corresponding structures and mechanisms disappear. By arguing that the relationship between actors A and B is connected, positively or negatively, to the relationships between A and C and between B and D, they dismiss the importance of power structures and mechanisms which manifest themselves at the dyadic level. In spite of its analytical importance, the notion of connectedness is misleading because connections are described not just as a problem for researchers who take the dyad as the unit of analysis, but also as a source of power increase or dependence reduction for a given actor. From a critical realist standpoint, what is more concerning is that researchers do not realise that this argument bounds what they address as empirical results.

Researchers argue that the network does not determine one's decisions for two major reasons. First, because it is a boundless system or structure enacted differently by different actors. Second, because it is always being transformed by the actions and interactions of other actors. Such complex representation leads researchers to nominate plurality and decentralisation as the two main characteristics of networks. Grounded on the seductive bottom-up representation of strategy popularised internationally by Mintzberg and associates (Mintzberg, 1994; Mintzberg *et al.*, 1998), industrial network researchers represent actors as equally capable of attempting to use and transform the network in accordance with their own interests. They understand that things happen this way because it is almost impossible for any single actor to grasp and control a given network.

Given the possibility of having supply chain management as the only theory in the field and given the divide between positivists and interpretivists, or between postmodernists and positivists (Ackroyd and Fleetwood, 2000), and the strength of the principle of incommensurability within business academia (Deetz, 1996; Alvesson and Sköldberg, 2000: 280), industrial network researchers have not faced many obstacles to legitimising their theory and corresponding methodological choices as a sort of second school in the international literature (see McLoughlin and Horan, 2000).

However, under the criterion of relevance, both schools share a serious problem. Both argue that networks are more effective than other governance modes, but their researchers have not tested such an argument properly because they impose their network logic on empirical investigations and corresponding texts. The underlying problem is that they fail to distinguish reasons and causes, or causal relationships and logical relationships (Archer, 1998). This is a central point for critical realists. They argue that research is not a neutral or 'natural' concept. More specifically they argue that 'what social reality is deemed to consist of (and what is deemed non-existent) do affect how explanation is approached' (Archer, 1995: 16).

A major issue in this respect is that researchers of both schools do not problematise the use of language when they represent the reality of networks and their constituents. Easton reminds us that when we analyse and interpret, 'we do so through language use that is, in turn, a socially conditioned tool' (2000: 215). Accordingly, it is argued here that the non-problematisation of language use from a critical realist standpoint impedes those researchers in discovering and expressing a more plausible representation of the real agency–structure interplay in networks.

The treatment that both schools give to the dyad comprised of the key customer and the first-tier supplier is a major and problematic issue. By giving priority to the system, both schools impose particular theories of time to represent processes within networks, which in the end suppress power structures and mechanisms at the dyadic level. Supply chain management researchers prescribe dyadic consensus before decisions are made while industrial network researchers disclaim it by arguing that consensus may happen *a posteriori* as a result of interactions and enactment processes governed by complex structures and mechanisms, either known or not known by actors.

However, researchers in the field of networks should take into account that causality in decision processes is difficult to unravel in retrospective research, not only because of the hindsight effects and biases in causal attribution (Schwenk, 1995) and in the process of deciding itself (Das and Teng, 1999), but also because of the deep ambiguities involving managers' acting and talking (Cohen *et al.*, 1972; March, 1987). Decisions comprise symbolic (Feldman and March, 1981) and context- or culture-dependent constructions (Chia, 1994; Brunsson, 1982; Geertz, 1973) that constrain and enable managers and organisations when they rationalise, justify, legitimise or make sense of both prior and future actions (Hendry, 2000: 956). Accordingly, biased attributions in the recollection of decisions are very common (Schwenk, 1986), as much as problems of interpretation for researchers, and have different causes. They may be the result of a deliberate intention held by managers and organisations to create the impression that things are under control (Salancik and Meindl, 1984), or a lack of freedom of managers within organisations to tell what they know (Brunsson, 1993), or cognitive misconceptions of managers and organisations in trying to make sense of reality (Huff and Schwenk, 1990).

Researchers of both schools have neglected this linguistic character of decisions, pointed out by researchers of other fields, because of the principles and knowledge they created or reproduced to represent networks of firms. These principles enable industrial network researchers, for instance, to appropriate and impose the representation of 'disjointed incrementalism' (Lindblom, 1959) to describe what actors do in networks, and the representation of 'logical incrementalism' (Quinn, 1980) to explain and theorise 'real' network phenomena, structure and mechanisms (see, for example, Anderson *et al.*, 1994). They disregard those linguistic issues in causal attribution that may affect both informants and themselves, and also other structures and mechanisms that may influence decisions and outcomes.

Conversely, the assumption that a network is a centralised and hierarchical system enables supply chain management researchers to appropriate the representation of deliberate strategy to every empirical phenomenon. More specifically, empirical investigations of cases of success are presented as if the 'eventual outcome was the intended all along' (Macy and Flache, 1995: 83) by the key customer firm. As a result, they represent key customer firms as much smarter and more powerful than they really are. This bias reproduces their main concern in prescribing rules from a top-down perspective and in exporting them to firms and managers located in any part of the world.

In both cases the major effect is that of double hermeneutics (Giddens, 1979). Researchers of both schools merely reproduce certain theoretical and linguistic representations they bring with themselves, in spite of their consciousness of this. In this respect Easton warns us that when we collect data 'we use our perceptions of the world to decide what to collect and we only recognise what we have concepts for' (2000: 215). Based on such an argument, one may argue that it is very likely that researchers of both schools end up imposing particular meanings on decisions, actions and episodes in supply networks. It is also likely that these researchers cannot discover or express power and contextual issues in the world out there because of those theoretical and linguistic representations they bring with them. Unfortunately one could also argue that this state of affairs in the novel field of networks reproduces the problems of misrepresentation in social research (Denzin, 1994: 503), that remain unchallenged due to the difficulties that researchers face in getting some 'critical distance' (Mingers, 2000) from their academic background.

Critical realists argue that concepts should not acquire meaning from the role they play in a given theoretical framework, because this means the imposition of theories, a typically positivist attitude (Chalmers, 1993: 27). They argue then that the researcher should discover causal structures and mechanisms, which can be unknown by social actors, rather than imposing some representation of reality. A first issue to be recognised is that social phenomena and reality exist 'independently of the researchers who study them' (Ackroyd and Fleetwood, 2000: 11). A second is that inquiry must start from the standpoint of agents, since social phenomena and structures 'do not exist independently of the agents' conceptions of what they are doing in their activity' (Bhaskar, 1989: 38). These are key issues to differentiate critical realists and positivists. They also represent a contentious point within critical realism (Hamlin, 2000) for two reasons: first, because it has not been made clear how the researcher can know what social actors actually know; and second, because it has not been made clear how researchers can be sure that what social actors recount represents what they actually know.

The major argument put forward so far by critical realists is that what is accounted by social actors cannot be equated with reality for two reasons: first, because social phenomena exist independently of their identification; and second, because their conceptions may be flawed (Ackroyd and Fleetwood, 2000: 11) for different reasons. Based on the assumption that the conceptions of social actors, as lay agents, are 'fallible and corrigible' (Lawson, 1998: 146), they argue that the researcher should discover the conditions that impede social actors in accounting those intransitive structures and mechanisms that really cause phenomena of interest.

Accordingly, it is argued here that the field of networks requires the construction and use of proper epistemological guidelines grounded on critical realism. It is also argued that a major challenge to the researcher is to find ways of getting knowledge of what managers actually know about social phenomena and causal structures and mechanisms. This is not an easy task in retrospective investigation. The researcher must find ways to decipher what managers actually mean, and why, when they account what happened in a particular way, before imposing some structure that has not been meant by managers. As a result the researcher will be in a position to discover the real interplay of agency and structures, and also how and why this may differ from the knowledge of managers. In the following section three major epistemological guidelines are developed.

Epistemological guidelines and research procedures

Guidelines to investigate power within networks

As noted in the previous section, supply chain management and industrial network researchers tend to dismiss important power and contextual issues. The Anglo-Americans represent networks as tightly coupled and centralised structures, composed of a limited number of firms who share goals and strategies. Accordingly, value-adding demands coming from the market of end consumers and passed by key customer firms to the supply network are described as strategic 'opportunities' for first-tier suppliers. These manager firms are expected to co-operate with the key customer firm in order to enhance the viability of the network, and to maintain or even to upgrade their position within networks. Moreover, they are expected to spread the correct rationale towards lower-tier suppliers and to develop value-adding projects with them.

Embedded in a particular and socio-cultural context, industrial network researchers disclaim such managerial rationale used by Anglo-American researchers. They represent networks as more loosely coupled, decentralised and boundless structures, composed of an uncertain number of semi-autonomous actors. Accordingly, value-adding demands coming from a given customer are situations the first-tier supplier may use in order to make the network more effective (Hakansson and Johanson, 1993). However, this type of co-operative response cannot be interpreted by the researcher as being caused by the authority of the key customer firm. In rough terms, such co-operative response actually depends on the particular way the first-tier supplier enacts and mobilises the network.

Accordingly, these theories are not sufficient in explaining why first-tier suppliers co-operate with key customer firms and lower-tier suppliers. These situations are particularly important not just for enhancing the viability of networks but also for economic development. In order to address power properly the researcher adopted a basic model of change in networks developed by Easton and Lundgren (1992), called the 'flow through nodes'. Given the objective of the investigation and the arguments developed so far in this chapter, the model has three main advantages. First, it provides a framework within which one can analyse the managerial options available to a manager firm which has to respond to a demand for change from a key customer firm. The model says that demands can be reflected, absorbed within the dyad, or transmitted, either directly or through some transformational intention, to the next stage of the network. As such, it does not force the researcher and researched into any known network logic or reasoning. Rather it helps managers to construct narratives, a form of expression more likely to reveal 'truth and unsettle power' (Ewick and Silbey, 1995: 199) than hegemonic tales. Second, the model allows the researcher and managers to conceive that effective responses, apparently caused by demands of the key customer firm and in accordance with the logic used by supply chain management researchers, may actually be caused by other interests or mechanisms, either known or not known by manager firms. Third, it allows the combination of depth and focus in management research (Eisenhardt, 1989). Its limited scope provides the researcher with a safe ground in undertaking in-depth investigation of how decisions are actually made and also for the proper understanding of meanings mobilised by actors.

The 'flow through nodes' model does not problematise contextual issues. Industrial and national issues were then taken into account in this investigation for three reasons. First, because researchers have demonstrated that managers make sense of reality, decide and act in particular ways in different industrial sectors (Spender, 1989) and national contexts or cultures (Hofstede, 1991). Second, researchers have demonstrated that different higher-order structures enable individual firms to use and legitimate power use in particular ways (Whittington, 1990; Meyer and Whittington, 1996). Third, because researchers have demonstrated that managerial or organisational actions that seem to cause organisational effectiveness are actually caused by higher-order structures, such as industrial or national ones, rather than by the actions undertaken by organisations or managers (Wilson, 1992).

Guidelines to investigate the knowledge of managers

Critical realists argue that experience, reason and causal mechanisms are placed in distinct levels of reality (Bhaskar, 1989: 12). Reality itself is constituted not only by events and reasons, but also by structures, powers, mechanisms and tendencies that 'underpin, generate or facilitate the actual phenomena that we may (or may not) experience, but are typically out of phase with them' (Bhaskar and Lawson, 1998: 5).

Unlike positivists, critical realists view social systems as open systems. Accordingly, causal laws are viewed as tendencies, 'which may be possessed unexercised and exercised unrealised, just as they may of course be realised unperceived (or undetected) by people' (Bhaskar, 1989: 9). Therefore it is not unlikely that social actors do not know or have misconceptions of the real causal mechanisms and structures that enable or constrain their actions or the actions of others. However, researchers should take into consideration that such structures and mechanisms may or may not be reported in their accounts for at least two reasons, besides those already addressed in this essay. First, managers are very busy people; they are thus not expected to tell the researcher everything they know unless they realise that the research can be useful for them. Second, the subjects of management research are very likely 'to be more powerful than the researchers themselves ... within organisations that are fairly tightly structured and controlled' (Easterby-Smith *et al.*, 1991: 45). As a result researchers must take into account these power and contextual issues that inhibit the full expression of knowledge by managers.

Accordingly, a first major task of the critical realist researcher is to develop conditions to make managers account for what they knew at the time things were happening. A second major task is then to discover the real causal mechanisms and structures. A third is to discover conditions that enable or constrain the production of knowledge by managers. In other words, besides identifying lack of knowledge or misconceptions, the analyst should explain why these occur. Finally the researcher should communicate these discoveries to managers, given the emancipatory assumption that the knowledge of deeper levels 'may correct as well as explain knowledge of more superficial ones' (Bhaskar, 1989: 12).

As reviewed in this chapter, the major problem is that theoretical and linguistic representations mobilised by the researcher tend to misrepresent the knowledge and agency of social actors. In order to overcome such problems, the ethogenic model (Harré and Secord, 1972: 9) was adopted in this investigation. This model was construed by its authors to elucidate the underlying structures of episodes in social life, through an investigation of the meanings and reasons that actors bring to the constituent acts. Its major guideline is to not take the social actor as a single individual, but rather consider him as 'made up of a fairly consistent set of inner and outer responses to his fellows and to the social situation ... backed up by accounts for his actions in terms of a unified set of rules and plans and a coherent system of meanings' (Harré and Secord, 1972: 6–7). Accordingly, informants from first-tier supplier firms, for instance, are not expected to account for things that challenge the key customer firm. Power issues are not easily disclosed in organisational settings (Pettigrew, 1973; Eisenhardt and Bourgeois, 1988: 738). Therefore the discovery of what managers know requires the researcher to play a more active role and adopt a less 'scientific' attitude during fieldwork.

Guidelines for investigating decision processes

In the field of strategy the use of more adequate representations of time by researchers has resulted in the discovery of how decision processes actually take place. Accordingly, contextualists argue that what happens, how it happens, why it happens and what results it brings about in strategy processes are dependent on 'when it happens, the location in the processual sequence, the place in the rhythm of events characteristic for a given process' (Pettigrew, 1992: 8). Halinen and Törnroos argue that time remains a major research issue in the field of networks because researchers tend to disregard the fact that time is not only physically determined 'but also socially constructed' (1995: 496). They also argue that time is dependent on cultural, organisational, relational and individual issues, which must be taken into account by the researcher.

The concept of critical episodes has been fruitfully used in studies of business relationships (Halinen *et al.*, 1999). Although this is indeed an important guideline for the investigation of decision processes in networks, researchers tend to misrepresent reality because they impose the standpoint of the network system. More specifically they impose a diachronic representation of time and causation that takes change as mere succession of events. For this they deny the possibility that 'some changes are *in* rather than between things' (Sayer, 1992: 157, italics in original). Critical realists argue that such atomistic representation is nonsensical since 'both motion and rest must occupy time as *duration* to be discernible' (Sayer, 1992: 156). Only with an ontology which admits 'both external and internal relations, internally structured and differentiated objects having causal powers and liabilities is it possible to distinguish between qualitative change and mere successions of events and hence between necessary or causal changes and relationships and accidental ones' (Sayer, 1992: 157).

Accordingly, a critical episode should be used not just to represent processes happening in time from the standpoint of the network system but also to represent processes taking place in time. A critical episode that takes place in time from the standpoint of a focal net, for instance, takes time from the standpoint of the focal firm or of the focal dyad. Therefore, besides getting the accounts of a given process from the standpoint of the network, the researcher should take into consideration and ask managers what was happening at that time within the focal firm or within the focal dyad.

In accordance with such a critical realist standpoint, horizontal and vertical dimensions of time have to be considered (see Table 9.1). Longitudinally, relationship episodes were taken as an embedded unit of analysis, more closely related to the focal net of firms. A stream of interaction episodes was taken as an intermediate embedded unit of analysis, more closely related to the dyadic domain. Individual episodes were taken as individual units of analysis, more closely related to the focal firm. Correspondingly, time was addressed from three vertical standpoints: that of the focal net of firms; that of the focal dyad; and that of the focal firm. Moreover, these representations were taken as subject to the influence of the contextual structures contemplated by the researcher.

The fieldwork and the interviews

The extensive in-depth investigation, undertaken from 1995 to 1997, was grounded on embedded case studies (Miles and Huberman, 1994). Each case study was comprised of a key customer firm, a first-tier supplier firm and a second-tier supplier firm. In Brazil, the empirical research took place mainly in the state of São Paulo. In the UK, it was undertaken in the West Midlands region. Both regions are important automotive industrial districts. In Brazil a case

Table 9.1 Representations of time and corresponding types of unit of analysis

Longitudinal representation	*Type of unit of analysis*	*Vertical representation*
Relationship episodes	Embedded	Focal net of firms
Stream of episodes	Intermediate	Focal dyad
Individual episodes	Individual	Focal firm

in the telecommunications sector was also investigated. The focal nets investigated in the UK and Brazil had two different European key customer firms. In Brazil, two local and one French first-tier supplier firms were investigated, while in the UK a local and a US first-tier supplier firm were investigated.

Fieldwork started in the UK, where the researcher was doing his PhD at business school, in 1995 and totalled seventy hours of contacts and interviews with managers of firms involved in each of the five firms. Fifty-one visits to their corresponding sites in both countries were made. Given the research question, the 'key customer' firms that agreed to take part in the research project were asked to suggest four suppliers with which they had extreme and interesting cases of co-operation. Three to four first-tier suppliers were contacted and corresponding access negotiations followed. The subsequent selection of focal suppliers for each key customer followed the rationale of polar cases (Pettigrew, 1992), and were selected by the informants of the firms.

The investigation of each case started with a brief account of the selected situation of interests by the informant. Subsequently, the key informant was asked to select three to four critical episodes (see Easterby-Smith *et al.*, 1991), from his or her standpoint. Subsequent semi-structured and in-depth interviews, most of them made in the working site of the informants, were grounded on these critical episodes and were accompanied by observations and informal conversations. The devil's advocacy procedure was used as much as possible in the interviews. The use of critical episodes provided a more coherent ground for both informants and the researcher. It made it more difficult for the key informant to misrepresent reality, and was useful in reducing the risks of misunderstandings and misrepresentations by the researcher.

In order to avoid the imposition of particular logical reasoning, the researcher followed the strategy of taking the focal firm, the focal dyad and the focal net as units of analysis. Such a strategy allowed informants and the researcher to address power and contextual issues not only at the level of the system but also at individual and relational levels of analysis. Accounts produced by informants of the focal firm were contrasted with and added to the accounts produced by informants of the key customer firm. The same procedure applied to the secondary dyad, composed by the first- and the corresponding second-tier supplier firm.

The key informant and the focused interview procedures were used for data collection (Merton and Kendall, 1946). The key informant was the first interviewed and, subsequently, informants of the other firms of the focal net were interviewed. The researcher prepared each interview before meeting informants, in accordance with what was being discovered and tested.

When the focal firm was taken as the unit of analysis, key informants were asked why their firms behaved in a specific way instead of choosing some other option. Based on the 'flow through nodes' model and the research question, those critical episodes were approached by the researcher as situations of agency or choice, in which the focal firm 'could, at any phase in a given sequence, have acted differently' (Giddens, 1984: 9).

When the focal dyad was taken as the unit of analysis, the informants of other net firms were asked about the causes that led the focal firm and the key customer firm to decide in a particular way instead of choosing some other option. Suspicious matches or mismatches between accounts were taken as critical issues to be further investigated. In most of these situations the researcher had to go back to the key informant and to the other informants to test the plausibility of each explanation.

When the focal net was taken as the unit of analysis, the researcher asked the informants of a particular case about reasons and motives accounted by informants in other cases in order to test those structures and mechanisms. These procedures followed in a particular way the basic tenets of critical realism:

> one has in science a three-phase schema of development in which, in a continuing dialectic, science identifies a phenomenon (or range of phenomena), constructs explanations for it and empirically tests its explanations, leading to the identification of the generative mechanisms at work, which now becomes the phenomenon to be explained, and so on.
>
> (Bhaskar, 1989: 12)

In some situations the researcher had difficulty choosing the most plausible explanation from those accounted by different informants. In those situations the researcher followed the strategy of not attributing discrepancies to network complexities. Power, control and symbolic issues that underlie the mobilization of information by managers and organisations (Feldman and March, 1981) were the major causes of discrepancies. In order to deal with this judgement issue, the researcher had to collect and use secondary information and knowledge produced by other disciplines such as global sociology and international political economy. Moreover he had to discuss those matters with researchers and also with non-academic social actors.

Major results and discoveries

Discovering the power of corporations inside and outside 'networks'

The first surprising result, although not that surprising given the aversion of Anglo-Americans to accounting power issues (Kotter, 1978; Kanter, 1979), was that Brazilian informants had much less difficulty in disclosing power in their use of narratives than UK informants. What was particularly surprising was that they accounted for power issues not just at the inter-firm level but also at the corporate and global level. Two fieldwork episodes in Brazil demonstrate how their narratives surprised the researcher.

In the first episode a key informant argued, ironically, that negotiations, at both inter- and intra-firm levels, never happen without bluffs. He also argued that his company was not used to following accounting procedures espoused by the business literature and the specialised media. Finally, he said that researchers should not trust what companies and managers in general say. The researcher then asked himself whether any informant could be telling any truth, either in this particular research or in any other research, and why. The researcher also reflected upon what to do with such epistemological questioning since taking it seriously would mean putting the research at risk. At that time he actually started to realise that it was one thing to develop and use proper research methods in order to discover reality, but another thing to have certain discoveries accepted by his superiors and peers in the UK.

In the second episode, a key informant interrupted an interview to ask the researcher if he had any working experience in the industrial sector. This interruption expressed his annoyance with the researcher's insistence in finding a more sophisticated or acceptable explanation to why his firm chose to co-operate with the key customer firm. This Brazilian informant expressed overtly what other informants in Brazil and in the UK had addressed already in a more covert manner. He mobilised a representation of stratified political economy to explain network phenomena that surprised the researcher.

For this informant the major cause was very clear: his firm decided to 'co-operate' because it was a medium-sized local firm pursuing survival, and the key customer was a large European transnational corporation (TNC) pursuing capital accumulation in the telecommunications sector, which was going through a controversial and fairly aggressive process of privatisation in the most 'attractive' country in South America. The second major cause was very clear as well: the net 'co-operated' because the second-tier supplier firm was not in a position to choose any other option. This local firm was going through a dramatic process of decline, as were many other local firms. To make things more complicated, it was located in a region in São Paulo that was going through a process of decline. The main cause of such decline was that major national firms were going bankrupt and international corporations were leaving that region and moving to other more attractive regions in Brazil, or to other countries in South America. Although this was not a point made in the interviews, it was clear for him that this scenario of industrial and regional decline actually started in the early 1990s, when the Brazilian government started the deregulation and privatisation of several industrial sectors and, accordingly, many TNCs decided to 'capture' not only the Brazilian market but the South American market as a whole. At the time, in Brazil and many other countries that were getting into globalisation, state and business 'were united in their belief that the protectionism of the past could no longer be maintained' if they were to enter the global economy (Sklair, 2001: 117). The informant was overtly critical of such discourse and of the outcomes brought by the new 'networks' formed by corporations and governments.

In the automotive sector the picture was much the same. Since the early 1990s, the few automobile makers who have controlled the Brazilian market for at least four decades announced that they would move their plants to less unionised regions and rebuild their supply networks. They announced that they would include supplier firms based in diverse parts of the world, and invite a few of them to establish new industrial districts in those less unionised regions. This was facilitated because, in parallel, major local suppliers were being acquired by transnational groups. Actually, in the absence of an industrial policy led by the state, Brazil became a land of 'global opportunities', not only to corporations but also to members of local government. Accordingly, mayors and public officers of less unionised regions in Brazil competed fiercely among themselves (Arbix, 2000) to attract these corporations by promising very attractive benefits. Conversely TNCs deployed overtly the strategy of 'shopping for a place', and abandoned former commitments with suppliers, workers and local governments in more unionised regions.

To the researcher's surprise the informant was aware that TNCs are used to 'playing-off' one regional or national government against another in their attempts 'to bargain for favourable conditions such as tax rebates, subsidies, infrastructure and telecommunications support' (Ruigrok and van Tulder, 1995: 104). This type of practice was becoming more common in Brazil at the time because the local public administration and its administrators were being 'infected' by the neo-liberal principles of the so-called 'managerial state' (Clarke and Newman, 1997) and of corresponding Anglo-American frameworks related to Reaganism and Thatcherism (Silver, 1987).

Managers were quite aware that public administrators and authorities should recognise that neither the market nor individual enterprises 'can be left to themselves' (Whittington, 1993: 142). Such awareness explained why they were so concerned with the establishment of that kind of 'new network order' in Brazil. Their civic posture surprised the researcher, since his interests and attention were bounded by an academic background in business. In the end the researcher realised that these local informants were not speaking as mere managers; rather, as citizens they proved to be consciously aware that, by bidding against each other to attract corporations, countries undermine each other's standards and 'expose their populations to predatory practices' (Monbiot, 2000: 355).

At the time these discoveries seemed very interesting indeed, because they revealed causal networks and mechanisms that are not problematised by the most-known schools on networks, nor by business academics in general. Nevertheless the researcher realised that it would be almost impossible to bring them from Brazil to a business school in the UK, not just because they were new, but also because they were quite critical on practices undertaken by TNCs in developing countries. In other words the major obstacles were not just academic mechanisms of stratification between researchers of developing countries and of developed countries (Stavenhagen, 1993); the major obstacle was that the researcher was aware that TNCs were becoming increasingly influential on cities or towns, such as Sunderland and Southampton (Oliver and Wilkinson, 1992; Monbiot, 2000: 93), and also on business schools and universities in the UK (Monbiot, 2000: 287) and particularly in North America (Epstein, 2001: 197; Tuldiver, 1999).

The researcher then tried to figure out why the knowledge accounted by informants in the UK did not express such a reality. The most obvious explanation was that people in the UK do not experience to the same degree political economic problems caused by TNCs and globalisation. Nevertheless, the researcher noticed a curious pattern: Brazilian and UK informants used critical episodes in their narratives in different manners. It led the researcher to realise that causality is a social construction enabled and constrained by distinct theories of time and language in different contexts. Brazilian informants 'connected' critical episodes in general to higher-order structures and mechanisms, while UK informants typically 'connected' a critical episode to the preceding, or the following, one in accordance with the linearity of the English code (Hickson, 1996). Besides, UK managers seemed to be more disciplined by the frameworks challenged by Brazilian managers. A critical episode was narrated in Brazil as caused mainly by synchronic generative mechanisms and structures, while in the UK it was accounted as caused mainly by diachronic generative mechanisms and structures. The researcher concluded that these linguistic and disciplinarian features constrained managers in the UK from expressing the same type of knowledge accounted by managers in Brazil. What was more concerning was that these features tended to affect researchers of all nationalities, given the hegemony of the English language in the field of business.

Enabled by such a particular code of language and of knowledge, besides representing networks of firms as stratified political economies at both national and international levels, informants in Brazil also represented networks, overtly, as political economies led by TNCs and other members of the transnational capitalist class, comprised of chief corporate executives and members of the local elite. Such representations challenged the most well-known schools on networks, (re)produced and transferred towards practitioners and citizens in every corner of the world by business scholars and corresponding institutions. A fieldwork episode illustrates this pattern well.

In this episode, an informant of a key customer firm challenged the assumption that local managers and subsidiaries play a major role in decisions that mobilise the interests of transnational corporations in Brazil. In saying so he actually challenged the more typical representations of reality reproduced by the management discipline in general and by the network literature. The informant then recollected controversial situations from the recent past. First, he stressed that TNCs were complaining that Brazil was a protectionist state, although they had been some of the most benefited and supportive agents of such regimes. Second, he pointed out that things were getting a bit more problematic in this respect in the 1990s, because TNCs developed a greater degree of freedom in Brazil. Third, he stressed that the current situation was more dramatic than in the past because managers were becoming even more powerless. In sum, he was aware that Brazil, in geopolitical terms, was essentially important for the expansion and consolidation of the supra-network led by TNCs and other powerful global agents in South America.

He was more conscious of the practices, strategies and resilience of the transnational capitalist class than the researcher and the academic knowledge that informed him and his peers and superiors. The transnational capitalist class is a concept largely ignored, not only by the network literature but also by business scholars in general. It has been represented in the field of global sociology (Sklair, 1995) as a sort of centralised network. According to Sklair, its inner circle makes system-wide decisions and connects in a variety of ways with subsidiary members in communities, cities, countries and supranational regions. The make-up of this class is 'intrinsically bound up with the globalising of the corporations and their control over the global economy that has been emerging over the last few decades' (Sklair, 2001: 35). Accordingly, this is a causal issue that researchers should not neglect in explaining the economic performance and effectiveness of TNCs, supply networks, industries and even countries.

The researcher then discovered that the type of bargaining and political relations outside networks of firms, as accounted overtly by informants in Brazil, has been addressed by political scientists, political economists and students of public administration and economic geography (Ruigrok and van Tulder, 1995: 91) but not by management academics. Correspondingly, the researcher noticed two serious issues behind such phenomena. First, these disciplines, and history in particular, are not part of management curricula (see Gibson *et al.*, 1999). Second, large organisations gained influence in the 1990s over the curriculum in the UK, and on programme design and assessment of managerial courses, 'by influencing government departments' (Fox, 1992: 88). The realisation of these issues led the researcher to call into question the contemporaneous belief that management discipline and the corresponding institutions are necessary means to collective welfare or worldwide development. For this reason a major problem for the researcher was quite surprising: what to do with such discoveries that came from outside the business academy?

Major conclusions and implications

Grounded in the major tenets of critical realism, this chapter has shown that the construction and use of epistemological guidelines that problematise power and contextual issues in a proper manner are important to enable managers to express what they know about reality. They are even more important for pushing researchers in the field of business to transcend or transgress undesirable disciplinary boundaries (Knights and Willmott, 1997). Accordingly, this chapter suggested that both practitioners and researchers became victims of the type of knowledge diffused and (re)produced internationally by business academics and corresponding institutions. What is more concerning is that researchers seem to be more affected than practitioners. Three major obstacles, of particular interest to critical realists, seem to explain such an outcome: (a) researchers are used to treating the knowledge of social actors as inferior, in order to legitimise their professions and productions; (b) researchers do not problematise the use of English as a sort of universal linguistic code; and (c) researchers take the transfer of knowledge from the academy towards social actors for granted.

Moreover, researchers must take into account the influence of transnational corporations. This cannot be disregarded. Actually, the dismissal of power and contextual issues by both European and US researchers on networks seems to have been influenced by the uncritical interests of TNCs in legitimising a particular representation of networks. Such a representation established the idea, flowing from the academy towards societies, that networks could sort out problems of development in every corner of the world and replace the ineffectiveness of national states. One may argue, then, that with the help of researchers TNCs imposed a 'particular view of the business world' (Mills and Hatfield, 1999) that misrepresents the roles, practices and responsibilities of managers, local firms, TNCs and the state.

One may argue that such a problematic outcome has been facilitated by structures and mechanisms which have been impeding the formulation of international and national codes of conduct for TNCs (Sklair, 2001; Ruigrok and van Tulder, 1995). It is unsurprising, then, that neither researchers in networks nor business researchers in general, especially those who work in better-known universities, question the power of corporations (see Mokhiber and Weissman, 1999: 26). These researchers do not see 'globalisation' and 'global competition' as contemporaneous representations of imperialism, and TNCs as its most important agents and benefactors (Deetz, 1992). It can be argued that the elimination of history and political backgrounds from business school curricula, in both taught and researched degrees, remains a central impediment to the understanding within the business academy that imperialism is not a practice of the distant past, and that colonialism is not an interest or ideology exclusively pursued by nation-states that only existed in a 'pre-democratic world' (see Munck, 1994).

Correspondingly, it is not surprising that schools on networks which have been challenged in this investigation by managers, produced in developed countries, overlook power and political issues and mechanisms at the home–host, state–corporation and academy–practice boundaries. It is also not surprising that these schools do not fit the way managers, as persons or citizens, live, work and make sense of their local realities.

These points call into question both the relevance of management knowledge and corresponding institutions, and the commodification, diffusion and internationalisation of them. For this reason business researchers should incorporate more societal, political and philosophical knowledge grounds into their frameworks and practices. They should set up a more realistic dialogue with the depreciated area of public administration, in order to build a necessary relevance and some autonomy for their practices. Political and educational institutions should then recognise that the uncritical diffusion and internationalisation of management knowledge, pushed by the supra-network, seems to be leading to a problematic process of colonisation, mystification and deception, rather than to 'development' or 'democracy' (Sklair, 1994).

Accordingly, the increasing power of TNCs and the transnational capitalist class over local political economies, and the low autonomy of subsidiaries of TNCs and of researchers in general, are issues to be problematised by citizens, researchers and public authorities. The current discourse that networks are more effective than other governance modes to promote socio-economic development (e.g. Kenis, 1991), by being more socially driven and by building the effective integration of the state and the market, should be critically addressed by citizens, researchers and public authorities. This is a central issue in developing countries. From a critical realist standpoint this should be addressed as a global problem rather than a local one, for two main reasons. First, because it actually involves and impacts on both developed and developing countries, even though it is much more problematic in the latter than in the former. Second, because developing countries in general are expected to have much less bargaining power *vis-à-vis* TNCs and other members of the supra-network than developed countries (see Ruigrok and van Tulder, 1995: 104).

References

Ackroyd, A. and Fleetwood, S. (2000) 'Realism in contemporary organisation and management studies', in S. Ackroyd and S. Fleetwood (eds), *Realist Perspectives on Management and Organisations*, London: Routledge.

Alvesson, M. and Sköldberg, K. (2000) *Reflexive Methodology*, London: Sage.

Anderson, J., Hakansson, H. and Johanson, J. (1994) 'Dyadic business relationships within a business network context', *Journal of Marketing*, 58: 1–15.

Araujo, L. and Easton, G. (1996) 'Networks in socio-economic systems: a critical review', in D. Iacobucci (ed.), *Networks in Marketing*, London: Sage.

Arbix, G. (2000) 'Guerra Fiscal e Competição Intermunicipal por Novos Investimentos no Setor Automotivo', *Dados – Revista de Ciências Sociais*, 43 (1): 5–43.

Archer, M. (1995) *Realist Social Theory: The Morphogenetic Approach*, Cambridge: Cambridge University Press.

—— (1998) 'Introduction: realism in the social sciences', in M. Archer, R. Bhaskar, A. Collier, T. Lawson and A. Norrie (eds), *Critical Realism: Essential Readings*, London: Routledge.

Astley, W. and Fombrun, C. (1983) 'Collective strategy: social ecology of organisational environments', *Academy of Management Review*, 8: 576–87.

Axelsson, B. and Easton, G. (eds) (1992) *Industrial Networks: A New View of Reality*, London: Routledge.

Baehr, P. (1990) 'Review article: critical realism, cautionary realism', *Sociological Review*, 38 (4): 765–77.

Bertodo, R. (1991) 'The role of suppliers in implementing a strategic vision', *Long Range Planning*, 24 (3): 40–8.

Bhaskar, R. (1989) *The Possibility of Naturalism: A Philosophical Critique of the Contemporary Human Sciences*, 2nd edn, Hemel Hempstead: Harvester Wheatcheaf.

Bhaskar, R. and Lawson, T. (1998) 'Introduction', in M. Archer, R. Bhaskar, A. Collier, T. Lawson and A. Norrie (eds), *Critical Realism: Essential Readings*, London: Routledge.
Bhaskar, R. and Norrie, A. (1998) 'Introduction: dialectic and dialectical critical realism', in M. Archer, R. Bhaskar, A. Collier, T. Lawson and A. Norrie (eds), *Critical Realism: Essential Readings*, London: Routledge.
Brunsson, N. (1982) 'The irrationality of action and action rationality: decisions, ideologies and organizational actions', *Journal of Management Studies*, 19 (1): 29–44.
—— (1993) 'Ideas and actions: justification and hypocrisy as alternatives to control', *Accounting, Organisations and Society*, 18 (6): 489–506.
Chalmers, A. (1993) *What is This Thing Called Science?*, 2nd edn, Buckingham: Open University Press.
Chia, R. (1994) 'The concept of decision: a deconstructive analysis', *Journal of Management Studies*, 31 (6): 781–806.
Chumer, M., Hull, R. and Prichard, C. (2000) 'Introduction: situating discussions about "knowledge" ', in R. Prichard, R. Hull, M. Chumer and H. Willmott (eds), *Managing Knowledge: Critical Investigations of Work and Learning*, New York: St Martin's Press.
Clarke, J. and Newman, J. (1997) *The ManagerialState: Power, Politics and Ideology in the Remaking of Social Welfare*, London: Sage.
Cohen, M., March, J. and Olsen, J. (1972) 'A garbage can model of organizational choice', *Administrative Science Quarterly*, 17 (1): 1–25.
D'Cruz, J. and Rugman, A. (1992) 'Developing international competitiveness: the five partners model', *Business Quarterly*, 56 (4): 101–7.
Das, T. and Teng, B.-S. (1999) 'Cognitive biases and strategic decision processes: an integrative perspective', *Journal of Management Studies*, 36 (6): 757–78.
Deetz, S. (1992) *Democracy in an Age of Corporate Colonization*, Albany, NY: SUNY Press.
—— (1996) 'Describing differences in approaches to organization science: rethinking Burrell and Morgan and their legacy', *Organization Science*, 7 (2): 191–207.
Denzin, N. (1994) 'The art and politics of interpretation', in N. Denzin and Y. Lincoln (eds), *Handbook of Qualitative Research*, London: Sage.
Dore, R. (1983) 'Goodwill and the spirit of market capitalism', *British Journal of Sociology*, 34: 459–82.
Easterby-Smith, M., Thorpe, R. and Lowe, A. (1991) *Management Research: An Introduction*, London: Sage.
Easton, G. (1996) 'Review article – only connect: network and organizations', *Organization Studies*, 3 (2): 291–310.
—— (2000) 'Case research as a method for industrial networks', in S. Ackroyd and S. Fleetwood (eds), *Realist Perspectives on Management and Organisations*, London: Routledge.
Easton, G. and Lundgren, A. (1992) 'Changes in industrial networks as flow through nodes', in B. Axelsson and G. Easton (eds), *Industrial Networks: A New View of Reality*, London: Routledge.
Eisenhardt, K. (1989) 'Building theories from case study research', *Academy of Management Review*, 14 (4): 532–50.
Eisenhardt, K. and Bourgeois, L. (1988) 'Politics of strategic decision making in high velocity environments: toward a midrange theory', *Academy of Management Journal*, 31: 737–70.
Epstein, B. (2001) 'Corporate culture and the academic left', in G. Philo and D. Miller (eds), *Market Killing: What the Free Market Does and What Social Scientists Can Do About It*, Harlow: Pearson Education.

Ewick, P. and Silbey, S. (1995) 'Subversive stories and hegemonic tales: toward a sociology of narrative', *Law and Society Review*, 29 (2): 197–226.
Feldman, M. and March, J. (1981) 'Information in organizations as signal and symbol', *Administrative Science Quarterly*, 26: 171–86.
Fox, S. (1992) 'What are we? The constitution of management in higher education and human resource management', *International Studies in Management and Organization*, 22 (3): 71–93.
Geertz, C. (1973) *The Interpretation of Cultures*, New York: Basic Books.
Gibson, J., Hodgetts, R. and Blackwell, C. (1999) 'The role of management history in the management curriculum: 1997', *Journal of Management History*, 5 (5): 73–84.
Giddens, A. (1979) *Central Problems in Social Theory: Action, Structure and Contradictions in Social Analysis*, London: Hutchinson.
—— (1984) *The Constitution of Society: Outline of a Theory of Structuration*, Cambridge: Polity.
Granovetter, M. (1985) 'Economic action and social structure: the problem of embeddedness', *American Journal of Sociology*, 91 (3): 481–510.
Hakansson, H. and Johanson, J. (1993) 'The network as a governance structure', in G. Grabher (ed.), *The Embedded Firm: On the Socioeconomics of Industrial Networks*, London: Routledge.
Halinen, A. and Törnroos, J.-A. (1995) 'The meaning of time in the study of industrial buyer–seller relationships', in K. Moller and D. Wilson (eds), *Business Marketing: An Interaction and Network Perspective*, Norwell, MA: Kluwer Academic.
Halinen, A., Salmi, A. and Havila, V. (1999) 'From dyadic change to changing business networks: an analytical framework', *Journal of Management Studies*, 36 (6): 779–94.
Hamlin, C.L. (2000) 'Realismo Crítico: Um Programa de Pesquisa para as Ciências Sociais', *Dados – Revista de Ciências Sociais*, 43 (2): 373–98.
Harland, C. (1996) 'Supply chain management: relationships, chains and networks', *British Journal of Management*, 7: s63–s80.
Harré, R. and Secord, P. (1972) *The Explanation of Social Behavior*, Oxford: Blackwell.
Hendry, J. (2000) 'Strategic decision making, discourse, and strategy as social practice', *Journal of Management Studies*, 37 (7): 955–77.
Hickson, D. (1996) 'The *ASQ* years then and now through the eyes of a Euro-Brit', *Administrative Science Quarterly*, 41: 217–28.
Hofstede, G. (1991) *Cultures and Organizations*, London: HarperCollins.
Huff, A. and Schwenk, C. (1990) 'Bias and sensemaking in good times and bad', in A. Huff (ed.), *Mapping Strategic Thought*, Chichester: Wiley.
Johnsen, T., Wynstra, F., Zheng, J., Harland, C. and Lamming, R. (2000) 'Networking activities in supply networks', *Journal of Strategic Marketing*, 8: 161–81.
Kanter, R. (1979) 'Power failure in management circuits', *Harvard Business Review*, 57 (4): 65–75.
Kenis, P. (1991) 'The preconditions for policy networks: some findings from a three-country study on industrial restructuring', in B. Marin and R. Mayntz (eds), *Policy Networks: Empirical Evidence and Theoretical Considerations*, Frankfurt/Main: Campus.
Knights, D. and Willmott, H. (1997) 'The hype and hope of interdisciplinary management studies', *British Journal of Management*, 8: 9–22.
Kotter, J. (1977) 'Power, dependence, and effective management', *Harvard Business Review*, July–August: 125–36.
Lamming, R. (1993) *Beyond Partnership: Strategies for Innovation and Lean Supply*, London: Prentice-Hall.

—— (1996) 'Squaring lean supply with supply chain management', *International Journal of Operations and Production Management*, 16 (2): 183–96.

Larry, G. (1994) 'Public–private partnerships in economic development: a review of theory and practice', *Economic Development Review*, 12 (1): 7–15.

Lawson, T. (1998) 'Economic science without experimentation', in M. Archer, R. Bhaskar, A. Collier, T. Lawson and A. Norrie (eds), *Critical Realism: Essential Readings*, London: Routledge.

Lindblom, C. (1959) 'The science of muddling through', *Public Administration Review*, 19 (2): 79–88.

McLoughlin, D. and Horan, C. (2000) 'The production and distribution of knowledge in the market-as-networks tradition', *Journal of Strategic Marketing*, 8: 89–103.

Macy, M. and Flache, A. (1995) 'Beyond rationality in models of choice', *Annual Review of Sociology*, 21: 73–91.

March, J. (1987) 'Ambiguity and accounting: the elusive link between information and decision-making', *Accounting, Organization and Society*, 12: 153–68.

Mattsson, L.-G. (1989) 'Development of firms in networks: positions and investments', *Advances in International Marketing*, 3: 121–39.

Merton, R. and Kendall, P. (1946) 'The focused interview', *American Journal of Sociology*, 51: 541–57.

Meyer, M. and Whittington, R. (1996) 'The survival of the European holding company', in R. Whitley and K. Kristensen (eds), *The Changing European Firm*, London: Routledge.

Miles, M. and Huberman, A. (1994) *Qualitative Data Analysis*, London: Sage.

Mills, A. and Hatfield, J. (1999) 'From imperialism to globalization: internationalization and the management text', in S. Clegg, E. Ibarra-Colado and L. Bueno-Rodriguez (eds), *Global Management: Universal Theories and Local Realities*, London: Sage.

Mingers, J. (2000) 'What is to be critical?', *Management Learning*, 31 (2): 219–37.

Mintzberg, H. (1994) *The Rise and Fall of Strategic Planning*, Hemel Hempstead: Prentice-Hall.

Mintzberg, H. and Waters, J. (1985) 'Of strategies, deliberate and emergent', *Strategic Management Journal*, 6: 257–72.

Mintzberg, H., Ahlstrand, B. and Lampel, J. (1998) *Strategy Safari: A Guided Tour Through the Wilds of Strategic Management*, New York: Free Press.

Mokhiber, R. and Weissman, R. (1999) *Corporate Predators: The Hunt for Mega-Profits and the Attack on Democracy*, Monroe, ME: Common Courage Press.

Monbiot, G. (2000) *Captive State: The Corporate Takeover of Britain*, London: Macmillan.

Munck, R. (1994) 'Democracy and development: deconstruction and debates', in L. Sklair (ed.), *Capitalism and Development*, London: Routledge.

Nohria, N. 1992, 'Is a network perspective a useful way of studying organizations?', in N. Nohria and R. Eccles (eds), *Networks and Organizations*, Boston, MA: Harvard Business School Press.

Oliver, N. and Wilkinson, B. (1992) *The Japanization of British Industry*, 2nd edn, Oxford: Blackwell.

Pettigrew, A. (1973) *The Politics of Organizational Decision Making*, London: Tavistock.

—— (1992) 'The character and significance of strategy process research', *Strategic Management Journal*, 13: 5–16.

Piore, M. and Sabel, C. (1984) *The Second Industrial Divide: Possibilities for Prosperity*, New York: Basic Books.

Quinn, J. (1980) *Strategies for Change: Logical Incrementalism*, Homewood, IL: Irwin.

Ruigrok, W. and van Tulder, R. (1995) *The Logic of International Restructuring*, London: Routledge.

Salancik, G. (1995) 'Wanted: a good network theory of organization', *Administrative Science Quarterly*, 40: 345–9.

Salancik, G. and Meindl, J. (1984) 'Corporate attributions as strategic illusions of control', *Administrative Science Quarterly*, 29: 238–54.

Saunders, M. (1994) *Strategic Purchasing and Supply Chain Management*, London: Pitman/CIPS.

Sayer, A. (1992) *Method in Social Science: A Realist Approach*, 2nd edn, London: Routledge.

Schwenk, C. (1986) 'Information, cognitive biases, and commitment to a course of action', *Academy of Management Review*, 11 (2): 298–310.

—— (1995) 'Strategic decision making', *Journal of Management*, 21 (3): 471–93.

Silver, J. (1987) 'The ideology of excellence: management and neo-conservatism', *Studies in Political Economy*, 24: 105–29.

Sklair, L. (1994) 'Capitalism and development in global perspective', in L. Sklair (ed.), *Capitalism and Development*, London: Routledge.

—— (1995) *The Sociology of the Global System*, 2nd edn, Hemel Hempstead: Harvester Wheatsheaf.

—— (2001) *The Transnational Capitalist Class*, Oxford: Blackwell.

Spender, J.-C. (1989) *Industry Recipes: An Inquiry into the Nature and Sources of Managerial Judgement*, Oxford: Blackwell.

Stavenhagen, R. (1993) 'Decolonializing applied social sciences', in M. Hammersley (ed.), *Social Research: Philosophy, Politics and Practice*, London: Sage.

Sternberg, R. (2000) 'Innovation networks and regional development: evidence from the European regional innovation survey', *European Planning Studies*, 8 (4): 389–409.

Tuldiver, N. (1999) *Universities for Sale*, Toronto: James Lorimer.

Waarden, F. (1992) 'Dimensions and type of policy networks', *European Journal of Political Research*, 21: 29–52.

Wensley, R. (1995) 'A critical review of research in marketing', *British Journal of Management*, 6: s63–s82.

Whittington, R. (1990) 'Social structures and resistance to strategic change: British manufacturers in the 1980s', *British Journal of Management*, 1: 201–13.

—— (1993) *What is Strategy – and Does It Matter?*, London: Routledge.

Wilson, D. (1992) *A Strategy of Change*, London: Routldege.

Womack, J., Jones, D. and Roos, D. (1990) *The Machine that Changed the World*, New York: Rawson Associates.

Wynstra, F., van Weele, A. and Axelsson, B. (1999) 'Purchasing involvement in product development: a framework', *European Journal of Purchasing and Supply Management*, 5: 129–41.

Young, R. and Francis, J. (1994) 'Small manufacturing firms and regional business networks', *Economic Development Review*, 8 (1): 77–84.

10 Competence theories

Clive Lawson

Introduction

Recent years have seen a growing concern, from within a variety of (especially economics-related) disciplines, to develop concepts and categories that are of clear relevance to applied research. This concern has not been simply an interest in 'conceptualisation for conceptualisation's sake'. Rather, close inspection shows that it is driven by a dissatisfaction with the tendency of existing theories to treat various central categories, such as firms, regions, learning and technology, as closed black boxes. Implicitly, then, the relative plethora of new concepts has as its main feature, although rarely acknowledged, a realist or ontological orientation.

The aim of this essay is to clarify and develop a particular branch of such conceptualisations, i.e. competence theories, and set these more explicitly within a particular realist position. Elsewhere, I have argued for a competence theory of the region to mirror, and draw from, the more prominent competence theory of the firm (Lawson, 1999). However, in so doing, I left unclear the ontological underpinnings of the competence perspective for which I was arguing, and this has caused several recent contributors either to misunderstand or ignore important aspects of that account. Moreover, it has become clear that the competence theory of the firm, although prominent, is far from a homogeneous, well-understood set of ideas. And although the connection between the competence theory of the firm literature and that on regions appears to remain a fruitful one, there is a need to provide a general account of competences or competence theory, from which specific applications (to firms, organisations, regions or whatever) can be made. However, one implication of starting from very general (realist) categories, rather than drawing upon existing competence (theory of the firm) accounts, is that there is no clear reason to prioritise the idea of a competence over and above other similar concepts (such as capacities, capabilities and dispositions). More specifically, I shall argue that although such terms refer to the same *kinds* of thing, they increasingly need to be distinguished once more substantive issues are addressed. This need (and the fuller typology suggested) is illustrated by referring to recent research on technical consultancies in the Cambridge region.

System competences, powers and mechanisms

The term competence has received a considerable amount of attention,[1] and it is now generally accepted that it is possible to talk about a coherent (and well-established) 'competence perspective' (see especially Foss and Knudsen, 1996). I have argued elsewhere that the common denominator in this perspective is the focus upon the way that things are structured, which gives rise to potentials that cannot be reduced to events or states of affairs (Lawson, 1999, 2000). However, although essential (as discussed later), this feature remains largely unnoticed or misunderstood. Given this, it appears necessary, first, to focus upon what I believe to be the most coherent underpinning of such ideas – that is to briefly indicate the main features of critical realism.

Powers, mechanisms and critical realism

Introductory accounts of critical realism are now sufficiently numerous as to make a detailed introduction unnecessary – although see Fleetwood's and Sayer's contributions to this volume. Here I focus upon a small set of ideas. Critical realist accounts are a response to, and extension of, developments in the philosophy of science. The relevance of these accounts for social sciences lies, in the main, in identifying underlying presuppositions of the contemporary practice of social science. Thus although few practising social scientists openly embrace any form of positivism, critical realist accounts have sought to show exactly what such conceptions imply and how various prominent practices rely implicitly on them. In particular, these accounts have shown how a form of empirical realism is typically assumed, i.e. where reality consists of experiences and the direct objects of experience (e.g. events, states of affairs). In contrast, explicitly realist accounts add a layer of reality that consists of underlying causal factors (powers, mechanisms, tendencies) that are responsible for, or generate, such events (and experiences).[2] It is primarily this aspect (the elaboration of a structured ontology) that makes critical realism of particular relevance to a discussion of competence theories.

Perhaps the key point is that the structure of explanatory accounts cannot be primarily deductive. Or, put another way, the important task here is to unpack the different senses in which we can talk about the fact that something 'may' happen. To elaborate, several terms need to be distinguished. To say that some domain of reality is structured means that it consists in more than one ontological level. A power simply indicates what a certain kind of thing can do (a cup can hold tea, a bicycle can transport its rider, a violin can be used to play music or perhaps even table tennis) in virtue of it being structured in the way that it is; the ability to *do* (or be used in a certain way) is located in the structure of that thing. For example, it is the structure of the violin, and of the materials that it is made from, which allows it to vibrate and create sound in certain ways (or hit ping-pong balls!). But a power may be exercised or not, and designates what something *can* do. Like a power, a mechanism is 'a real something over and above and independent of patterns of events' but, in contrast, it is best thought of as a power in motion (Bhaskar, 1978: 50). Actual events or states of affairs may be co-determined by numerous, often countervailing, mechanisms. This idea of continuing activity is captured by the idea of a tendency. Tendencies carry on acting even though the effects we attribute to them (say, in experimental situations) do not always come about. As Collier puts it, 'while the word "power" draws attention to the existence of unexercised powers, the word "tendency" draws attention to the existence of exercised but unrealised mechanisms' (Collier, 1994: 63). As Lawson points out, this notion of a tendency clearly differs from many of its interpretations in the economics literature:

> A statement of a tendency ... is not about long-run, 'normal' usual, or average outcomes at the level of events. Nor is it reducible to a counterfactual claim about events or states of affairs that would occur if the world were different. Indeed, it is not a claim about anything at the level of the actual course of events at all.
>
> (Lawson, 1997: 23)

In short, a statement of a tendency is a *transfactual*, not a counterfactual statement. It is a statement about a power being exercised (whatever events follow), rather than what might occur under certain circumstances. Given that reality is structured in this way, and that causal mechanisms cannot simply be 'read off' from events or patterns in events, there is a concern, in realist accounts, with a different form of inference to the more common induction and deduction. Whereas the latter are concerned with movements at the level of events from the particular to the general and vice versa, retroduction involves moving from a conception of some phenomenon of interest to a conception of a different kind of thing (power, mechanism) that could have generated the given phenomenon. Thus science, on this account, is concerned with identifying powers and mechanisms that produce or facilitate phenomena at a different level.

Now, the social realm too is structured in the above sense. If the social can be understood to be that realm which depends, at least in part, on human activity for its existence, then to say that the social world is structured is to say that it consists in more than such observables as human behaviour. It also consists in social rules, relations, processes, systems, etc.[3] These features are ontologically distinct from (or irreducible to) behaviour. Such features that do not reduce to behaviour can be termed social structures, consisting in their entirety as social structure. In the social realm, then, the distinction between appearances and events and underlying powers/mechanisms is maintained, along with the view of science as primarily concerned with retroduction to the latter of these. The main issue, then, is how these powers and mechanisms differ from those in the natural world, and the implications that follow from such differences. In short, the main differences between natural and social structures follow from the latter's dependence upon human agency. As with natural structures, social structures underlie, constrain or generate certain activities or events. However, unlike natural structures, they also exist through, or are emergent from, such activities. Thus social structures are emergent phenomena in the sense that there is some lower level out of which something has arisen which, although dependent upon that lower level, is not predictable from it or reducible to it.

Firm and region powers and mechanisms

How, then, does talk of powers and mechanisms and of the nature of social reality tie together in a discussion of the 'powers' of social systems such as firms, trade unions, organisations, national and regional economies, etc.? In short, such systems can have powers in a similar way that 'things' or natural kinds do because of the manner in which they too are structured. On this account social systems are conceptualised as an 'ensemble of networked, internally related positions with their associated rules and practices' (T. Lawson, 1997: 165). Because of the nature of the relations, rules and positions that constitute some particular system, it will have powers (that may be unexercised) and tendencies (that may be unrealised).

Now it does seem to me that, although not presented in this way, the main contribution of the firm competence literature is that it treats firms in just this way. Firms are regularly conceptualised in terms of their routines, which are understood to facilitate capable reactions to changing market conditions, to the emergence of new technologies, etc. Because of the way a firm is structured, it has numerous competences, each of which can remain unexercised or unrealised or be realised/manifest in various ways (in products, market positions, etc.). Learning processes of individuals, knowledgeable behaviour that draws upon encoded routines, etc., are simply different manifestations of such structures (see especially Foss and Knudsen, 1996; Rumelt, 1994; Oinas, 1999).

If firms can indeed be meaningfully and fruitfully conceptualised in terms of their competences, it would seem that other social systems can also be so conceptualised to good effect. For example the region can be understood as systems of competences (Lawson, 1999). Both regions and firms are constituted by rules, relations and positions that are either reproduced or transformed through individual action. And both regions and firms are emergent features of social activity. Distinguishing between regions and firms must then be a more substantive issue, resting upon the identification of the manner in which interaction, constitutive of the competence in question, is reproduced or transformed. In this, a crucial difference between the two (which other differences may often reduce to in practice) will be the relevance of contractual/legal rights and obligations. Firm competences are crucially constituted by interaction confined (or defined, along with membership, identity, etc. of those within the firm) by such contractual/legal considerations (the main insight of the contractarian tradition). However, these are not likely to have much direct bearing upon the kinds of interaction constitutive of regional competences. Thus, when focusing upon regional competences, there is a particular onus to account for any coherence (reproduction) of relationships observed. Furthermore, much of the relevant interaction will tend to take place between organisations and between different types of organisation. As such, the different means by which relationships emerge and are sustained between organisations becomes a central concern.

In order to illustrate the advantages of conceptualising firms and regions in terms of competences it is useful to consider one specific example – the ability to learn. This is one of the most discussed qualities of productive systems[4] focused upon in the recent literature. Moreover, most accounts stress the importance of the *collective* nature of learning. However, ambiguities and tensions arise because of a failure to distinguish different senses in which the collective-ness of learning is emphasised. More accurately, there are two essentially quite different processes at work – the first can be termed 'learning within an epistemic community', the second 'system learning'.

In the case of learning within an epistemic community, the focus is upon the way in which the individual learns *in virtue* of being a member of a particular community, i.e. in virtue of the particular social position that he or she occupies within some collectivity. Knowledge is settled upon through the interaction of the community's members. This interaction is enabled by the use of existing ideas, languages and conceptions (acquisition of which is crucial for membership) in order to formulate (socially construct) knowledge. Indeed, any group or community must use an existing stock of concepts, languages, perspectives, etc. in order to develop new concepts, to innovate and to learn. Central to this form of learning is the manner in which situated individuals *transform* the existing ideas and conceptions with which they are confronted. This is not to say that knowledge is *merely* constructed. Reality does, so to speak, kick back, producing all manner of constraint upon the form of construction possible. But this external reality is conceptualised and learned about using the discourse, prior knowledge, etc. of that community. These phenomena, such as the existence of new technologies, competitive conditions and other members of the group, provide the basis for the real *interaction* of the community, but this interaction is always manifest in some socially specific context using the conceptual materials to hand.[5] The point is that, although social factors are crucial to the ability to learn (learning would not be possible were it not for the relationships in which that individual stands), it is the individual that learns, rather than some organisation or group.

The second sense in which learning is understood as collective, system learning, involves enabling or successful routines becoming incorporated as part of what the system/group/organisation actually is. The emphasis here is not so much on what the individuals learn as on the processes by which the successes and failures that individuals experience become encoded into the routines and practices of the collectivity of which they are a part. Knowledgeable behaviour is made possible by some individual acting in accordance with or utilising the routines constitutive of the collective. Learning or problem solving by members is still important, but the emphasis is upon how this leads to a change in the constitutive routines of the community. Members of the community, by acting within the boundaries of what is acceptable or legitimate (in accordance with routines and procedures of the community), thus have access to the knowledge obtained by other members without either having access, necessarily, to the actual histories in which knowledge is obtained or consciously formulating their understanding of the processes involved. The knowledge is stored or encoded in the routines of the group, and it is the organisation or group that is portrayed as learning. Routines are the things encoded. Routines in this sense act much as, say, the rules of the highway code. Individuals, by serving an apprenticeship and becoming part of a particular community, become familiar with rules that embody the learning of past members, enabling the new member to act capably, to safely travel from one destination to another. The structure of rules is constantly undergoing change as some elements are found to work better than others, as new technological needs/conditions emerge, and as the values and targets of the community change. But access to the lessons of history is provided in a way that access to that history itself is not. The community is often viewed as having a 'collective memory', the store of routines, and so a form of intelligence. But the routines are not merely a 'stock'. Existing routines influence how individuals actually learn from direct experience, how such experience is interpreted, and how learning comes about from the experience and practice of others. It is not always clear what is learned by the individual agent. The emphasis is, instead, on the importance of tacit (procedural, uncodified) knowledge in explaining how agents act capably, rather than knowledgeably.[6]

The main point to make, then, is that there is a tension between uses of the word learning. In focusing upon the first, commentators have noted (and committed themselves to the view) that learning is a very human 'process'. Shared language, meaning, identity, understanding, etc. play a vital role in the process of learning which is contrasted with 'transfer' conceptions in which learning is the simple transmission of abstract knowledge from the 'head of the one that knows to the head of the one that does not'. The second sense of learning does not require a human 'knower' at all – rather, just capable action. This tension is perhaps most noticeable in the organisational learning literature, as developed by, amongst others, Cyert and March (1963) and Nelson and Winter (1982). Although general statements of the domain of organisational learning appear concerned solely with learning of the second type (system learning – to illustrate this see especially the review paper by Levitt and March (1996)), the main ideas involve a reference to both types in an almost completely undifferentiated manner. This failure to distinguish quite different processes appears to underlie much of the confusion in this literature over the question of whether learning is really occurring – if learning requires knowledge and 'a knower', can we then talk of such things as learning firms or learning regions (Asheim, 1996; Morgan, 1997; Simmie, 1997)?

Such confusion can be avoided if, instead, we attempt to understand such processes in terms of the powers and mechanisms of systems and people in something like the above manner. Indeed, in part, the attractiveness of competence theories does seem to arise from the ease with which such conceptual tensions can be resolved. To return specifically to the issue of learning, regions differ from firms in involving interaction between individuals who are members of quite different epistemic communities. Individuals, such as suppliers, providers of financial or technical services and local support agencies, are brought together, generating, if you like, communities across communities. Although there is at least the possibility of a greater benefit from the cross-fertilisation of ideas, issues of identity and the motivation for continued co-operation and interaction will doubtless be more conscious to those interacting, and more fluid than those within the firm.

It is also in this light, in attempting to identify the analogue, at the regional level, of the firm routines that become encoded with the lessons learned by members (and then act to facilitate the actions of other members, etc.), that much of the regional literature can best be understood. For example, the literature on collective learning, inspired by the work of the GREMI economists, is certainly best understood this way.[7] This literature focuses on the nature of a particular 'innovative milieu' within which firms operate, and the kinds of learning that are made possible because of membership of such a milieu. For example, skilled labour mobility within the local labour market, various kinds of customer–supplier relations, as well as relations to all kinds of service firms, and new start-ups through direct or indirect spin-out activity, feature as crucial channels whereby system learning takes place.

Now, just as knowledge is embedded in firm routines, so too is it embedded in the structure of the labour market, in the structure of localised inter-firm relations and in the institutional framework within which firms not only interact but come into being. Indeed these features become the main repositories for knowledge that enable system learning at a particular level/scale, underlying the nature of the competences of that system (firm, region, nation, etc.).

To take stock, conceptualisation of social phenomena in terms of competences seems to follow quite naturally from the social ontology developed within critical realism. Not only does this have the advantage of grounding the basic categories of competence theories, it seems already to clarify existing tensions. However, linking competence theories to this particular social ontology would also seem to offer general implications for the nature of research directed at such social systems, all of which would seem to be important for a coherent, consistent competence approach. First, social systems are constituted by sets of rules, relations and positions, and social science is typically bound up with identifying conditions (rules, relations, resources, motivations, etc.) for (and perhaps unintended consequences of) some particular social activity. Second, the discovery of empirical regularities is likely to be rare and, where identified, will tend to be partial. Regularities as such are best understood not as constituting explanations but as the first stage in an explanatory process. Third, as with natural science, the mode of inference is predominantly retroductive, moving from events and states of affairs to the rules, relations, etc. that govern, condition or facilitate them. Fourth, research is typically backward looking in the sense of starting analysis from already identified (agreed upon) phenomena of interest. Fifth, research will need not only to involve the identification of particular structures, but to explain the reproduction of such structures to actually explain the phenomena in question. Sixth, the emphasis must be on explanatory, rather than predictive, criteria for theory assessment. And finally, perhaps the major epistemological challenge likely to be faced by applied research is that of disentangling or differentiating the myriad, often internal, relations that constitute the social researcher's object of study (see also Fleetwood in this volume).

Capacities, capabilities, competences and dispositions

We are now in a position to address several misconceptions and confusions concerning the nature of system competences that have arisen in response to earlier attempts to frame such ideas within a competence perspective (especially those arising in response to Lawson, 1999).

The main point to make is that most commentators have read this earlier work as making a primarily substantive contribution. For example, it was read as defending the importance of localised network relations in general, or making a case for the regional level being the most important for explaining competitive advantage (Helmsing, 2001; Kloosterman and Musterd, 2001; Oinas, 2002); arguing that production is increasingly associated with vertical integration (Freel, 2002); pointing out that competences span corporations (Juniper, 2001), or that 'thick' regional competences can compensate for 'thin' firm competences (Malecki, 1999). However, it should be clear from the above that the main contribution of this account is not really substantive at all. Whether or not there happens to be such coherence at the regional level, or whether clusters are a viable form of competition simply does not follow from a focus on competences. It does seem to be the case that such substantive issues would need to be addressed using something like a competence approach, but there is little else that can be said at this level of generality. Instead the point of the above is to highlight the fact that the powers and mechanisms that underlie or generate the social outcomes observed are not likely to be open to the kind of positivistic modelling, of a deductive sort, that is so predominant in current economic research. Any sort of approach which relies on constancy or endurability at the level of events is not only likely to be unsuccessful, if the above is correct, but is also in stark opposition to the kind of competence approach defended here. Case study and ethnographic research, which are primarily retroductive and explanatory, are likely to be indispensable.

A series of further, more specific, points also follow from the above. First, some accounts have, at least implicitly, adopted the position that only firms and individuals have competences, and regional competences are simply an extension of 'industrial strategies to the environment' (Danson, 2000; Torre and Gilly, 2000). It should be clear that, whatever the merits of these accounts, they are not about regional competences; rather, they tend to mix up individual and system powers. Elsewhere, regional competences have been viewed as some kind of meta-competence – a different kind of thing operating at some different level than other competences (Malecki, 2002; Foss, 1996). However, it follows from the above account that regional competences are neither over and above other competences, nor are they simple extensions of firm competences. Instead, both firm and regional competences refer to the same kind of network of interdependent rules, relations, practices, etc. viewed from or under different aspects.

However, the main problem has been preoccupation with the substantive issues raised in the earlier work. Even where the main point of a layered ontology seems to have been explicitly discussed, there has been an inability to escape valuing the approach in terms of the substantive issues raised in the illustrations that accompany it (e.g. MacDonald, 2000). In other places, the arguments are viewed simply as an empirical application of the competence approach (e.g. Lorenzen, 1999). One explanation for all this lies in the very focus upon the term competence itself. Is it not the case that the primary use of the term competence, which is itself essentially substantive, encourages such overly substantive interpretations (of what is essentially a very general framework)? Although I have used the term competence almost exclusively (Lawson, 1999, 2000, 2002), this has for the most part been a strategic matter, drawing upon existing accounts that historically have been in terms of competences. However, given the generality of the present account, the main categories that feature are powers and mechanisms. When a move is made to a more substantive level, it would seem that various further distinctions need to be made that situate more correctly the idea of system competence.

The further distinctions I am suggesting are between capacities, capabilities, competences and dispositions. Although in the existing literature these terms, where used, tend to be used interchangeably, they actually have quite different meanings which turn out to be particularly useful in talking about the different structural characteristics encountered once applied, substantive research is engaged in. Let me here attempt to systematise these usages.

The term *capacity* is used for the more passive power of a structure to attract, contain or receive. Thus a cup has a capacity to hold half a pint of water, I may have a capacity for drinking a certain amount of alcohol or being exposed to a certain amount of direct sunlight without being ill. There is no learning or skill involved in this. Of course cups can be modified, and I can increase my tolerance to alcohol or sunlight – but these actually require a change in physical makeup. There is something about the usual usage of the term capacity that signifies, relative to such basic constitutional changes, an endurability or a lack of change. At the system level the relevant focus is upon how a system attracts or retains its members or constituents. The term *capability* is used to refer to an ability which is possible but has not yet been attained or acquired – a general ability which is not yet realised. I may have the capability of becoming a brain surgeon, but I am not yet one. I have good eyesight, two hands and an interest in how brains work, and so the learning needed is likely to be within my field of possibility (even though my bad memory may make it impossible). Either way, I have not yet acquired the skills/knowledge in question. At the system level, perhaps the main focus will be upon the networks of interconnections that enable such skill or knowledge acquisition (or competences) to take place.

The term *competence* refers to an ability (requiring skills and knowledge) that has actually been acquired. I may be a competent pianist, teacher or brain surgeon, although of course, as with all these terms, I may simply do something else instead. I may be a competent brain surgeon but may be suffering from mental illness or a bad cold, the operating conditions may be substandard, etc., thus compromising my attempts at successful surgery. But the competence has been acquired. At the system level the focus is likely to be upon the abilities of systems to perform certain kinds of jobs, master particular kinds of technology and so on. The idea of a competence is always going to be more substantive than the idea of a capability, although there will be large overlap between these terms depending on the question to hand.[8] Finally, a *disposition* or *propensity* is a way of acting or being that that thing is likely or inclined to pursue or do. I may thus find it difficult to resist playing the piano or fruit machines, and may be disposed to do so at any opportunity. Alternatively, people with headaches are disposed to be less friendly or tolerant. They are capable of becoming competent at many things but they will tend to act, or be disposed to act, in certain ways. It may also be the case that such dispositions are driven by some existing internal tension or inconsistency. In other words, there is a potential that really is likely to be realised, because of internal conditions. Similarly, at the system level, a disposition is any characteristic that is likely to be manifest in a certain outcome. This is not to say that some external forces (such as market conditions) are likely to make only one outcome possible (this is not some kind of single exit idea). The point of a disposition is that it is a way of acting that is likely to be realised because of the way that structure is constituted.

Of course, these terms have clearly been used to mean different things, and even under the above definitions will overlap in certain contexts. But this kind of typology does seem be a useful first step in developing an appropriate language of system powers. To illustrate, I shall draw on research into the activities of technical consultancies in the Cambridge region.[9]

An illustration: technical consultancies in the Cambridge region

The following account briefly summarises findings from a recent study that focused upon the activity of technical consultancies (Lawson, 2002). The aim of the study was to detail the activities of technical consultancies and show how, in alleviating a series of commonly identified constraints on the development of learning and innovation, technical consultancies have contributed to the success of the region, especially in terms of the commercialisation of research and development.[10] Central to Cambridge's development has been the emergence of firms that are sufficiently small as to require special links with other firms to survive. Thus the explanation of these firms' ability to learn, diffuse ideas and innovate occupies a central role in explaining the success of the region more generally.

All the region's consultancies have evolved from one particular consultancy, Cambridge Consultants Limited (CCL), which took form at the end of the 1950s and early 1960s. CCL, set up by a group of newly graduated scientists and engineers, intended to 'put the brains of Cambridge University at the disposal of … British Industry' (Dale, 1982). To do so, it quickly started up its own labs and workshops and effectively commercialised technology itself. The particular culture that emerged in CCL in this period was absolutely crucial to the later success of the region more generally. Each of the other main consultancies is aware both of the influence of CCL on their own corporate culture, and also that this culture has been essential to sustaining its competitive position. A cultural norm of combining knowledge of technology and management emerged in CCL that is clearly in evidence in the other main consultancies.

Another central feature of this corporate culture is the predominance of multi-disciplinary teams and sub-communities interacting within the consultancy. Although each consultancy clearly values the general cultural advantages of multi-disciplinary teams, the main advantage of such interaction seems to be that individuals are forced to articulate their own, often tacit, background knowledge, and that this is often a spur to new ideas or profitable re-combinations of existing ideas. The creation of such multi-disciplinary forums is formalised in a variety of different ways ranging from different processes for monitoring the performance of ongoing projects to, in one case, the setting up of an internal labour market. In this latter case, people are constantly both trying to sell themselves within the firm and carefully monitoring the performance and skills of others.

All consultancies recruit from outside the region, and indeed outside the country, but the (frequent) movement of these recruits after joining the consultancy tends to be to another firm within the locality. Thus, consultancies effectively act to channel new employees into the region. In general, employees are highly skilled, often young (and single) and very motivated by the idea of using and commercialising new technology. These characteristics are viewed as giving rise to a greater propensity to get bored by any particular job and a wish to move on. In response, each firm attempts to keep key personnel by giving them appropriate tasks and responsibilities, which in some part explains the emergence of forms of internal organisation with flatter management structures and all kinds of incentive opportunities for employees to 'take up and run' with particular technical ideas. This need has also lead to the increasingly formal procedure appearing within consultancies, discussed below, for new firms to be incubated and spun out.

An account of the client relationship, and its potential benefit to the consultancy, is clearly a central part of consultancy activity. Clients provide sets of problems that the consultancy must solve, information about the development end of the market, general needs which the firm itself is trying to fulfil as well as very specific information about the state of technology and the merits of existing technologies or solutions (both product and process). Interaction with the client prompts personnel from the consultancy to learn new languages, technologies and ways of thinking. Such interaction not only facilitates the finding of solutions to the problem at hand, but builds up the stock of skills and competences that the consultancy can draw upon more generally. There appears to be a strong two-way exchange of knowledge, culture and technology, which emerges in response to a well-defined problem that forces different individuals to draw upon, and communicate, vastly different background skills and knowledge.[11]

Without doubt, the most important aspect of the technical consultancies' activities is the large number of firms they have spun out. As spin-outs have been taken more seriously, over time, as a means for increasing revenues, firms began to devise a variety of organisational structures in which spin-out activity could be encouraged. Such activities feature, in the cases of the most recent consultancies, as integral parts of the firm's mission statement. Small batch, exploratory production is obviously an important part of a consultancy's activities, but the commercialisation of technology via its embodiment in particular products needs large amounts of financial investment as well as a quite different organisational structure to that most conducive to its success as a consultancy. As the main consultancies have dealt more with the development of new products (rather than the more traditional consultancy role), they have had to cope with, and incorporate, this basic organisational tension between design and development in ways conducive to the performance of the firm. An important way of doing this has been to let the project team that has designed a new technology or product be transformed into something else – a firm, which is itself conducive to the realisation or development of some idea or technology in the form of a product. Thus it is easy to see how many of the more recent consultancies have increasingly formalised the process of spin-out as an integral part of the firm's core activities. This formalisation has meant, in practice, incubation. The spin-out uses legal, administrative and advisory resources of the parent, often staying on site for a matter of years. The parent tends to help find partners, secure access to funding and help protect IPR. But for several reasons, including the need for independence to attract investment, any managerial role for the consultancy quickly disappears (although, of course, the consultancy will usually continue to profit financially from licensing agreements, equity stakes, etc.).

The similarities between many of these spin-outs is striking. Each firm's core technology is a fairly direct consequence of client work.[12] Most received huge support in spinning out, allowing them to avoid all kinds of early mistakes. Such support ranged from basic technology and goodwill to, more recently, very comprehensive incubation activities involving the provision of everything from the project team to feasibility studies, to premises and telephones, and the setting up of shareholder agreements (well captured by one interviewee as the provision of 'a fantastically sophisticated garage'). These firms all benefited, at least in their early phase, from local links with other firms that had also spun out from the same parent (or, often more importantly, the grandparent), as well as the reputation of the parent.[13]

Regional capacities, capabilities, competences and dispositions

An obvious point to make, in light of the above account, is that not all the structural characteristics at work can be captured by the idea of a competence. The region has a particularly strong *capacity* to attract both skilled workers and new ideas. Personnel are regularly drawn to consultancies in the region which act as high-profile centres of high technology activity. Once in Cambridge, the local surroundings, good schools, etc. act as significant factors keeping personnel in the area. Thus, although personnel often leave individual firms (in fact there seems to be a fairly high firm turnover rate), they tend to remain in the region (going to other firms, or starting up new ones). Additionally, the consultants' reputation outside the region attracts large, leading-edge firms as clients. Client relations act to channel ideas, including knowledge of the current state of technology, existing problems, etc., into the region. This knowledge is then diffused within the region via existing networks, movement of personnel setting up firms, and so on. Such mechanisms also manage to overcome a problem frequently observed in industrial districts of 'negative entropy'.[14]

These networks have emerged and are reproduced through a variety of means. Clear channels of communication are open because of historical ties to the university, and previous firms, not to mention the fact that 'Cambridge is a small place'. Crucially, personnel, in sharing in all manner of cultural norms, find communication easy. Moreover, consultants by moving between different firms act as networks themselves. Such activities manage to overcome transcoding problems (Camagni, 1991) to do with the flow of ideas as well as the proprietary problem outlined by Antonelli, Arrow and others.[15] As for the consultants themselves, there clearly is not an exploitation/exploration trade-off as outlined by March (1991), as the main tasks of consultancies are both developing new ideas and diffusing them. The interrelated networks that emerge from such activity, along with other factors leading to the emergence of such networks, are the main constituents of the region's *capabilities*. The point is that very general mechanisms are in place to diffuse information as well as to deal with a whole host of other problems. How these structural capabilities are realised in particular organisational or technological competences is another matter. The region does have a host of firm-level competences, such as IT, ink-jet printing and magnetic sensing. It has also developed competences in spinning out and especially incubating new firms that act to commercialise ideas in quite different ways (as well as setting up further networks). But such competences appear to be rather short lived in the Cambridge case, as opposed to those found in the more commonly identified industrial districts. Indeed, it does seem to be the case that Cambridge has excelled, supported by technical consultancies, at the capability rather than the competence level.

To provide another example, a general advantage of the spin-out activity found was that it facilitated a very healthy mix, at the regional level, of continuity and disruption.[16] But it seems difficult to understand such a feature as a competence. The quality of combining continuity and change would seem to be understood better as a general capability enabling the acquisition of a variety of particular competences. Furthermore, the region and firm levels are continually interacting. For example, a series of firm-level dispositions appear to have consequences for regional capabilities and competences. Notably, spin-outs can be understood as a firm disposition which arises from the basic tension within consultancies to combine product development with a service structure. Of course, there is no necessity that firms will be spun out as a result. But given the structure of the consultancies themselves, new ideas, products and technologies emerge which call out to be developed or commercialised, but cannot be within the existing organisational structure of the consultancy. Spinning out firms, embodying such technology, is a likely response to such a tension. Similarly, the tension felt by particular personnel (resulting from boredom and a lack of hierarchy to progress along) results in the high intra-regional labour mobility noted above, thus also reproducing the networking capabilities of the region.

Unpacking the structural characteristics of a region, in this manner, suggests further implications for research at the level of method. *A priori* it would seem to be the case that not all research techniques are of equal importance with respect to the categories focused upon (i.e. capacities, capabilities, competences and dispositions). For example, capacities may well be relatively amenable to quantitative methods. Personnel can be counted and their subsequent movement inside or outside of the region can be monitored. The consultancy client base, and its importance inside and outside of the region, can be easily assessed too. For different reasons, dispositions also would seem more easily identifiable. The point here is that dispositions are potentials that really do tend to occur in practice. Thus, finding empirical regularities is often likely and worth pursuing (although clearly not in any overly strict or exclusive manner). It is, however, capabilities and competences that are most likely to bear the most influence of the factors noted above as implications of a mechanisms and powers approach. Thus, the need for detailed, ethnographic case studies emphasising retroduction, etc. is most likely to be strongest in the latter case. However, as the above has made clear, it does seem to be the case that it will be at the level of capability and competence that the main explanatory forces are to be found. This would then suggest that case study and ethnographic research are at the very least likely to be indispensable.

Of course, any particular study that involves coming to know different capacities, capabilities, competences and dispositions will need a mixture of techniques and methods. But something like the above typology would seem to be a useful first step if it is accepted as is argued above that social phenomena cannot be treated in a primarily deductive way, and must be understood in terms of underlying structures and mechanisms. Although this does seem to be at the core of the popularity of the competence perspective, it is rarely, if ever, presented in this way.

Concluding remarks

The main aim of this chapter has been to clarify and develop the nature and scope of what may be termed competence theorisation. In particular, some attempt has been made to make explicit the particular ontological presuppositions upon which competence theories are best seen as resting. In so doing, the idea of powers and mechanisms irreducible to events has been central. In the particular case of the social sciences, such powers and mechanisms result from the nature of relationships, rules and practices that constitute particular social systems. At this level of generality the approach seems equally applicable to a variety of social systems including firms, organisations, regions and economies.

However, in applying these ideas to a specific substantive case, it has been found that the idea of a competence does not actually describe well all the main structural characteristics in operation. Rather, the idea of a competence has to be augmented with similar terms – in particular capacities, capabilities and dispositions. A consequence of this further step is that attention is drawn to the likely need for a wide range of analytical tools, required even for quite well-defined and small-scale investigations. The importance of retroductive and primarily explanatory methods, however, would seem to be unavoidable.

Notes

1 Several recent volumes are completely given over to the task of clarifying the history of and connections between different conceptions and types of competences (e.g. Hamel and Heene, 1994; Montgomery, 1996; Foss and Knudsen, 1996).
2 The original source for these ideas is the work of realist philosophers of science such as Harré, Madden and Secord (Harré, 1970; Harré and Madden, 1975; Harré and Secord, 1972).
3 Social rules are conceptualised as something other than the patterned behaviour they govern. The motorist who does not stop at a red light does not lead us to doubt our understanding of the rule 'when at traffic lights stop if the light is red'. Neither does it force us to consider such a rule as an 'average' or 'normal' description of what people do, even though most people may indeed stop at red lights. But the rule is not, and cannot be evaluated as, a prediction of actual behaviour. It is something different in kind. Second, whilst there is clear agreement that the social world is highly rule-governed, the existence and role of relationships are not so generally accepted. However, once it is accepted that different rules, rights, obligations, etc. are not equally applicable to all, it is difficult to avoid some notion of relations and positions. The sorts of activities allowed or constrained for foremen is different to those for a manager or employee. Each has different responsibilities and rights in virtue of the position they occupy. Moreover, the activities constrained or enabled tend to be orientated towards some other group, thus indicating a causal role for certain forms of relationship. Of particular importance here are internal relations, where two objects are what they are by virtue of the relationship in which they stand to each other. For example, with a wife and husband, landlord and tenant, it is not possible to have one without the other. For each couple the relation defines what each is and does.
4 The term 'productive systems' rather than the more common 'production systems' is used in order to emphasise the idea of potential noted above (see Wilkinson, 1983).
5 In short, an ontological realism is combined with an epistemological relativism. The most fully elaborated philosophical account, and defence, of this position is that

provided by Bhaskar (1989; see also T. Lawson, 1997). For an extended substantive account of the processes by which membership occurs and conditions learning in relationship to such issues as apprenticeships, see Lave and Wenger (1991).

6 For a general discussion of the idea of tacit knowledge, etc., see Fleetwood (1995).

7 The term 'collective learning' appears in a wide range of contributions where the meaning attributed to the term is often quite vague, usually being understood as a quite general counterpart to a notion of *individual* learning. The term has been used in relation to the idea of core competences (Prahalad and Hamel, 1990) and firm-specific competences (Pavitt, 1991: 42), and as part of a general discussion of organisational learning (Dodgson, 1993). However, the term acquires a distinctly regional orientation and some precision in the work of the GREMI economists (see especially Camagni, 1991; Capello, 1999).

8 Despite the overlap, there seems to be scope for using these terms to categorise a range of existing systems. For example, consider the many attempts to distinguish between industrial districts and other kinds of cluster. Such attempts that have focused on the relative importance of craft-based skills or new technology have been unsuccessful. It does seem that a distinction between competences and capabilities does seem to capture much of what is essential here.

9 I am aware that in giving such an illustration, and indeed in expanding on the illustration provided in my 1999 paper (Lawson, 1999), I may well be encouraging the kind of substantive interpretations noted above. But there seems to be no other way of illustrating the distinctions I have in mind here.

10 The survey was undertaken by the ESRC Centre for Business Research in Cambridge between July 1998 and October 1999. It involved a series of interviews with all four of the main technical consultancies in the region as well as shorter interviews with other, younger, consultancies and at least two spin-outs from each consultancy. Several of the consultancies were interviewed more than once, talking to different people within the organisation. Several interviews with a variety of other key local individuals were undertaken to get a wider perspective on the activities of these consultancies over a now quite long period (from the early 1960s to the present day). No attempt was made to accumulate quantitative data. Fairly structured questionnaires formed the basis of exploratory discussions in which the emphasis was upon getting at quite general mechanisms of how various events had come about. Central in all the interviews was a discussion of the difficult or transitional phases of the consultancies' development.

11 Consultants are keen to play down the role played by clients in developing technology for obvious intellectual property rights reasons. However, when considering the histories of particular technological developments, it becomes clear that there has been a tendency amongst consultants to move from the specific technical solutions provided for particular clients to general off-the-shelf solution products. This has led to changing attitudes within the firm to such factors as: the amount of time that each employee is expected to spend working directly for clients, relative to time spent developing ideas within the firm; and corporate strategies pursued in tandem with more 'normal' consulting activities. It was clear that clients provide a huge amount of the information needed to develop new ideas and technologies (a point made much more explicitly in newer consultancies), even though the need to retain client trust (and avoid IPR disputes) provides important limits to the usefulness of such interaction over time.

12 Typically, older spin-outs tended to confirm that they started up after the development of technology with clients who had got into financial problems or of technology that did not really suit its intended application. More recent spin-outs seemed to result from relatively systematic moves by the consultancy to develop competences in one particular area which had come to fruition prompted by at least one particular project.

13 Even those spin-outs which deviated from this pattern in significant ways (e.g. those that went on to become rival consultants) benefited from links between the new consultancy and old colleagues, other spin-out firms, subcontractors and so on, just as much as the 'normal' spin-outs.
14 Essentially, the problem here is that to maintain a region's integrity or coherence, some degree of independence from external influences needs to be maintained, but without such influences the region tends to stagnate (see Camagni, 1991).
15 See Lawson (2002) for a full elaboration of these problems.
16 The disruption was argued to be especially healthy in avoiding the negative entropy problem noted above as well as provoking the kind of recombination of existing ideas and technology thought to be essential to novel or innovative behaviour (see Lawson and Lorenz, 1999).

References

Asheim, B. (1996) 'Industrial districts as "learning regions": a condition for prosperity?', *European Planning Studies*, 4: 379–400.
Bhaskar, R. (1978) *A Realist Theory of Science*, Brighton: Harvester.
—— (1989) *The Possibility of Naturalism*, Brighton: Harvester.
Camagni, R. (ed.) (1991) *Innovation Networks: Spatial Perspectives*, London: Belhaven Press.
Capello, R. (1999) 'Spatial transfer of knowledge in high technology milieux: learning versus collective learning processes', *Regional Studies*, 33 (4): 353–65.
Collier, A. (1994) *Critical Realism: An Introduction to Roy Bhaskar's Philosophy*, London: Verso.
Cyert, R.M. and March, J. (1963) *A Behavioural Theory of the Firm*, Englewood Cliffs, NJ: Prentice-Hall.
Dale, R. (1982) *From Ram Yard to Milton Hilton*, Cambridge Consultants Ltd.
Danson, M. (2000) 'Debates and surveys', *Regional Studies*, 34 (2), 169–80.
Dodgson, M. (1993) 'Organisational learning: a review of some literatures', *Organisation Studies*, 14 (3): 375–94.
Fleetwood, S. (1995) *Hayek's Political Economy: The Socio-economics of Order*, London: Routledge.
Foss, N.J. (1996) 'Higher-order industrial capabilities and competitive advantage', *Journal of Industry Studies*, 3 (1): 1–20.
Foss, N. and Knudsen, C. (eds) (1996) *Towards a Competence Theory of the Firm*, London: Routledge.
Freel, S. (2002) 'Innovation networking and proximity: sectoral patterns and policy implications', *mimeo*, University of Aberdeen.
Hamel, G. and Heene, A. (eds) (1994) *Competence-based Competition*, New York: Wiley.
Harré, R. (1970) *Principles of Scientific Thinking*, London: Macmillan.
Harré, R. and Madden, E. (1975) *Causal Powers*, Oxford: Basil Blackwell.
Harré, R. and Secord, P. (1972) *The Explanation of Social Behaviour*, Oxford: Basil Blackwell.
Helmsing, A. (2001) 'Externalities, learning and governance: new perspectives on local economic development', *Development and Change*, 32 (2): 277–308.
Juniper, J. (2001) 'Universities and collaboration within complex, uncertain knowledge-based economies', paper presented at The University in the New Corporate World, Adelaide, July.
Kloosterman, R. and Musterd, S. (2001) 'The polycentric urban region: towards a research agenda', *Urban Studies*, 38 (4): 623–34.
Lave, J. and Wenger, E. (1991) *Situated Learning: Legitimate Peripheral Participation*, Cambridge: Cambridge University Press.

Lawson, C. (1999) 'Towards a competence theory of the region', *Cambridge Journal of Economics*, 23 (2): 151–66.
—— (2000) 'Collective learning and epistemically significant moments', in D. Keeble and F. Wilkinson (eds), *High Technology, Networking and Collective Learning in Europe*, Aldershot: Ashgate.
—— (2002) 'Technical consultancies and regional competences', in C. Dannreuter and W. Dolfsma (eds), *Globalisation, Social Capital and Inequality*, Cheltenham: Edward Elgar.
Lawson, C. and Lorenz, E. (1999) 'Collective learning, tacit knowledge and regional innovative capacity', *Regional Studies*, 33 (4): 305–17.
Lawson, T. (1997) *Economics and Reality*, London: Routledge.
Levitt, B. and March, J. (1996) 'Organisational learning', in M.D. Cohen and L.S. Sproull (eds), *Organisational Learning*, Thousand Oaks, CA: Sage, pp. 516–41.
Lorenzen, M. (1999) 'Regional competitiveness, localised learning, and policy', *Copenhagen Business School, Working Paper*, 99 (13).
MacDonald, K. (2000) 'Use and valuation: information in the city', *Urban Studies*, 37 (10): 1881–92.
Malecki, E. (1999) 'Knowledge and regional competitiveness', paper presented at International Symposium, Knowledge, Education and Space, Heidelberg, September.
—— (2002) 'Hard and soft networks for urban competitiveness', *Urban Studies*, 39 (5–6): 929–45.
March, J.G. (1991) 'Exploration and exploitation in organisational learning', *Organisation Science*, 2 (1): 71–87.
Montgomery, C. (1996) *Resource-based and Evolutionary Theories of the Firm: Towards a Synthesis*, Boston: Kluwer.
Morgan, K. (1997) 'The learning region: institutions, innovation and regional renewal', *Regional Studies*, 31: 491–503.
Nelson, R. and Winter, S. (1982) *An Evolutionary Theory of Economic Change*, Cambridge, MA: Harvard University Press.
Oinas, P. (1999) 'Activity-specificity in organizational learning: implications for analysing the role of proximity', *Geojournal*, 49 (4): 363–72.
—— (2002) 'Competition and collaboration in interconnected places: towards a research agenda', *Geografiska Annaler*, Summer.
Pavitt, K. (1991) 'Key characteristics of the large innovating firm', *British Journal of Management*, 2: 41–50.
Prahalad, C. and Hamel, G. (1990) 'The core competence of the corporation', *Harvard Business Review*, 68 (3): 79–91.
Rumelt, R. (1994) 'Foreword', in G. Hamel and A. Heene (eds), *Competence-based Competition*, New York: Wiley, pp. xv–xix.
Simmie, J. (ed.) (1997) *Innovation, Networks and Learning Regions?*, London: Jessica Kingsley.
Torre, A. and Gilly, J. (2000) 'On the analytical dimension of proximity dynamics', *Regional Studies*, 34 (2): 169–80.
Wilkinson, F. (1983) 'Productive systems', *Cambridge Journal of Economics*, 7: 413–29.

Part III

Substantive contributions

In this section are some examples of recent substantive social science research into work and organisation informed by a critical realist point of view. In some obvious ways the work reported on here is entirely new. These research reports are concerned with new types of organisation or new types of management practice that have hitherto not been studied. For example, Chapter 12, the second in this section, reports a study of the organisational behaviour found in call centres. Call centres are a type of organisation offering a kind of work that did not exist twenty years ago, and so have been little studied until quite recently. Similarly, in Chapter 15, the last chapter in this section and the last chapter of the book, the authors are concerned with reporting the findings of a research project into the activities of the human resource professionals who recruit new graduates for large organisations. Although, clearly, graduates were recruited in the past, this activity definitely was not organised in the sort of way reported on here. In this report, graduate recruitment is the full-time activity of a new sub-type of professional worker. This again is a type of work that scarcely existed even a few years ago, and so could not have been studied by researchers before. Even those essays in this section that deal with traditional institutions, such as the factory considered in Chapter 11, or the hospitals that are analysed in Chapters 13 and 14, are dealing with aspects of management and organisation that are new, and their existence, never mind their effects on the experience of work, could not have been imagined by an earlier generation of researchers.

But it is only a small part of the contribution of these essays that they are analysing new types of work and new patterns of work organisation. What they also do is offer accounts of the organisations under study as structures and systems of relationships combined with really penetrating analysis of what actually happens in them. At one level the accomplishment of the research reported on here is its revelation of the way people at work actually behave, and its consideration of the way work is experienced and understood by participants. It is characteristic of this work that the unique behaviour of the workgroups actually found is exposed and we are given an account of some of the relevant detail – sometimes extending to describing the personalities involved and the ways they behave. It is also a feature that the analysts here often show how individuals and groups can make a difference. It is part of the research design of several of the projects reported here that they compare and contrast the attitudes, behaviour and informal organisation of different work groups, that are in many respects similar in their formal characteristics. It is shown that what appear to be some quite subtle differences between the personalities found in different groups and their relationships can actually make an impact on what occurs in organisations.

In the first chapter of this series, for example, Rick Delbridge presents some of the findings from his, by now, celebrated ethnographic research into factories in South Wales. What he shows is that, although many factories these days are described as operating with similar patterns of organisation and managerial arrangements, the way they actually function varies a good deal. Delbridge compares the behaviour found in a car components factory with that in a Japanese transplant, both supposedly examples of 'high performance' factory regimes, and finds both the scope for informal organisation in the factory and the actual extent of it much greater in the British factory by comparison with the Japanese. Delbridge shows that, within the same factory, only slight differences of personnel can make a considerable difference to what workgroups do and the level of their effectiveness and performance. Other writers have argued forcefully that high performance regimes are actually very effective, and close down the scope for informal organisation amongst industrial workgroups and discipline behaviour very effectively. Again Delbridge shows very effectively that informal organisation is extensive even where management is highly experienced and highly developed, and in many ways management does not succeed in mobilising group sentiments as a way of reinforcing group discipline. In this respect, the work of Delbridge and that of several other authors in this section is the basis for a powerful corrective to the conclusions of those researchers who think that 'high performance' factory regimes work as expected by management and that they effectively suppress employee dissent.

The next chapter, by Phil Taylor and Peter Bain, comes to some similar conclusions. In this study too, comparison is built into the research design in that their work compares different call centres. Here it is shown that in organisations that might appear to be of the same type, there are marked variations that have effects on behaviour and performance. There are call centres in which the client base is large and in which the problems dealt with by operators are very similar. In such contexts, it is possible for work to be highly routinised, and so what would traditionally be defined as white collar or clerical work can become much like work in a factory. Even where these conditions do not apply, the technology in use in call centres is such that it makes possible a much higher level of monitoring and control of work performance than is often possible in other work situations. For these reasons it is reasonable to expect, as many commentators on modern work have predicted, that a high level of effective control by management, not only of the procedures and routines through which work is done, but also of the non-work behaviour of workers, will be achieved. In particular, it is thought that such control will extend to the way employees engage with their employing organisation, and the ways in which they identify with other employees. The work of Taylor and Bain shows very clearly that, here again, people and groups make a difference. In one of their research sites, the organisation of the work is conducive to the emergence of group solidarity, but it is also the case that the particular people involved have also given impetus to the emergence of effective self-organisation. In their research generally, there is evidence of the development of some degree of self-organisation in call centres, despite high levels of surveillance by managements.

In the next two chapters, both of which consider change in the contemporary National Health Service (NHS), the focus shifts somewhat to the consideration of organisations employing professional and semi-professional employees. The perspective also shifts away from exclusive concern with the effects of work organisation on those at the bottom of the hierarchy to examine the dilemmas of management and particularly processes of strategic change. In Chapter 13, Ruth Kowalczyk discusses the results of her study into a hospital merger, in which three hospitals were brought together, the aim being to serve a larger population, to take advantage of opportunities for greater specialisation and to realise economies of scale. Kowalczyk shows that, although the decision to undertake the merger was in line with government policy and had a clear economic justification, there were considerable difficulties in actually bringing the merger about in a satisfactory way. Kowalczyk makes reference to the evidence from her research, and argues that management had to reconcile not only the different patterns of organisation but also the different methods and practices found in the organisations that were party to the merger. In addition, however, at a more fundamental level, there was a problem arising from the relationships between the professional groups in these organisations. Hence, bringing about a new pattern of activities for the merged institution according to a rational plan was the least of the problems encountered. There was also the question of how to engineer agreement between different professional groups which had their own hierarchies and loyalties. Kowalczyk argues that what happened in the hospital merger must be understood against the background of a set of particular relationships within occupational groups (how, for example, doctors have organised themselves) and between them (how doctors, nurses and administrators worked together in the past). Here again the behaviour of particular groups of clinicians and managers clearly makes a difference to the outcome of attempts to produce strategic change.

In the next chapter, by Carole and Peter Kennedy, which is also about the NHS, the authors take an explicitly theoretical attitude towards their subject. While they do consider the findings of their own existing research into the attitudes and behaviour of nurses to illustrate their points, one of their main concerns is how best to interpret such data. In thinking about this issue, Carole and Peter Kennedy take very seriously the possible contribution of the Foucauldian perspective on professional organisation, which can be brought to bear on the nurses within the NHS. They consider the implications of this perspective sympathetically and suggest, rightly, that it is helpful in many ways in illuminating management practice with regard to the professions within hospitals. They refer, among other things, to the way professionalism features self-regulation. Professionals impose self-discipline and internalise their own standards of conduct. This makes professionals vulnerable to work intensification. If, for example, managers control key aspects of nursing work, such as the numbers of patients admitted to hospital, they can greatly increase the work of nurses without any need for direct control of their activities. Now it must be said that the insights of Foucault, which have preoccupied many British academics working on O&M studies, have often been neglected by critical realists. This, arguably, is because the discursive (or linguistic) 'turn' has often gone hand in hand with a strong social constructionist ontology and relativist position. But, as Carole and Peter Kennedy show, the analysis of discourse is not actually incompatible with a critical realist account of professions and their relationships. They argue, however, that discourse analysis needs to be contextualised; that is, used in conjunction with other modes of analysis. In the conclusion of their chapter, the authors draw on concepts from critical realist-inspired theory, arguing that discourse analysis is most valuable and insightful in the context of a more materialist analysis of the resources available to groups of actors.

In the last chapter of this section, we are again considering the work of groups of professionals. Drawing on their research into graduate recruitment, Anthony Hesketh and Phil Brown analyse what is going on when graduates are selected for employment. They show how a new group of experts who claim expertise in the recruitment of graduates for large organisations has emerged. Such professionals operate in an overfull employment market (there are many more graduates with good qualifications than there are jobs for them to fill) so recruiters have the difficult task of selecting those they believe are most eligible. The recruiters have developed claims to expertise in selection. This is in no small way a matter of technology. By using and adapting psychometric tests, and by developing a whole set of selection techniques and procedures, these professional workers try to take the guesswork out of recruitment. They also develop a rhetoric that suggests that they have succeeded in developing tools that allow efficient selection of the most suitable candidates from the large numbers seeking employment. Hesketh and Brown show, however, that the uncertainty is not removed, despite the technology and the time taken to make selections. As the professionals themselves acknowledge, there are usually residual elements of discretion in the choices made between candidates. Also, and more controversially, the professional selectors have reckoned without the adaptations that graduates make to the procedures of selection. Graduates soon become familiar with the tests and procedures brought to bear on them. Here again the investigators have looked closely at the attitudes and behaviour of the participants, and they show very clearly that many of the graduates subject to selection techniques have responded by acting out the kind of personal attributes that they believe recruiters value, thus trying to subvert the rational basis of the recruiters' professional expertise. Once again this analysis shows that the actual behaviour of people can make a difference to outcomes, that the outcome of social processes is not determined by the structure of institutions.

The point of work of the kind presented here is not simply to show that people can make a difference to the outcome of organisational processes. Looked at in some ways, the overall assessment on this score is not too impressive. The conclusion to be drawn from research is not only that people and groups can make a difference, but also that, often, they do not. Even when they do make a difference, the difference is usually quite small. Typically these differences amount to quite marginal deviations from the general trend of events. Yet, theoretically understood, any impact at all, any deviation from the main drift, is extremely important. It would be wrong to decide that marginal differences to outcomes do not matter and can be safely ignored. The point to note is that the propensity for people and groups to exercise their human agency, to act innovatively in their own interests (as they define them) and to resist manipulation and control, seems to be ubiquitous. Despite the limited impact of such tendencies, they are incorrigible. Innovative behaviour will not go away, despite the attempts to work round it, incorporate it or eliminate it. It may grow and/or, in the right circumstances, the effect it has may be large rather than small.

Finally, although the research presented in this section is new in the ways we have considered above, in another sense it is not new. The continuities of this research with the kind of work done by earlier generations of social scientists are also obvious. Although the present research occurs in new types of organisation and looks at new management practices, the analysis of them has many similarities with the work of earlier generations of researchers, and builds on their insights.

11 Working in teams

Ethnographic evidence from two 'high performance' workplaces

Rick Delbridge

Introduction

Discussion of 'high performance' or 'high commitment' workplaces has abounded in recent years and these discussions have been dominated by a positivist approach using the deductive method. There have been numerous attempts to test the relationship between establishment level performance and particular management practices (for example, Arthur, 1994; Huselid, 1995; MacDuffie, 1995). Each of these studies has sought to identify a set of practices that lead to high performance. However, as Cappelli and Neumark (2001) note in a recent overview of the existing research on work practices and organisational performance, there is considerable variation in what different researchers regard as constituting 'high performance' work systems. For example, Becker and Gerhart (1996) report twenty-seven different variables used as proxies for high performance work practices across just five studies.

Notwithstanding these variations, the key feature of this literature is the centrality of employee involvement in contributing to higher organisational performance. Work reform efforts focus on employee involvement through teamwork or other small group activities (Appelbaum and Batt, 1994), and teamwork is 'by far the most common practice across the studies' (Cappelli and Neumark, 2001: 742). Thus in their review Cappelli and Neumark (2001: 742) conclude that the 'central hypothesis being tested ... is whether employee involvement is associated with improved organisational performance'.

There are some inconsistencies in research findings with regard to certain outcomes associated with team working. While some industry-based surveys have reported clear positive results between teams and operational performance (Pil and MacDuffie, 1996), others have found a mixed picture (e.g. Lowe *et al.*, 1997). In addition, a number of surveys have found positive workforce outcomes as reported by management and/or trade union representatives, at least in some plants with teams (e.g. Bacon and Blyton, 2000; Park *et al.*, 1997). More recently there have been attempts to differentiate aspects of high performance work practices through refining survey analyses, for example, see Delbridge and Whitfield (2001) on different forms of employee participation scheme, and the degree to which they contribute to heightened perceptions of employee job influence.

These debates have been dominated by positivist analyses of quantitative survey findings and there is a price to be paid for this: a paucity of *explanation*. The deductive reasoning *assumes* a causal link between increased employee involvement and organisational performance but can do no more than uncover statistical associations. Contradicting these assumptions, the (at least implicitly) critical realist case research conducted in this area of study repeatedly reports certain negative effects of team working and evidence of worker dissatisfaction, particularly regarding peer pressure and its tendency to fragment any shopfloor collectivity (Delbridge, 1998; Graham, 1995; Rinehart *et al.*, 1997). In this essay, I suggest that these case study findings indicate a greater need for attention to the internal social processes and dynamics of teams, and for these to be contextualised through consideration of various organisational factors and the broader environment. In short, what is needed is a research approach that seeks to explain what positivists can only record. The focus is then to uncover how actors understand and make their choices; to place centrally the active role of agency. Such a research focus encourages a particular research method – ethnography – and the study reported here was conducted under a critical realist ontology (for details see Delbridge, 1998: 13–17). Thus agency is informed by enduring social-structural conditions, what Godard (1993) calls 'generative mechanisms', which give rise to 'empirical tendencies' rather than definite outcomes. As Fleetwood notes in Chapter 1 of this volume, it is 'an empirical (not a philosophical) question to discover which of these tendencies are actualised at any point in time'.

In the following section I discuss some recent research findings from projects looking at team working in various manufacturing sectors and identify some issues that arise from those researches. I leave to one side the extent to which research findings in manufacturing settings may or may not be applicable to the experience of workers in other sectors of the economy. Nelson (1998) has provided a recent analysis of the similarities and differences between manufacturing and service work. While this is a useful avenue for discussion, there is a danger of over-stylising the contrasts between these spheres of work. I then discuss a key aspect of team working – inter-worker relationships – drawing on previously published ethnographic research conducted in two manufacturing facilities (Delbridge, 1998). Through a detailed analysis of the causes and consequences of peer pressure as a control system, it is possible to discern certain features of these cases that contribute to the specific character of shopfloor relations. In a further section, these dynamics are contextualised before some discussion linking this work to other studies of team working concludes the chapter.

Recent research

Team working has attracted considerable attention in recent years, and discussion of teams and their workers has been hampered by a tendency to collapse empirical difference and conflate terms and meanings. It has become increasingly obvious that there are various forms of team working which deal with different types of work, are structured differently, have different implications for workers and have different objectives for management. In addressing these problems, various authors have sought to characterise or classify teams based on aspects of what the team does (Cutcher-Gershenfeld *et al.*, 1994; Thompson and Wallace, 1996); what management intends to achieve through team working (Mueller, 1994); or how the team is organised (Lowe *et al.*, 1997; Murakami, 1995). These represent useful attempts to bring some common understanding and pattern to research but, as Bacon and Blyton (2000: 1428–9) remark, taxonomies 'imply a separateness or bifurcation when in practice elements often significantly overlap. Such taxonomies can also encourage an oversimplification of reality and debate about that reality.'

In addressing the need for a fuller and more holistic analysis of team working, Bacon and Blyton (2000) propose to research the *inter-linkage* of the objectives, structure and outcomes. This is a positive step since it is evident that much research on team working has taken a limited or narrow view of what is important in understanding what the team does, how it does it and what outcomes are observed. For instance, something that is commonly underplayed in the literature is the question of what work is actually conducted by the team as a team, rather than by individuals under its umbrella. This point is made by Delbridge *et al.* (1998) in regard to electronics plants and by Rinehart *et al.* (1997) in their book on a car assembly plant. This suggests greater attention should be paid to the detail and difference of team working in each workplace setting.

From their survey of workplace trade union representatives in the UK steel industry, Bacon and Blyton (2000) outline a contingency model to consider the relationship between management rationale, type of team working and organisational and human resource outcomes. This model advances a dichotomy between types of team working – 'high road' and 'low road'. High road team working is associated with management having economic, cultural and social objectives (see Mueller, 1994) and is seen as capable of delivering benefit to the organisation and the workforce (Bacon and Blyton, 2000). Low road team working arises from management having purely economic objectives and is postulated to result in a limited and narrow range of organisational outcomes with a less positive outcome for workers.

Bacon and Blyton's results suggest that it is with the adoption of a more fully developed form of team working – the high road – that a greater positive impact on both organisations and employees is effected. Where management had broader objectives than the purely economic, the trade union respondents in the survey report that improved operational performance was being achieved through team working and in conjunction with improvements in workers' motivation towards, interest in, and enjoyment of their jobs. The Australian Centre for Automotive Management report some similar findings from their survey of the Australian automotive sector, although in that study trade union representatives were more ambivalent on the positive impact of team working on job satisfaction (Park *et al.*, 1997). Both of these projects concentrate on a specific industrial sector, but still suggest significant variation in the implementation and impact of team working. What these survey-based studies are unable to address adequately is *why* these results are found and what it is about the changes in the nature of work and working that encourage positive (or negative) outcomes. This is where case-based, critical realist research makes the key contribution.

Much of the recent case study research appears to have taken place in 'low road' plants. The study of the GM–Suzuki joint venture in Canada is a good example (Rinehart *et al.*, 1997). In their book, *Just another Car Factory?*, the authors report worker surveys as well as shopfloor observation and interview data which suggest that team working at that plant was not viewed as having wholly positive outcomes by the workers themselves. In particular, Rinehart *et al.* are critical of any notion that teams in contemporary manufacturing might be considered 'self-managing' or 'autonomous'. In addition, they follow others (e.g. Lowe *et al.*, 1997) in questioning the degree to which teams may be considered essential for operational success. It is clear from the work of Rinehart *et al.* that the experience of team working cannot be divorced from the other factors influencing worker perceptions and attitudes in their day-to-day work. Nonetheless, there are certain issues which are directly associated with team working.

A key feature of team working regularly reported in case study research is peer pressure. Rinehart *et al.* (1997: 89) report that '[t]eams provide a lateral control system in which peer pressure is combined with more traditional supervision' and in Graham's (1995) study of the Subaru-Isuzu car assembly plant in the US, workers often pushed each other to complete work, work to speed and not make mistakes. Graham (1995: 100) reports that this peer pressure may arise from the threat of having one's job intensified in order to cover a team member or from the team's sense of pride in their work. She concludes that peer pressure is central to the means of management control and that it acts to extend management prerogative over workers. Graham (1995: 133) identifies social, cultural and economic objectives in the use of teams in the Japanese model, and argues that a 'psychological tension' results for workers.

While case research of team working has consistently emphasised the significance of normative controls exerted by the team members upon themselves and each other, there has been relatively little detailed discussion of the sources, nature and outcomes of peer pressure on the shopfloors of contemporary manufacturers. This is central since it would appear that inter-worker relations are a critical aspect in the success of team working, both in terms of operational and workforce outcomes. I discuss this in the following sections by referring to research conducted in a Japanese consumer electronics plant (Nippon CTV) and a European auto components maker (Valleyco), both situated in the UK. These two plants had the trappings and practices generally associated with 'high performance workplaces', including team working, employee involvement schemes and lean production techniques such as just-in-time and total quality management. The primary sources of data are periods of participant observation at the two plants; details of the research are published elsewhere (Delbridge, 1998). Before considering the nature of team working in the two plants, I briefly overview the organisational context in each.

Valleyco

Valleyco was a European-owned automotive components maker operating in the South Wales valleys. It supplied a variety of electrical and plastic components to a number of car makers located both in the UK and continental Europe. Part of a very large multinational, the plant itself was a medium-sized operation of around 225 employees at the time of the research about ten years ago. The majority of these employees were direct and indirect shopfloor workers, predominantly women. The plant was organised around product lines, each constituting a team led by a charge hand. There were three managers responsible for different areas of manufacturing and these reported to the manufacturing director.

The plant had what might be best described as 'traditional British workplace' industrial relations. There were three trade unions on site, two representing shopfloor workers in collective bargaining. The plant itself had operated for over twenty years, but in that time had been owned and managed by several different companies. Thus the workforce had seen different managers and ideas come and go on a regular basis. This contributed to a certain cynicism on the shopfloor.

The labour process was typically very simple, involving a job cycle time of less than a minute and often of only a few seconds. The operators were paid on an individual daily piece rate set by time study engineers. In practice the system had many of the characteristics reported of similar systems elsewhere – variably accurate timings that mock the notion of 'scientific' management, game playing between timers and operators, workers conspiring to achieve the best rewards, and so on (Roy, 1955; Lupton, 1963). The timings specified maximum and minimum earnings and on some jobs the targets were relatively straightforward. On these, workers would achieve the maximum bonus well before the end of the shift. Other timings were deemed unachievable and workers consequently worked at a desultory rate and accepted that they would make the minimum.

In the period preceding the research, the company had sought to introduce aspects of lean production, particularly just-in-time (JIT) and total quality management (TQM). Companies in the motor industry had been heavily influenced by the success of Japanese car makers during the late 1980s and 1990s. This led to wide-scale pressures to adopt 'Japanese' manufacturing methods. The plant's manufacturing director described JIT as 'Japan induced terror'.

While much of the high performance work systems literature reports the beneficial impact of the adoption of lean manufacturing practices (e.g. MacDuffie, 1995), the result of JIT and TQM adoption at Valleyco was far removed from the popular expectations of quality and productivity improvements. Operations were riddled with ambiguity and uncertainty. The plant's attempts to sustain routines and maintain quality were undermined by uncertainty, particularly from unreliable and fluctuating demand schedules from customers and because of unreliable component quality from suppliers. One quality controller commented:

> You just can't win with this job. They play hell if you stop production, but they play hell if you let through faulty goods. So you just do this and do that and think, 'It's only another hour and I'm out of here.'

The problems of unreliable scheduling information and poor incoming quality were contributing to, and compounded by, a strained working relationship between managers and workers. Workers routinely criticised their managers as 'useless' or worse and absenteeism was a significant problem. Managers were forced to take *ad hoc* and reactive decisions to 'fire-fight' problems, and this undermined their own competency and thus their legitimacy in the eyes of their workers.

The combination of these factors led to high uncertainty on the shopfloor and I have characterised this as 'directed chaos'. It is directed in the sense that customer orders are completed, but chaotic in the process by which this is achieved. 'Progress chasers' (not a role or title to be found in Japanese plants) were left to frantically negotiate with the individual charge hands for the completion of their order ahead of others. The daily build schedule circulated by planning was regularly ignored on the shopfloor since it would include things already produced and in stores, or products for which there were not sufficient components or materials. On occasion I was told it scheduled the production of items the plant no longer made!

In a similar fashion, quality 'standards' became flexible due to unforeseen problems, uncertainty and delivery imperatives. At the time of a 'panic job', managers would instruct workers to disregard the quality control requirements in order to rush through orders and avoid penalties for late delivery to the car makers. These crises completely undermined previous attempts to establish a greater quality consciousness among the operators. Communication and training on the importance of quality were disregarded, often against the judgement of the workers themselves. As one operator commented after being told to use parts she felt were substandard, 'Well, it's on their backs, they said to use them. I wouldn't want them on my car.'

The chaos of the plant was informally directed through the taking of largely arbitrary decisions over the reprioritisation of batches and the acceptable level of quality, while formal systems and procedures failed and were then ignored.

Nippon CTV

Nippon CTV was a Japanese-owned plant making television sets in the south of England. The plant had around 1,000 employees at the time of the research. As at Valleyco, the vast majority of shopfloor operators were female. The main operations were automated component insertion, manual component insertion and final assembly of the circuit boards, tube and cabinet. The research was conducted primarily in the manual insertion area, the 'panel shop'. About 400 people worked in the panel shop, organised around nine main insertion lines/teams and some smaller sub-lines. Each line was run by a team leader.

Each main panel line would have about forty people in the team. The management structure was flat with wide spans of control. Each of the nine team leaders reported directly to the panel shop manager and her assistant. The company had established a single-union, no strike deal when it started operations in the early 1980s. There was no formal collective bargaining, but the company operated an advisory board of elected representatives. There were also daily team meetings and monthly plant meetings to communicate information to the workforce.

In the panel shop, work speed was driven by a moving conveyor line. Each operator had a set number of components to insert as the printed circuit board moved across in front of them. Typically the time per component was 2.7 seconds and each worker would usually have ten to twelve pieces, giving a job cycle time of around half a minute. At the end of the line there were inspectors checking that all the necessary components were correctly in place. A record of each individual's quality performance was displayed above their work station. Defects were recorded on colour-coded charts with green signifying the worker as 'good', yellow denoting 'warning' and red for 'danger'. If a worker made more than twenty mistakes in a month from a total number of insertions typically exceeding 200,000, then the procedures required a red sign to be posted. Moreover, the team leader would then be expected to 'counsel' the worker about their performance and the reasons for it. Workers saw a 'counselling' session as a form of disciplinary procedure rather than a supportive or developmental experience. Regular failure to meet performance targets would lead to the worker facing dismissal.

In distinct contrast to Valleyco, Nippon CTV had been successful in establishing JIT and TQM systems. These had been implemented from the outset when the Japanese parent company had first set up the plant. In many ways, the outward appearance of the organisation was as an exemplar of manufacturing 'best practice'. The plant ran to high levels of quality and produced large numbers of television sets efficiently and at low cost. The most obvious variation from the textbook view of JIT was that the plant was buffered from the external sources of potential uncertainty that had undermined Valleyco's operations. Rather than being tightly coupled to suppliers and the marketplace, the company ran with significant inventories of incoming components and finished goods. However, internal stocks were kept to an absolute minimum. The overall effect was that the plant had a 'bounded JIT' system.

In summary, both plants operated with lean production regimes and in particular the Japanese plant ran with very low buffers of inventory, tight manning and extremely close monitoring of quality. At each of the plants, workers were grouped into teams with a team leader, but the language of team working was most advanced in Nippon CTV where all workers were 'members' and underperformers were 'counselled' over their future work performance. Both plants recognised trade unions; Valleyco had a traditional bargaining arrangement with two different shopfloor unions, while Nippon CTV had a single union agreement. Most shopfloor workers in the two cases were women.

In the brief discussion above, I have tried to indicate the major similarities and differences between the way apparently similar systems of production were operating. Reference only to management completion questionnaires would likely have given the impression of great consistency between the two plants as exemplars of high performance workplaces. The shopfloor reality was rather different. In the following sections, I concentrate on the reported experiences and observations of team working in the two plants.

Team working in a low trust, high surveillance environment

For workers, the social relationships they form with each other are key in their perceptions of their workplace. Throughout the research, those workers who spoke favourably about the plant in which they worked tended to single out their fellow workers as the most significant plus. For example, one of the younger male workers at Nippon CTV was fairly non-committal about the work itself; he said his job was 'OK'. His main view of his own workplace experience centred around co-workers: 'They're a good group here, that's what it's all about.' He elaborated this by explaining that people 'pulled their weight' before noting that if they did not there could be 'problems'. A further indicative example can be drawn from Valleyco. One woman left to work at a nearby Japanese transplant because the money was better, but she soon returned to Valleyco and her friend commented that, 'The work was OK but she didn't like the girls on the line.'

Both the individual personalities and the actions of workers and managers are important in understanding the detail of the workplace relations in the plants. Many workers regarded individuals of the same formal level and authority in a different way depending upon how they perceived them to act in practice; this was particularly the case with regard to the first line of supervision. For example, a young testing operator at Nippon CTV complained to me about his team leader. He felt that she had not treated him with respect when he first started on the line. Consequently, he had complained to the shop superintendent, the team leader's superior. He told me, 'I had her [the team leader] in the coffee lounge [where workers are "counselled"]. We'd all worked this overtime for her to clear the piles of panels all on the trolleys, but she never even said "thanks".' While the tester cited a lack of respect on the part of the team leader as the cause of conflict, he also added that she 'sticks to the [rule] book too tightly'. In the eyes of the worker, it was the individual *application* of the rules and procedures that determined his experience of these.

Throughout the research and across both plants, workers talked about specifics and individuals in describing and interpreting their experiences at work. Nonetheless, a 'structured antagonism' provided the context and pervaded these discussions.

The persistence of resistance

While it has been argued that team working will contribute to workers identifying with company goals and will lead to these being internalised as their own

(Barker, 1993; Sewell and Wilkinson, 1992; Sewell, 1998), workers at both plants took steps to at least symbolically demonstrate that they did not share management's objectives and values. At Nippon CTV, the clearest examples were an unwillingness to wear the company uniform, workers' reluctance to work overtime and the rush to leave the premises at the end of the shift. These (in)actions may be fairly limited in their consequences for management but were clear demonstrations of resistance. At Valleyco, the divisions between management and labour were even more evident with workers actively withholding effort and regularly voicing their opposition to management.

Moving specifically to the issue of employee involvement central to arguments surrounding 'high performance workplaces', the evidence is clear. At both plants workers failed to participate in any discretionary activities. Take shopfloor worker contributions to problem-solving and continuous improvement. In each case employee suggestions for improvement were virtually non-existent. Nippon CTV had abandoned quality circle activity and Valleyco had never had small group problem-solving. Workers were organised in teams but this did not prompt employee involvement or contributions to improvement processes. Team meetings or briefings were almost entirely one-way channels of communication.

While there was a uniformity of resistance to voluntary participation at the two plants, it would be wrong to assume workers simply did the minimum required. Again, the nature and character of individuals helps explain action and interaction. There are a number of aspects to the relationships between workers themselves and between workers and managers which can help in understanding workers' behaviour. One particularly interesting feature was the attitude workers displayed to co-workers who fell behind with their work and needed assistance. During the research it became clear that workers were selective in whom they would help out and whom they left to struggle alone. A central feature of this was workers' perceptions of the effort that their co-workers were putting in. Workers seen as 'doing their best' would be assisted, others would be ignored and even derided as 'lazy cows', and the like. Indeed, some members of the team came under considerable pressure to work harder and more accurately, particularly when fellow workers felt they were 'not trying'. This element of peer pressure is consistent with the expectations of Barker, Sewell and others, but it is important to note that this was not a universal phenomenon in either plant. Rather, individuals were reasoning and calculative in their actions, sometimes helping, sometimes cajoling, but also sometimes collectively withholding effort. This was particularly the case at Valleyco where the reliance on informality provided more opportunity.

This individualistic interaction was also a feature of relations between workers and their supervisors. A distinguishing characteristic of who could expect help was the extent to which the workers felt their own position was understood and sympathised with by their superiors. A very clear example of how workers tended to empathise with, and be supportive of, those who were sympathetic to their own position came in the moulding shop at Valleyco, where there were two quality inspectors working – Adam and Calum. They carried out the same tasks, one on the morning shift and one on the afternoon shift. However, Adam was extremely unpopular with the setters and operators in the moulding shop and was commonly regarded as 'knowing fuck all'. In sharp contrast, Calum was respected and seen as very effective in his job – 'You can't hide anything [of poor quality] from Calum, he'll find it at the bottom of the bag.' Paradoxically, Calum did not apply the quality levels to the letter and told me that if possible he would let things pass his inspection, 'If it's not alright then I'll stop it. My job is to stop the rubbish. But if they [the operators] say, "That's the best we can do" then I will pass them. It is very rare for me to take things to my boss.' It was Calum's willingness to recognise the constraints on the operators that won him respect. Paradoxically, his acceptance of the limitations on quality performance had led him to have a reputation as being able to locate and stop poor quality products. On the other hand, Adam was seen as petty and stupid, without an understanding of the machines and their limitations or the problems that the setters and operators had. Thus his actions were not seen as legitimate by the workers, whether or not he was actually good at identifying defective work.

Adam's unpopularity went well beyond the verbal abuse regularly directed his way; a supervisor once said to me quite seriously, 'Someone'll knife him one day.' On the last day before the Christmas break, Adam was tied up and thrown in a skip, and his supervisor told me that 'If I hadn't found him down in assembly, he'd have been there all Christmas.' On another occasion, he was tied up and dumped in a box and put on a lorry, 'If the security bloke hadn't found him at the gate he'd have gone to Birmingham.'

Both quality inspectors had formally set procedures and quality standards to follow. It was the method of application and the nature of the interaction between inspector and workers that defined the relationship between them.

Shopfloor fragmentation

The relationships that form between workers and their superiors are only a part of the social situation; to a very significant extent, what workers do must be understood in relation to their interaction with their fellow workers. The practical significance of these relations was particularly evident at Nippon CTV and the areas of Valleyco where some form of team working had been fully implemented. In these situations, the actions and attitudes of individual workers were seen to have an effect, often directly, on the work experience of other workers. Under group-based work systems with reduced buffers of time or inventory, this increased coupling of worker activity resulted in heightened potential for inter-worker tension and disagreement, with a resulting potential for fragmentation in workplace relations among these workers.

Thus management's attempts to tighten control, extend surveillance and intensify work placed further strain on the structured antagonism of the capitalist workplace. Nonetheless, within this context individual attitudes and agency were important. The attitudes of workers to their peers were informed by three factors: their respective personalities and whether they 'got on'; whether the person in question was seen as 'trying' hard enough (meeting effort norms); and the extent to which the individual's actions had a direct and negative effect on their fellow workers. The first of these is left as largely intangible here, although one of the line workers who received a lot of help in maintaining her quality levels from fellow workers commented that, 'They only spot [and correct] the mistakes of the people they like.' An element of this would again centre on whether the co-worker was perceived to be 'doing their best'. At Nippon CTV, all quality performance is monitored at the individual level, and the informal checking of workmates allows some operators to avoid disciplinary action for exceeding the very strict defect levels.

The second and third elements were constantly demonstrated during the interactions of workers. For example, and against simplistic 'us and them' expectations, line workers at Nippon CTV would side with the senior member against a fellow worker if they felt that worker had not been meeting commonly accepted effort norms. Graham (1995: 100) describes a situation when 'team members cooperated with the team leader in an attempt to force compliance from another team member concerning his job performance'. Such a situation arose with one of the component insertion workers. She was moved from quality inspection because she had been letting through too many rejects. However, she could not keep to the linespeed on insertion. She did not receive any sympathy nor any additional help from her workmates. This necessitated a transfer of some of her workload onto another, more experienced, line worker, and this clearly caused resentment. Descriptions of the worker as a 'fat' or 'lazy cow' abounded from the other line workers with comments such as, 'Look at her, she's not even trying' or, 'It's no wonder she can't keep up, moving at that speed.'

The extra work the experienced worker took on did not seem to cause her undue problems, but that was not the point in the workers' eyes. It was clear that the failure to work at a certain speed (the speed that the other members felt co-workers should be working at) led to peer group pressure to increase speed, and triggered resentment and conflict. Through the research it became apparent that the nature of peer relations and the degree of peer pressure to conform to management expectations was at least partially determined by workers' view of the effort of their co-worker. In effect, as long as the worker appeared to be trying and 'doing their best', it did not seem to matter if they were 'hopeless' or 'useless' and needed help. Workers who were fairly popular could expect to be helped with little comment made, so long as the assistance required did not inconvenience fellow workers unduly or for a prolonged period of time.

As with other conflicts over whether workers were working 'too fast' or 'too slow', this example indicates that workers have an appropriate level of effort in mind when interpreting their workmates' activities. The vast majority of workers at both plants did not simply avoid activity, nor did they seek to do the minimum, but rather they had some accepted level of effort which was seen as legitimate or 'fair'. As a consequence, individual workers at both plants occasionally came under peer pressure to work faster. Equally, a worker at Valleyco came under pressure to work slower and any 'rate-busters' also came under peer pressure to conform to workspeed norms. These features of capitalist workplaces have been widely reported (for example, Lupton, 1963). What is important to note is that the effort norms were collectively established by the groups and were neither determined by, nor did they mirror, management expectations.

The context of worker relations

The previous section has shown how workers interpret each other's behaviour and establish expectations and perceptions that shape interaction. These interactions must be contextualised through an examination of both their organisational and wider contexts. A central finding from workplace studies has been that worker interrelationships are shaped by the nature of the production system within which they are operating. In the cases reported here, informal personal dynamics are compounded in their importance because of the 'blame mechanisms' which are part and parcel of quality control systems, especially at plants like Nippon CTV where every error must be attributed to an individual worker. In contrast to expectations surrounding survey-based arguments in support of high performance work systems, tight control at Nippon CTV undermined the prospect for employee participation. It also placed a greater strain on inter-worker relations.

Not surprisingly, the most deep-seated rifts along the line were between workers at different points in the quality inspection process, and the situations which led to the most directly confrontational behaviour between workers surrounded the monitoring and recording of quality. This is similar in some respects to the instances of open hostility between Adam and the setters and operators in the moulding shop at Valleyco reported above, although at Nippon CTV quality inspection is carried out by fellow team members rather than a white-collar specialist. At Nippon CTV, workers regularly became embroiled in disputes with each other over whether they should have a defect 'booked' against them.

During one period when I was observing the end of line inspection, there were particular disagreements. One of the inspectors claimed that another inspector was booking defects against her (the work of inspectors is inspected), 'She's always booking everything and getting other people into trouble for things that aren't their fault.' Her fellow inspector then said, 'I'll drag her by her hair into the coffee lounge if she gets me booked for that.' Later one added, 'We don't work as a team here do we?'

The inspection worker had been warned by the team leader about her work performance and was under pressure to improve. At one stage she complained to the team leader that she had to help one of the other line workers who had a problem with poor quality incoming parts. The lack of slack in the production system, and the pressure to perform their own tasks successfully, led to individual workers blaming *each other* for problems that arose. It is not just the quality system with its onus on ascribing blame for faults that structures the relations between workers. The pressure of a lean manufacturing system, with its unremitting high speed and limited or no informal breaks, exacerbates the difficulties for workers and further aggravates conflicts.

The self-policing elements of peer surveillance in quality control are also evident in the Valleyco case, but the lack of an effective and integrated information system means that divisive and fragmenting 'blaming' behaviour is not such an important factor in inter-worker relations at that plant. This evidence supports others that have concluded that, at least in part, it is the function of the team and the management system within which it operates that is important in interpreting team working (e.g. Cutcher-Gershenfeld *et al.*, 1994).

However, there are other factors that are important. Space does not permit a full discussion here, but it is clear that the history of the plants contributed to what Chung (1994) called 'factory consciousness' – the shared norms of the shopfloor. The attitudes of the workers at the two plants were very different in a number of ways, including the willingness to voice discontent to management and to show overt resistance. This in turn might be related to aspects of local community and the local history of industry and employment. Lupton's (1963) study contrasting workers and workplace relations in a garment manufacturer and an electrical plant attributes variation to a 'lack of will to control' and a deep-seated belief in 'looking after No. 1' that has historically been present in the garment industry. These factors in turn influence individual worker's perceptions and interactions.

Equally, the formal industrial relations arrangements at the two plants were very different and it is evident that these may have an impact. In the cases reported by Rinehart *et al.* (1997) and Graham (1995), the trade union had exerted considerable influence at times and this included direct organised resistance to the introduction or implementation of certain management practices. Such action was not seen at either of the two plants reported here during the time of the study. Again, reflection upon the local, historical and structural features pertinent to the specific case helps to interpret these variations.

Finally the plants themselves must be put in context. Each is part of a major multinational corporation making high volume products for mass consumption markets. One of the outcomes of the high surveillance, low trust regime at the two plants was a consistent unwillingness on the part of the workforce to participate in any discretionary work activity such as continuous improvement. In the area of innovation, the plant was not delivering. These plants may be seen as 'branch plants' in an international division of labour that sees production migrate to lower-cost bases while higher value-added activity involving higher skills and better wages remains in the country of origin (Delbridge *et al.*, 1998). This clearly influences the production system and the experiences of workers.

Discussion

Individual accountability for defects and workers' mutual loyalty can lead to informal behaviour that actually improves plant quality performance in line with management wishes. Each time someone corrects an up-line worker's error to save that defect being booked against their name, the quality of the product is improved. Quality is an important element in the control of labour at the two plants since it has a certain inherent legitimacy. Workers may more readily identify with the goal of good quality than with other management objectives. Management, and customers, are able to draw on this legitimacy in attempting to secure compliance from the shopfloor. Nevertheless, the research presented here suggests that workers are active in choosing whether they will assist a fellow worker through the correcting of faults, and it is their orientation to their fellow workers rather than the product which determines this. The detailed empirical data generated through ethnographic research clearly demonstrates that workers at Nippon CTV did not prioritise management objectives over their own independent social interaction and personal choices; the defects of some workers were not corrected irrespective of the detrimental impact upon product quality.

These findings differ from those of Barker (1993) who discusses the development of a system of 'concertive' control in a plant as management introduces team working. Concertive control is an example of normative control and, according to Barker, includes the following features: increased employee motivation and commitment; peer pressure as the primary mechanism through which members of the team are controlled; workers that are 'relatively unaware of how the system they created actually controls their actions' (Barker, 1993: 434); and enacted values that over time develop into 'rational rules'. Under such circumstances workers manage and discipline themselves, 'proper' behaviour is inferred from value-based discourse, and these rules of behaviour become incorporated as an integral part of the workers' sense of self (Fleming and Stablein, 1998: 10). Fleming and Stablein argue that under concertive control, an *illusion* of autonomy and flexibility develops.

The data reported here demonstrate that, at least under certain conditions of team working, workers remain aware of, and active in taking, choices over how to act and interact. Most importantly, research which underplays the active agency of workers may neglect to consider that normative control can be exerted in such a way as to subvert management goals as well as promote them. This oversight contributes to a common criticism that Foucauldian accounts of workplace relations fail to anticipate the prospects for resistance (Thompson and Ackroyd, 1995). This criticism may be levelled at Barker, and also Sewell (1998) whose assessment of the impact of team working privileges management and its discourses, in assuming peer pressure will be exerted in line with management objectives.

In practice, workers may establish pockets of solidarity that are effective in seeking support and creating meaningful patterns of resistance, or at least mechanisms for surviving the working day. Little detail is given, but Rinehart *et al.* (1997: 107) report that workers at the CAMI plant increasingly recognised the negative consequences of peer pressure and acted to encourage team solidarity. That said, successful collective resistance is highly problematic under the conditions found at a plant like Nippon CTV with its combination of a highly regimented lean production regime, an acquiescent trade union and unfavourable local economic and labour market conditions (see Delbridge, 1998, for a fuller discussion).

Conclusion

This essay has presented ethnographic evidence of workers' experiences under 'new' management practices. While on the face of it the two plants may have appeared to operate similar production and work organisation systems, workers' perceptions and experiences were rather different in the two cases. A self-evident conclusion must be, then, that the presence or absence of practices does not in itself define 'high performance'. This demonstrates the problem of positivist, survey-based studies that fail to capture the essence and nuance of the negotiated application of workplace practices. Such studies may obscure or omit more than they reveal.

The detailed case research has allowed a greater assessment of one of the key issues in team working under contemporary manufacturing practices such as JIT and TQM: that of peer pressure. It has been shown that management systems that seek to extend control, intensify the labour process and heighten surveillance can place inter-worker relations under extreme fragmentary pressure. However, what must be acknowledged within this broader conclusion is that workers remain active in evaluating their situation and acting accordingly. The nature of peer pressure involves an assessment of co-workers' efforts against collectively constructed norms, the extent of the negative consequences of co-worker (in)action, and whether the individuals enjoy generally friendly relations. It must be noted that the *direction* of peer pressure is part of what is informed by these issues. Sometimes workers may pressure others to work faster or more accurately; on other occasions the pressure may be to work less diligently. The prospects are constrained by aspects of the management control systems and informed by wider organisational and contextual features. Post-structuralist studies that downplay the structured antagonism of capitalist workplace relations (e.g. Barker, 1993), or presume a misplaced hegemony for management's objectives (e.g. Sewell, 1998), will assume away the contest, conflict and resistance that bring life to, and constitute the 'reality' of, workers' own shopfloor experiences. Nevertheless, the importance of workers as active agents in interpreting and determining their own behaviour requires us to reflect upon how and why these views are formed and sustained or modified through interaction. Here notions of identity will be important.

References

Appelbaum, E. and Batt, R. (1994) *The New American Workplace: Transforming Work Systems in the United States*, Ithaca, NY: ILR Press.

Arthur, J.B. (1994) 'Effects of human resource systems on manufacturing performance and turnover', *Academy of Management Journal*, 37: 670–87.

Bacon, N. and Blyton, P. (2000) 'High road and low road teamworking: perceptions of management rationales and organizational and human resource outcomes', *Human Relations*, 53 (11): 1425–58.

Barker, J. (1993). 'Tightening the iron cage: concertive control in self-managing teams', *Administrative Science Quarterly*, 38: 408–37.

Becker, B. and Gerhart, B. (1996) 'The impact of human resource management on organizational performance: progress and prospects', *Academy of Management Journal*, 39: 779–801.

Cappelli, P. and Neumark, D. (2001) 'Do "high-performance" work practices improve establishment-level outcomes?', *Industrial and Labour Relations Review*, 54: 737–75.

Chung, Y. (1994) 'Conflict and compliance: the workplace politics of a disk-drive factory in Singapore', in J. Bélanger, P. Edwards and L. Haiven (eds), *Workplace Industrial Relations and the Global Challenge*, Ithaca, NY: Cornell University Press, pp. 190–223.

Cutcher-Gershenfeld, J. *et al.* (1994) 'Japanese team-based work systems in North America: explaining diversity', *California Management Review*, 37 (1): 42–64.

Delbridge, R. (1998) *Life on the Line in Contemporary Manufacturing*, Oxford: Oxford University Press.

Delbridge, R. and Whitfield, K. (2001) 'Employee perceptions of job influence and organizational participation', *Industrial Relations*, 40: 472–89.

Delbridge, R., Kenney, M. and Lowe, J. (1998) 'UK manufacturing in the twenty-first century: learning factories and knowledge workers?', in R. Delbridge and J. Lowe (eds), *Manufacturing in Transition*, London: Routledge, pp. 224–41.

Fleming, P. and Stablein, R. (1998) 'Normative control in organizations: a review', paper presented at Critical Management Workshop, San Diego, August.

Godard, J. (1993) 'Theory and method in industrial relations: modernist and postmodernist alternatives', in R. Adams and N. Meltz (eds), *Industrial Relations Theory: Its Nature, Scope and Pedagogy*, New Jersey: Rutgers University Press, pp. 283–306.

Graham, L. (1995) *On the Line at Subaru-Isuzu*, Ithaca, NY: Cornell University Press.

Huselid, M.A. (1995) 'The impact of human resource management practices on turnover, productivity, and corporate financial performance', *Academy of Management Journal*, 38: 635–72.

Lowe, J., Delbridge, R. and Oliver, N. (1997) 'High performance manufacturing: evidence from the automotive components industry', *Organization Studies*, 18 (5): 783–98.

Lupton, T. (1963) *On the Shopfloor*, Oxford: Pergamon Press.

MacDuffie, J.P. (1995) 'Human resource bundles and manufacturing performance: organizational logic and flexible production systems in the world auto industry', *Industrial and Labor Relations Review*, 48 (2): 199–221.

Mueller, F. (1994) 'Teams between hierarchy and commitment: change strategies and the "internal environment" ', *Journal of Management Studies*, 31 (3): 383–404.

Murakami, T. (1995) 'Introducing teamworking: a motor industry case study from Germany', *Industrial Relations Journal*, 26 (4): 293–318.

Nelson, B. (1998) 'Square pegs into round holes? The pitfalls of applying manufacturing-based theory to service organizations', paper presented at the Academy of Management Meeting, San Diego, August.

Park, R. Erwin, P. and Knapp, K. (1997) 'Teams in Australia's motor industry: characteristics and future challenges', *International Journal of Human Resource Management*, 8 (6): 780–96.

Pil, F. and MacDuffie, J. (1996) 'The adoption of high-involvement work practices', *Industrial Relations*, 35 (3): 423–55.

Rinehart, J., Huxley, C. and Robertson, C. (1997) *Just another Car Factory? Lean Production and its Discontents*, Ithaca, NY: Cornell University Press.
Roy, D. (1955) 'Efficiency and "the fix": informal intergroup relations in a piecework machine shop', *American Journal of Sociology*, 60: 255–66.
Sewell, G. (1998) 'The discipline of teams: the control of team-based industrial work through electronic and peer surveillance', *Administrative Science Quarterly*, 43: 397–427.
Sewell, G. and Wilkinson, B. (1992) 'Someone to watch over me: surveillance, discipline and the just-in-time labour process', *Sociology*, 26 (2): 271–89.
Thompson, P. and Ackroyd, S. (1995) 'All quiet on the workplace front? A critique of recent trends in British industrial sociology', *Sociology*, 29: 615–33.
Thompson, P. and Wallace, T. (1996) 'Redesigning production through teamworking: case studies from the Volvo Truck Corporation', *International Journal of Operations and Production Management*, 16 (2): 103–16.

12 Humour and subversion in two call centres

Phil Taylor and Peter Bain

Introduction

Kelly (1998) has recently described the typical contemporary workplace as one in which employee discontent has grown alongside distrust of management, while Bryson and McKay (1997: 28) have demonstrated that there has been a significant underlying deterioration over time in employees' perceptions of workplace relations. In this chapter we report on research that contributes to the growing weight of evidence and argument of this kind supporting the thesis that oppositional attitudes and subversive behaviour continue to be widespread in the workplaces of late modern capitalism.

The evidence we shall bring forward derives from extended empirical investigations of call centres studied in research, funded in one case by the ESRC's 'Future of Work' programme.[1] It leads us to be in broad agreement with a diverse range of authors who have emphasised the persistence of oppositional practices, continuing union relevance and 'the resilience of adversarialism' (Thompson and Ackroyd, 1995; Bradley *et al.*, 2000) in the contemporary workplace. Our research has uncovered manifold and vigorous forms of individual, quasi-collective and collective resistance (Bain and Taylor, 1999, 2000; Taylor and Bain, 1999, 2001a, 2001b) rooted in part in the experience of work in this 'unique working environment' (HSE, 2001). Discontent with the experience of task performance, employment conditions and the 'managerial regime' are certainly integral to the use of humour by workers in the two call centres on which this essay is based.

In contrast with our view, various commentators have implied or asserted the end of oppositional attitudes and behaviour. It is true that certain general indicators apparently suggest a reduction in conflict. For example, UK statistics suggest that strike activity fell to record low levels in the 1990s (Davies, 2001: 302). Further, despite slight increases in recent years, the long-term decline in trade union membership is statistically established (Hicks, 2000). Added to this, much managerial and academic writing has concluded that the weakening of organised labour, combined with the effects of new systems of 'panoptic' surveillance (Sewell and Wilkinson, 1992) or 'involving' human resource management practices, have created a cowed and/or a contented workforce. A particularly persuasive view of events has involved the utilisation of the 'electronic panopticon' metaphor to describe new workplaces and particularly the call centre (Fernie and Metcalf, 1998). In this account, supervisory power has been 'rendered perfect' and worker resistance is nullified. This has sometimes been allied to a post-Foucauldian version of labour process theory (e.g. Knights and McCabe, 1998), which reduces the possibilities for resistance to highly individualistic and self-contained acts, where workers can seek only 'spaces for escape'. Using these kinds of evidence and ideas, it has widely been inferred that conflict and misbehaviour have all but disappeared from the contemporary workplace.

Proclamations of the death of resistance are, however, clearly mistaken. Almost everywhere, the arguments of those who claim the disappearance of resistance are eminently contestable, on both empirical and theoretical grounds. It is obviously problematic, for example, to impute the decline of oppositional attitudes and behaviour from the trend of strike statistics (Blyton and Turnbull, 1998: 288). It is presumptuous to infer that workplaces are harmonious or conflict-free, particularly if the definition of conflict includes a range of activities short of strike action. Nor can union decline be taken to be 'synonymous with the disappearance of workplace resistance and conflict' (Ackroyd and Thompson, 1999: 146). We would contend that arguments about the decline of conflict emanate from authors with little actual contact with the typical contemporary workplace, affinity with the experience of real workers, or understanding of the work environment. Reeves (2001: 188) exemplifies this reality avoidance, asserting that work is 'the happy pill' and that employees, 'holding the means of production in their heads, are working with enthusiasm, ambition and with themselves nominated as chief beneficiaries'.

Theory and philosophy

Our approach to research is rooted in a materialist and broadly Marxist framework and tradition. We think that the social relations between capital and labour in the workplace are of 'structured antagonism', although capital's requirement to generate some degree of creativity and co-operation from labour means that in response, worker resistance overlaps and co-exists with accommodation, compliance and consent. In essence, though, the workplace is a contested terrain. Accordingly, in our call centre research, we have adopted a conceptual framework derived from core labour process theory (LPT). Thompson and Smith's (2000: 56–7) identification of core elements of LPT includes the necessity for a control imperative in the labour process, in order for capital to secure profitable production and to translate labour power into actual labour and a surplus. These theoretical underpinnings have informed our specific analysis of work organisation and management control in call centres. We conclude that call centres embody novel and extensive forms of control, albeit reflective of the enduring influence of scientific management (Bain and Taylor, 2000; Taylor and Bain, 1999; Taylor *et al.*, 2002). It is also argued that much call centre work is experienced as repetitive, intensive and frequently stressful.

To a considerable extent also, our approach is consistent with the emerging critical realist approach to social science. As has been argued by some of its supporters, this is not a new approach but a rearticulation of some of the basic ideas of social science from its inception (Ackroyd and Fleetwood, 2000). In this account, we also reject both positivism and postmodernism, accepting the long-established conviction in the social sciences that social structures, as well as the meanings which actors bestow upon their situation and activities, must be taken into account in explaining events. Accordingly, in Ackroyd and Fleetwood's preliminary discussion (2000: 5) realism is a broad church, embracing diverse major thinkers (Marx, Weber, Chomsky *inter alia*). Included in this roll call is not only Braverman (1974) but also numerous subsequent labour process analysts.[2] Thus, in this inclusive and basic sense we also may be considered critical realists.

More fundamentally, from readings of Bhaskar (1979, 1986, 1989), Collier (1994) and other critical realists (Ackroyd and Fleetwood, 2000; Brown *et al.*, 2002), we also endorse the aspect of the ontology of critical realism which proposes that social phenomena exist independently of us and our investigations, and reject the relativism of postmodernism, particularly the reduction of reality to mere accounts of reality. In particular, in the context of this essay we suggest the following. Call centres, the economic imperatives which create and sustain them, the class relations which underpin their productive process and the reconstitution of the mode of customer service delivery which they involve, are produced by actors, yet crucially these still exist externally to them. As we demonstrate, there is an identifiable type of call centre regime which, as a pre-existing structure, influences and shapes the behaviour of groups who work within them. Following Bhaskar, we also accept the transformational model of social action which recognises that agents contribute to the re-creation, reproduction and more rarely to the transformation of those pre-existing structures.[3] Indeed, the actions of call centre agents in both of our cases studies, in contrasting ways, re-created or transformed those social structures given to them.

Methodology and techniques of data collection

This enquiry is concerned not merely with description but explanation. Hence our work implies the importance of the stratified and transformational ontology of critical realism, and recognises the significance of the distinctions between the domains of the real, actual and empirical for adequate explanations (Tsoukas, 2000: 29). We argue that explanation requires penetration behind the surface appearance to identify the underlying generative mechanisms in the domain of the real. Complete explanation, in fact, is achieved where the mechanisms connecting social and economic structures (real), and the powers and relations of particular entities (actual) at work behind the flux of perceived and actual events (empirical), are revealed (Fleetwood, 2002: 5). We argue that the crucial linkages are between the real and the actual domains, and showing their connectedness is crucial to the plausibility of particular explanations. Showing the links here is the basic 'raison d'être of realism', as Easton puts it (2000: 208). Thus it is suggested that, despite the general trend of economic change, particular behaviour and the extent and nature of worker self-organisation (in the domain of the actual) may affect the outcome from, and the effectiveness of, particular managerial regimes.

Thus, in our conception, realist explanation is far from being deterministic. What occurs often depends on particular contingencies. For this reason, realist method is often contrastive (Lipton, 1993: 35, cited in Fleetwood, 2002: 68–9). Thus, in this chapter, we give serious attention to the particular case study contexts, and attempt to specify the actual patterns of behaviour involved in them. Indeed, in order to acquire data on workplace behaviour in sufficient detail it is necessary to gain access to the rich fabric of social interaction between workers, and between workers and managers. Researchers must acquire an intimate knowledge of an organisation's underlife, and gain a high degree of trust from workers, if behaviour is to be adequately understood. It seems obvious that resistance to management – especially in subtle manifestations – may be completely missed by investigators. As Ackroyd and Thompson observe, 'Finding reliable evidence for misbehaviour has never been an easy task, if only because the tendency to misbehave is usually hidden' (1999: 100). An understandable suspicion that reports of misbehaviour might be relayed to management inhibits such acts being revealed to researchers.

In the research now being reported, the contrastive approach was adopted. In it we examined the operation of two call centres, which did not differ very much in formal aspects of their organisation. The data utilised here come from two different call centres. Findings from one call centre, Excell, are contrasted with what was observed to happen in another (to which we give the pseudonym 'T'). At both, we were able to focus on the informal organisation of the workplace, and to understand dynamics of workplace culture, including the use of humour. Access to this hidden world was achieved through the use of slightly differing techniques of data collection. In 'T', between October 1999 and May 2000, we were able to observe the work very directly, listening to calls while sitting alongside agents and discussing their task performance with them. However, field notes recorded not only direct observations of work performance; also available were the results of informal interviews with agents, supervisors and managers. Researchers had full access to 'shop floor' activities and, through sustained contact, gained the confidence of key informants. Consequently, the study method here draws mainly on ethnographic techniques. As in anthropology, however, the method of participation is concerned not merely to produce description of behaviour but also to identify the structural factors providing the context of human agency. In this respect, Porter (2000: 141–60) has demonstrated the possibility of using critical realism to overcome some of the epistemological weaknesses associated with participant observation, which is the key ethnographic method of investigation

Research at Excell commenced in 1998. To date, studies have focused on surveillance, control and employee resistance (Bain and Taylor, 2000) and the growth of collective organisation (Taylor and Bain, 2001b, 2002). Here research could not involve direct observation, but relied upon the testimony and recollection of workers interviewed off-site. This generated three qualitative data sets. The first consists of transcriptions of frequent meetings of a group of between four and twelve employees. In effect, these are the proceedings of an informal, loosely structured committee, striving to build a union in circumstances of employer hostility, and whose debates and decisions were recorded against a background of conflict. The authors documented twenty-seven such meetings between October 1998 and May 1999. Second, fifteen concurrent interviews were conducted with agents, ex-employees and supervisors, exploring, in detail, perceptions of the labour process and employee relations. Third, from late 1999 into 2000, ten interviews, each lasting two hours, were conducted with workers who were encouraged to reflect on the earlier period when they first organised themselves in the Communication Workers Union (CWU). These lengthy accounts by key informants generated thoughtful reflection on the purpose and effects of workplace humour. Although based on data from separate studies, the common organisational setting of the call centre enables pertinent comparisons to be made and contrasts drawn.

By these contrasting methods, we have arrived at a similar level of understanding of events in 'T' and Excell. Further we suggest that in our interpretation of events in these workplaces we demonstrate the value of substantive critical realist research. Despite the particularities of these studies, they nonetheless exhibit properties that are exemplary for understanding the general case of the persistence of dissent and subversion in workplaces of a certain type.

Call centres, 'managerial regimes' and self-organisation

Call centres are a distinctive kind of new workplace, and one which offers many new opportunities for the effective surveillance of work activity. Some early accounts of work organisation in call centres emphasised the ubiquity of such features. Fernie and Metcalf (1998) characterised call centres *toute courte* as regimes of all-encompassing electronic surveillance, in which employee resistance was impossible. However, it is increasingly recognised that, despite the common integration of computer and telephonic technologies, important differences exist between and within call centres (Bain *et al.*, 2002; Batt, 2000, Hutchinson *et al.*, 2000; Taylor and Bain, 2001a; Taylor *et al.*, 2002). At the risk of over-simplification, contrasts exist in the complexity of agent/customer interaction, the degree of routinisation/customisation, the 'hardness' of quantitative targets, the length of call handling times and the extent of employee discretion. In short, differences in volume and value reflect managerial prioritisation of quantity or quality. Contingent factors include industrial sector, market conditions and the value of the customer base (Batt, 2000). One model locates individual call centres along a spectrum defined by quantitative and qualitative characteristics (Taylor and Bain, 2001a: 45), but recognising diversity should not lead to the conclusion that call centres are equally distributed between 'quality' and 'quantity' operations. They tend to be concentrated at the highly controlled, quantitative end of the spectrum (Callaghan and Thompson, 2001; Taylor and Bain, 2001a).

Operations at 'T' and Excell both fell into this 'quantitative' category, with agents expected to handle the greatest number of routine calls in the shortest possible time. Further, agents exerted little control over task performance and faced a battery of numerical and quality targets. The daily reality for all agents at Excell, and most at 'T', was of repetitive and regimented work. While it is not suggested that the labour process constitutes the *sole* defining feature of these managerial regimes, experience of task performance provides an important contextual influence on the character of humour. Both call centres fell within the 'low trust'/'high regulation' quadrant of Ackroyd and Thompson's 'managerial regime' typology (1999: 88). Consequently, forms of misbehaviour and humour were likely to be characterised by 'recalcitrance/militancy', the predicted outcomes in regimes of direct control.

Despite common characteristics, contrasts exist. First, although both organisations were outsourcers, they differed in relation to their respective client bases and labour utilisation strategies. 'T', a multi-business centre, operating services on behalf of fifteen clients, combined a minority of high-value accounts with low-cost, routine operations, and pursued cost reduction through exploiting flexible internal labour markets. Excell, a telecommunications outsourcer, operated customer inquiry services for cable and mobile phone companies. Cost control was pursued primarily through a labour intensification strategy, so that targets were more rigorously enforced, and monitoring more pervasive than at 'T'. For example, directory inquiry agents took calls every 30 seconds, with call handling times measured to hundredths of a second and agents obliged to spend 97 per cent of working time on 'switch'. 'T' and Excell were comparable managerial regimes, but the latter exercised direct control *in extremis*.

The second contrast concerns employer attitudes towards trade unions and employee representation. Neither company recognised unions, but while 'T' senior management adopted a pragmatic approach, Excell, an Arizona-based multinational, was implacably hostile. Antipathy to unions, rooted in the ideological convictions of the company's founders, was sustained by the business logic driving telecommunications outsourcing. Excell has sought to attract clients through undermining or circumventing existing union agreements. No account of the Excell regime is complete without understanding their antipathy to trade unionism and, indeed, to all forms of dissent. The denial of any employee 'voice', other than through ineffectual internal communication fora, contributed to particular expressions of worker humour.

Third, differences existed in the nature of worker self-organisation. At Excell, a plethora of grievances concerning low pay, bonuses, health and safety, bullying managers, arbitrary disciplinaries and unrealistic targets hardened into a sense of collective injustice, as a group of workers coalesced round a determination to improve conditions (Bain and Taylor, 2000; Taylor and Bain, 2001b, 2002). However, the catalyst for CWU recruitment was managerial malpractice in relation to the emergency services which Excell provided for non-BT companies. To simplify a complex narrative, because management had neglected to update customer records, emergency calls frequently meant that 'fire engines, the police and ambulances were sent to wrong addresses' (Meeting, 29.11.98). The company's obdurate refusal to rectify this problem compelled this group of workers to campaign for remedial action, whilst simultaneously fighting to improve pay and conditions. As management lost legitimacy in many workers' eyes, union membership increased (to 30 per cent of the 350-strong workforce by May 1999). The examples below come from this period of conflict, in which union activists realised that humour could be an effective weapon. In contrast, at 'T', no nascent collective organisation existed to give expression and direction to employee discontent over aspects of work and employment conditions. This absence of collective purpose, allied to a less pressurised experience of work and softer managerial styles, influenced differences in the manifestations of workplace humour at 'T' and Excell.

Humour and subversion/humour as subversion

In both call centres, subversion manifested itself in one of its important modalities as humour and the use of humour. But in Excell, the use of humour took a form quite distinctive from that found in 'T'. Findings from Excell confirm the view that contemporary workplace humour may often have a 'corrosive content', 'being targeted consistently on managerial activities' (Ackroyd and Thompson, 1998: 1). However, evidence from Excell suggests an additional dimension to joking that has yet to be fully acknowledged. Here, a group of workers consciously used humour as a tool to construct an effective opposition to management. They used it in a way that simultaneously sought to undermine management and to advance trade union organisation. There are similarities here with Rodrigues and Collinson's study (1995) in which they describe the utilisation of humour in a Brazilian trade union newspaper, *The Goat*. While they examine the relatively formalised way in which a union used humour 'to highlight inconsistencies in managerial practices and to resist [a] corporate culture campaign' (Rodrigues and Collinson, 1995: 758), we delve deeper by exploring the relationship between union organising and humour at the informal, workplace level. To make this point plausible, it is perhaps necessary to review briefly the workplace humour literature.

As Collinson (1988) and Ackroyd and Thompson (1999) observe, workplace humour has long been acknowledged as an important form of workplace misbehaviour. Ethnographic research has uncovered its persistence, although frequently as an unintended by-product of broader studies (Roy, 1958; Lupton, 1963). However, little agreement exists on the overall purposes and effects of workplace humour, although many commentators do not regard humour as subversive or even potentially so. Collinson (2002) refers to Radcliffe-Brown (1965), who believed humour contributed to consensus and harmony by defusing conflict and acting as a safety valve, and highlights the influence of the functionalist tradition, which rejects the possibility that workplace humour can be radical in its intentions or effects (e.g. Bradney, 1957; Coser, 1959). Hay (2000) provides a recent example of the continuing search for the 'functions' of humour. Others have argued prescriptively that humour can be a useful management tool (Barsoux, 1993) and that in the contemporary workplace managers might usefully utilise humour to motivate employees (Deal and Kennedy, 2000).

Even writers from a more radical and critical tradition have argued that humour acts to defuse tension and sustain hierarchical social relations:

> joking at work plays an important regulatory function by providing a means of expression that assists group cohesion, deflects attention from the dehumanising aspects of work and acts to preserve the existing power hierarchy. In this sense, humour is a vital factor in obscuring the social relations of production, and suppressing the alienating tendencies of work.
>
> (Noon and Blyton, 1997: 159–60)

In contrast, several authors dissent from these views. Linstead (1985) concluded that humour is often closely related to manifestations of resistance and sabotage, creating an informal world outside the strictures of managerial control. Collinson's seminal study (1988) suggested that joking was one way in which work groups defined their identity, distinct from management and other employees. There were three dimensions to workplace humour – resistance, conformity and control. Collinson, however, insisted there were limits to humour as resistance, as it expressed male identities, and a preoccupation with masculinity meant that, ultimately, the bonds established between the workers he studied were superficial. Consequently, Collinson valuably cautions against attempts to romanticise workers' use of humour, and warns us not to neglect sexist, racist and other divisive forms which might serve to undermine the radical potential of humour. In short, he argues, workplace humour is contradictory, combining elements of both resistance and control, so that while often subversive it can also be oppressive.

Ackroyd and Thompson (1998: 7) argue that 'applied humour' – aimed at, targeted at and making fun of someone – is very likely to be found in the workplace. Although the process by which jokes are applied is complicated, many have both butts (whoever the joke is about) and audiences (whom the joke aims to amuse or influence). They identify three types of applied humour – clowning, teasing and satire – differentiated in terms of distinctive butts, audiences, targets, contents and character, which are presented as a typology of joking (1998: 17). Ackroyd and Thompson make a distinctive contribution to the debate by, first, developing four analytical categories of misbehaviour: disagreement over 'the appropriation of work', 'the appropriation of the materials used in work', 'the appropriation of time spent on work' and 'the extent to which employees identify with their work activity and the employer' (1999: 25). This last category encompasses workplace humour and joking. Second, they argue that 'ironic, sardonic and satirical commentary on managerial initiatives … endemic in Britain, have become in the current context, significant forms of misbehaviour' (1999: 10). The gap between managerial rhetoric claiming to prioritise employee opinion, and unchanged work situations, encourages cynical comment. For Ackroyd and

Thompson (1998: 103), joking of this kind constitutes an increasingly prevalent 'undercurrent of satirical debunking of management pretensions'.

The case study evidence is analysed by reference to this critical theoretical context. It is informed by a rejection of the functionalist perspective and by an acknowledgement of the subversive potential of workplace humour. Throughout, a consistent attempt is made to integrate empirical data with the conceptual concerns of these critical authors.

Humour at 'T' – undirected subversion

Humour as relief from boredom and routine

As some workers did make themselves the butt of their own jokes, then clowning did take place. For example, following the company's Christmas party, Andy, who had 'got off' with the daughter of a senior manager, acted out a ritual of self-ridicule. Andy, nicknamed 'Mr Cheese', because of his unctuous telephone manner, clearly could remember his actions on the night in question, but feigned amnesia through excessive alcohol consumption (Observation, 13.12.99). Fellow workers peppered him with questions on both mundane and intimate details, to which Andy responded by acting the dumb fool. This charade was played out in front of fresh audiences as, throughout the day, other workers dropped by to interrogate the 'victim'.

Ackroyd and Thompson's categorisation of humour into clowning, teasing and satirical forms provides a valuable framework with which to observe and analyse manifestations of humour. However, it should be recognised that protagonists may combine different roles and utilise more than one form of humour, as this example of clowning/teasing also included satirical comment which was overtly critical of management. One agent remarked, 'That's the first time a Martin [the surname of manager/daughter] has been fucked over by anyone in here', a perception which highlights the distance between employees and senior management, and displays an appreciation of the realities of power and authority. However, teasing and satirical banter between agents, and between agents and team leaders, were the dominant forms of humour, rather than pure clowning, and took several identifiable forms.

Several agents commented that having a laugh was the only thing that 'kept them going'. In a sales section with particularly rigorous targets, Pat described the effects of incessant call handling, and how the regime was forcing her to 'exit' after eleven months.

> People are unhappy – lots of things but mainly the calls. It seems to go in cycles. A new lot come in bright and fresh, get disillusioned and some leave, then it's new lambs to the slaughter. I probably won't be here next week, because my job interview yesterday went very well. ... This place does your head in, if it wasn't for the jokers here it wouldn't be tolerable.
>
> (Interview, 27.2.00)

A 'community of comedians', to use Collinson's term, made work 'tolerable'. In this community, a hierarchy, based on an ability to make workmates laugh, was discernible, with Mark, Shona and 'Norrie the Hun' best at banter and 'the wind-up'. The community engaged in common practices motivated by the desire to relieve boredom and the frustration of task performance. Agents dealing with irritating, long-winded or slow customers would typically hit their 'mute' button and, when inaudible to customers, make sarcastic comments to close colleagues. Whenever Hughie hit the mute he would say 'What's that all about?' and burst out laughing, expressing amazement at customers' foibles (Observation, 10.12.99). Typical comments included 'Wait till you hear this one', 'That's a new one', 'See these customers, outrageous man!' and 'Thick as fuck!'. Frequently, whilst conversing, agents' eye contact, facial movements and body language would convey similar expressions of frustration and astonishment. Such comments and mannerisms were part of a ritual, creating a sense of expectation amongst fellow workers, eager to hear a full account of these interactions. If the volume of incoming calls was sufficiently low as to create longish breaks between calls (and no supervisor was close), an audience would gather and proceed collectively to 'rip the piss' out of customers, competing to recount examples of their folly. Since 'T' received calls from across the UK, opportunities arose to mimic regional accents, a source of considerable amusement. Catchphrases from a popular Scottish television comedy 'Chewing the Fat' were liberally borrowed, providing a shared medium of comic expression.

Undoubtedly, these are examples of humour as coping or survival strategies (Noon and Blyton, 1997). The primary purpose was to make the day more interesting, providing relief from the routine of call handling. But this behaviour also 'reflected and reinforced a shared sense of self and a group identity and differentiation' (Collinson, 1988: 185), indicating the presence of a distinct organisational subculture in sharp conflict with managerial values and priorities. Verbal abuse of customers, even at a safe distance, certainly ran counter to the principles of company culture. A delightful irony was that whilst agents 'slagged off' customers, suspended from the ceiling above their heads were notices bearing mission statements such as 'Committed to putting the customer's needs first'. In challenging management values, and undermining the customer service ethos, these rituals should be seen as subversive in their effects.

Humour and the erosion of team leader authority

Ackroyd and Thompson argue that workplace struggle is also 'concerned with the matter of identity' (1999: 101). Management, at least rhetorically, has an interest in obtaining greater levels of commitment from its workforce, an objective which may allow employees to express opinions. Of course, such encouragement to openness has sharply defined boundaries, and is permitted insofar as it benefits the organisation. Since the promise, suggested by cultures of openness, may clash with the unchanged reality of routine task performance, workers exploit these limited spaces, inserting expressions of their interests which conflict with management aims. Under these conditions, joking, which is excused from the normal conventions of serious discourse, becomes a means of conducting a satirical attack on management: 'Joking is ... perfectly appropriate when a group with power is espousing a willingness to be intimate, but is still incapable of admitting equality. It is in this sort of situation that joking becomes a useful tool' (Ackroyd and Thompson, 1999: 102).

The joking practices of agents at 'T' confirm these insights, most pointedly in the way that humour was directed at undermining team leaders' authority. Formally, team leaders were responsible for ensuring that the quantity and quality of an agent's call-handling were satisfactory. Unacceptable performance levels ostensibly were to be improved through coaching, although exhortation or chastisement were equally common responses. Most team leaders, recently promoted from the ranks, were encouraged by senior management to maintain informal social contact with erstwhile colleagues. It is the contradiction between team leaders' conventional and directive roles, and the compulsion to act as if they were still 'one of the gang', which gives a distinct edge to the banter directed towards them. Three examples follow.

Taking the piss

When call volumes were low, gossip quickly filled the gaps. On this occasion, the stimulus was the previous Friday's company 'do'. The main topic, inevitably, was employees' ill-behaviour; how drunk so-and-so had been, who had felt which part of whose anatomy and who had got off with whom. Although risqué, the language was never sexist or offensive, with both sexes participating as protagonists and 'victims'. Sanction was given by Monica, the team leader, who having excelled in the consumption of alcohol, was herself the butt of much verbal sparring. For example, 'That dress must have been cheap, you'd only have to pay for half of it, it had no back.' Although two agents, Linda and Mark, came in for 'a proper slagging', the sharpest barbs were directed at Monica. The greatest hilarity occurred when an on-call team member re-entered the conversation and, in trying to catch up, would ask deliberately naive questions, pretending not to know who was being discussed. This kept the joke going and enabled agents to replay their attacks on Monica.

The limits to tolerance

A humorous 'questionnaire' was designed and distributed by Hughie, following management permission, on the grounds that it was a pre-Christmas 'bit of fun'. Everyone was polled on questions like 'Who is the sexiest? The grumpiest? The scariest?' As questionnaires circulated, jokes proliferated as workers considered nominations for various categories. Once again, the principal targets were team leaders, with the unpopular nominated for unwelcome categories; 'Nurse Ratched' won the 'grumpiest' award. Evidently, the questionnaire almost crossed the line of unacceptability as defined by management, as this snatch of conversation reveals.

HUGHIE: We had a question in the first version 'Who is going to get the sack before Christmas?' but we had to take it out because they were cracking up.
AL: Who was cracking up?
HUGHIE: They [management] were cracking up because of what's happening to them (nodding over to campaigns team).
CLARE: That's because they're getting fucked. All temps in campaigns are to be laid off by December 19th.

Team leaders were ambivalent. Although approving the questionnaire, to the extent that some joined in discussing nominations, a line was drawn when it strayed from what was defined as harmless fun and touched on sensitive issues. Team leaders even attempted to stifle spontaneity by insisting that completed questionnaires were returned to Monica so that she could compile the results. Such an approach tacitly acknowledges that creative joking in a workplace regime of this kind can never be purely harmless. Completed questionnaires revealed how workers enthusiastically seized the opportunity to deride both team leaders and those agents regarded as 'yes men'.

Je ne parle pas Français

Astonishingly, the manager of a French language section was unable to speak the native tongue of the majority of team members. Inevitably, this generated operating problems and undermined supervisory authority. On one celebrated occasion, the manager sat beside an agent in order to monitor calls, asking him to translate customer queries and his responses. Months later, the memory of this farcical incident induced wholesale derision of both the hapless manager and the company (Observation, 19.3.00). Two agents, Diane and Saul, described how, after the failure of this monitoring exercise, the manager continued to hover near the French team, clearly within earshot of agents' conversations. Saul recollected that after a call had ended and the customer had hung up, he continued talking, pretending it was still live. He finished by saying, in French, 'Thank you very much for calling. We will send someone round to kill your wife and family.' Agents at adjacent workstations were scarcely able to contain their laughter. The manager's humiliation was complete when Saul reported, in English, how successful the call had been. It matters little that this story was embellished in the retelling. What is significant is that it continued, months afterwards, to be a source of great amusement, and had come to symbolise managerial incompetence. The French speakers constituted a work group with a high degree of self-organisation, and their scathing humour served to widen the gap between themselves and the company.

These examples reveal a deep undercurrent of distrust of management motives, and the medium of humour conveyed a subtle, but frequently overt, criticism of supervisory authority. Such evidence challenges Noon and Blyton's (1997) claim that joking always obscures the social relations of production. Management's attempts to close the gap between team leaders and agents, through encouraging familiarity, proved largely unsuccessful. Agents used humour in order to clarify exactly where the boundaries of authority lay, subverting the attempt to humanise supervisors through an 'all pals together' culture. Supervisors' efforts to sponsor fun, or control banter, tended to be counterproductive. Out of earshot, agents would share their minor triumphs in what was certainly a battle for identity, but was much more besides. Their actions invoked an older tradition of not letting the foreman get away with anything.

Cynicism about management in general

There is nothing novel in the circulation of cartoons, slogans, poems, stories and gobbets of home-spun philosophising, delivering pithy, humorous or ironic messages, frequently of the 'you don't have to be mad to work here, but it helps' kind. The proportion containing satirical attacks on management may have increased at the expense of the more anodyne, although it is difficult to be certain about this. Some are authored within the workplace and contain references unique to the organisation, while others are generic, passed by hand, or now, frequently, forwarded as email attachments or downloaded from the internet. Whilst such cyber-humour can be experienced by employees as oppressive (Collinson, 2002: 277) many of the examples intercepted at 'T' caused great amusement as they circulated through networks of trusted colleagues, and should be seen as subversive. They recurrently mock policies and values held dear by management, or draw attention to the reality of managerial controls on activities. Whatever their precise targets, they typically contribute to a sense of the distance between employees and employers.

Summary

The significance of humour at 'T' as a means of overcoming tedium, and providing some relief from work pressures, should not be underestimated. Nor should its satirical force, directed at managerial targets, be underplayed. Yet, for all the caustic wit and sarcasm, this was directionless subversion, unconnected to any conscious strategy of challenging managerial 'frontiers of control' or improving working conditions. This is not so say that the humour lacked purpose. The experience of the labour process, the relatively poor pay and rewards package, and the contractual insecurity of temps, guaranteed that, given any opportunity, barbs would fly at the employer and managers, who promised much and delivered little. The point is that undermining management through humour, though undeniably corrosive of authority, was not accompanied by a conscious and broader challenge to the employer, unlike that which developed at Excell. Two years on, despite sporadic leafleting forays by two unions, the workforce at 'T' remains unorganised.

Excelling in humour – conscious and directed subversion

The 'bad boys'

At Excell, managers and supervisors themselves were largely responsible for becoming the objects of relentless and unforgiving joking. The incessant pressure to meet targets and their intimidation of certain workers made some managers extremely unpopular. Further, management unwittingly contributed to the formation of an oppositional group by dubbing individuals seen as troublesome as the 'bad boys'. The more managers took petty disciplinary action against these malcontents, the more they cohered as a group and developed common forms of expression and identity through a set of shared beliefs. Humour facilitated the formation of this 'out group', uniting disparate individuals into collective organisation.

> I think it [humour] was the glue that initially made collective action possible. Without that, people had no obvious reason to feel warmth, or commitment, or comradeship for anyone else. We had to develop a sort of kinship and emotional feelings and support for each other because we were up against it … it didn't happen organically, it happened quite deliberately.
>
> (Interview, Gary, 12.12.00)

The fact that this group of dissidents was funny made them, and the union with which they were identified, more attractive.

> Once people saw they could sit and have a laugh with everybody who was involved, that was really important. And the common ground that people shared was their ability to laugh at these fools who were nominally controlling them.
>
> (Interview, Gary, 12.12.00)

Humour as part of a conscious strategy of undermining management

> Oh aye, it was always about a means to an end. It was never a case of misbehaving for the sake of it – well I liked misbehaving and having a laugh anyway – but it was done for a reason.
>
> (Interview, Jimbo, 22.6.00)

Management was ridiculed as part of a deliberate strategy of undermining authority. The activists' main objective was to demonstrate to fellow workers that nobody need be frightened of management. Belittling superiors, particularly those most deserving of retribution, without incurring subsequent reprisals, could successfully erode deference to authority. The jokes, mocking and lampoonery enabled serious messages to be communicated. The following examples demonstrate both the inventive ways in which authority was undermined and a sophisticated understanding of the role of the audience.

> We would turn the whole scenario of control on its head, so that fools could be kings for the day. If you say in front of a manager, 'I can't believe this man earns £20,000 a year, have you seen his shoes?' the allure can be shattered just by saying something as foolish as this.
>
> (Interview, Gary, 12.12.00)

> People like Sammy were really effective. He would develop a routine, which he would use at every opportunity to berate managers, but in a way that they couldn't discipline him because the questions he was asking were part of normal conversation. He would ask managers questions that made absolutely no sense, like 'What's your favourite colour Roy?' and the conversation would go like this 'I don't know, I don't have a favourite colour.' 'You must have a favourite colour, everybody's got one.' And when you ask managers questions like that they immediately become wary, because they don't know where it's leading. So Roy would walk away. Ten minutes later Sammy would be standing right next to him saying, 'Have you got that answer for me? What's the colour, Roy?' 'I don't know.' 'Come on, I'm asking you what your favourite colour is.' On and on like that. We would create a situation where people working beside us could see what it was like to make managers, who would normally humiliate them, seem inadequate. And it was really important because this was happening in a public space with an audience. It didn't have any meaning unless people could see it happening.
>
> (Interview, Colin, 15.6.00)

Such was the contempt for particular managers, that mocking rituals were interspersed with vicious humour, like this humiliation of a recently promoted and deeply unpopular individual.

> It was just before Christmas Eve, one of those nights when we were all in high spirits. … The others were saying to me, 'Do something to Frank'. So I ripped a Christmas card off one of the boards, scored out the name and used my left hand to write 'Merry Christmas, from your friends at Excell, you prick, enjoy your new career as a manager'. Jack had a condom, so we got chicken soup out of the machine, waited till it was cold, poured it into the condom, made a wee prick at the end so that the soup dripped out, stapled it to his Christmas card, folded it up and put it in his locker. When he came in next morning we were still on shift. He got the chicken soup over him and went mental. He didn't know who had done it, but I told everybody that it was me, so it must have got back to him but he never did anything.
>
> (Interview, Jimbo, 22.6.00)

No action could be taken against the suspected perpetrator, for this would have drawn attention to the manager's own humiliation, inviting further ridicule. Managers had 'tittle tattle' about their private lives thrown back at them. One received the following broadside after delivering a 'motivating' team briefing, 'Well, I know when you are not here you sit in the house all afternoon smoking dope. I can't believe you are not more laid back at work' (Interview, Dave, 20.2.00). Again a manager has been targeted as the butt and is powerless to respond. The banter has a serious subtext, which goes something like this, 'If you do not stop cracking the whip, we will let it be known to senior managers what you do in your spare time.' The most disliked managers, 'total company men', were given nicknames like the 'Crafty Christian' or 'Tricky Dicky', which served to reinforce group solidarity and sharpen the sense of distance between 'them' and 'us'. These examples hardly convey the full repertoire of parody and invective directed at individual managers in what the activists saw as a never-ending war of attrition.

Challenging the rules, subverting company culture

Ackroyd and Thompson's (1999: 105) suggestion that sets of values underpinning workplace humour are evidence of 'a distinct organisational subculture' is confirmed by workers' *mis*behaviour at Excell. So too is their observation that a distinctive subculture often becomes 'a more pointedly critical and overtly satirical counter-culture' whose existence is evident in workers' challenges to formal rules. Collectively, agents decided to conform to the company's dress code, which they regarded as both unnecessary and expensive, in a particular manner.

> When you were nominally following the rules, you would do so in such a way as to be subversive. The dress code changed and we were told, 'You have to wear a shirt and tie'. So we got word round, 'Tomorrow, wear shirts and ties that make us look as unprofessional as possible'. I wore a tie about four or five inches wide, illustrating the history and future of the motor car in glorious technicolour, along with a purple-checked shirt. Everybody dressed like this and there was nothing managers could do.
>
> (Interview, Gary, 12.12.00)

This incident reveals a remarkable degree of collectivity in both thought and deed, justifying the assessment that satire of this kind proves the existence of a vigorous counter-culture. One further incident, debunking Excell's corporate culture, demonstrates how even spontaneous acts were informed by powerful collective identities.

> One night a manager … was showing new starts round, and he passed the mission statement, which was prominently displayed on a wall. Suddenly, he remembered he had ten people in tow and he hadn't pointed it out to them. So he led them back and started reading it when, spontaneously, about ten

> of us stood up and saluted him, singing 'The Star Spangled Banner'. And, of course, these new starts got the message that there was no respect for either management or company.
>
> (Interview, Dave, 9.3.99)

The ace joker

A group of workers were defined by management, and defined themselves, as 'bad boys'. They shared a common identity, and the comic code which informed their activity was allied to the wider purpose of combating an employer they regarded as unjust. Notwithstanding the collective nature of this undertaking, the leading role of one individual in the unionisation campaign has been recognised (Taylor and Bain, 2001b, 2002). So must the unique contribution of Jimbo, as the initiator of many practical jokes, be acknowledged. He adopted the roles of clown, tease and satirist, sometimes combining all three to great subversive effect, and sporadically used humour of the blackest kind, as with the episode of Frank and the Christmas card.

> Sometimes it was quite frightening and disturbing stuff. For example, Jimbo would leave cards lying around on managers' desks with one word, 'liar', written on them, and then wait for a reaction. Or he would go through memos with a fine toothcomb correcting the grammar and send them back to management, asking them to correct them before he would consider reading them.
>
> (Interview, Gary, 12.12.00)

Openly gay, 'he would always use his campness as a way of undermining management and winning people over' (Interview, Dave, 8.3.00) and was simultaneously 'very funny, camp, bitchy and very hard, taking people on all the time'. A frequent ploy was to 'slaughter' a manager's dress sense or appearance, pushing what was permissible as banter to the very limits. Jimbo would also connect managers to the Samaritans or live sex lines and relish their embarassment. He could get away with all this because he would exploit both his own popularity and managers' stereotypical expectations of a gay man. He could say and do things that managers would not have tolerated in others. No manager contemplated disciplining him, for it would have been counter-productive. The range of misbehaviour that Jimbo, and those inspired by him, engaged in is impressive. Clowning and yearning to escape routine call handling certainly motivated much joking, but this was ultimately connected to the more serious purpose of undermining management.

Humour and trade union organisation

At Excell, the boundary between subversive humour and conscious trade union activity was frequently blurred as, for example, when internal communication forums were subverted.

> We would write our demands on flip charts, but not on the first page. They would [later] be giving a briefing, using the flip chart, and when they turned a page they would find 'Parity for Glasgow and Birmingham'. They knew my writing and accused me but I denied it. They would insist, 'It was your writing.' I would say, 'Did you see me writing it?' The manager would go 'No' and I would say, 'Shut up then.' And that would be that, because I would be backed up, and they couldn't prove it. We would always back each other.
>
> (Interview, Jimbo, 22.6.00)

Hundreds of union leaflets were photocopied during night shifts, slipped under keyboards or placed in mail bins, and in the morning managers would 'go ballistic'. The leaflets had a serious purpose, calling on management to solve '999' service problems, or raising demands over pay and conditions. They might contain confidential data on company profitability or turnover, information appropriated from managers' desks (an example of pilfering for collective purposes). However, the distribution of serious leaflets was interspersed with scathing satire in the form of poems or, in this case, 'a recipe':

Leaflet 1: 'A recipe for disaster'

– A RECIPE FOR DISASTER –

TAKE

ONE BUCKET OF TAX DODGING GRANTS
TWENTY HORSES ARSES TO RUN THE PLACE
ONE PRIZE COCKSUCKER (AMERICAN IS BEST)

CHOP TWO GRAND OFF THE AVERAGE CALL CENTRE WAGE
DICE WITH DEATH AND A FAULTY DATABASE
TENDERISE THE SAPS THAT BELIEVE YOU

SPRINKLE LIBERALLY WITH LIES AND DECEIT

PLACE THE LOT IN A FUCKED UP ECONOMY AND HEAT FOR FOUR YEARS UNTIL IT REACHES BOILING POINT. THEN SIT ON YOUR FAT FUCKING ARSES AND DO SWEET FANNY ADAMS DRIVING AROUND IN YOUR FUCKING FREE MERCEDES WHILE WE ALL GET REPETITIVE STRAIN SYNDROME IN OUR EARS FROM LISTENING TO THE SAME SHITE YEAR AFTER BASTARD YEAR, THAT YOU DON'T EVEN RECOGNISE.

THEN GO AND FUCK YOURSELVES.

By general agreement, managers' furious reaction to the 'recipe' made this Jimbo's most effective satirical act. The content is not only funny, but succinctly gets to the heart of corporate priorities and the realities of work. Two days later, union membership cards were placed under the same keyboards and in the same mail bins, as the activists consciously linked their satirical attack on Excell with an open appeal to join the union.

The evidence from Excell suggests a paradox, in that while the company was profoundly anti-union and hostile to dissent, managers appeared impotent in the face of this satirical onslaught. This can be explained by reference to several factors, which emerge from a fuller analysis of developments at Excell (see Bain and Taylor, 2000; Taylor and Bain, 2001b, 2002). First, during the period in which these examples of humour occurred, a delicate balance of power existed between union activists and management. Fearful of further public exposure of malpractice in relation to service provision by the activists, and unsure of the strength of an increasingly confident workplace union, management acted cautiously. So extensive was the support for these counter-cultural activities and their instigators that attempts to sack individuals could prove counter-productive. A recent attempt to discipline, with the intention of dismissing, a leading unionist had collapsed in the face of widespread opposition from fellow workers and an impeccably constructed defence. Following what was seen as union victory, a chastened management was forced onto the defensive, allowing union activists the space to continue their organising (and humourous) activities.

This amounted to no more than a temporary postponement of Excell's desire to rid themselves of troublesome elements. In March 2000, Excell embarked on a course of repression, dismissing two leading unionists for gross misconduct, following a television report exposing poor working conditions. However, the victimisations proved to be a Pyrrhic victory, as the attendant publicity further damaged the company's reputation, precipitating a decision by the main client to replace Excell with a new outsourcing company (Vertex). Significantly, in the longer term the campaign to unionise the workforce and gain recognition has proved successful. In March 2002, 99.4 per cent voted for union recognition across the three former Excell call centres, demonstrating both the widespread degree of identification with the union and the enduring legacy left by activists from the period we have examined.

Conclusion

The evidence from both case studies suggests that 'pure' clowning was relatively rare, and shaded into teasing and satire. Overwhelmingly, satire, sometimes vicious in character and directed at individual supervisors or management in general, was the most common form of humour. Long-acknowledged motives behind joking were also apparent, particularly relief from boredom and routine. On occasions, the attempt to escape alienation took call centre-specific forms, as with the denigration of customers at 'T'.

Similarly, Collinson's (1988) observation that humour reflected and reinforced a shared sense of group identity is confirmed. Humour and joking contributed to the development of attitudes standing in sharp contrast to managerial values and priorities. Workers created 'counter-cultures', in which alternative values were clearly articulated, although the process went further at Excell. Gary displayed a sophisticated understanding of how the deliberate use of humour bolstered an oppositional culture.

> The beauty of it was this. Managers didn't understand the humour, the workers understood it, which is a complete reversion of what normally happens in the workplace, where managers are briefed in advance in terms of how they are going to behave and disseminate information. We reversed the process, we knew what *we* were doing.
>
> (Interview, Gary, 12.12.00)

Both call centres witnessed the erosion of team leaders' authority. However, satire at 'T' tended to be opportunistic, more a reflex. Although ridiculing managers was often spontaneous at Excell, targets were frequently selected in advance and tactics planned.

There is no evidence from these cases that the subversive effects of humour were undermined by divisions created by sexism or narrow preoccupations with masculine identity, as Collinson found. From the perspective of gender analysis, the locations raise interesting comparisons and contrasts. In both, the gender composition was about 50/50, with little sexual division of labour amongst agents but, common to many call centres, women were strongly represented in front-line supervision. At 'T', women participated in joking rituals equally with men, and some were leading comedians. To the extent that sexist humour was present, the banter tended to be even-handed with women equally dishing it out but, for the most part, humour was risqué rather than sexist. At Excell, there was a 'laddish' element to the humour, which the union activists came to acknowledge and sought to combat, particularly when more women joined the CWU and some became leading members. However, as several participants recalled, more significant was the camp quality of much of the humour, stimulated by Jimbo's presence, which makes it difficult to squeeze the joking into a neat category of masculinity.

Overall, Ackroyd and Thompson's central propositions are confirmed, namely that sardonic and satirical humour is common in the contemporary workplace, and there is deep distrust of management motives which pretensions to openness encourages. Yet, this leaves open questions of explanatory purchase which a critical realist approach emphasises. Causal mechanisms operating in the 'real' domain include here the economic markets in which both outsourced call centres compete, the existence of forms of work organisation based upon quantitative imperatives and effected through managerial regimes of direct control, and distinctive strategies of labour utilisation. These, it is argued, were necessary but insufficient conditions for the generation of subversive humour amongst call centre agents in both locations. However, for their actualisation, it is necessary to consider the importance of the interaction between these 'managerial regimes' and workers' self-organisation. That is to say there was no pre-determined inevitability to the emergence of events of humorous dissent. It is only through the actions of agents – in both philosophical and literal senses – that there developed vigorous, creative and unpredictable forms of comic misbehaviour.

Yet the uses of humour differed between the locations. It was the contrasting combinations of managerial culture, labour process, company attitudes to trade unionism and dissent which helped impart a different character to humour at 'T' and Excell. Although subversive at both locations, humour was more biting, even nasty, at Excell, with activists seeking an audience of fellow workers to inflict the maximum humiliation on managers. Undoubtedly, there was more to rail against at Excell, but the most important factor was collective organisation, the presence of incipient workplace trade unionism, *the key aspect of agency*. The activists were instrumental in their use of humour, clear in the knowledge that it helped make them and the union popular, and served to weaken managerial authority and legitimacy. Subversive satire was allied to a wider collective purpose while, at 'T', despite the piss-taking and creative satire, the widespread use of humour against management and its values did not lead to trade union organisation. At Excell, union recognition and negotiated improvements in pay and conditions were long-term objectives. With the qualified exception of Rodrigues and Collinson (1995), the literature fails to consider the role that workplace humour can play in trade union organising campaigns.

It is impossible to disentangle the precise contribution that humour played in the ultimately successful unionisation campaign from that which derived from formal organising activities. However, the evidence does support the conclusion that the informal category of resistance and misbehaviour, and the formal category of organisation, should not be analytically polarised, where work groups are prepared to use an array of both creative and more conventional means to challenge managerial legitimacy. It was the relationship between the two which gave a distinctively effective edge to organising activities at Excell.

Finally, the efflorescence of humourous activities at a subterranean level, that is beneath the organisational surface, delivers a further blow to those who liken the call centre to an electronic prison. Resistance, disobedience and collective organisation have emerged in familiar and novel ways in these most contemporary of workplaces.

Acknowledgements

The authors would like to thank Stephen Ackroyd, Paul Thompson and David Collinson for helpful suggestions. Three anonymous referees made valuable critical comments which assisted the passage of an earlier version to *Organisation Studies*.

Notes

1 ESRC award number L212 25 2006, 'Employment and Working Life Beyond the Year 2000: Two Emerging Employment Sectors', undertaken by the authors and colleagues from the Universities of Strathclyde (Nick Bonzienolis, Dirk Bunzel, Kay Gilbert, Cliff Lockyer, Marks, Gareth Mulvey, Dora Scholarios, Aileen Watson and the late Harvie Ramsay), Stirling (Chris Baldry, Gregor Gall) and Aberdeen (Jeff Hyman).

2 Pratten (2000) has convincingly demonstrated the compatibility of critical realism with Marx's analysis of the labour process. Unfortunately, his summary dismissal of Braverman and subsequent labour process writers is unwarranted, and ignores the significant contributions made by, *inter alia*, Thompson, Burawoy, Friedman, Littler, Edwards and Armstrong to our undertsanding of the capitalist labour process, writers whose work may well also have been considered from a realist perspective.

3 It is striking also how closely this approach corresponds to the sense of Marx's well-known passage in *Surveys from Exile* about man making history but not in circumstances of their own choosing (Marx, 1973).

References

Ackroyd, S. and Fleetwood, S. (eds) (2000) *Realist Perspectives on Organization and Management*, London: Routledge.

Ackroyd, S. and Thompson, P. (1998) 'No laughing matter? on the practicality of practical jokes: teasing, clowning and satire in the workplace', paper presented at the Work, Employment and Society Conference, University of Cambridge.

—— (1999) *Organizational* Mis*behaviour*, London: Sage.

Bain, P. and Taylor, P. (1999) 'Employee relations, worker attitudes and trade union representation in call centres', paper presented at the 17th International Labour Process Conference, University of London.

—— (2000) 'Entrapped by the "electronic Panopticon"? Worker resistance in the call centre', *New Technology, Work and Employment*, 15 (1): 2–18.

Bain, P., Watson, A., Mulvey, G., Taylor, P. and Gall, G. (2002) 'Taylorism, targets and the quantity–quality dichotomy in call centres', *New Technology, Work and Employment*, 17 (3): 154–69.

Barsoux, J.-L. (1993) *Funny Business: Humour, Management and Business Culture*, New York: Cassell.

Batt, R. (2000) 'Strategic segmentation in front-line services', *International Journal of Human Resource Management*, 11 (3): 540–61.

Bhaskar, R. (1979) *A Realist Theory of Science*, New York: Harvester.

—— (1986) *Scientific Realism and Human Emancipation*, London: Verso.

—— (1989) *Reclaiming Reality*, London: Verso.

Blyton, P. and Turnbull, P. (1998) *The Dynamics of Employee Relations*, Basingstoke: Macmillan.

Bradley, H., Erickson, M., Stephenson, C. and Williams, S. (2000) *Myths at Work*, Oxford: Polity.

Bradney, P. (1957) 'The joking relationship in industry', *Human Relations* 10: 179–87.

Braverman, H. (1974) *Labour and Monopoly Capital*, New York: Monthly Review Press.

Brown, A., Fleetwood, S. and Roberts, J.M. (eds) (2002) *Critical Realism and Marxism*, London: Routledge.

Bryson, A. and McKay, S. (1997) 'What about the workers?', in R. Jowell and J. Curtice (eds), *British Social Attitudes: The 14th Report*, Aldershot: Ashgate, pp. 23–47.

Callaghan, G. and Thompson, P. (2001) 'Edwardes revisited: technical control and call centres', *Economic and Industrial Democracy*, 22 (1): 13–36.
Collier, A. (1994) *Critical Realism*, London: Verso.
Collinson, D. (1988) 'Engineering humour: masculinity, joking and conflict in shop floor relations', *Organization Studies*, 9 (2): 181–99.
—— (2002) 'Managing humour', *Journal of Management Studies*, 39 (3): 269–88.
Coser, R. (1959) 'Some social functions of laughter: a study of humour in a hospital setting', *Human Relations*, 12: 171–82.
Davies, J. (2001) 'Labour disputes in 2000', *Labour Market Trends*, 109 (6): 301–14.
Deal, T. and Kennedy, A. (2000) *The New Corporate Cultures*, London: Texere.
Easton, Geoff (2000) 'Case research as a method for industrial networks: a realist apologia', in S. Ackroyd and S. Fleetwood (eds), *Realist Perspectives on Management and Organization*, London: Routledge.
Fernie, S. and Metcalf, D. (1998) *(Not) Hanging on the Telephone: Payment Systems in the New Sweatshops*, London: London School of Economics, Centre for Economic Performance.
Fleetwood, S. (2002) 'What kind of theory is Marx's theory of value? A critical realist inquiry', in A. Brown, S. Fleetwood and J.M. Roberts (eds), *Critical Realism and Marxism*, London: Routledge.
Hay, J. (2000) 'Functions of humour in the conversations of men and women', *Journal of Pragmatics*, 32 (6): 709–42.
Hicks, S. (2000) 'Trade union membership 1998–99', *Labour Market Trends*, 108 (7).
HSE (2001) *Advice Regarding Call Centre Working Practices*, London: Health and Safety Executive, Local Authority Unit.
Hutchinson, S., Purcell, J. and Kinnie, N. (2000) 'Evolving high commitment management and the experience of the RAC call centre', *Human Resource Management Journal*, 10 (1): 63–78.
Kelly, J. (1998) *Rethinking Industrial Relations*, London: Routledge.
Knights, D. and McCabe, D. (1998) 'What happens when the phone goes wild? Staff, stress and spaces for escape in a BPR telephone banking work regime', *Journal of Management Studies*, 35 (2): 163–94.
Linstead, S. (1985) 'Jokers wild: the importance of humour and the maintenance of organisational culture', *The Sociological Review*, 33 (4): 741–67.
Lipton, P. (1993) *Inference to the Best Explanation*, London: Routledge.
Lupton, T. (1963) *On the Shop Floor: Two Studies of Workplace Organisation and Output*, Oxford: Pergamon Press.
Marx, K. (1973) *Surveys from Exile* (*Political Writings*, Volume 2), ed. and with an intro by D. Fernbach, Harmondsworth: Penguin; London: New Left Review.
Noon, M. and Blyton, P. (1997) *The Realities of Work*, Basingstoke: Macmillan.
Porter, S. (2000) 'Critical realist ethnography: the case of racism and professionalism in a medical setting', in S. Ackroyd and S. Fleetwood (eds), *Realist Perspectives on Organization and Management*, London: Routledge.
Pratten, S. (2000) 'Structure, agency and Marx's analysis of the labour process', in S. Ackroyd and S. Fleetwood (eds), *Realist Perspectives on Organization and Management*, London: Routledge, pp. 109–38.
Radcliffe-Brown, A.R. (1965) *Structure and Function in Primitive Society*, London: Cohen and West.
Reeves, R. (2001) *Happy Mondays: Putting the Pleasure Back into Work*, London: Momentum.
Rodrigues, S. and Collinson, D. (1995) ' "Having fun?" Humour as resistance in Brazil', *Organization Studies*, 16 (5): 739–68.

Roy, D. (1958) 'Banana time: job satisfaction and informal interaction', *Human Organisation*, 18 (1): 158–61.

Sewell, G. and Wilkinson, B. (1992) 'Human resource management in "surveillance" companies', in J. Clark (ed.), *Human Resource Management and Technical Change*, London: Sage, pp. 137–55.

Stephenson, C. and Stewart, P. (2001) 'The whispering shadow: collectivism and individualism at Ikeda-Hoover and Nissan UK', Sociological Research Online, 6 (3). Online at: http://www.socresonline.org.uk/6/3/stephenson.html

Taylor, P. and Bain, P. (1999) '"An assembly line in the head": work and employee relations in the call centre', *Industrial Relations Journal*, 30 (2): 101–17.

—— (2001a) 'Trade unions, workers' rights and the frontier of control in UK call centres', *Economic and Industrial Democracy*, 22 (1): 39–66.

—— (2001b) 'Two steps forward, one step back: interest definition organisation and dissipated mobilisation amongst call centre workers', paper presented at the 19th International Labour Process Conference, University of London.

—— (2002) 'Call centre organising in adversity: from Excell to Vertex', in G. Gall (ed.), *Union Organising*, London: Routledge.

Taylor, P., Mulvey, G., Hyman, J. and Bain, P. (2002) 'Work organisation, control and the experience of work in call centres', *Work, Employment and Society*, 16 (1): 133–50.

Thompson, P. and Ackroyd, S. (1995) 'All quiet on the workplace front? A critique of recent trends in British industrial sociology', *Sociology*, 29 (4): 610–33.

Thompson, P. and Smith, C. (2000) 'Follow the redbrick road: reflections on pathways in and out of the labour process debate', *International Studies of Management and Organization*, 30 (4): 40–67.

Tsoukas, H. (2000) 'What is management? An outline of a metatheory', in S. Ackroyd, and S. Fleetwood (eds), *Realist Perspectives on Management and Organization*, London: Routledge.

13 Tracing the effects of a hospital merger

Ruth Kowalczyk

Introduction to research area

This chapter focuses on the study of three hospitals in the process of a Trust merger. Fieldwork concentrated primarily on seeing the merger through the eyes of a developing directorate, the Critical Care Directorate. The directorate incorporated intensive care, accident and emergency, theatre and chronic pain services. The researcher's main access to this process was the observation of directorate meetings, initially between all head nurses and directorate management, and later involving clinicians. This was supplemented by interviews, particularly with those associated directly with intensive care. Whilst the prime focus of this research is the intensive care service, this chapter aims to analyse the success of the merger process by tracing its effects across the directorate.

Why critical realism?

Within realism there is an appreciation of the fact that mechanisms act differently depending on the context, and so the relationship between causal mechanisms and their effects is contingent rather than fixed. Pawson and Tilley (1997) propose a structured approach to realist research wherein the researcher identifies the mechanism, the context in which it is working and its outcome. Both the advantages and disadvantages of this approach stem from its simplicity.

There is some concern within realism about realism's usefulness to the researcher at a practical level. Pawson and Tilley's approach provides the researcher with a way of structuring realist research. However, this simplification does not encourage the researcher to consider what exactly mechanisms or context are. Context appears to subsume everything apart from one particular mechanism and its outcome, and hence subsumes the interaction of other mechanisms with the prime object of study. In addition, the approach takes no account of feedback or of the importance of time. If a mechanism interacts with an entity's structure, causal powers and interrelationships, then the effects of exercising such power will in many cases affect that entity's structure. Archer stresses both of these features. Archer (1995: 157) emphasises the importance of understanding the structures at time T1, that is before the mechanism has been

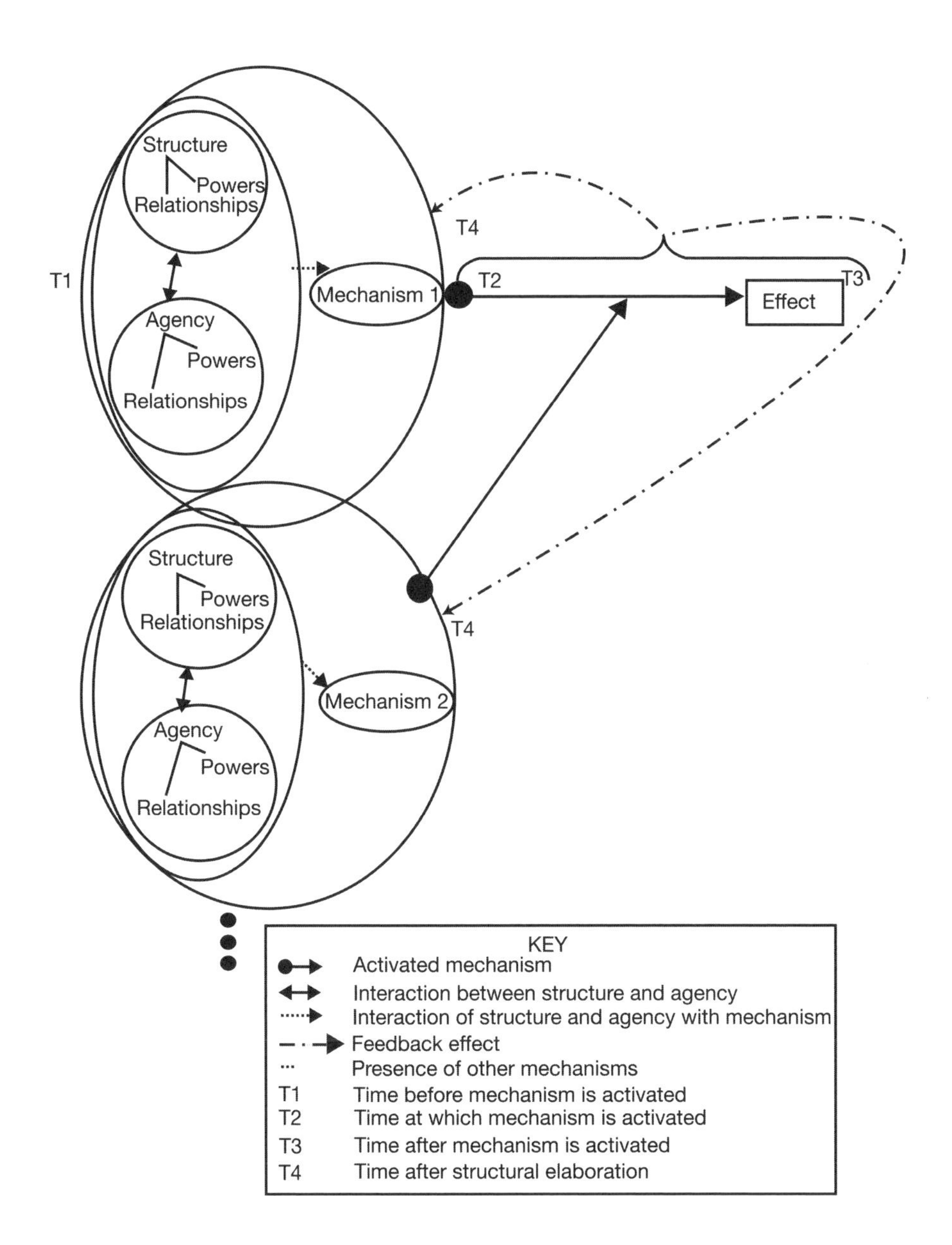

Figure 13.1 A practical realist approach to research

activated. The mechanism is then activated between times T2 and T3, followed by elaboration of the structure and potentially a changed structure at time T4. Archer's presentation incorporates both the effects of the mechanism's activation on structure and the importance of time, but focuses primarily on structural elaboration. As such, a combination of this work with that of Pawson and Tilley may perhaps be even more beneficial to the realist researcher undertaking practical research.

Figure 13.1 depicts the fact that within the immediate context of a mechanism are the structures and agents that interact with it. Within its wider context are other potentially interacting mechanisms, e.g. mechanism 2 and others, as well as those structures and agents interacting with these mechanisms. Dotted arrows represent feedback effects while T1–T4 represent the stages in time referred to in Archer's morphogenetic cycle. The diagram represents the fact that when a mechanism is activated it may be changed by its activation; the structures and their associated powers and interrelationships may be changed either by the activation of the mechanism or by the interaction of structure with agency; agents and their own powers and interrelationships may be changed either by their own actions or by the interaction of structure and agency. This elaboration of structure and agency applies equally to those mechanisms interacting with the prime object of study. One limitation of this presentation is the loss of the linearity of time, well represented in Archer's work. In addition there is an implication that structural change happens after the mechanism has been activated. Changes to both structure and agency might commence as soon as a mechanism has been triggered. Bearing in mind these limitations, this presentation aided the researcher in analysing the merger process.

The merger process

Pre-merger structure and relationships

Let me begin by providing a brief description of the three hospitals concerned. DGH1 and DGH2 were moderately sized district general hospitals while CH3 was a community hospital providing a much more limited range of services. To meet the Royal College's standards for junior doctors' training a certain diversity of service provision is required, and CH3 was not in a position to provide this. The same group of clinicians served DGH1 and CH3.

Whilst DGH1 was reasonably accessible from outside its natural catchment area, DGH2 was geographically isolated. The effects of this isolation could be seen in the problems DGH2 had with recruiting medical staff. While nursing staff tended to be drawn from the local population this could not be said for the medical profession and geographical isolation had led at times to a shortfall in medical staffing.

In addition DGH2 in particular had financial problems. The local health authority was under a lot of pressure, having the second lowest growth rate for income nationally because it had been adjudged by the RAWP (Resource

Allocation Working Party) formula to have too high an allocation per head of population, so growth monies were low until they came in line with the formula used.

> There is a longer term argument about whether it is appropriate to fund semi-rural areas in the same way as urban areas … there should be an allowance made for the fact that a Trust that is 50 miles long with three hospitals in it has fixed overheads that are very much larger than an urban population of the same size would be.
>
> (Clinical Director, Interview, January 1999)

The area served by both DGH2 and CH3 was largely rural, and the formula used to allocate funding in health care made no allowance for rurality.

The management structure of the three hospitals was very different. DGH1 had had a directorate structure for about two years at the time of the merger, with the Critical Care Directorate containing intensive care, accident and emergency, theatres and chronic pain services. Each department was responsible for managing a budget covering all their expenditure except medical staff. Responsibility for certain other management functions had been devolved to non-management staff. In intensive care, sisters each had areas of responsibility, such as health and safety. DGH2 had no directorate for anaesthetics or ICU, had absent or inadequate devolved budgets, and major decisions remained at chief executive level. This arrangement was both less structured and more centralised than that of DGH1. At CH3 there was a centralised management style with the hospital being run by the executive directors.

The under-development of management support at DGH2 and CH3 seemed to have led to under-development in other areas. The lack of devolvement of responsibility meant that staff at DGH2 and CH3 seemed to have less understanding of the 'system' and 'how to work it'. DGH2 also appeared to have been penalised financially; for instance, levels of staffing were noticeably lower. This had led to the needs of, for example, intensive care at the two sites being significantly different. When the two Directorate Nurses in intensive care were asked to identify areas of importance, they came up with significantly different areas of importance – while intensive care at DGH2 focused on basic needs, DGH1 were able to focus on development.

There was also a difference in culture highlighted to some extent by DGH2 staff's comments that before the merger DGH2 had a family atmosphere with most of the staff knowing each other, or their families, from outside work. Different areas tended to do each other favours, then return them.

Pre-merger positions suggested that DGH1 was in a dominant role. The financial and recruitment problems at DGH2 as well as their geographical isolation implied that DGH2 needed the merger more than DGH1 did. Since medics based at CH3 had their prime allegiance to DGH1, CH3 appeared to be in the least powerful position. However, there was an additional twist – whilst in general DGH2 could be seen to be in a subordinate position to DGH1, as far as the clinicians were concerned recruitment problems meant that it was important to 'try and keep them on board' (Clinical Director, Interview, January 1999).

Objectives of the merger

The Trust merger was originally presented as a management merger. The reasons given in the proposal were as follows:

- The maintenance and improvement of locally provided clinically effective services approved to national standards.
- To ensure the provision of high quality specialist services locally, e.g. cancer services.
- To continue to meet the very high training standards demanded by the Royal Colleges for junior doctors and other professional staff.
- To respond to financial pressures in the system which could threaten the future viability of local services.
- To make best use of all the available resources.

(Merger proposal, pre-April 1998)

Looking more closely at the proposal one could identify other intentions. These included:

- 'attracting clinicians'; and
- cross-site working.

Cross-site working seemed to apply not only to management but also to clinicians, as suggested by 'clinical teams working across the sites serving the total catchment population' and 'clinicians working in teams across [sites]' (Merger proposal, pre-April 1998).

The impetus for the merger was largely financial. 'An integral part of the formation of the new Trust was a comprehensive review of the financial standing of the new organisation resulting in the preparation of a three year Financial Recovery Plan' which included 'management cost savings' of £1 million over three years (Team brief, March 1999). The Trust's Financial Recovery Plan aimed to achieve recurrent financial balance by 31 March 2001.

Intended post-merger structure and relationships

The stated objectives of the merger suggest that Trust management intended to develop one integrated organisation existing across three hospital sites, with centralised management and a directorate structure. At all three sites the organisation would be financially secure, have no staffing problems and be able to meet both training needs and national standards. Service provision would be rationalised across the three sites.

Achieved post-merger structure and relationships

Looking at the Trust two years after the merger, Trust management has not achieved the unified organisation hoped for. While to a large extent management has been centralised and a directorate structure now exists across three sites, organisational links exist mainly between those with management functions. Some lines of responsibility continue to be based on the structure and relationships that existed before the merger. Although no individual hospital is now at risk of closure due to financial problems, overspending continues to occur. The Trust continues to have problems with medical staffing at DGH2. While the Trust is now able to meet junior doctors' training needs, slower progress has been made in improving standards on all three sites. Service provision has been rationalised to a limited extent by removing services from small hospitals.

Key questions for the researcher include:

- What potential ways were available to the Trust to achieve its objectives? Were they used?
- How did the pre-existing structure and relationships enable or constrain the Trust in achieving these objectives?
- Were there other forces in the context of the merger which either enabled or constrained the Trust in achieving these objectives?

Powers/potential of the pre-merger structure

There were six main powers or potential ways available to Trust management which, if activated by them, might achieve the objectives of the merger process:

- Centralisation of Trust management.
- Centralisation of other services.
- The development of a directorate structure, including the key role of Clinical Director. For the Critical Care Directorate this development was supported by the introduction of a directorate meeting.
- The devolution of budgets.
- The introduction of cross-site working, including the development of cross-site communication.
- Standardisation across sites.

In Figure 13.2, these powers are matched to those objectives of the merger they were most likely to impact upon.

One point to note is that there does not appear to be any potential way of achieving the development of specialist services. This may simply represent a limitation of observation, which focused primarily on critical care services rather than on medicine or surgery.

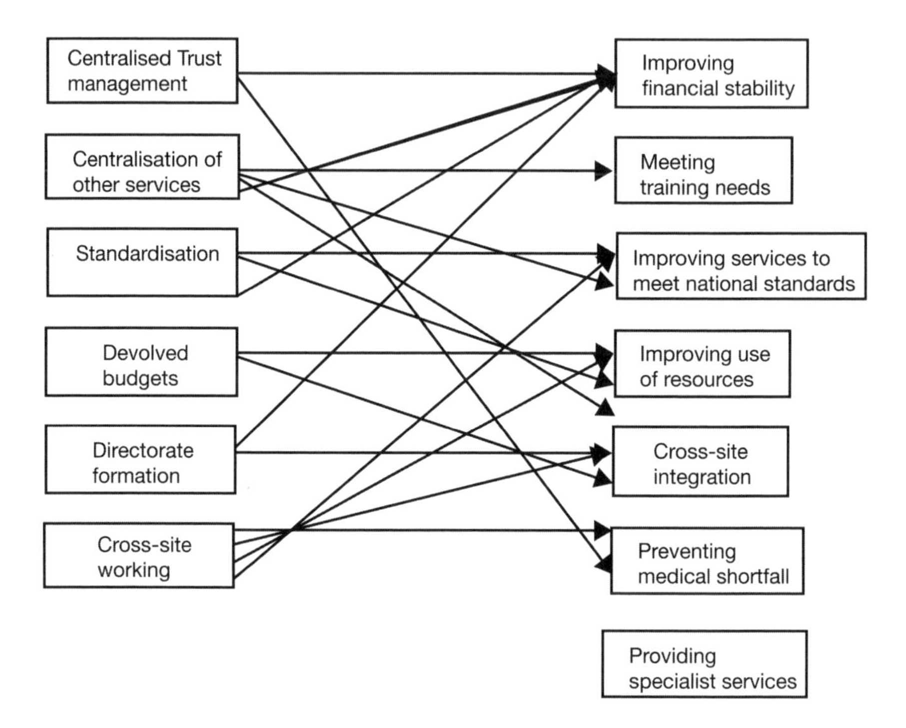

Figure 13.2 Potential ways for the Trust to achieve its objectives

The effect of context

The merger of the three hospitals took place within a national and local context. As Pfeffer comments 'The operations and decisions of organizations are inextricably bound up with the conditions of their environment' (1972: 382). The merger process can be seen as a causal mechanism in the development of a changed organisation. There were many other causal mechanisms in the organisation's context, some of which might affect the merger process. The researcher's skill comes from abstracting from the open system and selecting those mechanisms that were causally efficacious in relation to the merger process.

Government policy – introducing a business culture to the NHS

The merger can itself be seen as an outcome of another explanatory mechanism – the introduction of a business culture to the NHS. The financial impetus for this merger has already been highlighted. Even within the merger proposal, the rhetorical rationale that supports the business ethic by promoting it as in the interests of the patients was expressed – 'To free up resources for direct patient care by reducing the amount of money spent on management and administrative costs' (Merger proposal, pre-April 1998). Numerous recent mergers between Acute Hospital Trusts support the idea that the government is predisposed to hospital mergers. Gillett (2000) commented that forty-nine Trusts were working towards merger in April 1999, while Kjervik (1996) comments on the 'merger mania' trend within health care. One might assume that the government's prime motivation is to improve efficiency. However, Wallace *et al.* (2000: 26) comment that 'Economic analysts have stressed that there is probably insufficient slack in the system to produce large savings, particularly where there remains a need to keep a safe level of service on dispersed sites.' Another possibility is that mergers themselves can be used to progress the government's underlying agenda of introducing a business ethic to the NHS. This particular merger would support that view in that most of the potential ways for Trust management to achieve the objectives of the merger were themselves a part of the business agenda, for example the use of a directorate structure, devolution of budgets, the use of standardisation and greater centralisation.

Directorates have been introduced as part of this business-like culture, providing a structure that enables individual areas to 'develop some direct corporate idea of how decisions taken in a particular area will affect other areas in the Trust' (Clinical Director, Interview, January 1999). The creation of Trusts and new directorate structures devolves responsibility for decision making to the staff responsible for providing care. Thus the structure within which decisions are made has changed significantly, with directorates replacing the traditional hierarchical bureaucracy. Similarly, budgetary responsibility is devolved and there is a focus on business planning. Health care decision-making becomes more closely tied to the financial year and decisions are more closely linked to the Trust's financial needs than those of any individual directorate. Thus the reasons for which decisions are made have also changed with the focus being more on financial viability than on medical need. The emphasis on the corporate nature of the Trust is shown by the following example. After the directorate meeting at which the Critical Care Directorate's needs were prioritised, the Clinical Director was concerned that those within the directorate realised that the directorate's priorities might still not concur with the Trust's, resulting in a low directorate priority being funded while a high one was not. This highlights the difference between responsibility and control. While responsibility has been devolved to directorate level, ultimate control of their decisions rests at Trust level.

Recent government reforms with their focus on standards may also affect health care at a local level. Standardisation could work for the Trust by bringing all hospitals up to the level of the best one. The clash between this potential use of standardisation and the financial reality was highlighted:

> In the medium to long term strategies will have to be developed by the Trust to respond to these particular issues of standards of care. We won't be able to provide the standards of care on all three sites, it just wouldn't be financially possible to do it, so we are going to have to, in some services, decide you can only have them in one perhaps two sites, but often only one site.
>
> (Clinical Director, Interview, January 1999)

The potential for using these standards to justify changes to services was highlighted:

> What standards of care will do … they may be a way of circumventing the political process. Politics will always say you must have the general hospital with all its facilities in [DGH1] and in [DGH2] and as much as you possibly do in [CH3]. That's because the people demand it. … If you can't provide appropriate standards of care, the Chief Executive probably, with clinical governance, will have to make a decision to close down those services where he can't provide adequate standards of care, because otherwise he is clinically responsible for what happens there. That exercise of clinical governance and defined standards of care will really clarify the position for Trusts in a similar position to ourselves.
>
> (Clinical Director, Interview, January 1999)

The introduction of clinical governance to the NHS has major ramifications. Informal medical accountability for the care provided is supplemented by a formal and legal accountability by the Trust board for the quality of care provided.

The issue of further centralisation was of particular relevance to intensive care. The ICU at DGH2 did not meet national standards, and was not accredited as an ICU – it was inadequately staffed, as far as both medical and nursing staff were concerned, and equipment was poor. Alternatives included levelling up DGH2's facilities to DGH1's, closing beds and so increasing the staff/patient ratio, or closing the ICU necessitating the transfer of virtually all surgery to DGH1. As the Clinical Director commented 'If you end up with any significant changes in the service, other services become less viable' (Interview, January 1999). He explained the financial implications of current provision. At the time DGH1 had four beds and DGH2 had three beds:

> Economically 7 beds on one site is the logical solution to that purely because the fluctuation you get in bed occupancy around 4 beds and particularly 3 beds is astronomic … the more beds you have the more … that fluctuation disappears … till you get more efficient use of the beds you have. … There will come a point when the powers that be will have to say 'Well, how much money are we willing to put into this to keep it going?' before we decide 'No, we wont have that service here any more.'
>
> (Clinical Director, Interview, January 1999)

Medical power

Historically the NHS has been a very bureaucratic organisation. The medical profession was heavily involved in its conception, and to a large extent has managed to guard against intrusion into their areas of autonomy because of their privileged claim to clinical judgement. As Ackroyd comments 'Doctors have for many years successfully claimed the right to be the only party whose judgement is relevant to clinical decisions' (1992: 318). He points out that 'early management was subordinated to professional expertise, and, to a considerable degree in many areas, still is' (Ackroyd, 1992: 316). To some extent this has been modified in recent years. The introduction of a business ethic to the NHS, with the associated justification of limited resources and the need for rationing in health care, made initial erosion into medical power. But the greatest, though still very limited, effect on medical power appears to result from involving clinicians in management.

Recent structural change includes an increasing focus on primary rather than secondary care with the introduction of first fund holding and now Primary Care Groups. This has changed the balance of power within the medical profession. GPs are now in a much better position to demand the service they wish to have. This was of particular relevance to the Trust because of the isolated position of DGH2:

> You look at the populations and you say to the PCGs [Primary Care Groups] … 'Right we are going to move this specialty to [DGH2]'. And the PCG will say, 'You can move it where ever you like, but if it is not in [DGH1] we'll go to the next Trust because it is 20 miles away and [DGH2] is 47 … We'll change our contract.' So that will stop any development of specialties at [DGH2] absolutely stone dead. It will be a question of purchasers buying a service and they will not buy a service at [DGH2].
>
> (Clinical Director, Interview, January 1999)

DGH2 was approximately equidistant between DGH1 and the Trust's next nearest hospital. In effect DGH2's PCGs had no alternative while DGH1's did:

> [The] Trust would actually have to bow to the wishes of marginal constituents, if you like, PCGs around the edge who can switch. They would have to take their interests into account very seriously or otherwise the risk would be that [DGH2], [CH3] and [DGH1] would all fold up.
>
> (Clinical Director, Interview, January 1999)

Other attacks on medical power include the recent public outcry due to medical ineptitude, and the failure of the profession to police itself. However, despite all these attempts to reduce medical power, in secondary care, doctors remain the strongest group.

At their side is the nursing profession. Historically they have always been in a supporting role with the doctor as decision-maker. As Ackroyd (1992: 322) comments: 'Nurses were very much subordinated to medical control, taking over all of the routine and most of the distasteful aspects of care, but they also obtained involvement in significant aspects of management.' Mackay (1992: 184) suggests that doctors see nurses as supporting their role – they prescribe, nurses carry out. As Walby *et al.* comment, 'Medical staff want to have highly qualified and competent nurses, so long as they do not overtly challenge the domain of the consultant' (1994: 85). The introduction of general management to health care removed a major part of the nurses' role and 'nurses, as the weaker, dependent part in the old professional alliance, lost both function and status' (Ackroyd, 1992: 324). The impact of management change on nursing has been much more direct than on medicine. Ackroyd highlights the fact that 'nurses have not relinquished managerial function but have simply been excluded from those aspects of management which have become its key aspects under the regime of centralized policy management' (1992: 326). This erosion of nursing power might be expected to cause friction between nurses and managers. Friction appears to be limited perhaps because nurses form a much less cohesive body when under attack than do medics. Ackroyd comments that:

> Almost anything managers may seek to do, to improve the number of patients seen for example, requires the agreement and co-operation of clinicians to have any chance of success. The need to bring about the complicity of nursing in key decisions is much less, and for this reason they have been less often co-opted.
>
> (Ackroyd, 1998: 42)

The relationship between medicine and nursing remains hierarchical with nurses at times being seen in the role of 'handmaiden'. In intensive care, however, this relationship appears less so than in other areas. ICU is both very insulated and much more technical than other areas. The presence of the consultants on the unit for long periods of time is also distinctly different from other areas. In general intensivists tend to be anaesthetists originally. As a supporting specialty, traditionally anaesthetists are much lower down the medical hierarchy than surgeons. In contrast, intensive care nurses tend to be seen as the elite of their profession. This may contribute to the fact that the nursing profession in this area seems to be more highly regarded, with the nurses' opinions sought by medical staff, and medical and nursing staff working together as a team. A comment from the Clinical Director highlighted the limits of this difference between intensive care and other areas – 'I am not saying that we are all equal … that isn't the case, people have to be recognised for their strengths' (Interview, January 1999).

Powers – possessed, exercised or actualised?

In this section each potential way in which the Trust could achieve its objectives is focused on in turn. By studying whether these powers have been activated, and if so how, as well as the interaction of the merger process with other explanatory mechanisms, the effect of other mechanisms and human agency on achieving the desired objectives can be analysed.

Centralisation of Trust management

The prime source of financial savings from the merger was successfully achieved through centralisation of Trust management. However, the associated goal of greater integration was not. CH3 was chosen as the site on which to centralise Trust management.

> In terms of the use of [CH3], I think the movement of … managerial staff up to [CH3] was supposed to be seen in a positive way, i.e. we are actually committing ourselves to [CH3]. That was the rationale behind it because people were quite conscious that it could have been seen as a [DGH1] take-over because the Chief Executive came from here. And he certainly didn't want to create a Trust headquarters on the [DGH1] site and that's the reason that corporate services have been centralised on the [CH3] site.
>
> (Directorate Manager, Nurses' meeting, February 1999)

Staff at CH3 said poor communication was the problem. 'People have been told when things are happening and not been consulted beforehand … there's no explanations about why these things are being done, that's the big problem … you find out by default' (Directorate Nurse, Nurses' meeting, February 1999). Perhaps this actually reflects the loss of control felt by staff at CH3 as the merger process invaded their hospital.

For DGH2 there were significant job losses among junior administration staff. As Baker *et al.* (1999: 17) comment: 'The local community's vested interests in the hospital include accessible health care, a source of employment, and a contributor to quality of life.' For a hospital whose culture was closely integrated with the local community, this was particularly disruptive. The pre-merger dominance of DGH1 predisposed staff at DGH2 and CH3 to see the merger as a take-over. When combined with the subsequent disruption at DGH2 and CH3 and inadequacies in the communication process, the view of the merger as a take-over is a natural, though unintended, outcome of the merger process.

Centralisation of Trust management was also intended at directorate level with directorates having cross-site Directorate Nurses. However, the effect of devolved power to the directorates could counteract Trust strategy as directorate management chose how to implement Trust policy. The Critical Care Directorate did not have cross-site representation, and management suggested that they did not necessarily see the value of it and that directorates that already had this were probably not well represented because their representatives did not know the patch they were representing. The Clinical Director suggested that at that time 'the practices and personalities just wouldn't function' (Interview, January 1999), and he intended to introduce cross-site representation at different speeds in different groups. To date cross-site representation has not been progressed within the Critical Care Directorate.

Centralisation of other services

Centralisation of other services had the potential to improve services, enable the Trust to meet training needs, improve financial stability and improve the use of resources. Trust management chose to implement this in a limited way and only at DGH2 and CH3. As such its impact on the intended objectives was limited. The only objective fully realised was that the Trust as a whole now met junior doctors' training needs. A review of services at CH3 resulted in their reconfiguration. Some services were withdrawn while others were restricted. Some work was transferred to DGH1. At DGH2 satellite services in associated community hospitals were centralised on one site.

Examining this more closely the most obvious factor was that the work of medics was not adversely affected by these changes. DGH1's doctors served CH3 and DGH2's doctors provided DGH2's satellite services, so each change reduced the amount of work carried out by medics away from the main site. Again, from a medical viewpoint, the changes at CH3 enabled the Trust to comply with junior doctors' training requirements. CH3 experienced the most change. The absence of a medical presence at CH3 allowed this, highlighting the power of the medical profession and the limited power of the nursing profession when isolated from the medical profession.

In all the only area in which controversial decisions were made was the development of new services. So far in this analysis the role of the local community in health care decision-making has scarcely been alluded to. The potential for the local community to affect health service provision, whilst unlikely, is not impossible. 'Where trust merger is thought to be a Trojan horse for hospital reconfiguration, it is bitterly opposed by the public and staff' (Wallace *et al.*, 2000: 26). Whilst the closure of satellite services in associated community hospitals did not elicit a public response, the withdrawal of services at a district general hospital has much greater potential to do so. Therefore existing provision at DGH2 was not withdrawn because of the implications of doing so, but new services were less likely to be developed. For instance, the Clinical Director's ideas regarding rationalisation of intensive care onto one site were never implemented, but he chose not to increase intensive care provision at DGH2 since it was geographically too distinct to service the region.

Directorate structure

As the Clinical Director commented, the aim was to 'work towards some form of unified directorate structure' (Interview, January 1999). Directorate formation could be seen to encourage cross-site integration within the directorate but at Trust level was very divisive. This very divisiveness aided integration within the directorate. At directorate meetings interaction of the directorate with staff outside it was often discussed, in particular with respect to problems of directorate representation or involvement, and a team feeling regarding problems with those outside the directorate developed. Even at directorate level there was the potential for this change in management style to cause problems. As the Clinical Director commented, this model of management style was based on DGH1 – 'that in itself doesn't seem to have produced any particular problems with the rest of the Trust but potentially it can do' (Interview, January 1999). In the Critical Care Directorate the Clinical Director, Directorate Manager and Theatre Manager came from DGH1. They chose to continue to be based there. The Directorate Accountant and Assistant Directorate Manager, once appointed, were also based at DGH1.

To enable directorates to feed back into Trust management there was directorate representation for sub-committees of the Trust Management Executive, directorate representatives sitting on health and safety committees on each site, to reflect the management structure, and directorate representation at an executive level for nursing. In general cross-site committee membership seemed to encourage cross-site integration. However, the Clinical Director highlighted a communication issue: 'How do we get the directorate to fit with the Trust's strategies? It would certainly help if we knew what those were. ... No one really seems to be very clear' (Interview, January 1999). This again highlights the distinction between responsibility and control. Managers at directorate level were not necessarily able to take full control of their directorate's future because they were uninformed about the future direction of the Trust.

The Clinical Director commented: 'To move to Clinical Director [across all sites] doesn't really change that relationship very much except that you are doing it with rather more people and people you haven't met before' (Interview, January 1999). Pre-merger, this clinician was Clinical Director for the Critical Care Directorate at DGH1. As he commented: '[I have] got to be able to and be seen not to be taking partial decisions in [DGH1]'s favour always. I can't be seen to be doing that otherwise the whole thing will fail' (Interview, January 1999). In order to do this the Clinical Director had one clinical session at DGH2 to try to develop links with colleagues and gain experience of what the place was like to work in. He also had formal meetings with medical staff, and met informally with non-medical staff because of limited time. In relation to DGH1 the Clinical Director seemed to be very well respected by his colleagues and his role had enabled the acceptance of the directorate structure. But the lack of a pre-merger relationship with colleagues at DGH2 meant that his influence at best was limited, perhaps highlighted by the lower involvement of DGH2 consultants in the directorate meeting. Even at DGH1 at times, when the Clinical Director's role impinged on the clinical judgement of his colleagues, an adversarial response could be seen. In particular, when the Clinical Director decided two extremely expensive drugs should not be used in ICU in order to cut costs, his colleagues discussed closing beds instead – an approach to cost-cutting with a much higher political profile.

The directorate meeting initially involved head nurses from all specialties and sites within the directorate and directorate management (initially the

Directorate Manager and, once appointed, the accountant). Monthly meetings of the 'senior team' coincided with Trust board team briefing. Dates were set provisionally for twelve months, and it was agreed that meetings would rotate between the three sites. After this meeting had been in operation for six months the second stage of its development took place – Lead Clinicians were invited to attend, the idea being that in the future their attendance would continue at least intermittently. At the first joint meeting it was agreed that the Directorate Nurses should continue to meet monthly and Lead Clinicians would join them every three months. CH3 was chosen for the joint meeting, being situated between the other two sites. Suggestions for content included the budget, common problems, feedback from the Trust Management Executive, from the Trust board, on service developments, health and safety and from the nursing and midwifery group. Ground rules were set – meetings were to start on time, with or without people, were to have a time limit of one-and-a-half hours and refreshments would be provided. There would be a structured agenda and minutes would be provided.

The meeting between Directorate Nurses on the whole seemed to encourage cross-site integration, but to a large extent initial meetings were dominated by staff from DGH1, e.g. 'first meeting ... at [DGH1]' (Pre-meetings letter, October 1998). In that agenda items tended to be set by the Directorate Manager, then by those from DGH1; this domination continued to some extent. This might have been due in part to the fact that DGH1 staff were initially much more confident speaking in such a setting. Their familiarity with the directorate structure and decision-making within it suggest that staff at DGH1 benefited from their hospital's earlier compliance with the government's introduction of a more business-like culture. As the meetings progressed, staff, particularly from DGH2, also contributed to the agenda, and all staff contributed to discussion. Within one specialty this initial dominance caused particular problems. A Directorate Nurse from DGH1 commented that, when he was first appointed, the merger was about to happen and he contacted his counterparts in the other two hospitals for a coffee. He was met by 'Are you going to take us over?' (Post-meeting discussion, December 1998). This friction continued at times during the meetings and eventually this Directorate Nurse chose to largely withdraw from directorate meetings.

An interpersonal issue highlighted by the meeting was the interaction between the Directorate Manager and others. Problems in this relationship were accentuated by problems of cross-site communication. Staff commented on increasing problems with communication because of not knowing on which site a manager would be. There was an added distinction between the Directorate Manager and others, due to the distinction between a business and a nursing background. The Directorate Manager espoused a corporate view when compared to Directorate Nurses, e.g. on appraisal – 'We keep talking about personal development planning and personal development plans, what about work-based action plans in terms of what you expect them to achieve within the workplace?' (Nurses' meeting, January 2000). Directorate Nurses appeared confused by this interruption, suggesting that they thought this was what they were talking about, despite differences in the language used.

Despite these initial interpersonal problems at this level these meetings fulfilled a beneficial role providing scope for networking and a forum for learning about what else was going on in the organisation. Some beneficial practical work was done as a result of these meetings, for instance the development of a training strategy and the formation of a cross-site health and safety group. There were many other areas identified for joint working which did not materialise, perhaps because the work involved remained at Directorate Nurse level rather than being devolved down by the Directorate Nurses.

It appears that these meetings did aid integration at the level of Directorate Nurses but that this integration was not passed down to staff at lower levels. ICU Sisters at DGH1 spoke of what was intended compared to what they actually saw:

> You are all supposedly working together in one big family. ... At the end of the day, it's still another unit. You know, it's not like you can just suddenly be involved in what goes on there. ... I think in time, over quite a bit of time, we will work more closely with them, but I think it will take a long time.
>
> (Sister's interview, June 1999)

The directorate structure did not adequately address integration of staff below management level.

Looking at directorate meetings which included medical and nursing staff, the first meeting was well publicised and gained an almost complete attendance by very reluctant clinicians. The intentions of the Clinical Director and the Directorate Manager were that the clinicians should join the Heads of Services meeting every third meeting and that at this stage all Lead Clinicians and Directorate Nurses would be involved. The Clinical Director detailed the reasons why such a meeting should be considered:

> so that it hopefully breaks down the idea that I know exists in many circles that decisions are made in favour of one group at one end, in favour of another group at another end, in favour of [DGH1] versus [DGH2] or [DGH2] versus [DGH1].
>
> (First joint meeting, April 1999)

The meeting concluded with agreement to three-monthly meetings of all Lead Clinicians and Directorate Nurses, to follow the Directorate Nurses' meeting. These meetings have not been well managed as they have continued. The next meeting was postponed twice because doctors could not attend. From the memo: 'The Lead Clinicians will not be able to attend the above meeting due to prior commitments' (July 1999). Before the following meeting, the secretary said that some Lead Clinicians were on holiday and others 'could not be bothered' to attend. It was six months later that this meeting met and then the attendance from DGH2 was low. Only DGH1 consultants attended the third meeting, and in a pre-meeting discussion with a Directorate Nurse from DGH1 she suggested they attended because of pressure from the Clinical Director on the day. Various reasons were given for unwillingness to attend, including having to use their own time, not having a pre-prepared agenda and not seeing minutes. The difficulties in managing clinicians are highlighted by this example. The power which medics have historically had as professionals makes them a difficult group to control. Having agreed to the meetings in principle they chose to undermine them by their actions. The other obvious conclusion is that DGH2's doctors were less involved. Pre-meeting pressure might perhaps be applied in this direction also, although doing so is more difficult because of the lack of a pre-merger relationship. Wallace *et al.* (2000: 28) comment that 'there is a need to engage staff specifically in remote sites in strategic issues'. An increased focus within the Trust on the development of cross-site relationships between doctors may be needed. The potential for this forum to act as an integrative mechanism is there to some degree, but perhaps cross-site specialty meetings have greater potential and their development might feed into this group more productively.

Devolved budgets

> There are a lot of issues that in fact cover all of us … money affects us in different ways but nevertheless it is something that binds us all together. How … one would address overspends in a specialty in a site which affect the budget that everybody else has to contribute to, how would we resolve issues? … [I]f in fact the answer to the problem is not that you stop spending there but that you've got to absorb that somewhere else in the directorate, then decisions made there actually impact on everyone else, don't they?
>
> (Clinical Director, First joint meeting, April 1999)

The role of budgets as an integrating mechanism could be seen to work as both Directorate Nurses and Lead Clinicians became interested and to some extent protective of the directorate budget. As with directorate formation, at a Trust level devolved budgets could be divisive. This directorate was in a particularly difficult position because some parts of it did not have full control over their spending. In particular theatre services were to some extent at the mercy of surgeons, since equipment required for particular operations and even prostheses were ordered by surgeons and paid for by the Critical Care Directorate. These problems aided integration within the directorate. However, with devolved finance there was the potential for divisions within the directorate, e.g. on preparing capital bids: 'A&E versus Intensive Care versus Theatres versus [DGH1], [DGH2], [CH3] … so they've all got their boxing gloves at the ready' (Nurses' meeting, April 1999). To date this process has been relatively free from conflict. One clinician from DGH2 commented that he had 'noticed with that Capital Bids scheme the enormous potential for working together in strategy for equipment' (Joint meeting, April 1999). This lack of conflict may simply reflect the novelty of this process for these decision makers and their uncertainty when operating within it.

Devolved budgets have been less successful to date at improving the financial status of the Trust and improving the use of resources. While budgets for DGH1 had developed over the previous two years, devolved budgets were completely undeveloped at DGH2 and CH3. Progress in devolving these budgets was slow and remains incomplete, for instance training and development budgets are still held at Trust level at DGH2 and CH3. Initially the directorate did not have their own accountant. Also existing historical budgets were inaccurate and needed correcting. A final issue here was that while Directorate Nurses at DGH1 were used to managing a budget, this was a new experience for those at DGH2 and CH3.

A different view of budgets became visible when Trust overspending occurred. Within the directorate purse strings tightened and to some extent control over devolved budgets was restricted. The Clinical Director decided that two extremely expensive drugs should not be used in ICU in order to cut costs. This was imposed without consultation. This could also be seen at Trust level. The Directorate Manager spoke of discussion at Trust Board:

> He [the Chief Executive] was saying that there was a big discussion at Trust Board. And if it doesn't get pulled back within the next couple of months, never mind pulling it within the directorate, all requisitions were going to the Director of Finance … so that the individual specialties cannot sign for a thing.
>
> (Nurses' meeting, July 1999)

Willcocks highlights a similar problem:

> There is clear indication of power struggles, not only between individual clinical directorates, but between directorates and top management, the latter being reluctant to 'let go' and fully devolve power and decision making. These latter struggles are particularly evident when there are budgetary difficulties, for example, overspending.'
>
> (Willcocks, 1994: 31)

This reflects a pattern within the NHS of centralised control and devolved responsibility. At times of crisis this devolvement of financial control is pulled back, leaving only failed attempts at responsibility. As Berridge (1999: 27) comments in his history of health: 'This tension between local self-determination and central policy-making remained an ensuing issue within the NHS.'

Cross-site working

Cross-site working can include the involvement of a variety of different people, for example managers, doctors, nurses, directorate-based groups and specialty-based groups, and different types of working, for example meetings, audits and stock ordering. Cross-site working had mixed success in encouraging cross-site integration. Its power to improve services and the use of resources has not been fully realised because the use of cross-site working is limited.

At Trust level, work aimed at improving services included Trust-wide audit projects while work aimed at improving resource use included Trust-wide trials of equipment. Existing committees were replaced with committees with three-site membership, an idea that makes sense as a way of integrating sites. However, there were some problems. The most problematic committee replacement from the point of view of the Critical Care Directorate was the nursing and midwifery professional decision-making executive. This problem stemmed both from differences in the management structure pre- and post-merger, and from the choice made by the Critical Care Directorate management not to have cross-site Directorate Nurses. The Director of Nursing had prepared a paper about representation at an executive level for nursing. Other directorates, apart from the Critical Care Directorate, had a head nurse with cross-site responsibility. The Director of Nursing chose to circulate the paper in question to those already on this committee – a committee previously based at DGH1. This meant that in the Critical Care Directorate, Directorate Nurses at DGH1 received this document directly while Directorate Nurses at DGH2 and CH3 were forwarded the document, rather than receiving it officially:

> I would have thought it would have been better if the Director of Nursing had got us together from this side and said 'This is what has been run at [DGH1] and I want us all to go to the same. What do you think about it?'
>
> (Directorate Nurse, DGH2, Nurses' meeting, April 1999)

Within the directorate individuals seemed willing to share out representation on this committee, but the way in which this committee developed was a sensitive subject for one Directorate Nurse, perhaps reflecting the same problems as could be seen within the directorate meeting. From the researcher's point of view, the lack of anticipation of this problem by the Director of Nursing was surprising since he himself was from DGH2.

A prime example of cross-site working at directorate level was the directorate meetings. Directorate Nurses were involved in sharing ideas and working across sites to look at developing policy. A cross-site cross-specialty health and safety group was set up as a result of discussion at these meetings. The success of cross-site working within the directorate was affected by the pre-merger positions of the hospitals. In particular, when clinical supervision was discussed there was some defensiveness between areas suggesting perhaps that some areas had had other priorities. Perhaps this was because clinical supervision as an opportunity for development might not have been within the grasp of staff at DGH2 and CH3. This ties in with the view that their organisations' basic needs had not been satisfied pre-merger, leaving them unable to focus on developing further.

The idea of rotation of nursing staff between specialties and between sites was discussed at both Trust and directorate level. At the time DGH1 had a rotation programme for junior Staff Nurses between the specialties in the directorate. Senior nurses were interested in both cross-site and cross-specialty rotation. However, the further development of staff rotation at DGH1 into a cross-directorate rotation programme did not materialise, as the Critical Care Directorate was not included with surgery and medicine. The development of a similar scheme at DGH2 to that currently in use at DGH1 was frequently discussed at directorate meetings but has not happened. This is just one example of slow progress. Cross-site rotation of nursing staff, while discussed at directorate meetings, did not have the Clinical Director's support, has not yet been progressed and remains unlikely to be.

Medical rotation has also not happened. One doctor highlighted a problem of perception associated with this idea – although he himself was happy enough to provide cover at DGH2, he felt less sure about the DGH2 doctors providing cover for DGH1 (Interview, February 1998). It can be noted from this analysis that medical rotation was the only potential way in which the Trust could avoid having medical staff shortages at DGH2. 'As a unified Trust' this problem may be solved by secondment but that could lead to medics leaving (Clinical Director, Interview, January 1999). The power of clinicians is again highlighted. Despite medical rotation being the only way to avoid staff shortages, management chose not to implement it.

On the subject of communication, three main points deserve highlighting. The way in which in written communication and visits, e.g. ' "Year 2000 roadshow" – DGH2, 3, then 1' (Action notes from meeting, December 1998), DGH1 was mentioned after the other hospitals, must have appeared false when considered in light of their relative power. What people heard about each other's sites appeared at times to be restricted and at times not so. For example, staff complained about having to read about each other's sites and team briefing was split into core- and site-specific – a regressive step. By contrast, at directorate meetings some discussion seemed inappropriate, e.g. discussion of a medical post – 'Another little anaesthetist – our 12th in [DGH1]' (Nurses' meeting, January 1999). A final issue with respect to communication is that to a large extent it did not seem to filter down:

> I don't think people at grassroots actually understand what's happening at management level. I think there's still some anxieties about the future of services with the merger. I don't think enough's been said really, I don't think it filters down.
>
> (ICU Sister, DGH1, Interview, May 1999)

As far as intensive care is concerned, the Directorate Manager commented that the only joint working to date had been the occasional transfer of patients due to bed shortages. Suggestions for joint working included a joint audit into the use of haemofiltration, covering each other's sickness and joint ordering of stores. Both Directorate Nurses were keen to communicate cross-site on the subject of intensive care. They discussed the idea of their staff meeting socially. Limited progress has been made with these suggestions.

There are various practical problems with cross-site working, which, if anticipated, were not prepared for. The need for management to travel reduced their available time for problem solving. At directorate level one communication issue was the availability of directorate management. As part of the new directorate structure the Directorate Manager, Assistant Directorate Manager and Theatre Manager were to rotate between the three sites. Staff frequently reported problems getting hold of managers. Staff had problems because meetings were at a different site than they were. Increased funding was required because of travel.

Standardisation

Standardisation is focused mainly on standardising policies, practices and the use of resources. Unlike much of the government reforms, standardisation seems largely to be bought into by clinical staff, perhaps because of its partial emphasis on clinical effectiveness. At every directorate meeting standardisation was discussed in relation to a particular practice, equipment used or a particular policy. As such standardisation had the potential to improve services, financial stability and the use of resources.

Its impact on these objectives was limited. There was also an issue at both Trust and directorate level of whose standards were taken to be the standard. To some extent this appeared to have been shared out, but the most important features tended to be based on DGH1's practice thus supporting the idea that this was a take-over. One important feature that might appear to be based on DGH1's practice was the model of management style. Actually the directorate structure imposed had been imposed nationally by the government. At directorate level the Clinical Director commented that he tried to incorporate different styles and 'find ways to hopefully bring some of the good things from there [DGH2] over here [DGH1]' (Interview, January 1999).

The use of standardisation as a way of controlling staff might be more successful, particularly in the light of staff buying in to it. The Lead Clinician from ICU at DGH1 discussed the attempts to set up a joint audit with ICU at DGH2 into the use of haemofiltration. This was the Clinical Director's idea and the Lead Clinician felt that his opposite at DGH2 was trying to make doing this more difficult and being purposefully unhelpful. He believed this was because his colleague was using haemofiltration in an inappropriate way and the audit would show this up (Interview, September 1999). At times the use of standardisation as a control mechanism did not seem to benefit the directorate. For example, the Directorate Nurse for ICU at DGH2 had an approach to appraisal that differed significantly from that at DGH1 (Nurses' meeting, January 2000). In some ways it was more comprehensive than anything in use at DGH1 was. However, it did not neatly fit into the financial year. To stress the importance of this would in this case have been to the detriment of the use of appraisal in ICU at DGH2.

Summary

There is a need for the Trust to be able to justify the merger, for example when preparing the Directorate Business Plan – 'If some of these benefits could be tied back to the trust merger, so much the better' (Memo to directorates, January 1999). Unfortunately, apart from the objective of meeting junior doctors' training needs, other objectives have only been achieved in a limited way. In part this results from the interaction of the merger process with other causal mechanisms and in part from the role of human agency, as choices are made about if and how potential ways of achieving objectives are used.

The merger itself can be seen both as the outcome of and as a way to progress the government agenda of introducing a business ethic to health care. A key issue relating to this agenda is the distinction between locally held responsibility and centralised control. This distinction is seen within the Trust in that directorates are kept unaware of the Trust's future plans, and are overshadowed by the spectre of the removal of the limited financial control they have should a crisis situation occur. This lack of devolvement of the long-term view reduces the Trust's ability to satisfactorily achieve many of the merger objectives.

Medical power at times counteracts the merger process, though this is not done explicitly. Management at times chose not to implement certain policies, for example centralising services or introducing medical rotation, because of the fear of medical power. Medics themselves chose to undermine policies rather than directly challenge them. Public opinion had limited power only, although fear of it prevented greater rationalisation of services.

Whilst DGH1 obviously held a dominant position before the merger, careful use of both standardisation and the communication process might have prevented the natural outcome of staff at DGH2 and CH3 seeing the merger as a take-over. This view has limited the effectiveness of many of the Trust's attempts to achieve its objectives.

References

Ackroyd, S. (1992) 'Nurses and the prospects of participative management in the NHS', in K. Soothill, C. Henry and K. Kendrick (eds), *Themes and Perspectives in Nursing*, London: Chapman and Hall.

—— (1998) 'Nursing', in M. Laftin (ed.), *Beyond Bureaucracy?*, Aldershot: Avebury.

Archer, M.S. (1995) *Realist Social Theory: The Morphogenetic Approach*, Cambridge: Cambridge University Press.

Baker, C.M., Ogden, S.J., Prapaipanich, W., Keith, C.K., Beattie, L.C. and Nickleson, L.E. (1999) 'Hospital consolidation: applying stakeholder analysis to merger life-cycle', *Journal of Nursing Administration*, 29 (3): 11–20.

Berridge, V. (1999) *Health and Society in Britain since 1939*, Cambridge: Cambridge University Press.

Gillett, S. (2000) 'Turn of the screw', *Health Service Journal*, April: 22–4.

Kjervik, D.K. (1996) 'The urge to merge – will quality survive?' *Journal of Professional Nursing*, 12 (4): 195.

Mackay, L. (1992) 'Nursing and doctoring: where's the difference?', in K. Soothill, C. Henry and K. Kendrick (eds) *Themes and Perspectives in Nursing*, London: Chapman and Hall.

Pawson, R. and Tilley, N. (1997) *Realistic Evaluation*, London: Sage.

Pfeffer, J. (1972) 'Merger as a response to organizational interdependence', *Administrative Science Quarterly*, 17: 382–94.

Walby, S., Greenwell, J., Mackay, L. and Soothill, K. (1994) *Medicine and Nursing: Professions in a Changing Health Service*, London: Sage.

Wallace, L., Granne, A. and Boyle, G. (2000) 'Question of attitude', *Health Service Journal*, April: 26–8.

Willcocks, S. (1994) 'Organizational analysis: a health service commentary', *Leadership and Organisation Development Journal*, 15 (1): 29–32.

14 The moral management of nursing labour power

Conceptualising control and resistance

Carole and Peter Kennedy

Introduction

This chapter forms part of an empirical research of nurses' experience of professional work.[1] The focus of the research is on nurses' experience of contemporary forms of 'professionalism' in the context of the organisational turbulence affecting the NHS during the past two decades. The chapter discusses the key substantive and theoretical themes, which have informed data collection and analysis. We begin with an overview of key political and economic changes affecting public sector 'professionalism', with particular emphasis on nursing. The argument here is that broader economic changes have imparted a business ethos within the public sector that effectively draws professionalism under the influence of public sector managerialism in the attempt to maintain its own status and authority. The consequences for the nursing profession are then assessed. It is argued that modern developments in nursing professionalism are increasingly used as a means for processing the moral management of nursing labour power, in ways that strengthen the political/economic management, which nurses experience through the traditional medium of the management function. In support of this argument, the chapter considers ways in which the moral management of nursing is underpinned by a particular definition of nursing ethics that becomes inscribed in professional codes of conduct and competencies produced by the United Kingdom Council for Nursing, Midwifery and Health Visiting (UKCC). The chapter then assesses the contribution that discourse and critical realist approaches make in providing a broader understanding of issues of control and resistance. It is demonstrated that discourse, in over-emphasising control and docility, closes off an understanding of avenues of resistance, whilst critical realism extends an understanding of the ways in which control and resistance are internally related processes in the management of nursing labour power.

Background and wider context of the study

The contemporary capitalist economy has changed dramatically over the past two decades. Unsurprisingly, the nature and scope of the political, economic and social changes has been hotly debated. The recent past, present and near future of international capitalism signify the unstable transition between Fordism and post-Fordism (Ash, 1994; Bonefeld, 1991); the decaying forms of the Keynesian Welfare Nation State complex and the emergent, but as yet unfinished, Schumpeterian Workfare State (Jessop, 1999); and/or extremely uncertain and uneven forms of globalisation (Hirst and Thompson, 1996; Giddens, 1999). Despite the real differences between each perspective, there is an implicit consensus that the scope and extent of the changes under way are profoundly affecting social and economic policy, leading to a transformation in the ethos of public sector management across Europe and the USA. In the UK, for example, the power of financial markets to impose fiscal discipline on governments over public sector spending has had a strong influence on the reorganisation of social welfare. This fiscal discipline, alongside the increasingly global scope of corporate ownership of health and welfare products (Yates, 2001) and the emergence of private–public partnerships, have served to instil a *business ethos* within the public sector, whereby social welfare and professional aspirations to meet welfare needs are increasingly commodified (Ruane, 2000). The same forces have also provided a bulwark for the emergence of new forms of *managerialism*, which, although highly variable in practice from one public sector service to the next, represent a cultural shift towards the 'belief that the objectives of social services can be promoted at lower cost when appropriate management techniques are applied' (Clarke *et al.*, 2000: 9).

The combined effect of applying business ethics and forms of managerialism to the public sector has been to intensify the forces of instrumental rationality within public sector organisations even further, as witnessed by the pursuit of efficiency and cost-effectiveness, through a mixture of markets, modernisation and audit cycles, which combine as a new form of surveillance (Clarke *et al.* 2000: 251). One consequence is that any desire public sector professionals might express to serve the needs of the public is increasingly subverted by the logic of audit cycles to squeeze the 'best value' out of all resources, including public professional labour power (Ruane, 2000). This can be observed, for example, in the way contemporary forms of public sector professionalism are increasingly challenged by the wider objectives of public sector management. The terms of the challenge, as Clarke puts it, relate to who 'possesses the right to direct, coordinate or run public services in the UK' (Clarke *et al.*, 2000: 8). In this respect, managerialist discourse and practice seems intent on colonising traditional practices associated with public service professionalism, by making the efficient administration of resources a key definition of what is deemed to be 'good professional conduct' (Clarke *et al.*, 2000: 8). Labour governments, far from attempting to arrest this process, have extended the language of managerialism inherited from previous Conservative governments to include the idea of 'partnership' between stakeholders to promote further institutional change. In this instance the language of 'partnership' central to government texts such as *Working Together* (NHS Executive, 1998) and *The New NHS* (Department of Health, 1997) signifies the decentralisation of responsibility for the running of the NHS to the professionals concerned, and the centralisation of government control over resources and performance monitoring (Poole, 2000).

It is only within the wider context described briefly above that one can understand why the status and authority of professionalism in nursing is increasingly bound up with the fate and identity of those responsible for the management of the NHS. It is the particular argument of this chapter that modern forms of nursing professionalism are inseparable from the wider objective to harness nursing labour power to the requirements of the business ethos, which is shaping the development of the 'modern and dependable' NHS. The claim advanced below is that, while NHS *management* continue to attempt to exert political/economic control of nursing labour power, this control is being increasingly supplemented by forms of *moral management*, exercised by the nursing profession over its own members.

Managing nursing labour power

It is well documented how within the NHS the management function exercises political/economic control using a mixture of neo-Taylorist practices, including de-skilling and the use of core–periphery sourcing of an elite of highly skilled nurses and an army of assistants (Lloyd and Seifert, 1995). However, there are constraints on the ability to exercise control inherent to the deployment of neo-Taylorist practices to nursing, which necessitate the deployment of other forms of control, such as the redesign of shift working and reorganisations designed to increase patient throughput (Ackroyd and Bolton, 1998). The constraints on adopting wholesale neo-Taylorism have their root in what one Kings Fund Report termed 'the submerged tension' between 'quality of care' considerations and pressures for cost containment (Kings Fund Institute, 1990: 5). When the emphasis is on addressing quality of care considerations, there is a *systemic* need to ensure that nursing staff continue to be intrinsically involved in 'patient-centred' care. The latter becomes particularly acute in the context of increased litigation costs and the consequent necessity to 'manage risk' on the ward (Norman, 1997: 87), which took institutional form with the setting up in 1995 of Clinical Negligence Schemes for Trusts (CNSTs) (Faugier, 1997: 99). The latter set limits to the equally strong tendency to de-skill and 'task orient' nursing practice in the interests of increasing the quantity of 'care' provided. One outcome of this 'submerged tension', is that management must operate contradictory tendencies: they must impose forms of neo-Taylorism, but must also leave room for 'professional autonomy' (Ackroyd and Bolton, 1998). However, given the risk of litigation in the context of the need to intensify the use of nursing labour power, then professional autonomy must somehow be circumscribed and directed towards organisational needs. This is where the moral management of nursing labour power becomes crucial, in particular, the *moral management* of professional autonomy by means of *professional self-regulation*. Yet this area has remained under-researched. Crucial to an understanding of the forms of moral management nurses are being exposed to is an account of the relationship between (a) the increased concern to define the ethical underpinnings for nursing care; and (b) the growing concern, expressed by the UKCC and related professional nursing bodies, with institutionalising procedures relating to professional codes of conduct and the professional scope of competencies. This argument will now be elaborated upon.

The moral management of nursing labour power

Nursing ethics has been the object of growing interest over recent decades. One manifestation of this is the many journals dedicated to ethical nursing practice which have flourished (see, for example, *Nursing Ethics*, *The Journal of Medical Ethics*, *Bioethics*, *Philosophy and Health Care*, *Cambridge Quarterly Journal of Health Care Ethics* (Scott, 1998: 478). The interest expressed by these journals in defining an ethical basis for nursing has been supplemented by other nursing educator journals with a wider remit than ethics, which express a growing and sustained interest in nursing ethics around issues pertaining to training and professional practice. Examples here are *Nurse Education Today*, *Nursing Enquiry*, *Nursing Times* and *The Journal of Continuing Education in Nursing*. Scott (1998) attributes this concern with nursing ethics to two mutually exclusive reasons. On the one hand, the interest in ethics harbours a genuine concern to promote a more reflexive approach to nursing care. An example of this is the concern to promote de-professionalised notions of care (Fox, 1999) as well as neo-Aristotelian conceptions of care based on locality and virtuous action. One might speculate that this side of care expresses the empathetic emotional aspects rooted in nursing's professional autonomy as an embodied practice. On the other hand, argues Scott, the interest in ethics serves to underpin managerialist tendencies within the nursing profession, residing in professional nursing bodies such as the UKCC. In this respect, one might suggest (in light of what has been argued) that the kind of ethics cultivated by the UKCC has been instrumental in colonising professional autonomy through discourses associated with business ethics and managerialism.

Since 1979 the UKCC has made concerted efforts to prescribe a *Code of Professional Conduct*. Based around a limited number of fixed and determinate *categorical duties*, the prescribed codes of conduct exhort nurses to act, at all times, in such a manner as to:

- safeguard and promote the interests of individual patients and clients;
- serve the interests of society and justify public trust and confidence;
- uphold and enhance the good standing and reputation of the professions;
- be personally responsible at all times for one's practice and in the exercise of one's professional accountability.

Moreover, the UKCC, through its publication *Scope of Professional Practice* (SPP; UKCC, 1992b), has been concerned to elaborate, extend and *inscribe* the values of nursing *competencies* into every day nursing practice. One rationale behind the

SPP is not so much to challenge what professional nursing bodies perceive as the task-oriented, handmaiden culture of nursing as attempts to foster a willingness amongst nurses to 'go beyond contract', by engaging in *flexible working practices* on the basis of the 'life-long learning' of competencies (without the requirement for certification). Perhaps the crucial point to note here is that the SPP is one of a number of central texts that exhort the principles of *individual responsibility* and *self-regulation*. Through such texts nurses are morally positioned to be at all times accountable and responsible for attaining the prescribed codes and competencies, and for individualising risks of judgement as to whether, for example, they are sufficiently competent in any given situation.

The logic of individual self-regulation that lies behind the focus on codes and competencies is clear in both the SPP and the *Codes of Professional Conduct* (CPC; UKCC, 1992a). The SPP inscribes the requirement to extend the boundaries of nursing practice vertically (for example, into areas of medicine) and horizontally (into areas of administration), and then justifies this inscription as the *individual responsibility* of nurses. Meanwhile, the Codes of Professional Conduct (CPC) support and extend the latter by presenting *universal guidelines* on what is deemed to be *ethically* sound conduct. Those nurses who meet the guidelines are consonant with good 'self-regulatory practice', those who fall short of the guidelines are deemed 'un-regulated' offenders whose (mis) 'conduct' (read 'unethical practice') becomes punishable on the basis of clearly prescribed rules. As Heywood Jones reflects, '[t]he object is to encourage nurses to take a closer look at their own performance and, perhaps, to learn – *or be warned* – by others' mistakes' (Heywood Jones, 1990: xi, emphasis added).

There is also a particular relationship between the *professionalising impulse* and the expressed interest in defining an ethics of care that we need to consider too. It is to be noted in particular how the *self-regulating powers* of the UKCC's codes of conduct are predicated upon the acceptance of an *ethical accountability* that has a firm basis in Kantian-informed deontological approaches to an ethics of duty to care. The latter is particularly well-suited to the self-regulation of nurses because of its commitment to a set of *universal abstract principles of duty* (Winstanley and Woodall, 2000) that take no account of either the limitations imposed on the NHS by the wider social context, or the many institutional constraints nurses experience on the ward. In addition, such an ethics of duty is premised on a conception of society as an aggregation of atomic individuals, which facilitates the potential for *individualising responsibility* on the job and, therefore, deepening a nurse's sense of *individual culpability* to the NHS as well as their own professional bodies. It is this definition of ethics that provides a particularly potent form of professional self-regulation. The extent to which the latter succeeds in controlling nursing labour power by policing areas of professional autonomy is the purpose of our ongoing empirical research.

Establishing the substantive context has sharpened the research focus, which is to investigate nurses' experience of current forms of professionalism. However, to make sense of that experience – to be able to code the data in a way that meaningfully establishes the connection between the lived experience of nurses and the substantive context outlined above – requires the development of a suitable theoretical context. In what follows we evaluate the suitability of, first, discourse and, then, critical realist approaches.

Professionalism as discourse

A positive consequence of adopting a discourse approach is that it opens up the potential to 'supply an alternative framework for the analysis of professional power in nursing' (Fox, 1993: 62). In many ways *implicit* to the above account of the substantive context has been that professionalism in nursing acts as a disciplinary power over nurses, through the aforementioned *discourses* on appropriate ethical conduct, codes of practice and competencies. In this sense, the potential value of a discourse approach has, to a degree, already been demonstrated. However, at this point in the chapter a more explicit consideration is required.

Following Foucault, discursive power refers to systems of social representation, constructed by rules of conduct, talk, writing, symbols and social institutions, which regulate what can and cannot be known and produced (Foucault, 2000 [1972]). Systems of representation are then said to be the basis for the construction of various technologies of the self, which, through internalisation, induce forms of self-disclosure and confession as part of the process of the reconstruction of 'self' by a particular dominant discourse (Foucault, 2000 [1972]). Professionalism in nursing, for example, may usefully be conceived as a 'technology of the self', which nurses experience as forms of internal surveillance and as a means of 'confession' that makes visible, reconstructs and renders docile nursing practice. Moreover, as a 'technology of the self', professionalism in nursing may also be said to order and inscribe ways in which nurses 'know' and conduct themselves as the subjects of knowing.

Fournier's study of the accountancy profession (1999) may help us draw out the above, suggestive, remarks. Fournier's research draws attention to ways in which 'professionalism' is deployed in accountancy as a disciplinary logic in the management of professional relations. In particular, he describes how professionalism inscribes 'autonomous professional practices' as a means through which the governance of 'professional conduct' and accountability is to be achieved (1999: 280). Here the inscription of notions of professional competence become part of a number of other means of self-regulation that serve to colonise the 'autonomous space' left open when management concede areas of 'responsible autonomy' to professional accountants. In this way, argues Fournier, professionalism is able to exercise control (governance) over professional autonomy 'at a distance' (Fournier, 1999: 282). In short, professionalism 'allows for the reconciliation of control and consent', by establishing the '*responsibilisation of autonomy*', through mechanisms which emotionalise work, as the basis for 'instil[ling] professional like norms and work ethics, which govern not simply productive behaviour, but employees' subjectivity' (Fournier, 1999: 293).

Extrapolating from Fournier's ideas, one could argue that professionalism in nursing (complete with ethical codes of conduct and the various competencies that underpin the experience of 'professionalism') can usefully be explored as part of the panoply of *intellectual technologies of the self*, which reconstruct individuals as subjects and objects in such a way as to manage nursing labour power 'at a distance'. In this way professional autonomy becomes colonised by the moral agenda set by the NHS in the context of the earlier-mentioned shift in the public sector ethos. Moreover, one might suspect that the discourse of professionalism being pursued here could also operate to legitimise nursing as a profession *vis-à-vis* other official bodies, in an effort to maintain a sense of its own autonomy. This being the case, 'professionalism' in terms of discursive power is to be understood as an attempt to not only control nurses 'at a distance' but to keep official bodies 'at a distance' too. For example, to 'distance' central and local government, in the effort to limit the external regulation of nursing; or to 'distance' client groups as a means of limiting the threat of litigation and the encroachment of 'informal' care; and/or to 'distance' medicine in order to attain a position for the nursing profession in the power struggle *between* professionals involved in health care provision.

This 'distancing' aspect of professionalism in nursing is important because it influences the *form of the discourse* to which the nursing profession is subjected. For, clearly, what *particular* competencies and codes of conduct are specified and promoted by the nursing profession will be influenced too by the means used to maintain a sense of 'distance', and so autonomy, from outside influence and regulation. In this respect, the *particular form* that professional discourse takes in nursing through the UKCC's core texts on codes of conducts and related competencies, is both a means of controlling nursing labour power *and* assuring that a 'distance' is maintained between themselves and other powerful groups who may overlap or threaten their area of competency. The crucial point, however, is that, in the context of the business ethos and managerialism sweeping through the public sector (Clarke *et al.*, 2000), it is the professional nursing body's ability to morally manage nursing labour power that ultimately determines their success in maintaining a sense of 'distance' in the eyes of other external groups.

Research evidence

From the short overview above, it is clear that a discourse approach to professionalism in nursing offers a great deal of insight, but how well does it hold up empirically? The above review has suggested a number of issues relating to professionalism in nursing, which provide a useful focus for interpreting our focus group transcripts. Our own empirical research to date finds support for a discourse approach as well as evidence of its shortcomings in being able to account for nurses' ingrained resistance to some of the moral imperatives of professionalism. In this respect a number of key discourses based on approaches to professionalism, generalised to all focus groups, were clearly linked to the major discourse of moral management. We present brief extracts below related to their codes to demonstrate this line of argument. The code headings are as follows: *'being personally responsible'*; *'controlling levels of attachment'*; and *'rejecting detached instrumentalism'*.

'Being personally responsible'

If we recall, it has been argued that pivotal to the kind of moral management inscribed in nursing codes of conduct is an abstract and individualised duty to care, regardless of organisational constraints, and a sense of collective responsibility. In this respect, in answer to the question, 'where should responsibility lie for patient care on the ward?', a strong sense of individual blame, guilt and individual responsibility pervaded replies, which the following reply epitomises:

> I think it's quite an individual thing because like, if you didn't pick up on something, you know which you really should have. ... You really get to know them (the patient) if they are in, for a good few days. I just feel as if you miss something you would feel terrible and you wouldn't be looking for other people to blame, well I certainly wouldn't, if I knew the person and something happened to them and I didn't notice then I would take it really personal. ... I wouldn't be saying like, that someone else should have been watching them.
>
> (A)

The above quotation reveals amongst other things that the internalisation of an abstract duty to care is sustained by its ability to colonise an ever-present ethics of care based on patient familiarity. This *internalisation* comes across clearly in the following response to the same question:

> I think you know there comes a certain sense of responsibility because at the end of the day you are looking after their care, you're not looking after their treatment you are looking after their care ... it's just natural, I think it's instinctive and everyone should have that in them. It's not a job you would do for the money. ... It's something that you should care deeply about.
>
> (C)

'Controlling levels of attachment'

The individualisation of responsibility, referred to above, overlaps with the belief that, as responsible professionals, nurses need to learn to control their attachment and not get too involved with patients. As a conception of the 'good professional' this 'responsible' attitude is reinforced through constant moral supervision to the point of internalisation as a norm; as the responses to the following question demonstrate: 'Does your professional status influence your approach to patient care?'

> I was pulled up ... the other day for being *unprofessional*, lacking diplomacy and tact and that's coming from by the way, a *good* staff nurse, she's good at

> her job, but I've watched how she behaved on the ward and she does have this professionalism, you know, she's got very limited amount of contact talking with the patients, if she's got a task to do, if she's got to care for them, but its kept to a minimum, do you know what I mean?
>
> (G)

In this instance the attributes of 'the good professional', as defined in managerialist terms of tact, diplomacy and a business-like approach to patient care, are reinforced by external surveillance and through a 'role model'. The degree to which enforcement becomes increasingly internalised is evident in a response to the same question:

> Well, I had this patient, she got decanted to another ward and … you could always tell see, just before visiting every day she'd always come down to talk to me and see, at first I didn't mind and then it was going on, I don't mean I felt she was a nuisance, I felt no, she's getting too, and then one day it got so bad that her son came down to the ward and it was, my mum was actually wondering if she could have a wee word with you, could you go and see her? and it's about this doctor, he's done such and such and I thought no this has got to be too much and she's expecting me to go away to another ward to ask for her results … and I felt that was too attached. … It kind of taught me a lesson because I thought I had got too close.
>
> (L)

'Rejecting detached instrumentalism'

Another indication of the extent to which nurses have internalised the moral discipline implicit to professionalism is given by considering the expressed attitudes of respondents to what is defined as 'bad nursing' behaviour. As one might expect in an environment where the moral imperative to care is internalised, 'bad' nursing is presented as stepping over the invisible marker of the 'good professional' by becoming either too attached or too detached. Being too detached, then smacks of instrumentalism and lack of commitment. This is demonstrated in response to the question 'what would you define as bad nursing?'

> Someone that wants to just go in and do their job and come back out again, watching the clock until their shift finishes and … say their looking after someone that's not well and it's kinda ten past three, they're just burning to hand it over to the back shift, you know people out the door, you know, and that's my shift finished.
>
> (S)

Although the merest of snapshots, the above quotation does provide support for the efficacy of a discursive reading of the data. Yet, as one would expect, for every instance revealing a degree of discursive control we also unearthed clear examples of resistance to the dominant discourse. In this sense, the nurses we interviewed projected a sense of contesting the march of professionalism and asserting their own localised experiences of ethical approaches to nursing. Two themes in particular, *building nurse/patient alliances* and *reengineering professional codes*, reveal the internalised nature of nurses resistance to discourses of professionalism.

'Building nurse/patient alliances'

The embodied, emotional and gendered aspects of nursing come most to the fore to resist professionalism when nurses discuss their relationship to patients, as the response to the question 'Do you feel a sense of attachment to your job?' signifies:

> On the good side of it it's very satisfying, when you've had a good day and you're feeling great, you may go home feeling exhausted but you feel great if you felt that you had given somebody some care, but it's so far removed from the political situation, you know the new politics of the NHS, it's so far removed from your actual working day … because you're so involved with giving care to patients that the political and financial side of it as a student …
>
> (A)

In the above quotation one detects a strong sense of personal involvement and empathy with the patient, which overtly contradicts the pressure to maintain a position of 'controlled involvement'. Moreover, the following related responses to the same question are at least *suggestive* of the influence of cross-cutting powers of key 'positioned practices' such as gender and class on nursing practice discussed earlier:

> I had a staff nurse say to me don't put that dressing on, it's too expensive. I've never heard staff nurses talk like that, never. When a wound needs a particular dressing … you give the best that you can, but she was saying, ooh that's too expensive go back to the cupboard and I thought, what's happening!
>
> (V)

> I've been in trouble before for sitting on the patient's bed, you know the way you go and sit and talk, and I don't see anything wrong, I still don't see anything wrong.
>
> (H)

> I've always had that difficulty right through nursing, with people telling me you're too attached, you're too emotional, you're too talkative, you're too this, you're too that, and I've had it for years, sometimes you come across nurses that are like yourself though and they tend to be like that and you think I'm not a freak after all, but sometimes it ends up that you've got a kind of gang about you saying you're too this, you're too that.
>
> (B)

'Reengineering professional codes'

There is also clear evidence of how professional codes of conduct are used overtly by nurses to resist exploitation of their labour power by both nursing professionalism and the authority of medicine. Below is a sample of the responses to the following question that capture this: 'To what extent would you say that the UKCC codes of conduct influence your practice?'

> But see one of the main things that I've found anyway that's in your UKCC, it's to never do something to a patient or whatever, that you're not competent in doing, like you can actually refuse in your UKCC professional code of conduct see if someone asks you to do something and you've never been shown it and you don't know how to do it, you can refuse on those grounds that your complying with your professional code of conduct, so if a nurse was kind of, oh you'll do that because I've told you to do it, you can say on this ground I'm not doing it because I've not been shown, I don't feel confident.
>
> (F)

> See I never used to refuse to do anything, it wasn't until this placement and I did because I was told to go ... but I was told to go and lift this woman and she didn't even sleep in her bed, she was in this big Parker chair and there was the two of us going to lift her ... and then she was getting transferred and I said I'm not lifting her, it could never take my back ... and then after a couple of seconds he went oh right OK and then I said well where's the hoist and he said we don't have them on this ward.
>
> (G)

The limitations of a discourse approach

What comes across clearly is the sense that both control and resistance are internal to each other, which is a far cry from the kind of docility to professionalism projected by discourses of professionalism. Indeed the evidence suggests that, while the discourse approach offers a useful explanatory framework, it also has inherent limitations, which we need to discuss.

Chief among the limitations is the obvious one that discourse approaches to professionalism tend to stress the all-embracing and omnipotent nature of discursive power, in controlling individuals and rendering them as docile bodies. Yet, as evidence would appear to confirm, nurses exhibit resistance as well as conformity to current discourses of professionalism. Nurses, for example, continue to engage in industrial action (no matter how low key and spasmodic), in the full knowledge that it is in clear breach of professional codes of conduct (Castledine, 1995: 529). Moreover, high rates of job turnover in nursing indicate a high level of individual resistance, and so an awareness among nurses of the considerable gap between the rhetoric of professionalism and the reality of working life on the ward (Kings Fund Report, 1996–7).

Of course one could factor in resistance by arguing, as Knight and Willmott (1988, 1999) have done, that individuals are the subjects of multiple discourses, leading them to experience existential insecurities and so embrace and resist subjectivities, which promise freedom but deliver new forms of enslavement. Indeed this may open up an understanding of control and resistance that can enrich our analysis of the above data. However, if we reduce an understanding of resistance to discursive power – *even multiple overlapping forms of discursive power* – we are still left with a one-sided explanation of control and resistance. This is so because an approach that narrows its intellectual horizons to the analysis of discursive power tends too readily to perceive the *structural dominance* of docile bodies as *inevitable actualisations*, rather than as the *potentials* and/or *possibilities* that they are (May, 1996). The latter becomes common-sense knowledge once one appreciates the overlapping influences of key non-discursive forms of power, which bring to light the material origins and inequalities of relations and processes of power (Porter, 1996: 60). In particular, one might include those forms of power emanating from the broader structures of the capital/labour relationship, such as labour market power; or the power emanating from the ability to control employment law; or the power emanating from the wider industrial relations system (Thompson and McHugh, 1995).

In summary, the claim emanating from the above discussion is that multiple sites of power will contradict and limit, as well as support, discursive forms of power. Therefore, while a discourse approach can and does provide useful knowledge of the dynamics of power in organisations, it has its limitations: discursive forms of power, although crucial, are far from omnipotent in the face of alternative forms of non-discursive power. Moreover, once we do take account of other sources of power, then we become more sensitive to the sustained nature of the 'low intensity' wars of resistance against dominating discourses that are carried out by employees on a daily basis (Thompson and McHugh, 1995: 144). It should be added that we also begin to harbour an increased awareness of how 'forms of knowledge [discourses] are a key resource through which *resistance can be mobilised*' (Thompson and McHugh, 1995: 144). And, by implication, if we conceive discursive power more as *latent possibility* rather than *omnipotent actuality*, then discourse analysis can be of great value in understanding the increasing trend towards professionalism in general and its role in the self-regulation of nursing in particular. Porter (1996) has suggested, therefore, that research may usefully be guided by two related questions (which happen to be of special relevance to ethics and the discourse of professionalism in nursing). First, what must the social world be like for the exercise (or non-exercise) of disciplinary power to be possible? Second, what social mechanisms and countervailing powers must be in operation to account for the success and/or limitations of disciplinary power? Addressing these questions to nursing means 'bracketing back in' 'the social structural location of the actors involved' (Porter, 1996: 66). Below, we discuss ways in which critical realism can assist in these aims.

The contribution of critical realism

In what follows we will argue that critical realism (CR) offers a useful means of contextualising discourse analysis, providing a more adequate basis for its operationalisation for research into both control and resistance arising out of the imposition of professionalism in nursing. We are aware that CR has become an intellectual industry, which has grown more complex as it has defined and redefined its basic, and not so basic, philosophical principles. Therefore, it is not our intention here to provide anything like a detailed account of CR. The discussion that follows relates only to those core CR concepts that we believe to be central to illuminating our research topic: namely, CR's conception of society as a self-sustaining, complex, open entity, constituted by the activity of agents, structures, tendencies and mechanisms (Bhaskar, 1989).

Schematically, each of the above elements refers to different levels of social reality in terms of ontological importance. The 'empirical' and 'actual' level are where perceptions and events occur. They have their origin in a deeper level, where structures, mechanisms and powers operate. For CR, social structures emerge out of the specific relations that develop between the parts that constitute a social object. Power, then, is defined as the contradictory/complementary *capacities* located to the relations that make up a social object, as well as those pertaining to structures relating to the object. Of course the nature and scope of such power will differ (Bhaskar, 1989). Taking the example of the economy: while power is derived from the capital labour relation, this overlaps in complex ways with other sources of power derived from other social structures internal to the economy, such as inter-capitalist competition, patriarchal relations, etc. Also, because objects and structures can both complement and contradict each other's capacity to develop, then power is recognised as an *enduring potential*, in as much as it still exists even though it may not always be exercised at the level of the empirical/actual (Lawson, 1998). For example, patriarchal structures may complement the capital labour relation by helping to establish a reserve army of labour, which pegs back wage drift in such a way as to become a counteracting tendency against the 'law' of a declining rate of profit. Likewise the 'family wage' might contradict the capital labour relation by enhancing the above 'law'. Mechanisms, meanwhile, unlike objects, are not things in themselves, but moments of the structure/object that generate the link between structural power and the events and perceptions held by agents located at the less ontologically significant levels. The implication is that neither structure nor agency can be collapsed into each other (Archer, 1998). For the latter are both produced and reproduced by social activity that occurs within a multiplicity of *positioned practices* that result from the above relationship between structure and mechanism (Bhaskar, 1989). Finally, structure and agency are not just objects of social *reproduction* but are also potential objects of social *transformation* through positioned practices (Bhaskar, 1989). One can conclude from this that society is judged to be an open entity, constituted by a multiple of, often cross-cutting, sources of power relations, which provide social institutions and positioned practices with their internal complexity and, one might say, dialectical integrity.

A number of implications follow from this overview, which has implications for an understanding of the dialectic between control and resistance with reference to the moral management of nursing labour power. First, CR draws attention to how discourses are only one source of latent power within any given *positioned practice* alongside others. For example, hierarchical/bureaucratic power (Weber, 1968), patriarchal power (Tong, 1989) and the power exuding from capitalist relations of production (Marx, 1954), etc. To this degree, nurses as individuals and as a collectivity may become influenced by, and so may draw upon, any one or all of these sources of power in complex and overlapping ways. Second, and related, the relationships *between*, as well as those *internal* to, positioned practices, may at times complement or contradict each other. For example, from within the positioned practice of nursing, the discursive power of professional self-regulation may remain latent because nurses draw actively on the power of, say, class or patriarchy in ways that challenge and contradict the attraction of the discourse. Similarly, the relationship between the positioned practices of nursing and mothering may engender conflicts or complementarities, which render the discourse of professionalism either actual or little more than an unexercised potential. It is by reflecting on these implications that one can begin to provide a more adequate theoretical context for evaluating nursing practice.

The above claim becomes all the more clear if one clarifies the differences between *necessary* and *contingent* relations with respect to key positioned practices. In this respect CR draws our attention to how society is to be seen as a complex ensemble of structures with relations between each structure ranging from necessary/internal to the contingent/external (Sayer, 1992). For example, although nurses may be positioned as agents within discursive structures around an ethics of 'professionalism', they are *also* positioned as agents within structures that are *contingently* related (family, religion, education) and *internally* and *necessarily* related (class, gender, ethnicity, trade union membership). The crucial point here is that these structures can, variously, *complement, reinforce*, or act as a *countervailing power* to the management of nurses through professional self-regulation. Indeed, it is the concept of *internal* and *necessary* relations between structure and mechanisms and agents, that helps one clarify the importance of *embodiment* as a causal factor in setting limits to and contesting discourses of professionalism. One would imagine, for example, that the gendered nature, not to mention the intimate one-to-one nature of nursing may be just as likely to promote virtue as a guiding ethics, as re-enforce the discursive powers of an abstract ethics of 'duty to care' that are inscribed in related nursing competencies and codes of professional conduct. The point is, by incorporating embodied knowledge of ways in which alternative structural positions counteract or complement the prevailing discourse, *one begins to conceptualise the discourse itself as a contested positioned practice*, a practice that transmits, not only the power to discipline *and* resist, but just as importantly the power also to *transform* the discourse positively (i.e. in one's own interests).

A final implication of the above comments is that, while *all* structures may exhibit necessary *internal* relations (e.g. husband and wife in the family; nurse and patient on the ward; capitalist and worker in a capitalist economy), the tendential power relations and mechanisms which are generated by *particular* structures (and which lead to empirical events and actions) will vary in their importance for reproducing or transforming the historically specific *transitive* domain of society (for example, patriarchal relations). In this way CR draws our attention to ways in which one can *re*present a hierarchy of broader structural powers that bear influence upon the self-regulation of nursing. This allows one to contextualise and so re-interpret the nature, strengths and limits of the discursive moment of professionalism experienced by nursing. In this respect, for CR, it is both feasible and necessary to have a more comprehensive understanding of the limits and boundaries of the management of nursing labour power through self-regulation, that one bears in mind the hierarchy of countervailing/complementary, but *necessarily related*, structures with which this chapter began. By doing so we are in a much stronger theoretical position to make sense of the dialectics of resistance and control, when conducting and evaluating research into contemporary capitalist relations, and, in particular, the moral management of nursing labour power.

Note

1 The empirical aspect of the research, which is still ongoing, looks into nurses' experiences of and attitudes towards contemporary trends in professionalism, using a mixture of data derived from focus groups and interviews conducted at a university and a hospital in Glasgow. The data this chapter draws upon emerged from four focus group discussions involving twenty student nurses at the university campus, many of whom had considerable practical experience of nursing prior to their enrolment as student nurses.

References

Ackroyd, S. and Bolton, S. (1998) 'It's not Taylorism: mechanisms of work intensification in the provision of gynaecological services in an NHS Hospital', *Work, Employment and Society*, 13 (2): 369–87.

Archer, M. (1998) 'Realism and morphogenesis', in M. Archer, R. Bhaskar, A. Collier, T. Lawson and A. Norrie (eds), *Critical Realism: Essential Readings*, London: Routledge.

Ash, A. (1994) *Post Fordism: A Reader*, Oxford: Blackwell.

Bhaskar, R. (1989) *The Possibility of Naturalism*, 2nd edn, Hertfordshire: Harvester Wheatsheaf.

Bonefeld, W. (1991) *Post Fordism and Social Form*, London: Macmillan.

Castledine, J. (1995) 'Should nurses strike?, *British Journal of Nursing*, 4: 225.

Clarke, J., Gewirtz, S. and McLaughlin, E. (2000) 'Reinventing the welfare state', in J. Clarke, S. Gewirtz and E. McLaughlin (eds), *New Managerialism, New Welfare?*, London: Sage.

Department of Health (1997) *The New NHS: Modern and Dependable*, CM307.

Faugier, J. (1997) 'An exploration of clinical risk from a nursing perspective', *Nursing Times Research*, 2 (2): 97–105.

Foucault, M. (2000 [1972]) *The Archaeology of Knowledge*, London: Routledge.

Fournier, V. (1999) 'The appeal to professionalism as a disciplinary mechanism', *Sociological Review*, 47 (2): 280–307.
Fox, N. (1993) *Post Modernism, Sociology and Health*, Buckingham: Open University Press.
—— (1999) *Beyond Health: Post Modernism and Embodiment*, London: Free Association Books.
Giddens, A. (1979) *Central Problems in Social Theory*, Houndsmill: Macmillan.
—— (1999) *Runaway World: How Globalisation is Shaping Our Lives*, London: Profile.
Heywood Jones, I. (1990) *The Nurses Code: A Practical Approach to the Code of Professional Conduct of Nurses, Midwives and Health Visitors*, Basingstoke: Macmillan.
Hirst, P.Q. and Thompson, G.F. (1996) *Globalisation in Question: The International Economy and the Possibilities of Governance*, Cambridge: Polity.
Jessop, B. (1999) 'The changing governance of welfare: recent trends in its primary functions, scale and modes of coordination', *Social Policy and Administration*, 33 (4): 348–59.
Kings Fund Institute (1990) *Prospects for Nursing in the 1990s*, London: Kings Fund.
—— (1997) *Health Care UK 1996–7*, London: Kings Fund.
Knight, D. and Willmott, H. (1988) *New Technology and the Labour Process*, Basingstoke: Macmillan.
—— (1999) *Management Lives: Power and Identity in Work Organisations*, London: Sage.
Lawson, A. (1998) 'Economic science without experimentation/abstraction', in M. Archer, R. Bhaskar, A. Collier, T. Lawson and A. Norrie (eds), *Critical Realism: Essential Readings*, London: Routledge.
Lloyd, C. and Seifert, R. (1995) 'Restructuring in the NHS: the impact of the 1990 reforms on the management of labour', *Work, Employment and Society*, 9 (2): 359–78.
Marx, K. (1954) *Capital*, Vol. 1, London: Lawrence and Wishart.
May, T. (1999) 'From banana time to just in time: power and resistance at work', *Sociology*, 33 (4): 767–83.
NHS Executive (1998) *Working Together, Securing a Quality Workforce for the NHS*, consultation document.
Norman, S. (1997) 'Minimising risk while maintaining standards', *Nursing Times Research*, 2 (2): 86–7.
Poole, L. (2000) 'Health care: New Labour's NHS', in J. Clarke, S. Gewirtz and E. McLaughlin (eds), *New Managerialism, New Welfare?*, London: Sage.
Porter, S. (1996) 'Contra-Foucault: soldiers, nurses and power', *Sociology*, 30 (1): 59–78.
Ruane, W. (2000) *A Future for the NHS? Health Care for the Millenium*, London: Longman.
Sayer, A. (1992) *Methods in Science: A Realist Approach*, London: Routledge.
Scott, P.A. (1998) 'Professional ethics: are we on the wrong track?', *Nursing Ethics*, 5 (6): 477–85.
Thompson, P. and McHugh, D. (1995) *Work Organisations*, 2nd edn, London: Macmillan.
Tong, R. (1989) *Feminist Thought: A Comprehensive Introduction*, London: Routledge.
Weber, M. (1968) *Economy and Society: An Outline of Interpretive Sociology*, Vol. 1, ed. G. Roth and C. Wittich, New York. Bedminster Press.
Winstanley, D. and Woodall, J. (ed.) (2000) *Ethical Issues in Contemporary Human Resource Management*, London: Macmillan.
UKCC (1992) *Codes of Professional Conduct*, London, June.
UKCC (1992) *Scope of Professional Practice*, London.
Yates, N. (2001) *Globalization and Social Policy*, London: Sage.

15 I say tomato, you say tamato

Putting critical realism to work in the knowledge worker recruitment process[1]

Anthony Hesketh and Phil Brown

> That real things and generative mechanisms must exist can be established by philosophical argument. It is the job of the scientist to discover which ones actually do.
>
> (Bhaskar, 1998: 64)

A key idea today in popular thinking about both business and government concerns the importance of value added and the contribution of employees to this. Adding value in today's knowledge economy requires *inter alia* employees being problem solvers, not only having the capacity to identify new market opportunities, nor yet having the necessary sophistication and brokering skills to convince even the most circumspect of those opportunities, but also being adaptable 'symbolic analysts' (Reich, 1991). 'For the first time in history,' argues Castells, 'the human mind is the direct productive force, not just a decisive element of the production system' (Castells, 1996: 32). Given the key contribution of intellectual skill and knowledge in the economy, some envisage a developing *war for talent* in which 'talent is the critical driver of corporate performance and ... a company's ability to attract, develop, and retain talent [is] a major competitive advantage' (Michaels *et al.*, 2001: 2).

The war metaphor refers to the competition between organisations for what is perceived to be relatively scarce talent available in the contemporary knowledge economy. However, we must also envisage a *war for jobs*, or how individuals set out to secure the scarce jobs on offer, and the strategies they employ in achieving their aims. This aspect of the labour market has been largely overlooked by labour market researchers, certainly at least in the new and evolving knowledge-worker labour market. This chapter seeks to redress this imbalance, seeking to unpack the social dynamics at work when both sides of the labour market come together to thrash out who wins and who loses in the competition for jobs. Our focus is what happens during organisational recruitment events. As in the other chapters in this volume, a critical realist perspective is adopted, in this case for the analysis of the experiences of job applicants and company selectors and their impact on the outcome. Unlike the other chapters, however, what follows will also draw on some of the ideas of the French sociologist Pierre Bourdieu, to offer a different approach to critical realist-informed empirical analysis.

Players in the labour market and their powers

The employers and their interest in recruitment

Whether or not the rhetoric of the knowledge economy contains much truth, many organisations make significant investment in their professional and managerial employees. In these circumstances it is not unexpected for employers to seek reassurance about the suitability and capability of potential employees before making an offer of employment. What is unexpected, perhaps, is the scale of the investment of time and resources in selection processes, particularly in the selection of managerial and professional employees. Although there is now an array of recruitment tools to choose from when selecting employees, as Table 15.1 indicates, skilled manual workers are less likely to be asked to participate in an assessment centre than somebody applying for a management post (CIPD, 2000). There are also wide variations between the recruitment of managers and skilled manual workers in the use of personality testing or other psychometric tests. The more specialised and intensive forms of recruitment techniques are reserved for the jobs within the upper echelons of the new knowledge economy. Certainly, 83 per cent of organisations use assessment centres when recruiting graduates for their management training programmes (AGR, 2001, Table 2.1: 15). For those

Table 15.1 Selection methods used by organisations when recruiting staff (%)

Selection methods	All	Managers	Professionals	Skilled manual
Interviewing	99	98	99	81
Application forms	81	70	70	68
Résumés	74	70	71	45
Covering letter	63	61	61	41
Ability/aptitude test	54	39	37	24
Personality questionnaires	36	35	26	7
Assessment centres	26	22	15	2
Telephone screening	18	11	0	6
Biodata	7	5	5	2
Graphology	2	1	1	1

Source: CIPD (2000).

n = 262 (100%)

uninitiated in the business of recruitment and selection, an assessment centre is a recruitment event staged by an organisation or its agents (which may last several days) in which the strengths and attributes of potential employees are assessed using a variety of exercises and psychometric tools. The development of an institution such as an assessment centre is in itself significant testimony to the scale of the investment now made in the processes of staff recruitment and selection.

The use of specialised recruitment and selection techniques is spreading. Whilst the larger companies all tend to use assessment centres, mid-range organisations have also increasingly turned to this selection technique over the last decade (AGR, 2001). The principal reasons for the use of the assessment centre and associated techniques of selection are several. First, it is not clear from cursory inspection who will make a good employee or manager, especially in the longer term. The job of the manager in particular is felt to be both messy and ambiguous, with competence being viewed as largely emergent, as argued by Watson and Harris (1999), for example. Second, there are techniques of selection that are widely believed to be objective and effective that may be used to make recruitment more reliable. The evidence provided by psychometric testing and other techniques of selection such as job simulations are seen to be fair and objective. Indeed, the supposedly scientific status of the methods of testing used by recruiters is a key matter when employers consider the likely effectiveness of their recruitment procedures. Third, there is a new cadre of professionals who claim expertise in employee selection offering their services to employers. In sum, because of the perceived difficulty of the recruitment process, organisations have been persuaded to place a premium upon the assessments of potential recruits made by professional recruiters.

The recruiters and the legitimation of their activities

A significant recruitment industry has grown up rapidly in recent decades and is now worth several billion pounds annually. The industry has a growing professional membership which is employed both in the personnel departments of firms and in management consultancy organisations specialising in recruitment and selection. The industry rests on dual foundations: on the one hand there is the inherent difficulty of finding employees with significant talents and, on the other, there is the availability of techniques largely drawn from psychology and behavioural science that might provide superior, even 'scientific', insight into the qualities of candidates. Listing the benefits of its services, one well-known multi-national organisation providing selection services in over twenty countries points to its ability to provide 'independent reviews and assessments of individuals [which are] applicable when demonstrable objectivity is required [and] the process is open to outside scrutiny [and needs to be] seen to be fair and unbiased' (Thomas International, n.d.).

The government and its policies

We may contrast the view of recruiters (that it is possible for employers to identify and recruit superior talent in the labour markets) with that of government spokesmen and policy-makers. Here the rhetoric is equally ebullient but takes a different tack. Government ministers, in particular, never miss an opportunity to reiterate that higher levels of human capital bestow on their recipients' competitive advantage within the labour market:

> [R]esearch shows that if you look at the graduate labour market, all the evidence shows that higher education still represents a very good investment. The rewards for graduates are considerable. Earnings for those with higher level qualifications are around 40 per cent higher than the national average earnings *and going to university does make it easier to find a good job*.
>
> (Wicks, 1999: 1, emphasis added)

Such convictions are indeed used to support the policies of opening university provision to open competition and of allowing universities to charge premium fees.

Two caveats should concern anyone considering these attitudes and policies. The first concerns the basis of the calculation by researchers that graduates have superior earning power. The statistics referred to by the minister above refer to the labour market outcomes of a previous generation of graduates, those who have enjoyed the benefits brought about by a relative scarcity of their human capital. This is, of course, a luxury not afforded to the graduates of today's higher education, who now comprise over one-third of the relevant age group, with government targets aimed at ensuring at least half of their future contemporaries obtain the same experience.

Second, and related to this first concern, is the number of 'good' jobs available to new graduates now and in the future. An unprecedented upturn in the demand for graduates in the late 1990s has now given way to an equally precipitous downturn. Even at its height, the 350 major graduate recruiters in the UK only offered some 45,000 vacancies: hardly enough for the 450,000 graduates annually obtaining a first degree.[2] This '1:10 rule' has recently shifted in a downward direction, with estimates of graduate vacancies from the same source now currently projecting something in the region of just 20,000 graduate vacancies. The inevitability projected by the government's mantra of 'get a degree, get a career, get a higher salary' (Wicks, 1999) is being replaced by a new positional competition in graduate entry into today's managerial labour markets.

The duality of employability and the labour market

This observation leads Hirsch (1977) to forge the distinction between two dimensions in the quality of an educational commodity, let us say, for example, graduate status. On the one hand, there is the *absolute dimension* of a first degree, comprised of the quality added to the individual recipient by the course, the teachers and the institution at which the course has been completed. On the other hand, there is a *relative dimension*, 'in which the quality consists of the differential over the educational level attained by others' (Hirsh, 1977: 6). The policy rhetoric surrounding individual opportunity within today's knowledge economy most obviously applies to the first of these dimensions, implying that the relative dimension is unimportant if not irrelevant. The main point, according to government, is that acquiring high levels of human capital – measured by educational qualifications – renders an individual highly employ*able*. Success for highly qualified individuals is presented as inevitable. However, in conditions of job scarcity, the relative dimension of qualifications, inexorably, comes to be more and more important.

In general, employ*ability* is not employ*ment*, and this distinction highlights what we refer to as the *duality of employability*. By the use of this concept, we draw attention to the fact that employability does not necessarily translate into employment (Brown *et al.*, forthcoming). For example, two qualified brain surgeons being interviewed for the same post are employable by virtue of their medical degrees; that is, their vocationally specific human capital. But, ultimately, only one surgeon will be successful, rendering the other surgeon unemployed. Of course, our unsuccessful brain surgeon may well find employment elsewhere, but if there is no vacancy available and if one is not created, he/she will not only be unemployed but, in a basic sense, unemployable. This is hardly likely in the UK at present, given the shortage of highly qualified medical personnel, but it could be in a situation of oversupply of medical personnel, and a dearth of government funding. There is, however, no escaping the conclusion that the supply of jobs has relevance to employability (cf. Hillage and Pollard, 1998).

As we have already seen, graduates entering the managerial labour market for the first time have to find their way to jobs in a situation of scarcity and thus of intense competition from other candidates equally well-qualified as themselves. There simply are not enough jobs to go round. Far from being an absolute commodity, then, the employability of an individual turns on something other than merely their formally defined human capital. It is not simply a matter of raising oneself over an absolute threshold of human capital, as the policy and organisational rhetoric would have us believe. How then is it possible for employers to forge distinctions between individuals who are apparently equally qualified in absolute terms? If the employability of graduates is indeed relative, on what grounds is this relativity established and verified?

In the language of economists, the demand for labour is running far behind the supply of knowledge workers. For every management trainee appointed by organisations in the UK there are, on average, another thirty-eight disappointed applicants, seven of which will have been short-listed, with an average of five candidates interviewed (AGR, 2002, Table 2: 16). Hirsch (1977) describes this level of competition as an 'adding up problem' in which: 'Opportunities for economic advance, as they present themselves serially to one person after another, do not constitute equivalent opportunities for economic advance by all. *What each of us can achieve, all cannot*' (1977: 4–5, emphasis added). In circumstances of over-supply like these, economists would predict that both the salaries attached to new jobs, and the associated conditions of service, will decline; but they do not. This suggests that the knowledge employees have is indeed regarded as scarce and valuable to their prospective employers. Among other things, where the numbers of employees are few relative to the capital they use and the added value they create, there is a correspondingly high premium on securing high levels of responsibility and motivation.

The place of recruitment interventions

In these circumstances, professional recruiters have persuaded employers that they have the expertise to play an important role in the recruitment and selection of their professional and managerial employees. In the past there was a tendency for employers to take qualifications, such as a degree, pretty much at their face value as key evidence of the ability and general quality of a potential recruit. These days, however, with many more providers of degrees and a higher saliency attached to competence, the professional recruiter has no very hard task persuading employers that some other things are necessary in addition to qualifications. And further, they argue, without these there is little to guarantee employee quality. First, it is alleged that there is a broader conception of the skills that are desirable in recruits than qualifications alone. Second, the existence of these skills is verifiable, to a considerable extent, objectively and scientifically. Third, despite the fact that tests determining employees' abilities have objective elements, deciding on competence is not straightforward, but depends on professional skill in evaluating the complex data available from tests and assessment centres.

This brings us back to the supposed science of recruitment underpinning the industry. Labour market analysts highlight the relative attributes of potential employees and the social complexities of labour markets, and also recognise the methodological implications of this recognition (e.g. Peck, 2000). By contrast, the recruitment and selection industry confidently identifies the objectivity of selection processes. Validity, reliability, objectivity, accuracy and predictive measurement have become the touchstones of the recruitment industry. But few actually claim that this measurement, for all its refinement and supposed accuracy, is all that is needed, or that, for many purposes, the professional judgement of the selector is not also required. In the somewhat tautological language of one consultant, 'a test *should* measure what it is supposed to measure and predict what it is supposed to predict' (Bethell-Fox, 1989: 308, emphasis added), implying that they do not. According to another consultant, for example, the indeterminacy of tests is very clear:

> [T]he level of correlations between ratings given by different raters reporting on the performance of the same employees tends to only be of the order of 0.55 to 0.75, *which shows that a good deal depends on which rater is making the report.*
>
> (Handyside, 1989: 672, emphasis added)

There is, however, an understandable emphasis placed on the objectivity of selection tests in many circumstances. Soon-to-be graduates can read in the prospectuses of the organisations to which they are making applications how 'evidence of [their] competencies will be tested for objectively' (NHS, 2000). In the published pronouncements of recruiters, then, it is often simply claimed that the science of recruitment testing enables assessors to read off competencies through their tests and their observations of candidates' behaviour during recruitment events.

The changing basis of employment: from the currency of qualifications to narratives of employability

It is our contention that the rhetoric of recruiters has promoted a shift in the basis of selection processes away from a system based on the *currency of qualifications*, to a quite different mode of ordering and regulation based on what we shall call *narratives of employability*. By this we mean to draw attention to the reduction in the importance attributed to education based on acquired qualifications, which were formerly taken as reliable indicators of the acquisition of human capital. Qualifications were, formerly, in a literal sense, educational capital; and one could expect to purchase social esteem and employment with them. The currency of qualifications established a clear hierarchical and established *absolute* order, among other things reflected in the recognised hierarchy of credentials: a degree is absolutely better than an HNC, an HNC better than a clutch of A-levels, and so on. In contrast, in recent times, we have witnessed the rise to importance of the idea that valuable skills and capabilities are much less clear-cut, and of the belief in their being much more aesthetic and performative in nature. It is the professional recruiters, and their intervention in selection processes, that have been largely responsible for this change. It is no longer enough to simply differentiate between candidates in terms of the disciplines of their degree, or the class of degree obtained,[3] but it is necessary to examine their level of ability against behavioural attributes.

Drawing from all the evidence we amassed during an empirically based project examining the recruitment processes of new knowledge workers by fifteen leading-edge companies, however, it is clear that recruiters are also employing subjective judgement in their selections. In our studies of the graduate recruitment programmes of seven case study companies, we lay open to a new level of scrutiny the process of selecting individuals for jobs. Our approach was a longitudinal one: we interviewed graduate candidates both just before and just after they attended company assessment centres, whilst also observing their performance during the recruitment event in various group activities and face-to-face interviews. On the other side of the labour market divide, we have also examined how employers evaluated individuals before, during and after recruitment events, focusing primarily on the justificatory processes used by assessors to allocate individuals into employable or unemployable categories. In total, we have interviewed eighty graduates, re-interviewing half a few months after the

Table 15.2 An example of the selection criteria used by a case study organisation

Criterion	*Definition*
First impression	Well groomed and smart personal appearance
Personal presence	A powerful presence with real substance. Warm, gregarious, outgoing and full of energy. Earns respect from others without having to be 'loud'. A high–profile person who sets the standards by which others are judged.
Communication skills	An excellent communicator with customers, managers, subordinates and colleagues. Good at listening, speaking and making presentations.
Interpersonal skills	A diplomatic approach with service not servility. People - oriented and able to establish good relationships with others. A developer of people and someone who can manage others in a consultative rather than autocratic way.
Emotional resilience	Resilient and stable under pressure. Can plan and carry out work effectively under pressure without being driven to make hasty decisions. Does not become moody or irritable and is not over-sensitive to criticism.
Flexibility	Is adaptable and flexible in changing environments. Is prepared to try out new ideas and take calculated risks.
Drive and commitment	Someone who loves working on the sales floor, is totally committed to it and will put in that little extra effort when needed. Tenacious and self-motivated. Not constrained by self-doubt or lack of ambition. Keen on self-development.
Acceptance of responsibility	Prepared to accept a wide range of responsibilities and be judged on them. Will accept responsibility for own actions and not 'pass the buck'. Prepared to learn from constructive criticism and not be upset by it.
Intellectual substance	Can pull information together and make sense of it. Learns from experience. Analytical, inquiring and open. Is quick to learn, flexible and not rule-oriented.
Planning and organisation	Takes a structured approach through planning, setting priorities and thinking ahead. Can manage time, is good at administration and pays attention to detail.
Business awareness	Understands the need to know about products and customer requirements. Is commercially aware and 'in the know' about consumer trends.
Technical skills	Has good verbal, analytical and numerical skills. Can work accurately.

initial recruitment round to establish their success (or failure) in the labour market. In this chapter we focus mainly, though not exclusively, on the interviews conducted with the HR staff and graduate candidates attending the assessment events at our seven participating case study companies.

Irrespective of the economic sector, the type of graduate being sought or the numbers involved, there is a basically normative approach to recruitment being operated by the recruitment industry. Long lists of skills relevant to employability have been constructed by researchers (e.g. Bennett *et al.*, 2000) and practitioners (e.g. Woodruffe, 2000). By way of an example, Table 15.2 presents the list of twelve attributes used by one of our case study companies as its selection criteria. But, though tests of these skills are used, they cannot disguise the operation of judgement, justified by appeal to normative criteria, being used at crucial points in selection processes. This finding certainly emerges from a close study of the recruitment programmes of the UK's blue chip organisations. This is not entirely unexpected, of course. As in all professions, even those that are securely based on science, the scientific and the technical aspects of the job do not entirely close down the scope for professional judgement and discretion in decision-making. Although, in the rhetoric of recruiters, there is emphasis on the validity and reliability of measures of performance; there is no denying the role that professional judgements have in deciding which amongst many candidates are actually most employable.

Viewed in this way, the scientific discourse surrounding employability and its measurement used by the recruitment industry is a kind of rhetorical and persuasive language weaving behavioural measurements, other observations and judgements within frameworks having both logical and narrative aspects (Linstead, 2001). Narratives of employability, therefore, may be viewed as reflections of language used to justify and legitimate actual or potential power and exchange relationships on the one hand, whilst eliminating possible challenges to this power on the other (Gowler and Legge, 1981). The crucial observation we need to make here, however, is one that acknowledges that the majority of employers we have interviewed do ultimately believe in the capacity of recruitment methods to largely bypass such issues and other complexities. Even that recruits have acquired such rudimentary skills as making presentations is thought to be something necessarily assessed on an objective basis:

> We do need them to be able to do presentations, and perhaps we do ask for a little bit more of that now, but as a company we haven't changed our requirements. The emphasis might change, but I don't think we have put more emphasis on [presentations] now than what we used to do. As I said earlier, *we are now scientific about it and we are better at assessing it* [presentation skills] *because we have now got some better tools with which to do it.*
>
> (Graduate Recruiter, Car Manufacturer, emphasis added)

During our interviews with graduate recruiters we probed carefully about the extent of belief in the 'truth claims' and the supposed scientific validity of the recruitment decisions, asking respondents to comment upon whether they thought recruiting was, metaphorically speaking, best described as a 'science' or an 'art'. It was not difficult to get respondents to admit the judgemental aspects of these decisions:

> I guess [there is] a 'critical zone' or 'danger zone', but it is not that critical. I mean it is not absolutely hard and fast, and we don't say that if you have got three 3s [on a rising scale out of 7] compensated by good scores elsewhere then that is okay. Four 3s would never be compensated so it is not as hard and fast as that. *That is the kind of judgement element which comes in because it is not just an actuarial thing, it is very much a qualitative thing when you are going to make the final judgement as to whether somebody should be offered a post or not.*
>
> (Public Sector, emphasis added)

> It is because at the end of the day you have sort of got a jury system, you have your twelve men, good and true, deciding whether or not they are guilty enough. But you make sure that by having your assessment centre that they are assessed and each of the skills are looked at by a different person, and each of the skills is tested in a different way. You know you are going to have personalities [that] you are going to have at [an] assessment centre, 'Well, I liked him and I didn't like her!' 'Why?' 'I don't know!' That is going to happen we are all human, if it was a science I would just sit them all in front of the PC, given them tests and I would have a nice list of 400 people [from] 1,100 who I could give the job to.
>
> (IT and Consultancy)

Different responses to recruitment

Another reason why it would be imprudent to look on the techniques of selection used by recruiters as being entirely scientific, or even particularly objective, is that they have been far from neutral in their effects. The tools of the new forms of recruitment, the behavioural tests and the experience of assessment centres, have not acted on inert materials, but, on the contrary, have provoked adaptive reactions by the subjects to whom they are applied. The war for talent can be seen to have given rise to the war for jobs referred to at the start of this chapter. This is, as we will now show, a messy and undeclared guerrilla war, which not all recruiters are aware is being waged.

As will become apparent below, we have witnessed, on a number of occasions, individuals who have clearly sought to manipulate their own behaviour in the light of their experience of recruitment events, which has been guided by their own guesses about the criteria involved in selection tests. The writings of Pierre Bourdieu[4] on cultural taste are helpful here. Bourdieu makes a useful distinction between those who are equipped to understand only sense perception, which he calls 'the primary stratum of meaning' and those who are able to negotiate social situations because they are equipped with concepts at the secondary stratum of meaning:

> A beholder who lacks the specific code feels lost in a chaos ... without rhyme or reason. Not having learnt to adopt the adequate disposition, he stops short at ... the 'sensible properties'. ... He cannot move from the 'primary stratum of the meaning we can grasp on the basis of our ordinary experience' to the 'secondary stratum of meaning' i.e., the 'level of meaning of what is signified' unless he possesses the concepts which go beyond the sensible properties.
>
> (Bourdieu, 1984: 2)

Enacting recruitment events

Consider the following account offered by Janet, a candidate at one of the assessment centres we attended, a graduate who believes she has decoded the discourse of the recruiters:

> [I]t depends on what job. If it is management then I am very much into martial arts, and if it is a management position, I'm a 'go-getter' and I put things like that on there [the application form]. If it is dealing with vulnerable people ... then I take that off, so yes that changes as well. I found out all about the projects that they were running, found out the philosophies that they had, found out through people that had already worked there, were they male or female? What panel would be interviewing me and really geared it to that, went in there saying that I couldn't work for a company that didn't have the philosophy that they had, that I agreed with [Company x]. And that is really not what I think. ... I asked them to provide me with the literature and they did so and I just looked at it and went in there to be that person that they wanted. But I didn't believe any of it.
>
> (Janet, applying for a Public Sector Management Training Scheme)

Janet was not just capable of changing her own behaviour at assessment centres, but of matching it with the behavioural characteristics she imagined were influencing recruiters, so that they would see her in a positive light. She was also, to some extent, changing herself or, at least, repackaging her self, in such a way as to contribute to her success during the assessment centre. She was adopting what she felt was an appropriate personality, even though it was one she did not recognise to be her own:

> [T]hey are not going to get the true person. They are getting what they want to hear, and because we know what they want to hear, we are telling them that.
>
> (Janet, applying for a Public Sector Management Training Scheme)

Forbearing to enact

Compare now the strategy deployed by Janet with other graduate applicants for jobs in management:

> BT, Abbey National, Corus, I can't remember any more. [...] Oh I just send it, I can't be bothered changing my CV again and again. It's all there for them to read it.
>
> (Omar, a chemical engineering graduate, applying for a graduate management post)

> I've got a Chemistry PhD! Doesn't that tell you that I have numerical skills? Like everything else these days, it's all about spin. But I know I've got the skills so don't see why I should have to play that game.
>
> (Jamie, applying for a graduate management post)

Both Omar and Jamie choose not to see beyond the primary stratum of meaning *vis-à-vis* their employability. Omar adopts a 'scattergun' approach to his applications in a way that is very different to the changing chameleon-like strategy of Janet. Jamie, on the other hand, refuses to subjugate himself to the requirements of the recruitment process, suggesting that the performative requirement of assessment centres is nothing more than a game.

Being unwilling to enact

Maria, who attended the same recruitment event as Janet, also rejects the performative nature of assessment centres:

> I don't come off like someone's bullshitter basically, I am who I am and I can't be any different even for a situation as tough as that [i.e. assessment centre]. Some people can do it, some people are very, very good at presenting themselves in a different light to the way that they really are, and if that presentation is good enough on the day, then it will get them through. But I'm not a comfortable person in a different persona, so I can't do that, and if someone said to me if you said this and did this and acted like this then you would get in. But I couldn't, I'd blow myself, I'd blow my own cover because I know that I'm not good at presenting myself in a different way, but I know that people can do it.
>
> (Maria, applying for a Public Sector Management Training Scheme)

What is interesting about Maria is that she too sees through the primary stratum of meaning to the secondary stratum of meaning of employability. She is clearly aware of what is required of her but refuses to adopt a different persona, partly because she views it in some way as a betrayal of her 'authentic self', and partly because she does not feel that she has the capability to execute such a 'repackaging' of her personality.

This unwillingness to repackage oneself also highlights a central contribution to our understanding of employability made by critical realism. Even when individual candidates are familiar with at least some of the rules of the game as specified by recruitment consultants, have the requisite skills and are successful at being short-listed for assessment centres, they still fail; in some cases miserably. Why is this the case? Essentially it is because the labour market is an open system. Causal mechanisms work themselves out, but their precise effects will not occur in the same way in every single case. There are a number of reasons for this: it may be due to the countervailing action of another mechanism, or simply the effect of some contingent event.

The labour market balances the supply of jobs with the demand for them: it works as a mechanism to place people in jobs. A person may be employable, may appear in many respects employable, but their unwillingness to comply with what they clearly see is required puts them at a disadvantage. As Lawson puts it: 'events are typically unsynchronised with the mechanisms that govern them' (Lawson, 1997). Social constructionists would make a great deal about the variations in how people view what is in fact required, and attribute their success or failure to the individual performances. In the operation of labour markets, however, it is difficult to see how motives and intentions can explain outcomes adequately. Even where the emphases in the values of the recruiters and the traits they see as valuable are accurately assessed by candidates, the behaviour that is supposedly indicative of these things is frequently inappropriately mimicked by candidates; or they may refuse to comply with expectations. The capacity for self-conscious acting in the general population is limited. One way or another, it will be easy to make errors (from the recruiters' point of view) or activate latent prejudices.

Inviting identification

However, recruiters are clearly not deterred by the possibility of candidates perceiving and acting out what they take to be an appropriate personality type. Employers often place a heavy emphasis on candidates being able to project the right image. Indeed, in values-based recruitment, as it has become known, prospective employers or their agents provide a flavour of what it is like to work in a particular organisation, and encourage applications from people who supposedly have the particular traits appropriate for a particular type of job (e.g. Wood and Payne, 1998). Placing heavy emphasis on particular requirements can also be used as a means of deterring the unsuitable. Consider, for example, the following extract from a recruiter for one of our case study companies. The organisation had become increasingly concerned in recent months about the number of graduates applying for posts who are not aware of the demands of the jobs in which they would be employed:

> Let's be blunt. This job is not suitable for everyone. We're looking for men and women of the highest intellectual calibre. People who really care about the health service, with the strength of character to make tough decisions. People who not only cope well with change, but also lead and shape it. Excellent communicators, with the ability to lead through example and to influence others through persuasion and negotiation. In short, we are

> looking for people who will play a key role in determining the NHS of the future. Does this sound like you?
>
> (Public Sector, Management Training Scheme prospectus)

It takes a particular kind of individual to rise to the challenge of applying for a job presented in this way. It also requires a particular challenge in relation to selecting the 'right' people with the correct employability skills.

Failing to identify

Our data shows that the symbolic significance of aspects of the recruitment process and/or its physical location sometimes had a fatal impact upon how respondents reacted to the experience of an assessment centre:

> It was so bloody posh, like nothing before. I mean, I'd never stayed in an hotel like that one before! I disappeared up to my room as quickly as I could, got changed and went down for dinner at 7.00. I felt crap because everybody was there already, right. I just felt a complete dick, you know. I mean? I had to walk right across this massive room in front of everybody. There was this long table. I just felt like everybody was looking at me. All the applicants were on one side and the people from [the bank] were on the other. They'd said in the letter that we would all be dining together, but I didn't think it was going to be like, you know, so formal and regimented. Well, it scared the shit out of me, anyway!
>
> (High Street Bank Graduate Management Recruitment Event)

We can see in this example how the artefactual mode of reality (see Fleetwood, in this volume) comes into play. Artefacts represent 'a synthesis of the material, ideally and socially real [in which] actors interpret entities in various, and often diverse, ways'. Clearly, the layout of the furniture has had an impact on the perception of the occasion for this respondent. Of significance here is that the respondent need not have known why he felt uncomfortable in this situation, at least in terms of his description of the event, or have accurately gauged what impact his attitudes would have on his performance. For the social constructionist, whilst respondent's perceptions may have been noted, except in its symbolical aspects, the room layout, as an extra-discursive object, would not be a factor in the situation; indeed it would have no existence independent of the respondent. In its materiality, certainly, it would not be seen as having explanatory relevance.

It is also clear that, so far as all of the groups of actors we have considered in this account are concerned, it is beliefs and opinions (i.e. phenomena that are ideally real) which mainly shape behaviour. This is indicated by the way in which one employer assessed the merits of assessment centres. Did they always, in his view, produce an evaluation of the employability skills possessed by individuals, or were they open to abuse by those candidates who were familiar with the 'rules of the game' or had attended enough previous assessment centres to be 'clued-up' on how to perform?

> It depends how you look at it. I could say, 'Right, you have gone and done your research, so you have researched how you behave in an assessment centre, you have researched the skills we are looking for and you have researched them properly and that makes you competent enough to pass what I am looking for'. So why not?
>
> (IT Consultants Graduate Entry Programme)

There are several points to make about this. If, for example, all candidates are attempting to influence their employability, it will be more difficult for assessors to come to meaningful distinctions between the candidates. Hirsch (1977: 10) suggests: 'if everybody stands on tiptoe, nobody can see.' In these circumstances, the selectors run the risk of selecting the good performer in the sense of good actor, rather than the good performer in the sense of competent and efficient person. Here we see the socially real at work, in which outcomes are 'dependent on (some) human activity for their existence, that is, for their production, reproduction, and transformation'. We are now better able to understand (if not explain) the frustration felt by many who attend recruitment events; namely, that which arises from their lack of control of their employability, despite some limited control of their performances. Whilst being clued-up on what an organisation may necessarily be looking for at one of its recruitment events, the actions and employability strategies deployed by other participants can effectively render an individual's insight into an organisation's requirements superfluous. In an open system, which the recruitment process is, this is precisely what we would expect to find.

Conclusion

The contribution of critical realism to this consideration of the labour market for highly skilled labour is multifaceted. First, it promotes scepticism about the scientific basis of selection sometimes appealed to and invoked by the recruitment industry. It allows us to expose the recruitment industry as being based on pseudo-science which, interestingly, is acknowledged by practitioners themselves to be, in itself, an inadequate basis for distinguishing between the relative merits of candidates. Second, drawing attention again to the relative scarcity of employment for qualified people, discussed at the outset of this chapter, the actual role of recruiters and consultants in the recruitment process is a response to particular conditions of the employment market. The 'scientific' expertise of recruiters chiefly recommends itself as an important element in a rationing process. Through the exercise of this supposed expertise, some semblance of objectivity can be sustained in a situation where there is otherwise intense and unregulated competition for very few jobs. The narratives of employability, which, as we have seen, are inadequately rooted in the 'science of selection', are, nonetheless, sold to employers as a means of winning the 'war for talent'. Third, however, in contrast to the claims of the recruiters, the actual outcomes of recruitment events can be seen to be the product of the interactions of the policies and practices of the recruiters and the responses and innovations of the recruited. Instead of the science of selection, we have the war for talent, which has given rise to an extremely messy guerrilla war for jobs.

The consequences of this form of managed labour market, in which the recruiters' 'narratives of employability' are deployed, have led to a number of adaptive responses on the part of potential recruits. We are seeing the emergence of a group of self-conscious potential recruits who not only have the capability to see the rules of the recruitment game, but who also spend time learning how to act on them. This group, who we will refer to as 'the players', are willing to repackage themselves according to the expectations of the recruiters. We may contrast 'the players' with the 'the purists' who fail to operate beyond the primary stratum of meaning through a combination of ignorance of, or an inability to play, the emergent rules of the game. Whereas 'players' view the recruitment process from a market-based, winner-takes-all philosophy, and act accordingly, 'purists' prefer to sit back, viewing the recruitment process as meritocratic, relying on what they take to be the currency of their qualifications and the intrinsic value of themselves. Crucially, purists also buy into, at least to some degree, the notion of the objectivity of employability and the absolute status of their human capital.

By contrast, 'players' view the recruitment process as possessing nothing more than a veneer of objectivity, and where one learns to become 'competent at being competent'. Players reject the notion that they are square pegs attempting to fit themselves into round holes. On the contrary, players perceive their own employability – and, crucially, the definitions of employability held by employers – as malleable. Far from the notion of a formal contest between the relative merits of the human capital possessed by applicants, players are aware of the imperative of adding to their academic qualifications evidence of their having that something 'extra'. They attempt to exude the 'drive', 'character' and 'charisma' that employers require of their future managers. Crucially, there is no formal rule book. The rules concerning how individuals make manifest the skills they possess remain implicit in terms of what is involved. Being competent at being competent, therefore, says more about how individuals understand themselves, employability and social justice than it does for the relative merits of the policy declarations relating to employability. For some potential recruits the labour market is a 'technical puzzle', whereas for others it is a 'positional game', a matter of doing whatever it takes to secure a job.

But, the basic point to make from this realist analysis of the labour market is that it is not simply a social construction, emerging from the subjectivity of groups. As Roy Bhaskar suggests, *there is something else beyond individuals' constructions*:

> [P]eople do not create society. For it always pre-exists them and is a necessary condition for their activity. Rather society must be regarded as an

> ensemble of structures, practices and conventions which individuals reproduce and transform, but which would not exist unless they did so. Society does not exist independently of human activity (the error reification). But it is not the product of it (the error of voluntarism).
>
> (Bhaskar, 1989: 36)

Using Bhaskar's ideas, employability is not an outcome determined solely by the actions or thoughts of one individual or group of them. The contribution of critical realism to our understanding of employability, like that of constructionists, begins with the recognition that, in recruitment events, individuals may very likely experience the *same* event in *different* ways. This is because they are differentially implicated in the employment market, which is a mechanism that they do not fully comprehend. But our analysis does not conclude with this sort of observation. Operating beyond people's constructions of actual events exists a 'deeper' level in which processes work themselves out and affect outcomes regardless of whether they are conceived of or taken into account by individuals and groups. As Fleetwood argues in Chapter 1 of this volume, individuals do not need an adequate understanding of their existence for objects in the deep or real level to have an impact upon their lives: in this case, the factors influencing the decisions made about their employability. The purpose of this structured ontology of different 'domains' is not to seek constant event regularities or conjunctions in order to predict social outcomes or behaviour, but to identify and illuminate the structures and mechanisms, powers and tendencies that shape or facilitate the course of events.

Our explanation of what happens at recruitment events rests on our theoretical view of a mediated employment market for expert labour. In this, through their 'scientific expertise' and narratives of employability, recruiters set up a complex set of responses from the eligible people from whom they select. Despite these reactions, recruiters succeed in rationing employment allocations in ways that work so far as employers are concerned and which limit employment opportunities to a favoured few without provoking significant challenge. Thus, the ideas about employability that recruiters have contributed to the production of a certain form of mediated employment market structure. This structure may be seen as comprising of a number of other internally related elements (including the various reactions of the recruited, whose causal powers, when activated, underwrite their performances at recruitment events). Critical realism describes this process as a generative mechanism: 'a way of acting or working of a structured thing' (Lawson, 1997: 21).

Notes

1 An earlier version of this chapter was presented at the 2000 IACR Annual Conference in Lancaster (see Hesketh, 2000). The research, entitled *The Social Construction of Graduate Employability*, is sponsored by the Economic and Social Research Council (ESRC, RS000239101). Not all of the research team subscribes to the critical realist approach advocated by this essay.

2 These figures have been extrapolated from the Association of Graduate Rrecruiter's annual *Graduate Salaries and Vacancy Surveys*. Whilst these figures do not represent all of the organisations providing opportunities to graduates, they do largely comprise the traditional first target of those graduates applying for jobs in the first instance (see Brown *et al.*, 2003 for a more detailed explanation of these figures).
3 Although we acknowledge here the findings of Brown and Scase (1994) that the minimum class of degree required for entry to most graduate training programmes in organisations is an upper-second-class degree.
4 The ramifications of the application of Bourdieu's work for critical realism are discussed extensively by Hesketh (2000).

References

Association of Graduate Recruiters (AGR) (2001) *Assessment Centres*, AGR Briefing No. 4, Warwick: AGR.
AGR (2002) *2002 Graduate Salaries and Vacancies: Annual Review*, Warwick: AGR.
Bennett, N., Dunne, E. and Carré, C. (2000) *Skills Development in Higher Education and Employment*, Buckingham: Open University Press.
Bethell-Fox, C. E. (1989) 'Psychological testing', in Peter Herriot (ed.), *Handbook of Assessment in Organizations*, Chichester: Wiley.
Bhaskar, R. (1998) 'Philosophy and scientific realism', in M. Archer, R. Bhaskar, A. Collier, T. Lawson and A. Norrie (eds), *Critical Realism: Essential Readings*, London: Routledge.
Bourdieu, P. (1984) *Distinction: A Social Critique of the Judgement of Taste*, London: Routledge.
Brown, P. and Scase, R. (1994) *Higher Education and Corporate Realities: Class, Culture and the Decline of Graduate Careers*, London: UCL Press.
Brown, P. and Hesketh, A.J. (2004) *The Mismanagement of Talent: Employability and Jobs in a Knowledge Economy*, Oxford: Oxford University Press.
—— (forthcoming) 'Employability in a knowledge-driven economy', *Journal of Education and Work*.
Castells, M. (1996) *The Rise of the Network Society*, Oxford: Blackwell.
Chartered Institute for Personnel and Development (CIPD) (2000) *Recruitment: CIPD Survey Report No. 14*, London: CIPD.
Gowler, D. and Legge, K. (1981) 'Negation, abomination and synthesis in rhetoric', in C. Antaki (ed.), *The Psychology of Ordinary Explanations of Human Behaviour*, London: Academic Press.
Handyside, J.D. (1989) 'On ratings and rating scales', in P. Herriot (ed.), *Handbook of Assessment in Organizations*, Chichester: Wiley.
Hesketh, A.J. (2000) 'I say tomato, you say tamato: the role of critical realism in the labour exchange process', paper presented to the IACR Conference, Lancaster University.
Hillage, J. and Pollard, E. (1998) *Employability: Developing a Framework for Analysis*, Sudbury: DfEE Publications.
Hirsch, F. (1977) *The Social Limits to Growth*, London: Routledge.
Lawson, T. (1997) *Economics and Reality*, London: Routledge.
Linstead, S. (2001) 'Rhetoric and organizational control: a framework for analysis', in R. Westwood and S. Linstead (eds), *The Language of Organization*, London: Sage.
Michaels, E., Handfield-Jones, H. and Axelrod, B. (2001) *The War for Talent*, Boston, MA: Harvard University Press.

National Health Service (NHS) (2000) *Leadership in the NHS: Are You Ready? The NHS Management Training Scheme*, London: NHS.

Peck, J. (2000) 'Structuring the labour market: a segmentation approach', in S. Ackroyd and S. Fleetwood (eds), *Realist Perspectives on Management and Organisations*, London: Routledge.

Reich, R. (1991) *The Work of Nations: Preparing Ourselves for 21st Century Capitalism*, New York: Knopf.

Thomas International (n.d.) *The People Partnership*, Buckinghamshire: Thomas International.

Watson, T. and Harris, P. (1999) *The Emergent Manager*, London: Sage.

Wicks (1999) 'Get a degree, get a job', DfEE Press Release, London: DfEE.

Wood, R. and Payne, T. (1998) *Competency Based Recruitment and Selection: A Practical Guide*, Chichester: Wiley.

Woodruffe, C. (2000) 'Development and assessment centres: identifying and assessing competence', 3rd edn, London: CIPD.

Index of names

Index of subjects